2006
中国能源统计年鉴

中国统计出版社
China Statistics Press

（京）新登字 041 号

图书在版编目（CIP）数据

中国能源统计年鉴—2006/国家统计局工业交通统计司，
国家发展和改革委员会能源局编．
—北京：中国统计出版社，2006.4
ISBN 978 - 7 - 5037 - 5004 - 5

Ⅰ．中…
Ⅱ．国…
Ⅲ．能源经济 - 经济统计 - 中国 - 2006 - 年鉴
Ⅳ．F426.2 - 54

中国版本图书馆 CIP 数据核字（2006）第 032158 号

中国能源统计年鉴—2006

作　　者/国家统计局工业交通统计司　国家发展和改革委员会能源局
责任编辑/佘竞雄
装帧设计/艺编广告
出版发行/中国统计出版社
网　　址/www.stats.gov.cn/tjshujia
通信地址/北京市西城区月坛南街 57 号　邮政编码/100826
办公地址/北京市丰台区西三环南路甲 6 号

版　　别/2007 年 3 月第 1 版
版　　次/2007 年 3 月第 1 次印刷
书　　号/ISBN 978 - 7 - 5037 - 5004 - 5/F·2335
定　　价/150.00 元

《中国能源统计年鉴 2006》
编委会和编辑人员

主　　　编：许宪春

副 主 编：刘富江　赵小平　赵家荣　吴贵辉

　　　　　　周大地　耿　勤

编委会委员：（以姓氏笔划为序）

　　　　　　王化江　王祥进　许宪春　刘富江

　　　　　　吴贵辉　张苏平　周大地　孟合合

　　　　　　赵小平　赵家荣　耿　勤　董秀芬

总 编 辑：耿　勤

编辑部主任：孟合合　熊自力

编 辑 人 员：（以姓氏笔划为序）

　　　　　　王化江　王立群　王庆一　王祥进

　　　　　　朱　虹　佘竞雄　张苏平　孟合合

　　　　　　武　斌　陶　全　董秀芬　谢　欣

责 任 编 辑：佘竞雄

Chinese Energy Statistical Yearbook – 2006

DEITORIAL BOARD AND STAFF

编 辑 说 明

一、《中国能源统计年鉴》是一部全面反映中国能源建设、生产、消费、供需平衡的权威性资料书,从 1986 年开始,由国家统计局工业交通统计司主编,2000 - 2002 年版起由国家统计局工业交通统计司与国家发展和改革委员会能源局共同主编,中国统计出版社出版,向国内外公开发行。

二、为满足广大读者对中国能源统计数据的需求,提高数据应用的时效性,从 2004 年起,《中国能源统计年鉴》由每两年出版一册改为每年出版一册,封面的年份由数据年改为出版年份。根据第一次全国经济普查结果,2005 年《中国能源统计年鉴》对 1999 年以来的全国有关数据进行了调整。

三、《中国能源统计年鉴》信息量大,特别突出数据的权威性、完整性。全书共分为 8 个部分:1. 综合;2. 能源建设;3. 能源生产;4. 全国能源平衡表;5. 能源消费;6. 地区能源平衡表;7. 香港、澳门特别行政区能源数据;8. 附录:台湾省能源数据、有关国家和地区能源数据、主要统计指标解释以及各种能源折标准煤参考系数。

四、本书大部分资料来源于国家统计局年度统计报表及《中国统计年鉴》。全国性统计数字均未包括香港、澳门特别行政区和台湾省。能源平衡表均未包括非商品能源数据。

五、本书中,中国能源数据截止到 2005 年,世界和各国能源数据截止到 2004 年。

六、符号使用说明:年鉴各表中"空格"表示该项统计指标数据不足本表最小单位数、数据不详或无该项数据;"#"表示其中的主要项。

PREFACE

Chinese energy statistical yearbook is an annual statistical publication, which covers very comprehensive data in energy construction, production, consumption, equilibrium of supply and demand in an all – round way, established in 1986, edited by the department of Industrial and Transport Statistics of State Statistics Bureau. 2000 – 2002 annual is edited together by the industrial traffic statistics department of State Statistics Bureau and Energy Bureau of National Development and Reform Commission, China Statistics Press publishes, to the domestic and international public publication.

In order to satisfy the masses of readers´ demands for Chinese energy statistics, improve the efficiency and timeliness of the data use, from each of 2004, *Chinese energy statistical yearbook* is published one volume every year to change into and publish every 2 years, the year of front cover also switched over to publishing year. In Chinese energy statistical yearbook 2005, some National data is revised from 1999 according to The First National Economic Census.

The amount of information in *Chinese energy statistical yearbook* is large, especially stress the authoritativeness, integrality of the data. The book consists of seven chapters: 1. General Survey; 2. Construction of Energy Industry; 3. Energy Production; 4. Energy Balance Table of China; 5. Energy Consumption ; 6. Energy Balance Table by Region; 7. Energy data for the Hong Kong and Macao Special Administrative Region; 8. Additional information provided in the appendices include major energy data for Taiwan province, energy data for related countries or areas and explanatory notes of main statistical indicators and conversion factors from physical units to coal equivalent.

Annual statistical reports from the National Bureau of Statistics and the *China Statistical Yearbook* are the main data sources of this document. However, the national data in this book does not include that of the Hong Kong and Macao Special Administrative Region, the Taiwan province. Also, the data in the energy balance tables does not cover non – commercial energy.

The Chinese energy data were by the year of 2005 , energy data for the world and other countries were by the year of 2004.

Notations used in the yearbook: blank space indicates that the figure is not large enough to be measured with the smallest unit in the table, or data are unknown or are not available; "#" indicates a major breakdown of the total.

目　　录
CONTENTS

1

三、能源生产
Chapter 3　Energy Production

四、全国能源平衡表
Chapter 4　Energy Balance Table of China

五、能源消费

Chapter 5　Energy Consumption

六、地区能源平衡表
Chapter 6　Energy Balance Table by Region

七、香港、澳门特别行政区能源数据
Chapter 7 Energy Data for Hong Kong and Macao Special Administrative Region

八、附录

Chapter 8   Appendix

附录 1　台湾省能源数据

Appendix Ⅰ   Energy Data for Taiwan Province

附录 2　有关国家和地区能源数据

Appendix Ⅱ   Energy Data for Related Countries or Areas

一、综　　合
Chapter 1　General Survey

1-1 能源生产、消费与国民经济增长速度
GROWTH RATE OF ENERGY PRODUCTION AND
CONSUMPTION COMPARED WITH GROWTH RATE OF GDP

项　目　　　Item	2000	2001	2002	2003	2004	2005
国内生产总值增长速度（%） Growth Rate of GDP（%）	8.4	8.3	9.1	10.0	10.1	10.4
能源生产增长速度（%） Growth Rate of Energy Production	2.4	6.6	4.6	13.9	14.3	9.9
电力生产增长速度（%） Growth Rate of Electricity Production	9.4	9.2	11.7	15.5	15.3	13.5
能源消费增长速度（%） Growth Rate of Energy Consumption	3.5	3.4	6.0	15.3	16.1	10.6
电力消费增长速度（%） Growth Rate of Electricity Consumption	9.5	9.3	11.8	15.6	15.4	13.5
能源生产弹性系数 Elasticity of Energy Production	0.29	0.80	0.51	1.39	1.42	0.95
电力生产弹性系数 Elasticity of Electricity Production	1.12	1.11	1.29	1.55	1.51	1.32
能源消费弹性系数 Elasticity of Energy Consumption	0.42	0.41	0.66	1.53	1.59	1.02
电力消费弹性系数 Elasticity of Electricity Consumption	1.13	1.12	1.30	1.56	1.52	1.32

注：国内生产总值增长速度按 2000 年可比价格计算，能源生产增长速度和能源消费增长速度采用等价值总量计算。

a）GDP growth rate is calculated at comparable prices.

3

1-2 国民经济和能源经济主要指标
MAIN INDICATORS OF NATIONAL ECONOMY AND ENERGY ECONOMY

指　　标	Item	单位 unit	2000	2001	2002	2003	2004	2005
1. 年底人口总数	1. Year-end Population	万人 10^4person	126743	127627	128453	129227	129988	130756
城镇	Urban	万人 10^4person	45906	48064	50212	52376	54283	56212
乡村	Rural	万人 10^4person	80837	79563	78241	76851	75705	74544
2. 国内生产总值	2. Gross Domestic Products	亿元 10^8yuan	99215	109655	120333	135823	159878	183085
第一产业	Primary Industry	亿元 10^8yuan	14716	15516	16239	17068	20956	23070
第二产业	Secondary Industry	亿元 10^8yuan	45556	49512	53897	62436	73904	87046
工业	Industry	亿元 10^8yuan	40034	43581	47431	54946	65210	76913
建筑业	Construction	亿元 10^8yuan	5522	5932	6466	7491	8694	10134
第三产业	Tertiary Industry	亿元 10^8yuan	38943	44627	50197	56319	65018	72968
3. 全社会固定资产投资总额	3. Investment in Fixed Assets	亿元 10^8yuan	32918	37214	43500	55567	70477	88774
能源工业（国有）	Energy Industry (State-owned)	亿元 10^8yuan	2840	2622	2626	2876	3643	4760
煤炭采选业	Coal Mining and Processing	亿元 10^8yuan	199	199	233	310	420	624
石油和天然气开采业	Petroleum and Natural Gas Extraction	亿元 10^8yuan	365	375	158	236	301	279
电力、蒸汽、热水生产和供应业	Electricity,Steam Production and Supply	亿元 10^8yuan	2130	1861	2082	2158	2640	3451
石油加工及炼焦业	Petroleum Processing and Coking	亿元 10^8yuan	95	127	93	90	188	294
煤气生产和供应业	Gas Production and Supply	亿元 10^8yuan	60	58	60	82	95	113
4. 进出口总额	4. Total Value of Exports and Imports	亿元 10^8yuan	39273	42184	51378	70484	95539	116922
出口总额	Exports	亿元 10^8yuan	20634	22024	26948	36288	49103	62648
进口总额	Imports	亿元 10^8yuan	18639	20159	24430	34196	46436	54274
5. 煤炭保有储量	5. Coal Ensured Reserves	亿吨 10^8tn	10084	10202	10202	10212	10212	10212
6. 水利资源蕴藏量	6. Hydropower Resource	亿千瓦 10^8kW	6.76	6.76	6.76	6.76	6.76	6.76
可开发量	Developable Resources	亿千瓦 10^8kW	3.79	3.79	3.79	3.79	3.79	3.79
7. 海洋能源理论蕴藏量	7. Theoretical Sea-energy Reserves	亿千瓦 10^8kW	6.30	6.30	6.30	6.30	6.30	6.30
8. 一次能源生产总量（发电煤耗计算法）（＊）	8. Primary Energy Production (coal equivalent calculation)(＊)	万吨标准煤 10^4tce	128978	137445	143810	163842	187341	205876
一次能源生产总量（电热当量计算法）（＊＊）	Primary Energy Production (calorific value calculation)(＊＊)	万吨标准煤 10^4tce	122673	129794	135983	155947	177962	195518
9. 能源消费总量（发电煤耗计算法）	9. Total Energy Consumption (＊) (coal equivalent calculation)(＊)	万吨标准煤 10^4tce	138553	143199	151797	174990	203227	224682
能源消费总量（电热当量计算法）	Total Energy Consumption (＊＊) (calorific value calculation)(＊＊)	万吨标准煤 10^4tce	132469	135765	144155	167273	193990	214466

注：（＊）发电煤耗计算法是指电力按当年平均火力发电煤耗换算成标准煤。（下表同）

　　（＊＊）电热当量计算法是指电力按自身的热功当量换算成标准煤。采用的折标系数为1万千瓦时=1.229吨标准煤。（下表同）

　　（＊）Electricity is converted to TCE by average quantity of fuel used for power generation.（the same as in the following tables）

　　（＊＊）Electricity is converted to TCE by 10^4kW·h=1.229TCE.（The same as in the following tables）

1－3 平均每万元国内生产总值能源消费量
ENERGY INTENSITY BY GDP

年 份 Year	能源消费总量 （吨标准 煤/万元） Total Energy Consumption （tce/10⁴ yuan）	煤炭 （吨/万元） Coal （tn/10⁴ yuan）	焦炭 （吨/万元） Coke （tn/10⁴ yuan）	石油 （吨/万元） Petroleum （tn/10⁴ yuan）	原油 （吨/万元） Crude Oil （tn/10⁴ yuan）	燃料油 （吨/万元） Fuel Oil （tn/10⁴ yuan）	电力 （万千瓦小 时/万元） Electricity （10⁴ kW·h /10⁴ yuan）
国内生产总值按1990年可比价格计算 GDP is calculated at 1990 comparable prices.							
1991	5.12	5.46	0.35	0.61	0.61	0.17	0.34
1992	4.72	4.94	0.34	0.58	0.57	0.15	0.33
1993	4.42	4.61	0.34	0.56	0.53	0.14	0.32
1994	4.18	4.38	0.31	0.51	0.48	0.12	0.32
1995	4.01	4.21	0.33	0.49	0.46	0.11	0.31
1996	3.88	4.04	0.30	0.49	0.44	0.10	0.30
1997	3.53	3.57	0.28	0.50	0.45	0.10	0.29
1998	3.15	3.08	0.26	0.47	0.41	0.09	0.28
1999	2.90	2.82	0.23	0.46	0.41	0.09	0.27
2000	2.77	2.64	0.21	0.45	0.42	0.08	0.27
国内生产总值按2000年可比价格计算 GDP is calculated at 2000 comparable prices.							
2000	1.40	1.33	0.11	0.23	0.21	0.04	0.14
2001	1.33	1.26	0.10	0.21	0.20	0.04	0.14
2002	1.30	1.21	0.11	0.21	0.19	0.03	0.14
2003	1.36	1.31	0.11	0.19	0.19	0.07	0.15
2004	1.43	1.36	0.12	0.22	0.20	0.03	0.15
2005	1.43	1.38	0.14	0.21	0.19	0.03	0.16
国内生产总值按2005年价格计算 GDP is calculated at 2005 comparable prices.							
2005	1.22	1.18	0.13	0.18	0.16	0.02	0.14

1－4 能源加工转换效率
EFFICIENCY OF ENERGY TRANSFORMATION

单位:% （%）

年 份 Year	总效率 Total Efficiency	发电及电站供热 Power Generation and Heating by Power Station	炼焦 Coking	炼油 Petroleum Refinery
1991	65.90	37.60	89.90	98.10
1992	66.00	37.80	92.70	96.80
1993	67.32	39.90	98.05	98.49
1994	65.20	39.35	89.62	97.48
1995	71.05	37.31	91.99	97.67
1996	71.50	38.30	94.07	97.46
1997	69.23	35.89	92.08	97.37
1998	69.44	37.06	94.97	97.42
1999	69.19	37.04	96.21	97.51
2000	69.04	37.36	96.21	97.32
2001	69.03	37.63	96.5	97.92
2002	69.04	38.73	96.63	96.71
2003	69.40	38.83	96.13	96.80
2004	70.71	39.46	97.61	96.43
2005	71.16	39.87	97.61	96.86

1-5 人均能源生产量和消费量
ENERGY PRODUCTION AND CONSUMPTION PER CAPITA

年　份 Year	人均能源生产量 Per-Capita Energy Production				人均能源消费量 Per-Capita Energy Consumption			
	能源总量 Total Energy （千克 标准煤） （kgce）	原煤 Raw Coal （千克） （kg）	原油 Crude Oil （千克） （kg）	电力 Electricity （千瓦小时） （kW·h）	能源总量 Total Energy （千克 标准煤） （kgce）	原煤 Raw Coal （千克） （kg）	原油 Crude Oil （千克） （kg）	电力 Electricity （千瓦小时） （kW·h）
1990	915	951	122	547	869	930	101	549
1991	905	944	123	589	902	960	108	591
1992	915	958	122	647	937	979	115	651
1993	937	976	123	712	984	1022	125	715
1994	991	1040	123	779	1030	1078	125	777
1995	1065	1130	125	836	1089	1143	133	832
1996	1089	1147	129	888	1141	1189	143	884
1997	1056	1116	131	922	1123	1132	160	917
1998	991	1006	130	939	1064	1043	160	934
1999	1005	1022	128	989	1068	1038	168	982
2000	1021	1029	129	1074	1097	1045	178	1067
2001	1081	1086	129	1164	1126	1061	180	1158
2002	1123	1136	130	1292	1186	1106	194	1286
2003	1272	1337	132	1483	1358	1314	188	1477
2004	1445	1537	136	1700	1568	1494	245	1695
2005	1579	1691	139	1918	1723	1662	250	1913

注：本表按年平均人口数计算。

a）This table is calculed by anaual average population.

1-6 人均生活用能量
RESIDENTIAL ENERGY CONSUMPTION PER CAPITA

年　份 Year	全国人均生活用能量 Annual Average Residential Energy Consumption Per Capita						城镇人均 生活用能量 Urban （千克标准煤） （kgce）	农村人均 生活用能量 Rural （千克标准煤） （kgce）
	（千克 标准煤） （kgce）	煤炭 Coal （千克） （kg）	电力 Electricity （千瓦小时） （kW·h）	液化石油气 LPG （千克） （kg）	天然气 Natural Gas （立方米） （cu. m）	煤气 Gas （立方米） （cu. m）		
1990	139	147	42	1.4	1.6	2.5	298	83
1991	138	142	47	1.7	1.6	3.1	292	83
1992	133	126	55	2.0	1.8	4.4	267	85
1993	131	121	61	2.5	1.4	4.5	250	83
1994	129	110	73	3.2	1.7	6.3	238	86
1995	131	112	84	4.4	1.6	4.7	242	86
1996	145	118	93	5.8	1.6	3.9	260	97
1997	133	100	102	6.0	1.7	4.9	237	86
1998	116	72	107	6.2	1.9	6.0	207	72
1999	121	67	118	7.0	2.1	9.3	210	75
2000	126	63	132	7.8	2.6	10.0	215	77
2001	130	62	145	7.9	3.5	9.4	213	82
2002	137	59	156	9.1	4.0	9.8	216	87
2003	154	63	174	10.0	4.4	10.2	237	99
2004	164	63	190	10.4	5.2	10.7	243	109
2005	179	67	217	10.2	6.1	11.1	257	122

1-7 年末交通运输设备拥有量
NUMBER OF TRANSPORTATION EQUIPMENT(YEAR-END)

指 标　　　　Item	2000	2001	2002	2003	2004	2005
铁路机车合计(辆) Total Railway Locomotives(unit)	15253	15756	16026	16320	17022	17473
蒸汽机车 Steam Locomotives	911	699	374	343	263	193
内燃机车 Diesel Locomotives	10826	11081	11312	11355	11872	12114
电力机车 Electric Locomotives	3516	3976	3918	4622	4887	5166
铁路客车(辆) Railway Passenger Coaches(unit)	35989	37214	37942	38972	39766	40328
铁路货车(辆) Railway Freight Cars(unit)	439943	449921	446707	503868	520101	541824
民用汽车合计(10^4 辆) Total Civil Motor Vehicles(10^4unit)	1609	1802	2053	2383	2694	3160
载客汽车 Passenger Vehicles	854	994	1202	1479	1739	2132
载货汽车 Trucks	716	765	812	854	893	956
其它机动车(10^4 辆) Others(10^4unit)	4168	4724	6174	7109	7786	8595
公路部门营运车辆(10^4 辆) Motor Vehicles Owned by Highway Department(10^4unit)	703	764	826	925	1067	733
私人汽车(10^4 辆) Private Vehicles(10^4unit)	625	771	969	1219	1482	1848
民航飞机合计(架) Total Civil Aircraft(unit)	982	1031	1112	1160	1245	1386
民用运输船舶合计(艘) Total Civil Transport Vessels(unit)	229676	210786	202977	204270	210700	207294
机动船 Motor Vessels	185018	169329	165936	163813	166854	165900
驳船 Barges	44658	41457	37041	40457	43846	41394
私人运输船舶(艘) Private Transport Vessels(unit)	142117	121721	115108	114297	115503	95838

1-8 主要能源品种进、出口量
IMPORTS AND EXPORTS OF MAJOR ENERGY PRODUCTS

指标　　　　Item	2000	2001	2002	2003	2004	2005
进口量 Import						
煤（万吨） Coal（10^4tn）	212.0	249.0	1081.0	1109.8	1861.4	2617.1
焦炭（万吨） Coke（10^4tn）				0.2	0.5	0.5
原油（万吨） Crude Oil（10^4tn）	7027.0	6026.0	6941.0	9102.0	12272.0	12681.7
汽油（万吨） Gasoline（10^4tn）						
柴油（万吨） Diesel Oil（10^4tn）	25.9	27.5	47.7	84.9	274.9	53.2
煤油（万吨） Kerosene（10^4tn）	255.5	201.9	214.5	210.3	282.0	328.3
燃料油（万吨） Fuel Oil（10^4tn）	1480.0	1823.6	1659.7	2395.5	3059.2	2608.6
液化石油气（万吨） LPG（10^4tn）	481.7	488.9	626.2	636.7	641.0	617.0
其它石油制品（万吨） Other Petroleum Products（10^4tn）	161.5	201.3	384.3	432.1	384.2	443.4
天然气（亿立方米） Natural Gas（10^8cu. m）						
电力（亿千瓦小时） Electricity（10^8kW・h）	15.5	18.0	23.0	29.8	34.0	50.1
出口量 Export						
煤（万吨） Coal（10^4tn）	5505.0	9012.0	8384.0	9402.9	8666.4	7172.4
焦炭（万吨） Coke（10^4tn）	1520.0	1385.0	1357.0	1472.1	1501.2	1276.4
原油（万吨） Crude Oil（10^4tn）	1031.0	755.0	766.0	813.3	549.2	806.7
汽油（万吨） Gasoline（10^4tn）	455.2	572.5	612.0	754.2	540.7	560.0
柴油（万吨） Diesel Oil（10^4tn）	55.5	25.6	124.0	224.0	63.7	147.6
煤油（万吨） Kerosene（10^4tn）	198.9	182.2	170.0	201.7	205.0	268.7
燃料油（万吨） Fuel Oil（10^4tn）	33.4	44.1	64.0	76.1	181.7	230.0
液化石油气（万吨） LPG（10^4tn）	1.6	2.1	5.6	2.4	3.2	2.7
其它石油制品（万吨） Other Petroleum Products（10^4tn）	280.5	325.5	246.0	261.8	360.7	473.0
天然气（亿立方米） Natural Gas（10^8cu. m）					24.4	29.7
电力（亿千瓦小时） Electricity（10^8kW・h）	98.8	101.9	97.0	103.4	94.8	111.9

1-9 主要耗能产品的进、出口量
IMPORTS AND EXPORTS OF ENERGY INTENSIVE PRODUCTS

指标 Item	2000	2001	2002	2003	2004	2005
进口量 Import						
钢材（万吨） Steel Products(10^4tn)	1596	1722	2449	3717	2930	2582
钢铁丝（吨） Iron and Steel Wire(tn)	336300	353771	427554	465540		
铜及铜合金（吨） Copper and Copper Alloys(tn)	812126	954167	1330146	1562151	1381112	1415029
铝及铝合金（吨） Aluminum and Aluminum Alloys(tn)	914099	529419	581757	880735	1033422	636951
锌及锌合金（吨） Zinc and Zinc Alloys(tn)	129974	141159	211722	310221		
烧碱（吨） Caustic Soda(tn)	46458	27357	114834	104686		
纯碱（吨） Soda Ash(tn)	134953	68665	293685	301276	197174	70549
肥料 Chemical Fertilizers,Manufactured(10^4tn)	1189	1092	1682	1213	1240	1397
纸浆（万吨） Paper Pulp(10^4tn)	335	490	526	603	732	759
纺织用合成纤维（万吨） Synthetic Fiber Suitable for Spinning (10^4tn)	100	92	104	106	99	84
出口量 Export						
水泥（万吨） Cement(10^4tn)	605	621	518	533	704	2216
平板玻璃（万平方米） Plate Glass(10^4sq. m)	5592	6123	11359	12427	14464	19925
钢材（万吨） Steel Products(10^4tn)	621	474	545	696	1423	2052
钢铁丝（吨） Iron and Steel Wire(tn)	190122	224484	310992	401235		
铜材（吨） Copper Products	144484	123790	171710	232879	390023	463560
铝材（吨） Aluminum Products(tn)	130052	135630	188744	273874	430988	711484
锌及锌合金（吨） Zinc and Zinc Alloys(tn)	593336	562021	495987	484231	263149	146845
纸及纸板（万吨） Paper and Paperboard(10^4tn)	65	68	74	114	101	167

1-10 分地区工业废气排放量
EMISSION OF INDUSTRIAL WASTE GAS BY REGION

地 区 Region	工业废气排放总量 （亿标准立方米） Total Volume of Industrial Waste Gas Emissions （10^8 cu. m）				燃料燃烧工业废气排放量 （亿标准立方米） Waste Gas from Fuel （10^8 cu. m）			
	2002	2003	2004	2005	2002	2003	2004	2005
全 国 **National**	**175257**	**198906**	**237696**	**268988**	**103776**	**116447**	**139726**	**155238**
北 京 Beijing	2966	3005	3198	3532	1816	1825	1927	2015
天 津 Tianjin	3677	4360	3058	4602	2722	3467	2223	3380
河 北 Hebei	12743	15768	21696	26518	7079	8147	11556	13142
山 西 Shanxi	9402	12849	13351	15142	5786	7191	7976	8565
内 蒙 Inner Mongolia	5998	7961	13518	12071	4391	5273	8579	8802
辽 宁 Liaoning	10462	12774	13015	20903	6077	6814	6798	10640
吉 林 Jilin	3516	3869	4316	4939	2375	2456	2761	3405
黑龙江 Heilongjiang	4628	4841	4968	5261	3787	3943	4110	4276
上 海 Shanghai	7440	7799	8834	8482	3288	3377	3603	3564
江 苏 Jiangsu	14286	14633	17818	20197	8826	8981	11029	12748
浙 江 Zhejiang	8532	10432	11749	13025	5921	7208	8223	8148
安 徽 Anhui	5119	5383	5934	6960	3092	3281	3670	4478
福 建 Fujian	3565	4189	5020	6265	1845	2379	2819	3284
江 西 Jiangxi	2612	3202	3972	4379	1458	1812	2100	2138
山 东 Shandong	14306	16139	20357	24129	8987	10314	12355	14333
河 南 Henan	10645	11992	13103	15498	6536	7093	7728	9180
湖 北 Hubei	6440	6707	8838	9404	2963	3248	3626	3958
湖 南 Hunan	4190	4603	5527	6014	2048	2497	2750	2826
广 东 Guangdong	10579	11075	12543	13447	6575	6934	7805	9213
广 西 Guangxi	5693	6636	10656	8339	2425	2937	7223	4370
海 南 Hainan	528	533	634	910	291	294	342	552
重 庆 Chongqing	1979	2277	3541	3655	1185	1341	2490	2178
四 川 Sichuan	7287	6634	7466	8140	4021	3384	3840	4395
贵 州 Guizhou	3515	3477	4182	3852	1953	1822	2112	1933
云 南 Yunnan	3659	4197	4940	5444	1650	1978	2723	2939
西 藏 Tibet	14	14	16	13	9	9	10	13
陕 西 Shaanxi	3424	3861	4374	4916	1944	2505	2804	3140
甘 肃 Gansu	2972	4033	3690	4250	1598	2292	2191	2648
青 海 Qinghai	937	1002	1238	1370	241	312	324	345
宁 夏 Ningxia	1631	1727	2338	2844	957	1022	1273	1625
新 疆 Xinjiang	2512	2934	3806	4485	1930	2311	2755	3005

资料来源：《中国统计年鉴》。

Source：*Statistical Yearbook of China.*

1–11 分地区工业废水排放及处理情况
DISCHARGE AND TREATMENT OF INDUSTRIAL WASTE WATER BY REGION

单位:万吨 (10⁴tn)

地 区	Region	工业废水排放总量 Total Volume of Industrial Waste Water Discharged				工业废水排放达标量 Volume of Industrial Waste Water up to the Discharge Standards			
		2002	2003	2004	2005	2002	2003	2004	2005
全 国	**National**	**2071885**	**2122527**	**2211425**	**2431121**	**1830394**	**1892891**	**2005680**	**2217093**
北 京	Beijing	18044	13107	12617	12813	17745	13015	12442	12740
天 津	Tianjin	21959	21605	22628	30081	21898	21571	22482	29962
河 北	Hebei	106772	108324	127386	124533	97988	102609	122817	119920
山 西	Shanxi	30777	30929	31393	32099	26626	26939	28135	28526
内 蒙	Inner Mongolia	22737	23577	22848	24967	15759	15076	13968	16634
辽 宁	Liaoning	92001	89186	91810	105072	80819	81704	86234	99917
吉 林	Jilin	34783	31365	33568	41189	26782	24071	26668	33458
黑 龙 江	Heilongjiang	47983	50286	45190	45158	44515	47353	42339	41759
上 海	Shanghai	64857	61112	56359	51097	61521	58020	54255	49590
江 苏	Jiangsu	262715	247524	263538	296318	251997	241765	256210	288936
浙 江	Zhejiang	168048	168088	165274	192426	161873	163387	158556	185978
安 徽	Anhui	64577	63525	64054	63487	61827	60908	62076	61816
福 建	Fujian	78511	98388	115228	130939	75094	95633	111989	127874
江 西	Jiangxi	46119	50135	54949	53972	35786	41642	48720	49726
山 东	Shandong	106668	115933	128706	139071	102801	112590	124839	136606
河 南	Henan	114431	114224	117328	123476	103124	104480	109909	113518
湖 北	Hubei	98481	96498	97451	92432	82930	80848	83591	80926
湖 南	Hunan	111788	124132	123126	122440	86768	99127	102990	109879
广 东	Guangdong	145236	148867	164728	231568	130225	123453	138162	194284
广 西	Guangxi	97126	119291	122731	145609	81774	103212	106282	121873
海 南	Hainan	7170	7181	6894	7428	6712	6741	6464	6954
重 庆	Chongqing	79872	81973	83031	84885	71372	73663	77560	79507
四 川	Sichuan	117638	120160	119223	122590	93045	98313	103048	108195
贵 州	Guizhou	17117	16815	16119	14850	9720	9411	9374	10054
云 南	Yunnan	33696	34655	38402	32928	22186	24172	28697	26659
西 藏	Tibet	1063	612	993	991				
陕 西	Shanxi	30496	33526	36833	42819	25491	29138	33737	39704
甘 肃	Gansu	19677	20899	18293	16798	14218	15901	13390	12301
青 海	Qinghai	3583	3453	3544	7619	2148	2067	2223	3396
宁 夏	Ningxia	11534	10740	9510	21411	6461	6288	7676	14508
新 疆	Xinjiang	16426	16417	17671	20052	11189	9794	10847	11893

资料来源:《中国统计年鉴》。
Source: *Statistical Yearbook of China.*

11

二、能源建设

Chapter 2   Construction of Energy Industry

2-1 国有经济能源工业分行业固定资产投资
INVESTMENT IN FIXED ASSETS OF
STATE-OWNED UNITS IN ENERGY INDUSTRY

单位:亿元 (100 million yuan)

项 目 Item	1995	2000	2002	2003	2004	2005
能源工业 **Energy Industry**	**2025.28**	**2839.59**	**2626.17**	**2876.44**	**3643.01**	**4760.73**
煤炭采选业 Coal Mining and Processing	282.26	198.90	233.17	310.05	419.88	623.62
石油和天然气开采业 Petroleum and Natural Gas Extraction	499.68	355.55	157.57	236.37	300.73	278.78
电力、蒸汽、热水生产和供应业 Electricity,Steam,Hot Water 　Producing and Supply	1042.71	2130.30	2082.18	2158.03	2639.79	3451.47
石油加工及炼焦业 Petroleum Processing and Coking	161.64	94.81	93.16	89.74	187.66	293.97
煤气生产和供应业 Coal Gas and Coal Products	38.99	60.03	60.09	82.25	94.95	112.89

2-2 国有经济能源工业分行业固定资产投资构成
PROPORTIONS OF INVESTMENT IN FIXED ASSETS OF
STATE-OWNED UNITS IN ENERGY INDUSTRY

单位:% (%)

项 目 Item	1995	2000	2002	2003	2004	2005
能源工业 **Energy Industry**	**100.00**	**100.00**	**100.00**	**100.00**	**100.00**	**100.00**
煤炭采选业 Coal Mining and Processing	13.94	7.00	8.88	10.78	11.53	13.10
石油和天然气开采业 Petroleum and Natural Gas Extraction	24.67	12.52	6.00	8.22	8.25	5.86
电力、蒸汽、热水生产和供应业 Electricity,Steam,Hot Water 　Producing and Supply	51.48	75.02	79.29	75.02	72.46	72.50
石油加工及炼焦业 Petroleum Processing and Coking	7.98	3.34	3.55	3.12	5.15	6.17
煤气生产和供应业 Coal Gas and Coal Products	1.93	2.11	2.29	2.86	2.61	2.37

2-3 分地区国有经济能源工业固定资产投资
INVESTMENT IN FIXED ASSETS OF
STATE-OWNED UNITS IN ENERGY INDUSTRY BY REGION

单位：亿元 （100 million yuan）

地　区 Region	1995	2000	2002	2003	2004	2005
北　京 Beijing	48.33	54.14	49.23	32.41	52.98	99.83
天　津 Tianjin	120.62	30.67	36.86	48.41	41.95	46.76
河　北 Hebei	108.93	166.82	80.94	88.76	96.31	190.31
山　西 Shanxi	70.05	106.57	100.04	120.43	157.72	263.36
内　蒙 Inner Mongolia	73.62	33.36	47.55	110.81	225.18	382.06
辽　宁 Liaoning	133.08	179.51	108.15	99.80	109.92	123.89
吉　林 Jilin	44.26	66.45	42.68	42.97	34.08	46.85
黑龙江 Heilongjiang	163.08	72.04	68.23	66.48	87.79	114.20
上　海 Shanghai	75.72	76.10	66.78	74.86	93.17	108.43
江　苏 Jiangsu	49.28	202.11	194.00	269.97	310.33	311.16
浙　江 Zhejiang	56.44	91.08	83.31	108.66	199.30	291.11
安　徽 Anhui	76.87	54.25	72.98	63.64	107.11	170.18
福　建 Fujian	38.19	70.64	51.07	37.34	72.60	114.90
江　西 Jiangxi	18.65	50.71	35.68	37.55	57.29	81.04
山　东 Shandong	180.99	330.44	174.07	196.99	247.65	216.01
河　南 Henan	99.65	180.77	148.98	157.64	183.66	210.03
湖　北 Hubei	138.42	221.63	241.71	191.77	187.33	187.89
湖　南 Hunan	57.75	88.95	100.82	81.78	96.31	116.78
广　东 Guangdong	84.91	90.46	159.48	192.01	242.91	375.78
广　西 Guangxi	21.36	71.02	60.67	59.08	68.90	67.36
海　南 Hainan	1.53	13.01	4.92	7.65	24.00	70.77
重　庆 Chongqing		42.89	32.74	34.09	41.73	73.95
四　川 Sichuan	110.55	94.62	89.10	66.52	122.74	182.91
贵　州 Guizhou	26.83	67.38	114.03	140.41	169.84	179.64
云　南 Yunnan	22.63	49.37	75.30	55.99	86.00	140.51
西　藏 Tibet	9.01	9.73	14.65	20.65	15.33	15.05
陕　西 Shaanxi	40.35	94.33	91.26	124.88	183.73	237.74
甘　肃 Gansu	33.99	53.01	39.54	67.17	79.80	95.04
青　海 Qinghai	22.24	10.59	18.41	29.69	35.18	21.38
宁　夏 Ningxia	11.57	16.32	34.38	31.59	27.36	60.79
新　疆 Xinjiang	106.91	49.90	54.87	61.01	64.81	74.03

2-4 分地区国有经济煤炭采选业固定资产投资
INVESTMENT IN FIXED ASSETS OF STATE-OWNED
UNITS IN COAL MINING AND PROCESSING BY REGION

单位:亿元 (100 million yuan)

地 区	Region	1995	2000	2002	2003	2004	2005
北 京	Beijing	0.62	0.21	0.12			0.01
天 津	Tianjin	60.30					
河 北	Hebei	62.86	19.54	16.56	16.70	11.49	30.68
山 西	Shanxi	46.59	34.25	51.63	68.61	104.60	180.97
内 蒙	Inner Mongolia	35.26	2.49	6.55	13.72	17.88	31.74
辽 宁	Liaoning	6.09	7.95	7.62	11.46	9.38	15.34
吉 林	Jilin	2.86	0.84	1.99	2.23	3.00	5.07
黑龙江	Heilongjiang	14.12	7.46	8.32	11.53	14.33	22.48
上 海	Shanghai						
江 苏	Jiangsu	6.16	5.48	8.40	15.82	11.76	12.31
浙 江	Zhejiang	0.12			0.21		
安 徽	Anhui	34.64	13.16	21.51	35.44	56.19	91.42
福 建	Fujian	1.48	1.27	1.48	0.54	1.54	1.73
江 西	Jiangxi	1.72	0.89	2.83	4.62	2.41	4.40
山 东	Shandong	24.62	39.50	46.42	51.45	59.62	55.61
河 南	Henan	22.83	18.47	17.93	18.48	17.44	23.80
湖 北	Hubei	0.56	0.43	0.70	0.37	0.37	
湖 南	Hunan	3.38	1.04	2.00	1.69	3.07	4.16
广 东	Guangdong	0.99	0.17		0.04		
广 西	Guangxi	0.93	0.52	0.63	0.69	1.96	1.58
海 南	Hainan	0.01					
重 庆	Chongqing		1.08	1.00	1.19	1.63	5.06
四 川	Sichuan	6.61	2.21	2.43	3.87	3.66	6.90
贵 州	Guizhou	6.65	4.46	4.20	9.76	15.19	21.56
云 南	Yunnan	3.59	1.90	2.53	1.88	6.60	6.30
西 藏	Tibet	0.09					
陕 西	Shaanxi	8.38	3.20	6.12	8.36	12.61	12.93
甘 肃	Gansu	4.07	4.97	3.86	6.45	9.86	10.21
青 海	Qinghai	0.24	0.01	0.11	0.94	0.53	0.42
宁 夏	Ningxia	5.21	2.79	3.51	4.92	11.60	32.88
新 疆	Xinjiang	3.34	2.15	2.43	4.04	5.50	6.92

2-5 分地区国有经济石油和天然气开采业固定资产投资
INVESTMENT IN FIXED ASSETS OF STATE-OWNED UNITS
IN PETROLEUM AND NATURAL GAS EXTRACTION BY REGION

单位:亿元 (100 million yuan)

地 区	Region	1995	2000	2002	2003	2004	2005
北 京	Beijing					0.06	0.03
天 津	Tianjin	30.77	4.11	8.18	19.76	22.88	9.03
河 北	Hebei	3.06	3.35	0.48	0.02		2.09
山 西	Shanxi					0.02	
内 蒙	Inner Mongolia		0.70	0.60	5.46	14.84	18.05
辽 宁	Liaoning	54.91	67.50	13.88	14.24	16.52	21.58
吉 林	Jilin	17.39	20.85	5.49	5.95	0.62	0.14
黑 龙 江	Heilongjiang	103.85	0.40		2.00	3.29	7.52
上 海	Shanghai	0.07	2.17	0.28			
江 苏	Jiangsu	6.28	10.74	8.38	8.85	11.18	11.62
浙 江	Zhejiang						
安 徽	Anhui				0.01		
福 建	Fujian						
江 西	Jiangxi						
山 东	Shandong	79.97	132.95		0.15	0.45	
河 南	Henan	26.10	43.95	55.30	61.24	73.73	55.37
湖 北	Hubei	3.77	13.20	12.79	10.36	10.76	12.19
湖 南	Hunan						
广 东	Guangdong	6.28	0.72	6.64	6.95	0.75	0.47
广 西	Guangxi	0.04					
海 南	Hainan		5.00				
重 庆	Chongqing		0.09	0.32	1.15	0.61	0.28
四 川	Sichuan	24.11	6.87	6.13	5.00	12.74	13.65
贵 州	Guizhou			0.69	0.39	0.47	0.52
云 南	Yunnan		0.03				
西 藏	Tibet						
陕 西	Shaanxi	2.76	23.98	31.72	55.01	80.50	94.69
甘 肃	Gansu	4.29	6.57	0.08	3.15	5.09	5.76
青 海	Qinghai	6.00	1.76	4.44	19.02	28.22	4.54
宁 夏	Ningxia						
新 疆	Xinjiang	85.85	10.61	2.17	17.63	18.03	21.23

2-6 分地区国有经济电力、蒸汽、热水生产和供应业固定资产投资
INVESTMENT IN FIXED ASSETS OF STATE-OWNED UNITS IN
ELECTRICITY, STEAM, HOT WATER PRODUCTION AND SUPPLY BY REGION

单位:亿元 (100 million yuan)

地　区	Region	1995	2000	2002	2003	2004	2005
北　京	Beijing	36.72	35.85	33.77	19.65	42.47	76.39
天　津	Tianjin	23.28	21.18	26.05	25.48	16.43	28.15
河　北	Hebei	37.82	134.25	56.61	62.76	74.68	142.31
山　西	Shanxi	21.33	66.63	43.36	38.82	41.57	76.51
内　蒙	Inner Mongolia	32.63	29.17	38.22	87.92	180.07	307.59
辽　宁	Liaoning	41.63	85.64	67.06	62.54	64.94	77.01
吉　林	Jilin	19.95	43.46	34.69	34.38	28.70	40.89
黑龙江	Heilongjiang	25.76	58.69	45.66	49.13	55.85	76.40
上　海	Shanghai	57.17	61.71	58.57	63.23	79.93	103.29
江　苏	Jiangsu	29.18	172.25	166.52	232.25	280.85	284.34
浙　江	Zhejiang	53.58	89.68	79.29	104.85	171.93	261.32
安　徽	Anhui	26.96	39.05	49.66	25.35	40.62	65.70
福　建	Fujian	32.89	67.33	48.62	34.31	64.26	94.76
江　西	Jiangxi	14.28	47.42	30.23	29.59	49.07	66.36
山　东	Shandong	60.82	148.94	113.01	128.25	159.30	139.58
河　南	Henan	46.00	113.29	72.15	71.39	81.92	123.06
湖　北	Hubei	126.00	204.23	225.65	173.93	166.11	169.36
湖　南	Hunan	51.30	75.46	88.44	74.42	78.97	101.41
广　东	Guangdong	64.11	81.64	146.38	180.41	237.78	329.79
广　西	Guangxi	20.19	68.96	58.53	57.67	66.61	65.28
海　南	Hainan	1.51	6.43	4.86	7.59	10.23	8.10
重　庆	Chongqing		40.85	29.83	30.75	37.75	67.12
四　川	Sichuan	77.03	82.51	77.19	52.99	103.22	157.52
贵　州	Guizhou	19.98	62.37	108.71	129.31	153.61	157.07
云　南	Yunnan	18.58	47.18	72.38	53.51	78.24	130.40
西　藏	Tibet	8.92	9.73	14.65	20.65	15.26	15.05
陕　西	Shaanxi	25.12	63.09	47.75	50.20	76.60	110.00
甘　肃	Gansu	18.47	38.85	34.44	45.90	49.75	44.06
青　海	Qinghai	16.00	8.82	13.67	9.73	6.37	16.33
宁　夏	Ningxia	6.02	13.01	30.56	26.15	14.78	27.22
新　疆	Xinjiang	12.11	34.39	44.21	34.49	29.53	37.27

2-7 分地区国有经济石油加工及炼焦业固定资产投资
INVESTMENT IN FIXED ASSETS OF STATE-OWNED
UNITS IN PETROLEUM PROCESSING AND COKING BY REGION

单位:亿元   (100 million yuan)

地 区	Region	1995	2000	2002	2003	2004	2005
北 京	Beijing	6.95	5.59	1.63	1.38	3.88	12.37
天 津	Tianjin	5.17	1.48	0.07	0.15		6.94
河 北	Hebei	4.66	7.14	3.81	2.19	3.20	11.03
山 西	Shanxi	1.06	2.90	4.19	6.11	8.11	5.08
内 蒙	Inner Mongolia	5.59	0.26	1.31	1.82	11.15	23.24
辽 宁	Liaoning	28.90	16.59	18.63	9.54	16.18	5.82
吉 林	Jilin	3.15	0.55	0.51	0.41	0.66	0.25
黑龙江	Heilongjiang	16.74	4.26	11.86	2.88	14.12	7.09
上 海	Shanghai	10.05	5.33	5.30	6.93	10.80	0.97
江 苏	Jiangsu	6.80	12.24	6.17	8.72	4.08	1.55
浙 江	Zhejiang	1.36	0.24	1.90	0.11	0.15	0.44
安 徽	Anhui	14.39	1.42	0.69	0.40	6.88	9.79
福 建	Fujian	3.56			1.20	5.11	11.05
江 西	Jiangxi	1.87	1.76	2.38	2.78	4.42	9.13
山 东	Shandong	13.21	5.68	11.17	12.64	24.74	16.43
河 南	Henan	1.48	1.42	0.36	0.02	0.47	0.19
湖 北	Hubei	6.80	3.33	1.80	2.98	7.48	3.24
湖 南	Hunan	2.02	11.62	8.37	4.58	12.29	10.15
广 东	Guangdong	11.70	6.48	4.97	3.35	2.64	36.52
广 西	Guangxi	0.09	0.10	0.20	0.11	0.15	0.22
海 南	Hainan					13.62	62.53
重 庆	Chongqing		0.15	0.13	0.14	0.25	0.09
四 川	Sichuan	0.53	0.03	0.68	0.70	0.74	0.33
贵 州	Guizhou		0.07	0.01		0.07	0.13
云 南	Yunnan	0.05	0.06			0.54	0.66
西 藏	Tibet						
陕 西	Shaanxi	3.31	1.70	3.42	8.49	11.98	16.92
甘 肃	Gansu	6.64	2.26	0.64	10.22	14.47	34.22
青 海	Qinghai						
宁 夏	Ningxia	0.25	0.05			0.47	0.49
新 疆	Xinjiang	5.32	2.07	2.97	1.87	9.02	7.11

2-8 分地区国有经济煤气生产和供应业固定资产投资
INVESTMENT IN FIXED ASSETS OF STATE-OWNED
UNITS IN GAS PRODUCTION AND SUPPLY BY REGION

单位:亿元 （100 million yuan）

地 区	Region	1995	2000	2003	2004	2005
北 京	Beijing	4.04	12.50	11.38	6.56	11.03
天 津	Tianjin	1.10	3.90	3.02	2.64	2.63
河 北	Hebei	0.53	2.53	7.10	6.95	4.20
山 西	Shanxi	1.07	2.80	6.88	3.43	0.79
内 蒙	Inner Mongolia	0.14	0.74	1.88	1.24	1.44
辽 宁	Liaoning	1.55	1.83	2.02	2.90	4.15
吉 林	Jilin	0.91	0.76		1.09	0.50
黑 龙 江	Heilongjiang	2.61	1.22	0.93	0.20	0.71
上 海	Shanghai	8.43	6.88	4.71	2.44	4.18
江 苏	Jiangsu	0.86	1.41	4.33	2.46	1.32
浙 江	Zhejiang	1.38	1.16	3.49	27.22	29.35
安 徽	Anhui	0.88	0.61	2.44	3.41	3.27
福 建	Fujian	0.26	2.03	1.28	1.69	7.36
江 西	Jiangxi	0.78	0.64	0.56	1.38	1.14
山 东	Shandong	2.37	3.38	4.50	3.53	4.40
河 南	Henan	3.24	3.64	6.50	10.10	7.62
湖 北	Hubei	1.29	0.44	4.12	2.62	3.10
湖 南	Hunan	1.05	0.83	1.09	1.97	1.07
广 东	Guangdong	1.83	1.45	1.24	1.75	8.99
广 西	Guangxi	0.11	1.44	0.62	0.18	0.27
海 南	Hainan	0.01	1.58	0.06	0.15	0.14
重 庆	Chongqing		0.72	0.86	1.49	1.40
四 川	Sichuan	2.27	3.00	3.96	2.38	4.51
贵 州	Guizhou	0.20	0.49	0.94	0.51	0.36
云 南	Yunnan	0.41	0.19	0.60	0.62	3.16
西 藏	Tibet				0.06	
陕 西	Shaanxi	0.78	2.37	2.83	2.04	3.21
甘 肃	Gansu	0.52	0.36	1.45	0.62	0.80
青 海	Qinghai				0.06	0.09
宁 夏	Ningxia	0.09	0.47	0.52	0.51	0.21
新 疆	Xinjiang	0.29	0.68	2.97	2.73	1.50

21

2-9　城镇能源工业分行业投资
INVESTMENT OF URBAN IN ENERGY INDUSTRY

单位:亿元 (100 million yuan)

项　目　　Item	1995	2000	2003	2004	2005
能源工业 **Energy Industry**	**2369.16**	**3991.48**	**5159.94**	**7504.8**	**10200.15**
煤炭采选业 Coal Mining and Processing	285.60	211.39	436.43	690.42	1162.95
石油和天然气开采业 Petroleum and Natural Gas Extraction	503.82	789.41	945.99	1112.28	1463.56
电力、蒸汽、热水生产和供应业 Electricity Steam, Hot Water 　Producing and and Supply	1336.86	2744.47	3304.82	4854.41	6503.2
石油加工及炼焦业 Petroleum Processing and Coking	194.38	172.55	321.05	637.91	795.81
煤气生产和供应业 Gas Production and Supply	48.51	73.66	151.64	209.77	274.63

2-10　城镇能源工业分行业投资构成
INVESTMENT OF URBAN IN ENERGY INDUSTRY BY PROPORTIONS

单位:% (%)

项　目　　Item	1995	2000	2003	2004	2005
能源工业 **Energy Industry**	**100.00**	**100.00**	**100.00**	**100.00**	**100.00**
煤炭采选业 Coal Mining and Processing	12.05	5.30	8.46	9.20	11.40
石油和天然气开采业 Petroleum and Natural Gas Extraction	21.27	19.78	18.33	14.82	14.35
电力、蒸汽、热水生产和供应业 Electricity Steam, Hot Water 　Producing and and Supply	56.43	68.76	64.05	64.68	63.76
石油加工及炼焦业 Petroleum Processing and Coking	8.20	4.32	6.22	8.50	7.80
煤气生产和供应业 Gas Production and Supply		1.85	2.94	2.80	2.69

2-11 各地区城镇能源工业投资
INVESTMENT OF URBAN IN ENERGY INDUSTRY BY REGION

单位:万元 (10 000 yuan)

地 区	Region	1995	2000	2003	2004	2005
北 京	Beijing	580106	577931	350754	660309	1168557
天 津	Tianjin	592634	997416	1257903	1605499	1784199
河 北	Hebei	800280	2003185	1584197	2495757	4172805
山 西	Shanxi	727468	1572844	3046474	4930625	6027304
内 蒙	Inner Mongolia	737152	402299	2130454	4776237	7897228
辽 宁	Liaoning	1539475	1904716	1975754	2384310	3176630
吉 林	Jilin	444053	798735	913772	1079042	1598594
黑 龙 江	Heilongjiang	1634605	2253840	2196129	2598165	3353423
上 海	Shanghai	813844	1148266	940675	1183193	1390160
江 苏	Jiangsu	902150	2232172	3720192	5948967	5599103
浙 江	Zhejiang	697792	2150971	2201857	3596570	4780581
安 徽	Anhui	776267	813056	860286	1629053	2944666
福 建	Fujian	636218	1254552	808188	1577329	2467379
江 西	Jiangxi	253058	599004	559364	959438	1332836
山 东	Shandong	1955268	3931843	4778666	6194247	7641586
河 南	Henan	1329607	1879757	2682376	3926407	4978426
湖 北	Hubei	1458289	2389352	2457819	2694469	2866517
湖 南	Hunan	590819	961959	1175809	1487899	2485777
广 东	Guangdong	1744346	1819912	2863810	4462237	6739151
广 西	Guangxi	267558	873235	1116014	1563626	1870863
海 南	Hainan	238795	145957	99970	283286	825096
重 庆	Chongqing		498323	673475	1003519	1635491
四 川	Sichuan	1228031	1365482	1628038	3026056	4307259
贵 州	Guizhou	271653	717444	1624957	2167279	2692206
云 南	Yunnan	351856	572173	1022318	2128603	3712921
西 藏	Tibet	90070	97340	206532	154347	151232
陕 西	Shaanxi	418013	1058410	1527677	2342372	3007465
甘 肃	Gansu	340874	648601	948549	1127938	1399090
青 海	Qinghai	222683	303079	510611	823525	859577
宁 夏	Ningxia	117431	191842	403772	593805	1044530
新 疆	Xinjiang	1071295	1797885	2330512	3086140	3750842

23

2-12 分地区煤炭采选业城镇投资
INVESTMENT OF URBAN
IN COAL MINING AND PROCESSING BY REGION

单位:万元   (10 000 yuan)

地 区	Region	1995	2000	2003	2004	2005
北 京	Beijing	6186	2076	1292		4268
天 津	Tianjin		843			
河 北	Hebei	170999	199587	185274	114850	433600
山 西	Shanxi	473255	365317	903602	1045978	2587510
内 蒙	Inner Mongolia	352778	28201	204192	178826	1095432
辽 宁	Liaoning	60867	79575	143183	93848	250455
吉 林	Jilin	29953	8873	28021	30045	90245
黑 龙 江	Heilongjiang	142853	114599	180684	143279	407062
上 海	Shanghai					
江 苏	Jiangsu	61551	55179	158717	117632	133646
浙 江	Zhejiang	1153		2110		3400
安 徽	Anhui	346997	141949	399678	561885	1068059
福 建	Fujian	14812	13481	7115	15399	45356
江 西	Jiangxi	18561	9895	50593	24143	93675
山 东	Shandong	252635	403475	1055199	596210	1486334
河 南	Henan	231828	187061	217554	174400	1028782
湖 北	Hubei	5766	7809	17134	3653	39328
湖 南	Hunan	33756	12192	31860	30747	184244
广 东	Guangdong	9922	1712	6093		197
广 西	Guangxi	10419	5227	6854	19559	51838
海 南	Hainan	110				
重 庆	Chongqing		11115	31822	16342	236992
四 川	Sichuan	66415	28415	69094	36609	287369
贵 州	Guizhou	66497	53089	127172	151916	326942
云 南	Yunnan	36807	20673	37873	65954	370657
西 藏	Tibet	900				
陕 西	Shaanxi	87340	37459	129168	126132	366563
甘 肃	Gansu	40740	49806	68836	98645	130076
青 海	Qinghai	2379	130	13611	5315	25637
宁 夏	Ningxia	53710	28204	58373	116024	330303
新 疆	Xinjiang	33585	23451	78834	55013	160203

2-13 分地区石油和天然气开采业城镇投资
INVESTMENT OF URBAN
IN PETROLEUM AND NATURAL GAS EXTRACTION BY REGION

单位:万元 (10 000 yuan)

地　区	Region	1995	2000	2003	2004	2005
北　京	Beijing				639	271
天　津	Tianjin	307679	601436	881913	228759	1234110
河　北	Hebei	30600	33545	23998		248932
山　西	Shanxi				175	
内　蒙	Inner Mongolia		7003	56725	148359	221513
辽　宁	Liaoning	549104	675014	717609	165162	949040
吉　林	Jilin	173950	221980	435308	6150	663884
黑龙江	Heilongjiang	1038519	1394374	1136853	32908	1664434
上　海	Shanghai	654	21675	24702		16786
江　苏	Jiangsu	62806	107387	88482	111759	125712
浙　江	Zhejiang					
安　徽	Anhui			100		230
福　建	Fujian		1000	900		
江　西	Jiangxi					
山　东	Shandong	799717	1329483	1190383	4500	1176786
河　南	Henan	260967	439471	612420	737341	553712
湖　北	Hubei	37705	131998	104470	107584	128500
湖　南	Hunan					
广　东	Guangdong	62844	44097	205617	7530	102371
广　西	Guangxi	420				1600
海　南	Hainan	36213	50000	5378		
重　庆	Chongqing		3377	15691	6051	6831
四　川	Sichuan	242277	116256	65484	127389	158967
贵　州	Guizhou		1000	3927	4688	5216
云　南	Yunnan		300			230
西　藏	Tibet					230
陕　西	Shaanxi	31620	239757	550427	804999	957068
甘　肃	Gansu	42928	65748	115455	50881	61123
青　海	Qinghai	59969	169180	190245	282154	307284
宁　夏	Ningxia			950		
新　疆	Xinjiang	858475	1293814	1584775	180289	2620624

2-14 分地区电力、蒸汽、热水生产和供应业城镇投资
INVESTMENT OF URBAN IN ELECTRICITY, STEAM,
HOT WATER PRODUCTION AND SUPPLY BY REGION

单位:万元 (10 000 yuan)

地 区	Region	1995	2000	2003	2004	2005
北 京	Beijing	464034	384200	221579	424721	929197
天 津	Tianjin	222172	340961	324895	164301	404971
河 北	Hebei	541859	1661981	1171473	746765	2828692
山 西	Shanxi	222337	1054166	1304368	415723	2462847
内 蒙	Inner Mongolia	326587	354399	1614378	1800680	6027601
辽 宁	Liaoning	495116	890619	850267	649440	1157532
吉 林	Jilin	199538	546346	416588	286998	765137
黑 龙 江	Heilongjiang	257770	668546	591250	558502	1025050
上 海	Shanghai	582874	887196	661562	799273	1201932
江 苏	Jiangsu	687769	1873140	3257704	2808497	5104054
浙 江	Zhejiang	596495	2036481	1987327	1719265	4355204
安 徽	Anhui	269432	648320	393004	406213	1657247
福 建	Fujian	582995	1208401	760753	642589	2218134
江 西	Jiangxi	207855	564657	456831	490713	1064638
山 东	Shandong	738805	1899026	2069545	1593016	3729173
河 南	Henan	789102	1196424	1709460	819182	3033918
湖 北	Hubei	1303271	2176337	2234034	1661102	2438110
湖 南	Hunan	525130	813996	1047758	789702	2058720
广 东	Guangdong	1511922	1667758	2527506	2377757	5467997
广 西	Guangxi	254788	848859	1079966	666129	1750719
海 南	Hainan	138897	71397	84234	102334	171603
重 庆	Chongqing		467102	594546	377484	1301692
四 川	Sichuan	888303	1180216	1342195	1032245	3698944
贵 州	Guizhou	203109	648738	1471718	1536068	2316270
云 南	Yunnan	310470	546983	927028	782405	3212543
西 藏	Tibet	89170	97340	206532	152636	150922
陕 西	Shaanxi	256452	732021	662604	765983	1381443
甘 肃	Gansu	184703	501710	631574	497467	847820
青 海	Qinghai	160335	133689	304657	63673	518046
宁 夏	Ningxia	60259	145166	294489	147841	686629
新 疆	Xinjiang	122091	416024	444390	295302	546626

2-15 分地区石油加工及炼焦业城镇投资
INVESTMENT OF URBAN IN
PETROLEUM PROCESSING AND COKING BY REGION

单位:万元 (10 000 yuan)

地　区	Region	1995	2000	2003	2004	2005
北　京	Beijing	69456	66661	13770	38845	123662
天　津	Tianjin	51740	15221	16400		83060
河　北	Hebei	50918	76523	100033	31955	553303
山　西	Shanxi	21173	118894	761553	81061	940325
内　蒙	Inner Mongolia	56435	4941	136034	111539	510942
辽　宁	Liaoning	418895	237034	242772	161757	753221
吉　林	Jilin	31483	10852	29535	6644	32464
黑龙江	Heilongjiang	169346	62707	276382	141183	245530
上　海	Shanghai	100510	170589	114189	108001	55407
江　苏	Jiangsu	71219	174603	103939	40800	111081
浙　江	Zhejiang	82441	98553	154892	1540	88811
安　徽	Anhui	150488	14592	21283	68821	137351
福　建	Fujian	35853	10493	19793	51145	118019
江　西	Jiangxi	18737	17599	29329	44244	119265
山　东	Shandong	140387	259955	324315	247417	1042454
河　南	Henan	15346	17635	36734	4680	188418
湖　北	Hubei	98575	49743	48093	74838	96953
湖　南	Hunan	20210	124671	71868	122879	148925
广　东	Guangdong	118511	69631	83813	26361	716214
广　西	Guangxi	852	1416	16494	1515	25939
海　南	Hainan	55993	3768	400	136153	626503
重　庆	Chongqing		1470	8958	2450	30933
四　川	Sichuan	6654	1390	73807	7365	71518
贵　州	Guizhou		4779	9303	679	31813
云　南	Yunnan	458	2186	47762	5391	96213
西　藏	Tibet					
陕　西	Shaanxi	34818	20899	147840	119753	263344
甘　肃	Gansu	66450	27787	112628	144717	345513
青　海	Qinghai			98		
宁　夏	Ningxia	2536	8375	42490	4676	23654
新　疆	Xinjiang	54268	52535	166016	90238	377310

27

2-16 分地区煤气生产和供应业城镇投资
INVESTMENT OF URBAN
IN GAS PRODUCTION AND SUPPLY BY REGION

单位:万元 （10 000 yuan）

地 区	Region	1995	2000	2003	2004	2005
北 京	Beijing	40430	124994	114113	65605	111159
天 津	Tianjin	11043	38955	34695	26443	62058
河 北	Hebei	5904	31549	103419	69482	108278
山 西	Shanxi	10703	34467	76951	34262	36622
内 蒙	Inner Mongolia	1352	7755	119125	12394	41740
辽 宁	Liaoning	15493	22474	21923	29038	66382
吉 林	Jilin	9129	10684	4320	10921	46864
黑 龙 江	Heilongjiang	26117	13614	10960	2022	11347
上 海	Shanghai	129806	68806	140222	24380	116035
江 苏	Jiangsu	18805	21863	111350	24642	124610
浙 江	Zhejiang	17703	15937	57528	272243	333166
安 徽	Anhui	9350	8195	46221	34138	81779
福 建	Fujian	2558	21177	19627	16859	85870
江 西	Jiangxi	7905	6853	22611	13766	55258
山 东	Shandong	23724	39904	139224	35344	206839
河 南	Henan	32364	39166	106208	100988	173596
湖 北	Hubei	12972	23465	54088	26152	163626
湖 南	Hunan	11723	11100	24323	19733	93888
广 东	Guangdong	41147	36714	40781	17480	452372
广 西	Guangxi	1079	17733	12700	1820	40767
海 南	Hainan	7582	20792	9958	1483	26990
重 庆	Chongqing		15259	22458	14926	59043
四 川	Sichuan	24382	39205	77458	23788	90461
贵 州	Guizhou	2047	9838	12837	5062	11965
云 南	Yunnan	4121	2031	9655	6205	33278
西 藏	Tibet				631	80
陕 西	Shaanxi	7783	28274	37638	20422	39047
甘 肃	Gansu	6053	3550	20056	6240	14558
青 海	Qinghai		80	2000	623	8610
宁 夏	Ningxia	926	10097	7470	5094	3944
新 疆	Xinjiang	2876	12061	56497	27298	46079

三、能源生产
Chapter 3 Energy Production

3-1 一次能源生产量和构成
PRIMARY ENERGY PRODUCTION AND COMPOSITION

指　标　　Item	1995	2000	2001	2002	2003	2004	2005
一次能源生产量(万吨标煤)(电热当量计算法) Primary Energy Production（10^4 tce）（calorific value calculation）	123519	122673	129794	135983	155947	177962	195518
一次能源生产量(万吨标煤)(发电煤耗计算法) Primary Energy Production（10^4 tce）（coal equivalent calculation）	129034	128978	137445	143810	163842	187341	205876
原煤（万吨）Raw Coal（10^4 tn）	136073	129921	138152	145456	172200	199232	220473
原油（万吨）Crude Oil（10^4 tn）	15004	16300	16396	16700	19660	17587	18135
天然气（亿立方米）Natural Gas（10^8 cu. m）	179	272	303	327	350	415	493
水电（亿千瓦时）Hydro Power（10^8 kW・h）	1906	2224	2774	2880	2837	3535	3970
核电（亿千瓦时）Nuclear Power（10^8 kW・h）	128	167	175	251	433	505	531
构成(电热当量计算法)（%）As Percentage of Primary Energy Production（%）（calorific value calculation）							
原煤 Raw Coal	78.69	75.65	76.03	76.41	78.87	79.97	80.55
原油 Crude Oil	17.35	18.98	18.05	17.54	15.54	14.12	13.25
天然气 Natural Gas	1.93	2.95	3.11	3.19	2.99	3.10	3.35
水电 Hydro Power	1.90	2.25	2.65	2.63	2.26	2.47	2.52
核电 Nuclear Power	0.13	0.17	0.17	0.23	0.34	0.35	0.33
构成(发电煤耗计算法)（%）As percentage of primary energy production（%）（coal equivalent calculation）							
原煤 Raw Coal	75.30	71.95	71.80	72.25	75.07	75.96	76.49
原油 Crude Oil	16.60	18.05	17.04	16.59	14.79	13.41	12.58
天然气 Natural Gas	1.90	2.80	2.93	3.02	2.84	2.94	3.19
水电 Hydro Power	5.85	6.69	7.74	7.49	6.34	6.73	6.83
核电 Nuclear Power	0.39	0.50	0.48	0.65	0.96	0.95	0.91

3-2 分地区原煤生产量
COAL PRODUCTION BY REGION

单位：万吨 (10 000 ton)

地 区	Region	1995	2000	2002	2003	2004	2005
北 京	Beijing	995	553.00	880.95	822.57	1067.96	897.92
天 津	Tianjin						
河 北	Hebei	8101	5781.21	6083.70	6600.15	8651.97	8639.49
山 西	Shanxi	34731	19602.70	24361.30	29508.66	48392.72	55426.05
内 蒙	Inner Mongolia	7055	7247.29	8880.30	11959.35	21235.21	25607.69
辽 宁	Liaoning	5626	4454.89	5180.77	5870.69	6641.94	6395.03
吉 林	Jilin	2644	1636.71	1685.25	2037.63	2589.96	2715.11
黑 龙 江	Heilongjiang	7938	4974.36	5882.58	6669.20	8476.49	9503.20
上 海	Shanghai						
江 苏	Jiangsu	2651	2479.02	2593.59	2760.40	2763.13	2817.56
浙 江	Zhejiang	125	72.96	73.50	69.39	65.32	43.67
安 徽	Anhui	4444	4678.31	6137.84	6726.41	8147.86	8487.96
福 建	Fujian	1134	375.03	644.51	778.22	1492.61	1823.66
江 西	Jiangxi	2878	1813.76	1375.04	951.66	2871.75	2565.05
山 东	Shandong	8827	8038.59	13065.97	14667.27	14764.28	14030.00
河 南	Henan	10334	7577.90	9921.21	11871.01	16829.42	18761.42
湖 北	Hubei	1533	389.32	372.55	366.40	1016.62	1010.39
湖 南	Hunan	5565	1490.81	1845.42	2366.69	6016.57	5735.00
广 东	Guangdong	1069	161.71	168.71	202.34	557.35	383.38
广 西	Guangxi	1391	706.67	463.51	417.14	589.19	700.34
海 南	Hainan	1	2.00	1.26	2.00		
重 庆	Chongqing		1149.90	1211.73	1484.20	3654.61	3618.90
四 川	Sichuan	9561	2061.95	2753.89	3133.88	7651.35	8125.05
贵 州	Guizhou	5472	3676.75	5001.12	7802.51	7953.02	10795.50
云 南	Yunnan	2803	994.13	1219.34	1399.39	5045.03	6462.14
西 藏	Tibet		2.13	1.56	2.21	1.64	3.35
陕 西	Shaanxi	4248	1983.89	5859.31	7392.76	13068.42	15246.00
甘 肃	Gansu	2466	1632.71	2089.21	2603.27	3539.98	3619.84
青 海	Qinghai	278	145.44	249.77	310.57	452.26	595.66
宁 夏	Ningxia	1480	1581.00	1707.31	2047.90	2432.7	2607.86
新 疆	Xinjiang	2721	2745.82	1582.28	1845.71	3263	3855.66

3-3 分地区焦炭生产量
COKE PRODUCTION BY REGION

单位:万吨 (10 000 ton)

地 区	Region	1995	2000	2002	2003	2004	2005
北 京	Beijing	400.87	402.07	357.44	362.39	362.04	344.36
天 津	Tianjin	174.78	170.92	282.38	310.84	376.68	360.55
河 北	Hebei	937.54	792.47	972.61	1128.23	1941	2613.43
山 西	Shanxi	5297.62	4967.22	5852.00	6747.41	6582.31	7981.05
内 蒙	Inner Mongolia	394.50	393.65	506.74	805.25	877.85	1034.19
辽 宁	Liaoning	820.15	788.90	871.50	923.01	1013.77	1237.89
吉 林	Jilin	135.79	153.88	153.79	177.76	224.64	269.91
黑 龙 江	Heilongjiang	189.55	128.64	192.64	298.96	414.84	474.40
上 海	Shanghai	651.20	776.39	692.79	741.65	746.58	762.16
江 苏	Jiangsu	191.25	237.15	358.44	410.97	490.54	575.63
浙 江	Zhejiang	57.34	60.13	60.55	58.81	57.79	55.20
安 徽	Anhui	293.45	330.16	351.03	367.31	438.15	488.37
福 建	Fujian	38.89	44.89	45.77	49.09	68.69	90.94
江 西	Jiangxi	166.53	186.71	223.63	239.76	340.54	400.98
山 东	Shandong	464.75	361.99	369.73	596.56	1124.76	1709.34
河 南	Henan	488.74	355.22	427.51	527.34	833.63	1380.54
湖 北	Hubei	398.44	410.52	415.56	473.93	469.36	678.41
湖 南	Hunan	214.66	207.17	206.39	272	410.12	445.88
广 东	Guangdong	54.47	53.96	54.72	56.06	90.62	124.58
广 西	Guangxi	63.69	60.68	77.99	99.44	152.17	223.46
海 南	Hainan						
重 庆	Chongqing		136.41	136.18	153.17	196.62	222.74
四 川	Sichuan	707.76	382.22	486.13	606.51	819.09	827.94
贵 州	Guizhou	426.18	133.69	153.29	530.91	695.26	716.15
云 南	Yunnan	370.27	221.25	532.33	659.67	917.59	1213.72
西 藏	Tibet						
陕 西	Shaanxi	340.78	175.38	245.06	871.02	573.39	590.62
甘 肃	Gansu	94.62	126.22	117.39	136.18	149.64	221.85
青 海	Qinghai	1.47	1.50	2.00	0.03		1.59
宁 夏	Ningxia	42.96	29.58	27.88	45.21	98.93	117.08
新 疆	Xinjiang	91.78	95.06	106.34	126.25	152.03	248.74

3-4 分地区原油生产量
CRUDE OIL PRODUCTION BY REGION

单位：万吨   (10 000 ton)

地 区	Region	1995	2000	2002	2003	2004	2005
北 京	Beijing						
天 津	Tianjin	620.82	763.99	1215.94	1316.30	1446.21	1792.99
河 北	Hebei	517.02	518.26	503.26	511.01	537.78	562.45
山 西	Shanxi						
内 蒙	Inner Mongolia			3.73	5.00	113.22	
辽 宁	Liaoning	1552.68	1401.12	1351.15	1332.22	1283.19	1260.96
吉 林	Jilin	342.73	348.46	477.01	476.40	481.11	550.57
黑龙江	Heilongjiang	5601.49	5306.73	5029.35	4840.12	4666.49	4516.01
上 海	Shanghai		52.73	47.32	38.02	31.86	25.27
江 苏	Jiangsu	101.41	155.02	162.97	166.35	168.94	164.7
浙 江	Zhejiang						
安 徽	Anhui						
福 建	Fujian						
江 西	Jiangxi						
山 东	Shandong	3006.27	2675.69	2671.51	2665.51	2590.19	2694.54
河 南	Henan	601.96	562.18	568.06	549.77	523.41	507.16
湖 北	Hubei	85.03	75.11	78.30	77.53	165.02	78.11
湖 南	Hunan						
广 东	Guangdong	650.97	1393.17	1264.46	1275.70	1481.9	1470.03
广 西	Guangxi	3.65	3.29	3.52	3.28	3.59	3.43
海 南	Hainan	0.11		4.64	7.57	8.04	10.07
重 庆	Chongqing						
四 川	Sichuan	17.23	17.32	14.05	13.92	14.62	13.92
贵 州	Guizhou						
云 南	Yunnan	10.21				0.09	0.09
西 藏	Tibet						
陕 西	Shaanxi	166.95	746.44	1063.77	1267.43	1531.51	1778.16
甘 肃	Gansu	267.83	55.25	63.24	73.44	77.04	78.91
青 海	Qinghai	121.72	200.01	214.02	220.02	222.02	221.49
宁 夏	Ningxia	39.04	139.01			4.1	
新 疆	Xinjiang	1297.83	1848.24	2015.19	2120.39	2237	2406.43

3-5 分地区燃料油生产量
FUEL OIL PRODUCTION BY REGION

单位:万吨　　　　　　　　　　　　　　　　　　　　　　　　　　　　　　　　　　(10 000 ton)

地 区	Region	1995	2000	2002	2003	2004	2005
北 京	Beijing	220.31	78.95	68.32	69.21	73.36	75.29
天 津	Tianjin	142.38	40.60	32.60	50.17	102.02	29.38
河 北	Hebei	44.26	30.17	63.88	41.46	41.53	25.37
山 西	Shanxi						
内 蒙	Inner Mongolia	18.85		21.93	16.32	16.07	13.56
辽 宁	Liaoning	610.43	413.40	394.37	338.28	420.47	466.15
吉 林	Jilin	85.11	95.59	73.21	47.42	27.26	34.76
黑 龙 江	Heilongjiang	181.28	120.56	70.88	63.97	76.88	44.69
上 海	Shanghai	290.40	139.03	80.20	94.75	118.63	119.67
江 苏	Jiangsu	162.04	136.29	113.84	156.43	217.44	159.43
浙 江	Zhejiang	78.33	123.40	57.62	75.41	160.89	109.76
安 徽	Anhui	48.48	10.68	7.44	2.19	10.69	8.30
福 建	Fujian	10.44	10.01	11.56	19.27	105.1	8.86
江 西	Jiangxi	43.27	54.27	42.25	52.10	58.95	39.53
山 东	Shandong	334.33	274.66	338.73	421.08	429.98	602.62
河 南	Henan	19.56	30.42	23.58	37.96	47.54	40.02
湖 北	Hubei	95.49	40.24	26.59	20.03	35.7	28.38
湖 南	Hunan	55.29	33.95	18.04	23.42	32.8	31.55
广 东	Guangdong	214.73	186.13	181.65	246.04	279.49	248.08
广 西	Guangxi	3.60	4.37	7.22	10.58	17.47	9.16
海 南	Hainan		9.45	7.73	7.20		4.36
重 庆	Chongqing					0.06	0.06
四 川	Sichuan	3.58	4.10	4.36	1.87	0.23	
贵 州	Guizhou						
云 南	Yunnan	0.58				0.04	
西 藏	Tibet						
陕 西	Shaanxi	55.64	41.54	90.02	103.93	98.19	83.69
甘 肃	Gansu	101.21	91.65	66.33	71.48	73.38	39.57
青 海	Qinghai	19.72	6.39	2.50	1.97	2.75	2.11
宁 夏	Ningxia	10.24	10.54	2.03	5.28	3.59	3.23
新 疆	Xinjiang	111.22	67.26	38.62	27.02	28.58	33.61

3-6 分地区汽油生产量

GASOLINE PRODUCTION BY REGION

单位:万吨 (10 000 ton)

地 区	Region	1995	2000	2002	2003	2004	2005
北 京	Beijing	101.95	146.20	154.12	151.44	169.77	170.90
天 津	Tianjin	94.02	122.02	110.44	124.61	130.89	145.42
河 北	Hebei	135.11	159.04	135.22	173.76	210.79	223.60
山 西	Shanxi					0.03	
内 蒙	Inner Mongolia	23.43		30.44	39.20	40.2	44.99
辽 宁	Liaoning	398.22	683.88	766.86	823.04	925.79	965.60
吉 林	Jilin	147.88	159.45	160.43	172.93	155.48	164.72
黑 龙 江	Heilongjiang	261.72	347.46	391.27	395.43	405.27	384.85
上 海	Shanghai	111.00	263.69	268.01	297.94	290.56	263.45
江 苏	Jiangsu	108.07	171.53	184.94	215.18	219	233.25
浙 江	Zhejiang	124.15	178.98	198.94	245.05	292.47	288.69
安 徽	Anhui	74.11	79.38	66.86	71.90	86.99	86.00
福 建	Fujian	81.49	102.22	96.48	103.48	108.72	95.19
江 西	Jiangxi	64.56	82.51	73.99	78.46	83.19	86.10
山 东	Shandong	214.88	280.15	291.65	361.76	438.54	474.54
河 南	Henan	138.68	136.86	129.49	139.37	136.2	127.65
湖 北	Hubei	126.32	154.97	144.65	166.99	170.96	178.87
湖 南	Hunan	90.38	120.19	116.33	124.27	129.67	122.83
广 东	Guangdong	286.47	331.50	356.64	371.44	400.73	367.23
广 西	Guangxi	15.09	15.64	15.87	15.84	16.24	19.38
海 南	Hainan						
重 庆	Chongqing					0.01	
四 川	Sichuan	5.92	8.42	11.52	13.24	18.33	23.20
贵 州	Guizhou						
云 南	Yunnan						
西 藏	Tibet						
陕 西	Shaanxi	49.68	180.13	199.40	229.59	310.54	387.83
甘 肃	Gansu	166.84	150.92	168.50	193.71	226.94	229.30
青 海	Qinghai	29.48	20.78	20.89	22.57	26.32	29.40
宁 夏	Ningxia	23.57	26.91	29.06	38.77	48.51	58.17
新 疆	Xinjiang	178.53	211.86	197.87	220.88	235.85	238.06

3-7 分地区煤油生产量
KEROSENE PRODUCTION BY REGION

单位：万吨   (10 000 ton)

地　区 Region	1995	2000	2002	2003	2004	2005
北　京 Beijing	0.26				8.11	12.36
天　津 Tianjin	8.85	32.57	26.90	27.07	29.19	25.83
河　北 Hebei	4.83	12.69	8.71	11.43	12.08	11.94
山　西 Shanxi						
内　蒙 Inner Mongolia	0.02					
辽　宁 Liaoning	84.34	231.53	200.21	214.19	213.46	220.00
吉　林 Jilin	1.96	1.28	0.22	0.31	0.05	
黑龙江 Heilongjiang	22.27	23.27	22.61	22.07	20.53	19.28
上　海 Shanghai	35.84	48.38	65.62	105.06	137.05	144.25
江　苏 Jiangsu	50.64	67.21	66.94	59.16	69.18	99.41
浙　江 Zhejiang	32.31	107.28	100.40	110.31	130.69	130.97
安　徽 Anhui						
福　建 Fujian	3.49	8.64	4.93	5.24	5.64	5.81
江　西 Jiangxi	2.14	4.44	4.08	5.08	5.34	4.67
山　东 Shandong	24.89	44.96	46.73	50.85	59.44	34.65
河　南 Henan	21.10	17.04	17.55	15.88	28.2	20.07
湖　北 Hubei	13.64	16.38	17.47	12.93	8.59	8.85
湖　南 Hunan	7.49	8.57	8.25	7.17	10.45	10.99
广　东 Guangdong	72.28	147.68	160.45	145.23	165.25	156.29
广　西 Guangxi	0.55	0.05	0.01	0.01		0.01
海　南 Hainan						
重　庆 Chongqing			0.04	0.04	0.04	0.02
四　川 Sichuan	2.76	4.23	2.76	1.41	1.42	1.44
贵　州 Guizhou						
云　南 Yunnan						
西　藏 Tibet						
陕　西 Shaanxi	1.65	8.46	10.24	6.87	8.21	
甘　肃 Gansu	38.64	55.88	42.44	35.39	42.76	49.61
青　海 Qinghai						
宁　夏 Ningxia						
新　疆 Xinjiang	15.80	31.75	19.55	19.60	24.45	32.14

3-8 分地区柴油生产量
DIESEL OIL PRODUCTION BY REGION

单位:万吨 (10 000 ton)

地 区	Region	1995	2000	2002	2003	2004	2005
北 京	Beijing	79.20	183.92	174.05	170.17	180.74	199.41
天 津	Tianjin	119.44	246.82	259.89	278.71	310.24	364.54
河 北	Hebei	165.81	271.19	230.85	293.59	374.98	403.42
山 西	Shanxi	0.16				0.01	
内 蒙	Inner Mongolia	20.46		42.62	45.63	48.66	41.01
辽 宁	Liaoning	677.68	1202.07	1350.79	1567.72	1831.6	1899.60
吉 林	Jilin	99.83	178.81	226.89	290.52	332.73	367.43
黑 龙 江	Heilongjiang	379.68	532.61	593.85	596.76	616.8	627.52
上 海	Shanghai	129.13	401.30	452.46	571.35	637.89	717.86
江 苏	Jiangsu	207.31	408.69	369.26	433.99	544.96	725.87
浙 江	Zhejiang	201.52	387.40	488.88	549.69	688.46	728.09
安 徽	Anhui	98.87	151.85	134.89	146.31	181.39	177.36
福 建	Fujian	85.15	161.49	147.08	147.38	174.44	150.34
江 西	Jiangxi	83.17	127.09	112.82	116.62	137.25	132.53
山 东	Shandong	328.63	540.04	609.13	669.78	875.31	939.01
河 南	Henan	121.69	213.42	202.79	215.96	250.51	219.02
湖 北	Hubei	153.05	247.01	227.27	245.88	298.38	329.83
湖 南	Hunan	104.36	215.53	185.83	178.87	240.6	229.25
广 东	Guangdong	377.36	654.02	685.59	716.37	867.05	875.28
广 西	Guangxi	14.98	24.92	25.36	24.15	27.93	36.33
海 南	Hainan						
重 庆	Chongqing			0.01	0.01	0.38	
四 川	Sichuan	5.78	11.14	16.41	27.07	39.72	48.52
贵 州	Guizhou						
云 南	Yunnan						
西 藏	Tibet						
陕 西	Shaanxi	52.93	223.19	308.00	358.03	453.62	513.38
甘 肃	Gansu	188.59	276.23	336.94	364.34	442.53	535.67
青 海	Qinghai	20.99	22.63	25.27	26.41	36.14	44.31
宁 夏	Ningxia	24.92	33.44	33.10	50.73	63.24	76.57
新 疆	Xinjiang	231.88	364.79	429.40	446.78	523.1	697.27

3-9 分地区天然气生产量
NATURAL GAS PRODUCTION BY REGION

单位:亿立方米 （100 million cu. m）

地 区 Region	1995	2000	2002	2003	2004	2005
北 京 Beijing						4932
天 津 Tianjin	7.57	9.10	8.88	8.49	8.72	8.79
河 北 Hebei	3.49	5.14	5.90	6.34	6.63	6.92
山 西 Shanxi	0.47	1.14	2.06	2.50		3.24
内 蒙 Inner Mongolia		4.55	8.49		17.19	
辽 宁 Liaoning	21.12	14.70	13.31	13.28	10.3	11.72
吉 林 Jilin	1.83	2.05	2.41	2.32	3.44	5.40
黑 龙 江 Heilongjiang	25.91	23.04	20.22	20.96	20.34	24.43
上 海 Shanghai	0.00	2.60	4.33	4.97	5.73	6.04
江 苏 Jiangsu	0.19	0.24	0.23	0.33	0.53	0.64
浙 江 Zhejiang		0.04	0.05			0.03
安 徽 Anhui						
福 建 Fujian						
江 西 Jiangxi						
山 东 Shandong	12.85	6.88	7.50	8.10	9.25	9.25
河 南 Henan	11.38	14.95	19.36	20.14	18.55	17.62
湖 北 Hubei	0.76	0.91	0.91	0.94	1.08	1.12
湖 南 Hunan						
广 东 Guangdong	1.03	34.60	31.55	26.88	42.82	44.75
广 西 Guangxi						
海 南 Hainan					1.29	1.66
重 庆 Chongqing		1.94	1.94	2.23	4.69	3.27
四 川 Sichuan	76.64	88.60	100.06	113.43	114.03	142.3
贵 州 Guizhou		0.70	0.48	0.52		0.53
云 南 Yunnan	1.81	0.05	0.15	0.24	0.18	0.22
西 藏 Tibet						
陕 西 Shaanxi	0.22	21.10	40.04	52.86	74.46	75.46
甘 肃 Gansu	1.13	0.20	0.87	0.21	0.2	0.84
青 海 Qinghai	0.64	3.91	11.51	15.57	17.94	22.26
宁 夏 Ningxia	0.62	0.15				
新 疆 Xinjiang	11.81	35.38	46.08	49.84	57.23	106.71

3-10 分地区发电量
POWER GENERATION BY REGION

单位:亿千瓦小时

(100 million kW · h)

地 区	Region	1995	2000	2002	2003	2004	2005
北 京	Beijing	132.21	145.26	141.98	192.16	203.89	213.35
天 津	Tianjin	133.65	211.49	268.83	320.07	339.76	369.06
河 北	Hebei	607.17	844.42	1014.26	1088.34	1255.56	1338.63
山 西	Shanxi	505.97	620.31	842.01	965.01	1078.99	1311.97
内 蒙	Inner Mongolia	278.54	439.22	514.85	647.73	816.44	1056.59
辽 宁	Liaoning	540.08	645.58	725.27	837.11	874.85	904.21
吉 林	Jilin	284.60	313.50	295.65	338.83	386.19	433.43
黑 龙 江	Heilongjiang	388.01	426.73	459.28	493.78	501.83	596.02
上 海	Shanghai	403.42	553.09	608.92	687.63	705.02	733.97
江 苏	Jiangsu	700.41	909.70	1116.56	1336.77	1554.89	2120.00
浙 江	Zhejiang	401.48	624.83	778.20	1101.74	1231.9	1456.42
安 徽	Anhui	310.32	355.44	465.66	557.15	607.1	648.41
福 建	Fujian	261.55	403.73	533.08	610.70	674.64	778.25
江 西	Jiangxi	176.48	203.35	247.99	320.94	378.98	373.49
山 东	Shandong	739.24	1005.26	1220.84	1396.97	1688.19	1911.39
河 南	Henan	547.71	694.93	876.82	1025.10	1280.75	1414.68
湖 北	Hubei	452.74	559.12	606.57	780.46	1096.77	1289.80
湖 南	Hunan	332.94	354.42	425.54	537.76	651.11	644.41
广 东	Guangdong	821.06	1292.69	1525.53	1882.68	2141.23	2278.59
广 西	Guangxi	217.29	289.09	307.74	362.91	378.49	446.04
海 南	Hainan	31.53	39.05	50.11	58.59	65.7	82.19
重 庆	Chongqing		167.90	184.75	204.11	262.66	253.90
四 川	Sichuan	575.97	500.24	695.74	849.26	934.49	1018.77
贵 州	Guizhou	231.55	404.70	547.12	640.98	720.46	797.65
云 南	Yunnan	228.42	297.84	373.16	474.8	548.05	624.20
西 藏	Tibet	4.83	6.61	7.96		11.51	13.34
陕 西	Shaanxi	236.77	272.28	343.51	419.16	498.29	548.80
甘 肃	Gansu	237.75	253.52	340.18	404.87	455.34	506.17
青 海	Qinghai	60.42	133.79	139.49	130.48	172.51	215.89
宁 夏	Ningxia	107.77	136.61	171.02	206.13	253.66	312.87
新 疆	Xinjiang	120.43	182.12	195.37	233.53	263.84	310.11

3-11 分地区水力发电量
HYDRO POWER GENERATION BY REGION

单位:亿千瓦小时   (100 million kW·h)

地 区	Region	1995	2000	2002	2003	2004	2005
北 京	Beijing	3.18	8.64	4.10	6.52	3.96	4.71
天 津	Tianjin	0.21	0.14				
河 北	Hebei	12.63	4.70	3.64	3.01	4.02	5.61
山 西	Shanxi	7.11	13.04	18.83	19.29	21	20.32
内 蒙	Inner Mongolia	1.43	5.59	6.69	7.07	8.49	11.55
辽 宁	Liaoning	41.71	14.89	14.46	22.97	38.59	56.73
吉 林	Jilin	83.16	47.84	44.57	40.80	56.35	78.30
黑 龙 江	Heilongjiang	6.69	13.19	15.09	11.72	13.96	14.70
上 海	Shanghai						
江 苏	Jiangsu	0.35	0.13	1.03	4.00	3	2.66
浙 江	Zhejiang	78.25	65.23	95.29	125.00	95.38	135.11
安 徽	Anhui	11.39	4.58	10.51	15.60	18.11	12.52
福 建	Fujian	154.91	195.22	224.35	188.99	184.84	291.00
江 西	Jiangxi	55.13	53.50	61.51	47.64	75.55	67.88
山 东	Shandong	0.40	0.03	0.01	0.20	0.98	1.30
河 南	Henan	15.64	15.52	15.52	54.00	78.36	67.91
湖 北	Hubei	258.82	281.40	272.58	380.64	697.24	813.65
湖 南	Hunan	157.97	191.15	227.93	242.97	280.93	241.28
广 东	Guangdong	131.10	106.11	108.62	180.02	192.13	207.74
广 西	Guangxi	138.30	168.87	184.12	192.63	185.41	195.82
海 南	Hainan	11.32	11.54	13.74	13.22	9.23	10.64
重 庆	Chongqing		38.22	37.48	46.19	93.5	67.32
四 川	Sichuan	259.79	315.11	409.85	480.15	620.57	653.35
贵 州	Guizhou	114.90	183.44	221.53	208.25	226.05	213.35
云 南	Yunnan	162.05	196.53	209.24	280.90	299.83	349.19
西 藏	Tibet	3.04	5.54	6.88		10.32	12.10
陕 西	Shaanxi	25.43	34.80	25.92	46.75	42.49	50.54
甘 肃	Gansu	96.18	102.54	105.74	108.07	119.42	165.57
青 海	Qinghai	42.57	107.69	88.97	66.60	111.3	160.58
宁 夏	Ningxia	9.30	8.18	7.78	7.28	9.4	16.41
新 疆	Xinjiang	22.82	30.83	29.21	36.33	35.03	42.33

3-12 分地区火力发电量
THERMAL POWER GENERATION BY REGION

单位:亿千瓦小时 (100 million kW·h)

地 区	Region	1995	2000	2002	2003	2004	2005
北 京	Beijing	128.18	136.62	136.18	185.64	198.07	209.80
天 津	Tianjin	131.58	211.35	268.83	320.07	339.76	365.69
河 北	Hebei	593.72	839.53	1010.32	1085.17	1251.11	1332.17
山 西	Shanxi	498.85	607.27	823.18	945.71	1058	1291.65
内 蒙	Inner Mongolia	277.11	432.09	507.30	639.53	805.84	1042.28
辽 宁	Liaoning	496.63	628.00	709.29	812.30	834.48	845.00
吉 林	Jilin	201.45	265.48	250.37	297.39	329.15	354.16
黑 龙 江	Heilongjiang	381.30	413.54	444.19	483.12	484.98	581.13
上 海	Shanghai	401.93	553.09	608.92	687.51	703.77	728.74
江 苏	Jiangsu	698.42	909.57	1115.53	1332.77	1550.78	2114.03
浙 江	Zhejiang	300.67	539.18	630.12	827.50	915.34	1094.64
安 徽	Anhui	297.94	350.87	455.15	541.60	587.58	636.37
福 建	Fujian	106.60	208.45	308.50	421.46	489.52	486.88
江 西	Jiangxi	121.35	149.85	186.48	273.30	303.43	305.61
山 东	Shandong	738.83	1005.14	1220.73	1396.77	1681.78	1909.59
河 南	Henan	532.01	677.76	858.86	968.26	1200.87	1346.77
湖 北	Hubei	193.71	277.73	333.98	395.32	396.8	476.15
湖 南	Hunan	174.86	163.27	197.61	294.79	371.31	403.13
广 东	Guangdong	583.62	1038.61	1209.57	1399.46	1661.26	1764.53
广 西	Guangxi	78.99	120.21	123.61	170.28	192.02	250.23
海 南	Hainan	20.21	27.51	36.37	45.25	56.4	72.46
重 庆	Chongqing		129.68	147.27	158.18	168.99	185.81
四 川	Sichuan	316.18	185.13	285.65	368.45	313.79	365.42
贵 州	Guizhou	116.64	221.27	325.59	432.74	490.4	584.30
云 南	Yunnan	66.37	101.32	163.93	193.91	248.22	274.89
西 藏	Tibet	0.25	0.05	0.07		0.08	0.08
陕 西	Shaanxi	211.34	237.48	317.59	373.35	455.9	495.85
甘 肃	Gansu	141.56	150.98	234.26	295.95	334.71	339.70
青 海	Qinghai	17.85	26.10	50.52	63.88	61.21	55.63
宁 夏	Ningxia	98.48	128.43	163.24	198.85	243.99	295.19
新 疆	Xinjiang	97.27	149.29	164.43	195.10	226.34	265.48

3-13 分地区城市天然气供应情况
BASIC STATISTICS ON SUPPLY OF
NATURAL GAS IN CITIES BY REGION

地 区 Region	供气总量（万立方米） Total Gas Supply（10^4cu. m）			用气人口(万人) Population with Access（10^4 person）		
	2000	2004	2005	2000	2004	2005
全 国 National Total	821476	1693364	2104951	2580.98	5627.6	7104.4
北 京 Beijing	95740	270213	317397	295.30	738.0	880.0
天 津 Tianjin	23474	62350	68966	304.12	404.6	411.5
河 北 Hebei	4647	17123	25374	31.08	118.0	142.0
山 西 Shanxi	5611	10585	10802	35.68	44.3	50.2
内 蒙 古 Inner Mongolia		4021	9444		39.5	49.6
辽 宁 Liaoning	24923	37698	36817	409.88	575.9	566.6
吉 林 Jilin	13162	21131	17333	76.50	147.5	166.9
黑 龙 江 Heilongjiang	4185	16932	19555	55.71	89.0	103.7
上 海 Shanghai	25974	98268	174962	66.99	396.5	521.9
江 苏 Jiangsu		20976	87634		178.8	380.4
浙 江 Zhejiang		3052	10428		58.1	118.9
安 徽 Anhui	600	3839	11564	5.29	105.3	207.8
福 建 Fujian						
江 西 Jiangxi		123	1051		12.6	38.4
山 东 Shandong	84065	93978	116691	61.88	258.9	381.3
河 南 Henan	55018	36603	53337	185.89	346.6	398.7
湖 北 Hubei	1	5884	17422	0.20	14.2	263.9
湖 南 Hunan		1538	5632			61.6
广 东 Guangdong	339	4857	71597	4.00	19.7	78.5
广·西 Guangxi		168	84	0.12	1.4	0.5
海 南 Hainan		4632	6360		48.4	21.1
重 庆 Chongqing	68049	135173	164614	328.63	458.0	509.0
四 川 Sichuan	388394	582734	598531	556.00	911.7	966.5
贵 州 Guizhou	450	6199	6199	1.89	1.7	1.7
云 南 Yunnan	1533	14500	14500	2.00	4.9	4.9
西 藏 Tibet			808			15.4
陕 西 Shaanxi	17770	59153	76285	125.95	321.6	358.8
甘 肃 Gansu	78	13200	4100	1.60	88.8	117.6
青 海 Qinghai	2022	67456	63606	3.93	30.5	32.6
宁 夏 Ningxia	56	63749	68193	1.35	27.0	34.1
新 疆 Xinjiang	5385	37230	45665	26.99	186.3	220.4

3-14 分地区城市人工煤气供应情况
BASIC STATISTICS ON SUPPLY OF COAL GAS IN CITIES BY REGION

地 区	Region	供气总量（万立方米） Total Gas Supply（10^4cu. m）			用气人口（万人） Population with Access（10^4 person）		
		2000	2004	2005	2000	2004	2005
全 国	**National Total**	1523615	2137224.8	2558343	3944.45	4653.8	4368.6
北 京	Beijing	47310	16890	20211	82.94	28.0	21.9
天 津	Tianjin	9882	25800.0	28803	72.62	98.5	96.5
河 北	Hebei	45918	73647	78435	278.73	378.5	400.9
山 西	Shanxi	241869	77720.6	82291	295.07	396.0	394.7
内 蒙 古	Inner Mongolia	7485	6549.1	6887	77.93	88.9	92.9
辽 宁	Liaoning	81957	61112	63614	422.10	474.7	531.5
吉 林	Jilin	15508	12119.7	13755	149.88	154.2	169.2
黑 龙 江	Heilongjiang	30347	41726	40199	211.03	274.6	289.4
上 海	Shanghai	213147	207463.3	199744	449.95	719.4	662.3
江 苏	Jiangsu	362606	1027886.1	1290834	324.65	333.8	234.1
浙 江	Zhejiang	27796	33503.5	27686	47.77	110.8	83.3
安 徽	Anhui	22996	18510.7	8723	168.76	129.3	67.0
福 建	Fujian	12727	1537.2	1810	21.21	9.3	11.2
江 西	Jiangxi	39463	46473.8	31707	125.38	155.0	130.6
山 东	Shandong	43041	47103.9	47743	335.43	396.8	356.5
河 南	Henan	81775	95994.3	117592	136.31	142.3	142.4
湖 北	Hubei	14588	16618	9184	180.08	140.7	22.3
湖 南	Hunan	60375	44119	44064	81.29	102.2	74.6
广 东	Guangdong	12097	64345.9	29310	150.07	155.6	162.9
广 西	Guangxi	2817	4120.8	4483	14.51	23.9	24.9
海 南	Hainan						
重 庆	Chongqing	100			0.50		
四 川	Sichuan	111677	113863.0	128252	30.08	31.9	32.5
贵 州	Guizhou	8727	16929.0	19209	73.35	110.5	124.8
云 南	Yunnan	15407	16899.0	20287	99.60	127.1	177.3
西 藏	Tibet						
陕 西	Shaanxi	4447	4534.0	4365	32.67	29.8	27.4
甘 肃	Gansu	6691	4694	3802	70.24	26.3	24.0
青 海	Qinghai	24			2.50		
宁 夏	Ningxia	2838	2883.0	3013	9.80	10.9	8.8
新 疆	Xinjiang		54182.0	232340		5.0	5.0

3-15 分地区城市液化石油气供应情况
BASIC STATISTICS ON SUPPLY OF LPG IN CITIES BY REGION

地　　区	Region	供气总量（吨） Total Gas Supply（ton）			用气人口（万人） Population with Access（10⁴ person）		
		2000	2004	2005	2000	2004	2005
全　国	**National Total**	**10537147**	**11267119.9**	**12220141**	**11106.62**	**17559.2**	**18012.8**
北　京	Beijing	176460	431399	374358	252.69	418.0	340.8
天　津	Tianjin	44203	69779	61503	89.40	119.3	122.9
河　北	Hebei	189612	336674.1	327294	475.66	708.8	705.0
山　西	Shanxi	34152	38741.6	42004	102.28	168.2	169.7
内 蒙 古	Inner Mongolia	59425	144113	138348	191.86	266.7	294.5
辽　宁	Liaoning	379194	456355	402659	568.82	726.8	713.1
吉　林	Jilin	169062	210681	184659	350.34	447.4	493.0
黑 龙 江	Heilongjiang	601427	236835	228630	546.44	603.3	612.3
上　海	Shanghai	490561	446543	452613	421.15	702.5	710.9
江　苏	Jiangsu	705010	1226674.8	1129147	882.85	1712.1	1764.6
浙　江	Zhejiang	630895	1050666.6	1060572	555.11	1144.3	1135.2
安　徽	Anhui	458621	590159.1	613614	378.80	517.3	540.9
福　建	Fujian	737609	346659.6	378053	340.72	598.2	603.5
江　西	Jiangxi	164698	175642	174521	220.08	387.9	411.6
山　东	Shandong	276543	517235	572194	886.80	1750.9	1835.6
河　南	Henan	162199	171956.4	225864	429.88	544.3	573.8
湖　北	Hubei	296179	315009.2	311171	908.34	1224.1	1142.0
湖　南	Hunan	199873	300410.3	294718	460.65	592.9	647.6
广　东	Guangdong	3108612	3121280.1	4101990	1485.28	2908.3	3222.5
广　西	Guangxi	204904	271967.6	315998	373.57	506.1	550.9
海　南	Hainan	77856	68291	66866	116.53	91.1	113.4
重　庆	Chongqing	38769	96022.6	95577	35.05	75.1	71.7
四　川	Sichuan	66154	163946.8	164266	80.54	139.2	152.2
贵　州	Guizhou	28973	60465	53779	89.71	189.6	189.3
云　南	Yunnan	82954	95078.1	70436	137.50	184.1	141.0
西　藏	Tibet	16680	704.5	1500	13.80	12.5	2.8
陕　西	Shaanxi	79038	51448	121943	205.97	241.2	242.9
甘　肃	Gansu	783739	73240.2	71904	101.73	208.6	141.9
青　海	Qinghai	11496	17399	14339	29.50	35.8	36.9
宁　夏	Ningxia	18231	27217.2	22697	69.87	87.8	90.4
新　疆	Xinjiang	244018	154526.2	147314	305.70	246.9	240.2

3-16 分地区城市集中供热情况
BASIC STATISTICS ON HEATING SUPPLY IN CITIES BY REGION

地 区	Region	蒸汽供应能力（吨/小时）Capacity of Steam Supply（tn/hr）			热水供应能力（兆瓦）Capacity of Hot Water Supply（10^6W）		
		2000	2004	2005	2000	2004	2005
全 国	**National Total**	**74148**	**98262**	**106723**	**97417**	**174442**	**197976**
北 京	Beijing	3408	1384	2297	4755	23706	30115
天 津	Tianjin	9106	3407	3294	5608	10111	10563
河 北	Hebei	6427	8140	9290	8388	12866	13917
山 西	Shanxi	3316	2799	3133	5347	6627	8578
内 蒙 古	Inner Mongolia	1200	844	844	5687	10160	10887
辽 宁	Liaoning	11569	11844	12583	19154	30488	36051
吉 林	Jilin	3425	5763	4749	10564	18330	18925
黑 龙 江	Heilongjiang	4513	5690	5937	13750	22646	23952
上 海	Shanghai						
江 苏	Jiangsu	2554	17157	19744	8	228	200
浙 江	Zhejiang	1516	3583	4569		233	233
安 徽	Anhui	1915	2276	2006	214	135	135
福 建	Fujian		160		43	286	286
江 西	Jiangxi						
山 东	Shandong	12498	20054	22770	9206	13901	16744
河 南	Henan	3261	4602	4698	1334	1617	2118
湖 北	Hubei	775	1404	1404		78	78
湖 南	Hunan	493	105	105			
广 东	Guangdong						
广 西	Guangxi						
海 南	Hainan						
重 庆	Chongqing						
四 川	Sichuan		160	160			
贵 州	Guizhou						
云 南	Yunnan						
西 藏	Tibet						
陕 西	Shaanxi	1923	1983	2240	551	1499	1806
甘 肃	Gansu	3949	4774	4813	3611	5474	5791
青 海	Qinghai				89	158	173
宁 夏	Ningxia	662	646	646	2963	4822	5115
新 疆	Xinjiang	1638	1487	1441	6145	11077	12309

四、全国能源平衡表

Chapter 4   Energy Balance Table of China

4-1 中国能源平衡表（标准量）–2005

单位：万吨标准煤

项　目	Item	能源合计 Energy Total	
		（发电煤耗计算法） （coal equivalent calculation）	（电热当量计算法） （calorific value calculation）
一. 可供本地区消费的能源量	**Total Primary Energy Supply**	**223212.66**	**212995.66**
1. 一次能源生产量	Indigenous Production	205876.28	195517.87
水电	Hydro Power	13959.15	4879.34
核电	Nuclear Power	1866.58	652.45
2. 回收能	Recovery of Energy	2840.06	2840.06
3. 进口量	Import	26330.02	26215.42
4. 我轮、机在外国加油量	China Airplanes&ships Refueling in Abroad	622.05	622.05
5. 出口量（-）	Export（-）	-10868.39	-10612.38
6. 外轮、机在我国加油量（-）	Foreign Airplanes&ships Refueling in China	-579.48	-579.48
7. 库存增（-）、减（+）量	Stock Change	-1007.82	-1007.87
二. 加工转换投入（-）产出（+）量	**Input（-）& Output（+）of Transformation**	**-3719.60**	**-53449.08**
1. 火力发电	Thermal Power		-46822.74
2. 供热	Heating Supply		-2906.74
3. 洗选煤	Coal Washing	-1302.64	-1302.64
4. 炼焦	Coking	-658.20	-658.20
5. 炼油	Petroleum Refineries	-1304.78	-1304.78
6. 制气	Gas Works	-175.36	-175.36
#焦炭再投入量（-）	Coke Input（-）	-226.95	-226.95
7. 煤制品加工	Briquettes	-51.68	-51.68
三. 损失量	**Loss**	**6483.00**	**2546.87**
四. 终端消费量	**Total Final Consumption**	**214479.39**	**158470.11**
1. 农、林、牧、渔、水利业	Farming, Forestry, Animal Husbandry, Fishery & Water Conservancy	7978.28	5973.13
2. 工业	Industry	149638.94	109162.43
#用作原料. 材料	Noe-Energy Use	8618.19	8618.19
3. 建筑业	Construction	3411.07	2870.16
4. 交通运输. 仓储及邮电通迅业	Transport, Storage, Postal & Telecommunications Services	16279.32	15277.83
5. 批发和零售贸易业. 餐饮业	Wholesale, Retail Trade and Catering Service	5031.12	3282.56
6. 生活消费	Residential Consumption	23449.51	16332.06
城镇	Urban	14220.53	9642.53
乡村	Rural	9228.98	6689.53
7. 其他	Other	8691.15	5571.94
五. 平衡差额	**Statistical Difference**	**-1469.32**	**-1470.41**
六. 能源消费总量	**Total Energy Consumption**	**224681.99**	**214466.07**

48

ENERGY BALANCE OF CHINA – 2005 (STANDARD QUANTITY)

(10 000 tce)

煤合计 Coal Total	原煤 Raw Coal	洗精煤 Cleaned Coal	其他洗煤 Other Washed Coal	型煤 Briquettes	焦炭 Coke	焦炉煤气 Coke Oven Gas	其他煤气 Other Gas	其他焦化产品 Other Coking Products	油品合计 Petroleum Products Total
153213.55	**153058.51**	**154.55**	**2.32**	**−1.82**	**−1386.44**		**1983.44**	**35.53**	**46637.83**
157483.80	157483.80								25908.08
						1983.44			
1993.84	1343.48	647.51	2.85		0.52			116.06	24043.40
									622.05
−5220.04	−4742.62	−473.38	−1.07	−2.98	−1239.90			−80.53	−3539.46
									−579.48
−1044.06	−1026.16	−19.59	0.54	1.15	−147.06				183.24
−107737.13	**−112929.26**	**1451.25**	**3050.26**	**690.63**	**23549.87**	**2615.72**	**21.52**	**414.90**	**−4163.43**
−68428.79	−67372.22	−75.51	−981.07				−220.10	−376.31	−2296.06
−9443.61	−9326.04	−6.03	−111.54				−103.82	−224.74	−577.55
−1302.64	−31410.63	25258.35	4849.64						
−27512.82	−4182.11	−23296.82	−33.89		23469.11	2911.78	67.75	405.98	
									−1269.26
−997.59	−560.47	−428.75	−8.37		302.15	27.86	554.82	14.47	−20.56
						−221.40		−5.55	
−51.68	−77.79		−664.52	690.63					
									222.51
47264.51	**41624.78**	**1860.67**	**3085.18**	**693.88**	**21810.22**	**2605.21**	**2004.96**	**449.78**	**42244.82**
1809.36	1796.02		13.34		59.22				3024.94
36646.13	32172.75	1857.60	2528.01	87.78	21581.72	2295.95	1697.76	449.78	15801.68
2341.62	2136.27	95.48	106.18	3.70	863.27	23.40		114.47	4059.25
472.32	466.29	3.07	2.97		17.15				2057.50
638.22	635.59		2.62		1.00		0.65		13985.90
680.96	668.32		5.79	6.85	59.78	17.99	17.25		1363.20
6433.30	5335.73		500.03	597.54	84.27	271.50	289.30		2961.13
1785.59	1285.88		189.94	309.76	46.57	271.50	285.77		2329.17
4647.71	4049.85		310.09	287.78	37.70		3.52		631.96
584.22	550.08		32.42	1.71	7.08	19.78			3050.47
−1788.09	**−1495.53**	**−254.88**	**−32.61**	**−5.07**	**353.20**	**10.51**	**0.00**	**0.65**	**7.08**

续表

单位:万吨标准煤

项 目 Item		原油 Crude Oil	汽油 Gasoline
一.可供本地区消费的能源量	**Total Primary Energy Supply**	**42985.39**	**-850.89**
1.一次能源生产量	Indigenous Production	25908.08	
水电	Hydro Power		
核电	Nuclear Power		
2.回收能	Recovery of Energy		
3.进口量	Import	18117.13	0.01
4.我轮、机在外国加油量	China Airplanes&ships Refueling in Abroad		
5.出口量(-)	Export (-)	-1152.42	-823.48
6.外轮、机在我国加油量(-)	Foreign Airplanes&ships Refueling in China		
7.库存增(-)、减(+)量	Stock Change	112.60	-27.41
二.加工转换投入(-)产出(+)量	**Input(-) & Output(+) of Transformation**	**-41518.14**	**7992.94**
1.火力发电	Thermal Power	-30.40	-1.03
2.供热	Heating Supply	-0.47	-0.15
3.洗选煤	Coal Washing		
4.炼焦	Coking		
5.炼油	Petroleum Refineries	-41487.27	7994.12
6.制气	Gas Works		
#焦炭再投入量(-)	Coke Input (-)		
7.煤制品加工	Briquettes		
三.损失量	**Loss**	**219.66**	
四.终端消费量	**Total Final Consumption**	**1243.40**	**7139.98**
1.农、林、牧、渔、水利业	Farming,Forestry,Animal Husbandry,Fishery & Water Conservancy		335.46
2.工业	Industry	1243.40	678.18
#用作原料、材料	Noe-Energy Use	165.37	21.77
3.建筑业	Construction		253.29
4.交通运输、仓储及邮电通迅业	Transport,Storage,Postal & Telecommunications Services		3634.43
5.批发和零售贸易业、餐饮业	Wholesale,Retail Trade and Catering Service		440.52
6.生活消费	Residential Consumption		447.05
城镇	Urban		352.54
乡村	Rural		94.51
7.其他	Other		1351.04
五.平衡差额	**Statistical Difference**	**4.19**	**2.07**
六.能源消费总量	**Total Energy Consumption**		

50

Continued

煤油 Kerosene	柴油 Diesel Oil	燃料油 Fuel Oil	液化石油气 PLG	炼厂干气 Refinery Gas	其他石油制品 Other Petroleum Products	天然气 Natural Gas	热力 Heat	电力 Electricity	其他能源 Other Energy
93.49	−171.37	3528.42	1062.01	0.00	−9.23	6164.68	0.00	5490.45	856.62
						6559.56		5566.44	
							0.00	4879.34	
								652.45	
									856.62
483.12	77.58	3726.69	1057.72	0.00	581.16			61.59	
217.47	11.32	393.25							
−395.31	−215.13	−328.55	−4.58		−620.00	−394.88		−137.57	
−263.23	−33.95	−282.29							
51.44	−11.19	19.33	8.87		29.61				
1480.93	15625.14	678.91	2450.45	1247.02	7879.32	−783.90	7805.31	25161.76	−333.70
	−534.37	−1580.12	−0.21	−57.37	−92.56	−419.22		25161.76	−244.02
		−245.33	−5.42	−130.82	−195.36	−308.16	7805.31		−54.16
1480.93	16159.52	2524.92	2456.08	1435.21	8167.24				−35.52
		−20.56				−56.53			
			2.85			137.39	89.72	2097.25	
1584.46	15453.59	4214.20	3498.12	1243.53	7867.55	5298.25	7715.44	28554.40	522.51
2.35	2677.63	0.94	8.55				2.61	1077.01	
84.61	2512.81	2475.18	906.18	1243.53	6657.80	3880.41	5669.74	20616.75	522.51
9.87	47.49	119.96	98.86	10.69	3585.23	1166.14			50.03
	563.37	20.26	10.83		1209.75	19.82	15.87	287.50	
1298.39	7313.78	1658.63	80.66			76.74	46.44	528.89	
5.40	708.19	39.32	169.78			143.53	75.25	924.59	
37.46	198.75		2277.86			1056.42	1764.46	3471.69	
2.74	146.39		1827.51			1052.43	1764.46	2107.03	
34.73	52.37		450.35			3.99		1364.66	
156.25	1479.05	19.87	44.26			121.33	141.08	1647.98	
−10.04	0.19	−6.86	11.50	3.49	2.54	−54.86	0.14	0.55	0.41

4-2 中国能源平衡表(实物量) - 2005

项 目	Item	煤合计 (万吨) Coal Total (10⁴ tn)	原煤 (万吨) Raw Coal (10⁴ tn)
一. 可供本地区消费的能源量	**Total Primary Energy Supply**	**214462.14**	**214289.02**
1. 一次能源生产量	Indigenous Production	220472.91	220472.91
水电	Hydro Power		
核电	Nuclear Power		
2. 回收能	Recovery of Energy		
3. 进口量	Import	2617.11	1892.23
4. 我轮、机在外国加油量	China Airplanes&Ships Refueling in Abroad		
5. 出口量(-)	Export (-)	-7172.44	-6639.53
6. 外轮、机在我国加油量(-)	Foreign Airplanes&Ships Refueling in China		
7. 库存增(-)、减(+)量	Stock Change	-1455.44	-1436.59
二. 加工转换投入(-)产出(+)量	**Input(-) & Output(+) of Transformation**	**-154568.38**	**-163126.08**
1. 火力发电	Thermal Power	-103263.49	-101311.60
2. 供热	Heating Supply	-13542.00	-13322.92
3. 洗选煤	Coal Washing	-4582.11	-41880.84
4. 炼焦	Coking	-31667.06	-5717.18
5. 炼油	Petroleum Refineries		
6. 制气	Gas Works	-1276.96	-784.64
#焦炭再投入量(-)	Coke Input (-)		
7. 煤制品加工	Briquettes	-236.77	-108.90
三. 损失量	**Loss**		
四. 终端消费量	**Total Final Consumption**	**62154.13**	**53069.67**
1. 农、林、牧、渔、水利业	Farming, Forestry, Animal Husbandry, Fishery & Water Conservancy	2315.24	2289.84
2. 工业	Industry	48040.74	41018.77
#用作原料. 材料	Noe-Energy Use	3037.99	2723.65
3. 建筑业	Construction	603.56	594.50
4. 交通运输、仓储及邮电通迅业	Transport, Storage, Postal & Telecommunications Services	815.34	810.35
5. 批发和零售贸易业. 餐饮业	Wholesale, Retail Trade and Catering Service	874.39	852.08
6. 生活消费	Residential Consumption	8738.97	6802.81
城镇	Urban	2511.25	1639.44
乡村	Rural	6227.72	5163.37
7. 其他	Other	765.88	701.33
五. 平衡差额	**Statistical Difference**	**-2260.37**	**-1906.73**
六. 消费量合计	**Total Final Consumption**	**216722.51**	**216195.75**

ENERGY BANLANCE OF CHINA −2005（PHYSICAL QUANTITY）

洗精煤 （万吨） Cleaned Coal （10⁴ tn）	其他洗煤 （万吨） Other Washed Coal （10⁴ tn）	型煤 （万吨） Briquettes （10⁴ tn）	焦炭 （万吨） Coke （10⁴ tn）	焦炉煤气 （亿立方米） Coke Oven Gas （10⁸ cu. m）	其他煤气 （亿立方米） Other Gas （10⁸ cu. m）	其他焦化产品 （万吨） Other Coking Products （10⁴ tn）	油品合计 （万吨） Petroleum Products Total （10⁴ tn）	原油 （万吨） Crude Oil （10⁴ tn）
171.72	4.41	−3.00	−1427.26		689.70	30.79	32539.13	30089.17
							18135.29	18135.29
				689.70				
719.46	5.42		0.54			100.57	16732.31	12681.74
							430.84	
−525.98	−2.03	−4.90	−1276.41			−69.78	−2488.28	−806.68
							−399.80	
−21.76	1.02	1.90	−151.39				128.76	78.82
1612.50	5807.80	1137.40	25183.79	425.80	7.48	359.53	−3190.69	−29062.12
−83.90	−1867.99			−35.83	−130.85		−1602.02	−21.28
−6.70	−212.38			−16.90	−78.15		−407.61	−0.33
28064.84	9233.90							
−25885.35	−64.53		25100.65	474.00	23.56	351.80		
							−1166.67	−29040.51
−476.39	−15.93		311.05	4.53	192.93	12.54	−14.39	
			−227.91			−4.81		
	−1265.27	1137.40						
							155.42	153.76
2067.41	5874.29	1142.75	23377.93	424.09	697.18	389.76	29189.30	870.36
	25.40		63.47				2072.88	
2064.00	4813.42	144.56	23133.01	373.75	590.36	389.76	11245.03	870.36
106.09	202.16	6.09	925.32	3.81		99.19	3073.43	115.76
3.41	5.65		18.38				1502.19	
	4.99		1.07		0.23		9579.95	
	11.03	11.28	64.08	2.93	6.00		915.64	
	952.07	984.09	90.33	44.20	100.60		1794.43	
	361.65	510.15	49.92	44.20	99.37		1407.96	
	590.42	473.94	40.41		1.22		386.48	
	61.73	2.82	7.59	3.22			2079.18	
−283.20	−62.08	−8.36	378.59	1.71	0.00	0.56	3.71	2.93
28519.75	9300.39	1142.75	23605.85	476.82	906.19	394.57	32535.42	30086.24

项 目	Item	汽油 （万吨） Gasoline （10^4 tn）	煤油 （万吨） Kerosene （10^4 tn）
一. 可供本地区消费的能源量	**Total Primary Energy Supply**	**−578.29**	**63.54**
1. 一次能源生产量	Indigenous Production		
水电	Hydro Power		
核电	Nuclear Power		
2. 回收能	Recovery of Energy		
3. 进口量	Import	0.00	328.34
4. 我轮、机在外国加油量	China Airplanes&Ships Refueling in Abroad		147.80
5. 出口量（−）	Export（−）	−559.66	−268.66
6. 外轮、机在我国加油量（−）	Foreign Airplanes&ships Refueling in China		−178.90
7. 库存增（−）、减（+）量	Stock Change	−18.63	34.96
二. 加工转换投入（−）产出（+）量	**Input（−）& Output（+）of Transformation**	**5432.20**	**1006.48**
1. 火力发电	Thermal Power	−0.70	
2. 供热	Heating Supply	−0.10	
3. 洗选煤	Coal Washing		
4. 炼焦	Coking		
5. 炼油	Petroleum Refineries	5433.00	1006.48
6. 制气	Gas Works		
#焦炭再投入量（−）	Coke Input（−）		
7. 煤制品加工	Briquettes		
三. 损失量	**Loss**		
四. 终端消费量	**Total Final Consumption**	**4852.51**	**1076.84**
1. 农、林、牧、渔、水利业	Farming, Forestry, Animal Husbandry, Fishery & Water Conservancy	227.99	1.60
2. 工业	Industry	460.91	57.50
#用作原料、材料	Noe-Energy Use	14.80	6.70
3. 建筑业	Construction	172.14	
4. 交通运输、仓储及邮电通迅业	Transport, Storage, Postal & Telecommunications Services	2470.05	882.42
5. 批发和零售贸易业、餐饮业	Wholesale, Retail Trade and Catering Service	299.39	3.67
6. 生活消费	Residential Consumption	303.83	25.46
城镇	Urban	239.59	1.86
乡村	Rural	64.23	23.60
7. 其他	Other	918.20	106.19
五. 平衡差额	**Statistical Difference**	**1.41**	**−6.82**
六. 消费量合计	**Total Final Consumption**	**4853.31**	**1076.84**

Continued

柴油 (万吨) Diesel Oil (10⁴ tn)	燃料油 (万吨) Fuel Oil (10⁴ tn)	液化石油气 (万吨) PLG (10⁴ tn)	炼厂干气 (万吨) Refinery Gas (10⁴ tn)	其他石油制品 (万吨) Other Petroleum Products (10⁴ tn)	天然气 (亿立方米) Natural Gas (10⁸ cu. m)	热力 (万百万千焦) Heat (10¹⁰ kJ)	电力 (亿千瓦小时) Electricity (10⁸ kW · h)	其他能源 (万吨标煤) Other Energy (10⁴ tce)
−117.61	2469.85	619.50	0.00	−7.04	463.51	0.00	4467.41	856.62
					493.20		4529.24	
						0.00	3970.17	
							530.88	
								856.62
53.24	2608.63	617.00	0.00	443.36			50.11	
7.77	275.27							
−147.64	−229.98	−2.67		−472.99	−29.69		−111.94	
−23.30	−197.60							
−7.68	13.53	5.17		22.59				
10723.45	475.23	1429.42	793.57	6011.08	−58.94	228894.66	20473.36	−333.70
−366.74	−1106.06	−0.12	−36.51	−70.61	−31.52		20473.36	−244.02
	−171.73	−3.16	−83.25	−149.04	−23.17	228894.66		−54.16
11090.19	1767.41	1432.70	913.33	6230.73				−35.52
	−14.39				−4.25			
		1.66			10.33	2631.20	1706.47	
10605.71	2949.88	2040.55	791.35	6002.10	398.36	226259.28	23233.85	522.51
1837.64	0.66	4.99				76.48	876.33	
1724.53	1732.59	528.60	791.35	5079.19	291.76	166267.92	16775.22	522.51
32.59	103.96	57.67	6.81	2735.14	87.68			50.03
386.64	14.18	6.32		922.91	1.49	465.43	233.93	
5019.41	1161.02	47.05			5.77	1361.95	430.34	
486.03	27.52	99.03			10.79	2206.70	752.31	
136.40		1328.74			79.43	51743.58	2824.81	
100.46		1066.04			79.13	51743.58	1714.43	
35.94		262.70			0.30		1110.38	
1015.06	13.91	25.82			9.12	4137.21	1340.91	
0.13	−4.80	6.71	2.22	1.94	−4.12	4.18	0.45	0.41
10972.45	4242.06	2045.49	911.11	6221.75	467.63	228890.48	24940.32	856.21

4-3 综合能源平衡表

单位：万吨标准煤

项　目	Item	1980	1985
可供消费的能源总量	**Total Energy Available for Consumption**	**61557**	**77603**
一次能源生产量	Primary Energy Output	63735	85546
回收能	Recovery of Energy		
进口量	Imports	261	340
出口量（－）	Exports（－）	3058	5774
年初年末库存差额	Stock Changes in the Year	619	－2509
能源消费总量	**Total Energy Consumption**	**60275**	**76682**
在总量中：	Consumption by Sector		
1. 农、林、牧、渔业	Farming, Forestry, Animal Husbandry, Fishery Conservancy	4692	4045
2. 工　业	Industry	38986	51068
3. 建筑业	Construction	957	1302
4. 交通运输、仓储和邮政业	Transport, Storage and Post	2902	3713
5. 批发、零售业和住宿、餐饮业	Wholesale, Retail Trade and Hotel , Restaurants	518	766
6. 其他	Others	1205	2470
7. 生活消费	Residential Consumption	11015	13318
在总量中：	Consumption by Usage		
（一）终端消费	（Ⅰ）Final Consumption	57508	73586
#工业	Industry	38293	48021
（二）加工转换损失量	（Ⅱ）Losses in Processing and	1358	1491
#炼焦	Coking	644	572
炼油	Petroleum Refining	113	110
（三）损失量	（Ⅲ）Other Losses	1409	1605
平衡差额	**Balance**	**1282**	**921**

注：1. 村办工业包括在工业中（下同）。

2. 电力、热力按等价热值折算，因此加工转换损失量中不包括发电、供热损失量。

3. 进口量包括我国飞机、轮船在国外加油量；出口量包括外国飞机、轮船在我国加油量。

OVERALL ENERGY BALANCE SHEET

(10 000 tce)

1990	1995	1999	2000	2001	2002	2003	2004	2005
96138	**129535**	**132065**	**136535**	**140981**	**149082**	**172129**	**203344**	**223213**
103922	129034	125935	128978	137445	143810	163842	187341	205876
	2312	1694	1760	1859	1908	2043	2508	2840
1310	5456	9514	14334	13472	15769	20048	26593	26952
5875	6776	7051	9633	12020	11695	12989	11646	11447
−3219	−491	1974	1097	225	−710	−814	−1452	−1008
98703	**131176**	**133831**	**138553**	**143199**	**151797**	**174990**	**203227**	**224682**
4852	5505	5993	6045	6400	6612	6716	7680	7978
67578	96191	92840	95443	98273	104088	121771	143244	159492
1213	1335	1979	2143	2234	2544	2860	3259	3411
4541	5863	9340	10067	10363	11171	12819	15104	16629
1247	2018	2901	3039	3265	3520	4180	4820	5031
3473	4519	5563	5852	6096	6334	6819	7839	8691
15799	15745	15214	15965	16568	17527	19827	21281	23450
94289	124252	127814	132030	136486	144231	166633	194104	214479
63239	89473	87151	89266	91903	96864	113725	134442	149639
2264	3634	2228	2461	2325	2788	3378	3684	3720
905		516	525	518	541	769	527	658
326		648	781	607	1015	1092	1416	1305
2150	3289	3789	4062	4388	4778	4979	5439	6483
−2565	−1641	−1766	−2017	−2218	−2716	−2862	117	−1469

a) Data on industry include the data of village-run industry. (The sane as in the following tables).

b) Electric power and heat are converted on the basic of equal caloric value. Therefore, losses in processing and transformation exclude losses in power generation and heating.

c) Data on imports include the petroleum consumed by the Chinese airplanes and ships in refueling abroad. Data on exports include the petroleum consumed by the foreign airplanes and ships in refueling in China.

4-4 煤炭平衡表

单位：万吨

项　目	Item	1980	1985
可供量	**Total Energy Available for Consumption**	**62601.0**	**82776.6**
生产量	Output	62015.0	87228.4
进口量	Imports	199.0	230.7
出口量（-）	Exports（-）	632.0	777.0
年初年末库存差额	Stock Changes in the Year	1019.0	-3905.5
消费量	**Total Energy Consumption**	**61009.5**	**81603.0**
在消费量中：	Consumption by Sector		
1. 农、林、牧、渔业	Farming, Forestry, Animal Husbandry, Fishery Conservancy	1550.3	2208.6
2. 工　业 2.	Industry	43848.4	58613.3
3. 建筑业 3.	Construction	556.0	531.9
4. 交通运输、仓储和邮政业	Transport, Storage and Post	1934.4	2307.1
5. 批发、零售业和住宿、餐饮业	Wholesale, Retail Trade and Hotel, Restaurants	455.2	738.2
6. 其他	Other	1091.2	1579.5
7. 生活消费	Residential Consumption	11574.0	15624.4
在消费量中：	Consumption by Usage		
（一）终端消费	（I）Final Consumption	38804.2	52704.4
#工　业	Industry	21643.1	29715.0
（二）中间消费	（2）Intermediate Consumption		
（用于加工转换）	（Consumed in Transformation）	19461.6	25397.4
发　电	Power Generation	12648.4	16440.7
供　热	Heating		1462.3
炼　焦	Coking	6682.2	7303.8
制　气	Gas Production	131.0	190.6
（三）洗选损耗	（3）Losses in Coal Washing and Dressing	2743.7	3501.2
平衡差额	**Balance**	**1591.5**	**1173.6**

注：生产量为原煤产量。

58

COAL BALANCE SHEET

(10 000 ton)

1990	1995	1999	2000	2001	2002	2003	2004	2005
102221.0	**133461.7**	**127076.1**	**128297.1**	**130554.0**	**137060.8**	**163402.0**	**192265.5**	**214462.1**
107988.3	136073.1	128000.0	129921.0	138152.0	145456.0	172200.0	199232.4	220472.9
200.3	163.5	167.3	217.9	266.0	1125.7	1109.8	1861.4	2617.1
1729.0	2861.7	3743,9	5506.5	9012.9	8389.6	9402.9	8666.4	7172.4
−4238.5	86.8	2652.7	3664.7	1148.9	−1131.4	−504.9	−162.0	−1455.4
105523.0	**137676.5**	**130000.0**	**132000.0**	**135000.0**	**141600.5**	**169232.0**	**193596.0**	**216722.5**
2095.2	1856.7	1735.6	1647.7	1599.6	1622.9	1683.3	2251.2	2315.2
81090.9	117570.7	116500.0	119300.7	122518.3	129290.4	156168.5	180135.2	202609.1
437.6	439.8	522.5	536.8	525.0	553.6	577.2	601.5	603.6
2160.9	1315.1	1286.3	1132.2	1041.3	1055.0	1067.3	832.1	815.3
1058.3	977.4	896.2	814.6	810.9	809.1	860.4	871.8	874.4
1980.4	1986.7	651.1	661.0	664.7	667.1	700.6	731.0	765.9
16699.7	13530.1	8408.4	7907.0	7830.3	7602.6	8174.7	8173.2	8739.0
60205.9	66156.1	49714.2	46821.4	45611.7	42572.4	49044.8	59543.7	62154.1
35773.8	46050.3	36214.2	34122.0	33129.9	30262.2	35981.2	46083.0	48040.7
41257.8	69487.6	80285.8	85178.6	89388.3	99028.1	120187.3	134052.3	154568.38
27204.3	44440.2	52458.2	55811.2	59797.9	68600.0	81976.5	91961.6	103263.49
2995.5	5887.3	7961.0	8794.1	8951.5	8973.7	10895.5	11546.6	13542.0
10697.6	18396.4	15931.7	16496.4	17236.4	18624.7	23639.9	25349.6	31667.1
360.4	763.7	917.6	960.0	1002.1	973.2	1054.8	1316.4	1277.0
4059.3	2032.8	3091.5	3191.2	2450.5	1917.5	2699.3	3633.89	4582.1
−3302.0	**−4214.8**	**−2923.9**	**−3702.9**	**−4446.0**	**−4539.8**	**−5830.1**	**−1330.5**	**−2260.37**

a) Data on output refer to the output of raw coal.

4-5 焦炭平衡表

单位：万吨

项　目	Item	1980	1985
可供量	**Total Energy Available for Consumption**	**4315.3**	**4689.7**
生产量	Output	4343.0	4802.1
进口量	Imports		2.1
出口量(-)	Exports（-）	27.1	36.9
年初年末库存差额	Stock Changes in the Year	-0.6	-77.6
消费量	**Total Energy Consumption**	**4303.0**	**4689.7**
在消费量中：	Consumption by Sector		
1. 农、林、牧、渔业	Farming, Forestry, Animal Husbandry, Fishery Conservancy	10.6	20.8
2. 工业	Industry	4266.7	4627.7
3. 建筑业	Construction	11.9	7.8
4. 交通运输、仓储和邮政业	Transport, Storage and Post	8.2	5.7
5. 批发、零售业和住宿、餐饮业	Wholesale, Retail Trade and Hotel, Restaurants	0.9	2.7
6. 其他	Other	4.7	2.0
7. 生活消费	Residential Consumption		23.0
在消费量中：	Consumption by Usage		
（一）终端消费	(1) Final Consumption	4294.7	4677.9
#工业	Industry	4258.4	4615.9
（二）中间消费	(2) Intermediate Consumption		
（用于加工转换）	(Consumed in Transformation)	8.3	11.8
制气	Gas Production	8.3	11.8
（三）损失量	(3) Losses in Coal Washing and Dressing		
平衡差额	**Balance**	**12.3**	

COKE BALANCE SHEET

(10 000 ton)

1990	1995	1999	2000	2001	2002	2003	2004	2005
7085.8	**12207.1**	**10970.6**	**10892.3**	**11462.9**	**12830.5**	**15930.9**	**17863.2**	**23984.4**
7328.3	13424.5	12073.7	12184.0	13130.8	14253.3	17775.7	19937.6	25411.7
	0.1	0.0				0.2	0.5	0.5
129.0	886.1	997.4	1519.7	1384.6	1357.0	1472.1	1501.2	1276.4
−113.5	−331.4	−105.7	228.0	−283.2	−65.8	−372.9	−573.8	−151.39
6914.7	**10725.3**	**10460.5**	**10440.0**	**10999.2**	**12343.9**	**14503.8**	**17267.0**	**23605.8**
60.1	128.6	145.8	144.2	139.2	141.0	141.0	98.7	63.5
6808.8	10412.0	10094.9	10080.5	10638.4	11978.1	14149.8	16981.1	23360.9
5.2	10.8	17.1	19.0	23.9	23.4	20.8	16.8	18.4
4.1	10.1	10.1	11.2	11.7	11.4	10.8	1.8	1.1
7.7	25.7	36.5	35.7	39.7	42.6	47.5	53.4	64.1
1.9	6.4	13.0	12.2	12.1	12.3	11.4	10.1	7.6
26.9	131.6	143.1	137.2	134.2	135.1	122.5	105.2	90.3
6846.3	10648.0	10302.7	10297.1	10845.6	12206.6	14325.9	17072.7	23377.9
6740.4	10334.7	9937.1	9937.7	10484.8	11840.7	13972.0	16786.8	23133.0
68.4	77.3	157.8	142.9	153.7	137.4	177.9	194.3	228.0
68.4	77.3	157.8	142.9	153.7	137.4	177.9	194.3	228.0
171.1	1481.8	510.1	452.3	463.7	486.6	1427.1	596.2	378.6

4-6 石油平衡表

单位：万吨

项　目	Item	1980	1985
可供量	**Total Energy Available for Consumption**	**8794.5**	**9193.7**
生产量	Output	10594.6	12489.5
进口量	Imports	82.7	90.0
出口量(-)	Exports (-)	1806.2	3630.4
年初年末库存差额	Stock Changes in the Year	-76.6	244.6
消费量	**Total Energy Consumption**	**8757.4**	**9168.8**
在消费量中：	Consumption by Sector		
1. 农、林、牧、渔业	Farming, Forestry, Animal Husbandry, Fishery Conservancy	814.9	758.7
2. 工业	Industry	6203.2	6171.4
3. 建筑业	Construction	175.2	292.2
4. 交通运输、仓储和邮政业	Transport, Storage and Post	911.5	1176.4
5. 批发、零售业和住宿、餐饮业	Wholesale, Retail Trade and Hotel, Restaurants	29.0	38.1
6. 其他	Other	481.7	506.1
7. 生活消费	Residential Consumption	141.9	225.9
在消费量中：	Consumption by Usage	8757.4	
(一) 终端消费	(I) Final Consumption	6311.0	7063.3
#工业	Industry	3780.3	4462.0
(二) 中间消费	(II) Intermediate Consumption		
(用于加工转换)	(Consumed in Transformation)	2102.1	1745.6
发电	Power Generation	2065.4	1425.5
供热	Heating		285.6
制气	Gas Production	36.7	34.5
(三) 炼油损失量	(III) Losses in Petroleum Refining	81.5	112.9
(四) 损失量	Other Losses	262.8	247.0
平衡差额	Balance	37.1	24.9

注：1. 生产量为原油产量。
　　2. 进口量包括我国飞机、轮船在国外加油量；出口量包括外国飞机、轮船在我国加油量。

PETROLEUM BALANCE SHEET

(10 000 ton)

1990	1995	1999	2000	2001	2002	2003	2004	2005
11435.0	**16072.7**	**20981.3**	**22631.8**	**23204.7**	**24925.1**	**27540.5**	**32116.2**	**32539.1**
13830.6	15005.0	16000.0	16300.0	16395.9	16700.0	16960.0	17587.3	18135.3
755.6	3673.2	6483.3	9748.5	9118.2	10269.3	13189.6	17291.3	17163.2
3110.4	2454.5	1643.5	2172.1	2046.7	2139.2	2540.8	2240.6	2888.1
−40.8	−151.0	124.6	−1244.6	−262.7	94.9	−68.2	−521.9	128.8
11485.6	**16064.9**	**21072.9**	**22439.3**	**22838.3**	**24786.8**	**27126.1**	**31699.9**	**32535.4**
1033.6	1203.2	1422.1	1496.9	1568.5	1674.1	1681.4	2001.3	2072.9
7321.6	9349.3	10428.7	10918.5	10827.2	11803.4	12886.5	14857.3	14462.6
327.3	242.8	747.3	830.6	933.8	1096.6	1230.6	1422.3	1502.2
1683.2	2863.6	5004.3	5509.0	5692.9	6163.7	7093.2	8620.6	9708.5
77.6	333.9	537.2	545.0	567.4	593.0	682.3	818.7	915.6
757.8	1390.3	1800.3	1882.9	1953.7	1978.6	1916.4	2201.7	2079.2
284.5	682.0	1133.1	1256.5	1294.8	1477.5	1635.8	1778.0	1794.4
9304.7	13676.3	18664.7	19893.5	20357.0	21989.8	24062.8	28062.0	29189.3
5180.4	7095.5	8172.1	8530.0	8498.4	9168.3	9958.7	11344.1	11245.0
1630.4	2230.0	2222.2	2352.9	2292.0	2606.8	2901.4	3488.2	3190.7
1234.4	1358.5	1228.6	1178.2	1213.6	1275.6	1491.6	1864.1	1602.0
356.3	399.9	394.6	427.0	438.7	420.7	418.0	418.5	407.6
39.7	51.6	32.5	25.9	22.8	18.9	20.9	10.5	14.4
295.8	420.1	566.6	721.9	617.0	891.6	970.9	1195.1	1166.7
254.7	158.6	186.0	192.9	189.3	190.2	161.9	149.7	155.4
−50.6	**7.8**	**−108.5**	**192.5**	**366.4**	**138.3**	**414.4**	**416.3**	**3.7**

a) Data on output refer to the output of crude oil.

b) Data on imports include the petroleum consumed by the Chinese airplanes and ships in refueling abroad. Data on exports include the petroleum consumed by the foreign airplanes and ships in refueling in China.

4-7 原油平衡表

单位：万吨

项　目	Item	1980	1985
可供量	**Total Energy Available for Consumption**	**9222.9**	**9516.5**
生产量	Output	10594.6	12489.5
进口量	Imports	36.6	
出口量(－)	Exports (－)	1330.9	3003.0
年初年末库存差额	Stock Changes in the Year	－77.4	30.0
消费量	**Total Energy Consumption**	**9205.0**	**9509.5**
在消费量中：	Consumption by Sector		
1. 农、林、牧、渔业	Farming, Forestry, Animal Husbandry, Fishery Conservancy	8.0	0.8
2. 工业	Industry	9112.0	9389.9
3. 建筑业	Construction	28.8	74.0
4. 交通运输、仓储和邮政业	Transport, Storage and Post	50.1	44.3
5. 批发、零售业和住宿、餐饮业	Wholesale, Retail Trade and Hotel, Restaurants		0.1
6. 其他	Other	6.1	0.4
7. 生活消费	Residential Consumption		
在消费量中：	Consumption by Usage		
（一）终端消费	(I) Final Consumption	499.6	350.4
#工业	Industry	429.7	254.9
（二）中间消费	(II) Intermediate Consumption		
（用于加工转换）	(Consumed in Transformation)	8443.0	8929.7
发电	Power Generation	574.0	279.5
供热	Heating		61.3
炼油	Petroleum Refineries	7869.0	8588.9
（三）油田原油损失量	(III) Losses in Oil Field for Crude Oil	262.4	229.4
平衡差额	**Balance**	**17.9**	**7.0**

64

CRUDE OIL BALANC SHEET

(10 000 ton)

1990	1995	1999	2000	2001	2002	2003	2004	2005
11770.6	**14794.9**	**18947.2**	**21383.0**	**21537.2**	**22769.0**	**25187.1**	**29012.3**	**30089.2**
13830.6	15004.4	16000.0	16300.0	16395.9	16700.0	16960.0	17587.3	18135.3
292.3	1709.0	3661.4	7026.5	6026.0	6940.6	9102.0	12272.0	12681.7
2399.0	1822.7	716.7	1030.6	755.0	766.5	813.3	549.2	806.7
46.7	−95.8	2.6	−912.9	−129.7	−105.2	−61.6	−297.9	78.8
11762.2	**14886.4**	**18949.5**	**21232.0**	**21342.7**	**22541.1**	**24922.0**	**28749.3**	**30086.2**
0.2	10.1							
11653.8	14716.3	18775.2	21052.1	21168.2	22357.5	24768.4	28625.5	29959.4
55.2	2.7	3.2	3.3	3.4	4.2	4.0		
52.1	156.8	169.5	175.0	169.8	177.9	148.3	123.8	126.9
0.3	0.5	0.2	0.2	0.2	0.1	0.1		
0.6	1390.3	1.4	1.4	1.2	1.3	1.2		
402.1	309.9	519.4	636.8	654.1	681.3	812.2	844.9	870.4
333.4	274.7	495.4	612.3	630.8	658.0	793.0	844.9	870.4
11106.9	14419.4	18245.7	20404.3	20500.7	21671.3	23949.0	27755.6	29062.1
124.6	61.6	80.2	85.0	81.6	78.3	94.0	18.0	21.3
21.1	4.4	12.9	14.0	12.3	12.8	11.0	0.3	0.3
10961.2	14353.4	18152.6	20305.3	20406.8	21580.2	23844.0	27737.3	29040.5
253.2	157.1	184.4	190.9	187.9	188.5	160.8	148.8	153.8
8.4	**−91.5**	**−2.2**	**151.0**	**194.4**	**227.9**	**265.1**	**263.0**	**2.9**

4-8 燃料油平衡表

单位：万吨

项 目	Item	1980	1985
可供量	**Total Energy Available for Consumption**	**3096.1**	**2848.0**
生产量	Output	3142.0	2835.8
进口量	Imports	39.0	70.0
出口量（－）	Exports （－）	45.4	64.9
年初年末库存差额	Stock Changes in the Year	－39.5	7.1
消费量	**Total Energy Consumption**	**3073.7**	**2837.4**
在消费量中：	Consumption by Sector		
1. 农、林、牧、渔业	Farming , Forestry , Animal Husbandry , Fishery Conservancy	2.3	3.1
2. 工业	Industry	2937.4	2662.2
3. 建筑业	Construction	15.0	18.9
4. 交通运输、仓储和邮政业	Transport , Storage and Post	109.0	144.1
5. 批发、零售业和住宿、餐饮业	Wholesale , Retail Trade and Hotel , Restaurants	2.9	3.1
6. 其他	Other	7.1	6.0
7. 生活消费	Residential Consumption		
在消费量中：	Consumption by Usage		
（一）终端消费	（Ⅰ）Final Consumption	1617.9	1538.8
#工业	Industry	1481.6	1363.5
（二）中间消费	（Ⅱ）Intermediate Consumption		
（用于加工转换）	（Consumed in Transformation）	1455.8	1296.1
发电	Power Generation	1419.1	1042.3
供热	Heating		219.3
制气	Gas Production	36.7	34.5
（三）损失量	（Ⅲ）Other Losses		2.5
平衡差额	**Balance**	**22.4**	**10.6**

FUEL OIL BALANCE SHEET

(10 000 ton)

1990	1995	1999	2000	2001	2002	2003	2004	2005
3320.7	**3717.3**	**3901.1**	**3836.7**	**3836.9**	**3702.8**	**4291.1**	**4846.6**	**4237.3**
3267.9	2960.8	1959.4	2053.7	1864.4	1845.5	2004.8	2029.3	1767.4
167.3	859.1	1963.3	1704.3	2048.7	1915.2	2589.7	3269.2	2883.9
97.2	68.6	38.8	57.9	84.9	104.9	188.7	368.7	427.6
−17.3	−34.0	17.2	136.6	8.7	47.0	−114.7	−83.2	13.5
3367.8	**3693.7**	**3934.1**	**3872.8**	**3850.2**	**3873.9**	**4220.5**	**4783.5**	**4242.1**
2.9	8.4	0.4	0.4	0.4	0.4	0.6	0.7	0.7
3091.7	3406.2	3047.7	2975.1	2949.3	2950.9	3236.8	3570.4	3024.8
47.3	14.2	16.2	16.7	16.2	19.0	17.8	21.4	14.2
208.2	227.5	840.0	850.0	855.0	872.1	940.3	1150.4	1161.0
1.6	6.6	10.5	11.6	12.3	12.3	13.0	25.0	27.5
16.1	30.8	19.4	19.0	17.0	19.1	12.1	15.6	13.9
2042.6	2262.8	2694.0	2741.4	2689.3	2675.6	2882.1	3130.4	2949.9
1766.5	1975.3	1807.6	1843.7	1788.4	1752.6	1898.3	1917.4	1732.6
1325.2	1430.9	1240.1	1131.3	1160.9	1198.2	1338.5	1653.0	1292.2
977.3	1071.5	906.3	814.2	838.5	912.7	1056.7	1429.2	1106.1
308.3	307.8	301.3	291.2	299.6	266.7	260.8	213.3	171.7
39.6	51.6	32.5	25.9	22.8	18.9	20.9	10.5	14.4
−47.1	23.6	−33.0	−36.1	−13.4	−171.1	70.6	63.1	−4.8

67

4-9 汽油平衡表

单位：万吨

项　目	Item	1980	1985
可供量	**Total Energy Available for Consumption**	**999.4**	**1399.6**
生产量	Output	1079.0	1471.9
进口量	Imports		0.3
出口量（-）	Exports（-）	117.8	129.9
年初年末库存差额	Stock Changes in the Year	38.2	57.3
消费量	**Total Energy Consumption**	**998.6**	**1396.3**
在消费量中：	Consumption by Sector		
1. 农、林、牧、渔业	Farming, Forestry, Animal Husbandry, Fishery Conservancy	53.3	122.3
2. 工业	Industry	273.2	451.3
3. 建筑业	Construction	54.1	73.0
4. 交通运输、仓储和邮政业	Transport, Storage and Post	404.9	477.4
5. 批发、零售业和住宿、餐饮业	Wholesale, Retail Trade and Hotel, Restaurants	19.4	23.4
6. 其他	Other	193.7	238.3
7. 生活消费	Residential Consumption		10.6
平衡差额	**Balance**	**0.8**	**3.3**

GASOLINE BALANCE SHEET

(10 000 ton)

1990	1995	1999	2000	2001	2002	2003	2004	2005
1884.1	**2902.0**	**3379.8**	**3504.5**	**3606.9**	**3749.7**	**4072.3**	**4697.2**	**4854.7**
2173.4	3051.6	3741.3	4134.7	4154.7	4320.8	4790.9	5265.3	5433.0
16.9	15.9	0.0	0.0	0.0				
233.8	193.1	425.8	467.7	586.0	630.4	754.2	540.7	559.7
−72.4	27.6	64.3	−162.5	38.1	59.3	35.7	−27.4	−18.6
1899.5	**2909.6**	**3380.7**	**3504.9**	**3597.8**	**3749.7**	**4072.0**	**4695.8**	**4853.3**
145.9	179.7	178.1	184.5	190.6	187.9	195.0	220.1	228.0
589.3	812.4	646.5	602.0	618.1	631.6	617.9	507.4	461.7
89.5	103.6	113.8	115.6	116.7	122.3	123.7	156.5	172.1
620.1	982.3	1265.5	1387.8	1419.4	1503.5	1861.6	2308.5	2470.0
46.0	197.2	206.3	209.8	214.0	224.2	238.1	279.8	299.4
390.7	570.7	849.4	877.7	904.3	916.3	837.0	936.9	918.2
18.0	63.7	121.1	127.6	134.6	163.8	198.8	286.5	303.8
−15.4	−7.6	−0.9	−0.4	9.1	0.0	0.3	1.4	1.4

4-10 煤油平衡表

单位: 万吨

项　　目	Item	1980	1985
可供量	**Total Energy Available for Consumption**	**359.0**	**383.2**
生产量	Output	398.5	405.3
进口量	Imports		15.2
出口量(−)	Exports (−)	46.8	46.0
年初年末库存差额	Stock Changes in the Year	2.3	8.7
消费量	**Total Energy Consumption**	**365.9**	**385.5**
在消费量中:	Consumption by Sector		
1. 农、林、牧、渔业	Farming, Forestry, Animal Husbandry, Fishery Conservancy	2.3	3.3
2. 工业	Industry	15.7	20.1
3. 建筑业	Construction	0.8	1.3
4. 交通运输、仓储和邮政业	Transport, Storage and Post	31.4	56.2
5. 批发、零售业和住宿、餐饮业	Wholesale, Retail Trade and Hotel, Restaurants	0.2	0.1
6. 其他	Other	216.7	182.9
7. 生活消费	Residential Consumption	98.8	121.6
平衡差额	**Balance**	**−6.9**	**−2.3**

KEROSENE BALANCE SHEET

(10 000 ton)

1990	1995	1999	2000	2001	2002	2003	2004	2005
350.9	**486.4**	**848.6**	**880.9**	**894.2**	**914.8**	**914.5**	**1054.5**	**1070.0**
392.5	445.8	743.8	872.3	789.4	826.1	855.3	962.2	1006.5
26.1	115.7	272.2	322.5	298.6	324.3	317.4	421.0	476.1
55.5	62.4	162.8	256.3	246.4	240.9	275.9	331.5	447.6
-12.2	-12.7	-4.6	-57.6	52.7	5.3	17.7	2.7	35.0
350.9	**512.1**	**824.2**	**869.6**	**890.3**	**919.2**	**921.6**	**1060.9**	**1076.8**
3.1	3.6	1.4	1.5	1.5	1.4	1.4	1.1	1.6
20.6	44.9	78.4	84.0	86.0	87.4	87.8	60.9	57.5
1.3	3.5	3.9	4.0	3.5	0.0	0.0	0.0	0.0
93.4	250.0	505.6	535.9	560.7	616.7	621.7	819.7	882.4
0.6	8.5	11.5	12.0	12.5	13.0	11.2	3.6	3.7
127.3	137.3	152.7	160.1	151.1	140.0	143.2	148.2	106.2
104.6	64.3	70.8	72.2	75.0	60.7	56.4	27.4	25.5
	-25.7	**24.3**	**11.3**	**4.0**	**-4.4**	**-7.1**	**-6.4**	**-6.8**

4-11 柴油平衡表

单位：万吨

项　　目	Item	1980	1985
可供量	**Total Energy Available for Consumption**	**1663.2**	**1944.1**
生产量	Output	1827.8	2023.2
进口量	Imports	2.1	4.5
出口量（-）	Exports（-）	166.5	225.6
年初年末库存差额	Stock Changes in the Year	-0.2	142.0
消费量	**Total Energy Consumption**	**1663.2**	**1939.4**
在消费量中：	Consumption by Sector		
1. 农、林、牧、渔业	Farming, Forestry, Animal Husbandry, Fishery Conservancy	749.0	629.2
2. 工业	Industry	457.4	644.1
3. 建筑业	Construction	76.5	125.0
4. 交通运输、仓储和邮政业	Transport, Storage and Post	316.1	454.4
5. 批发、零售业和住宿、餐饮业	Wholesale, Retail Trade and Hotel, Restaurants	6.5	10.9
6. 其他	Other	57.7	74.0
7. 生活消费	Residential Consumption		
在消费量中：	Consumption by Usage		
（一）终端消费	（I）Final Consumption	1590.9	1827.4
#工业	Industry	385.1	532.1
（二）中间消费	（II）Intermediate Consumption		
（用于加工转换）	（Consumed in Transformation）	72.3	108.6
发电	Power Generation	72.3	103.6
供热	Heating		5.0
（三）损失量	Other Losses		3.4
平衡差额	**Balance**		**4.7**

DIESEL OIL BALANCE SHEET

(10 000 ton)

1990	1995	1999	2000	2001	2002	2003	2004	2005
2689.4	**4404.2**	**6204.3**	**6806.5**	**7272.0**	**7722.3**	**8467.5**	**9948.4**	**10972.6**
2609.0	3972.6	6172.6	7079.6	7485.6	7706.1	8532.8	9843.6	11090.2
233.8	645.3	56.0	51.9	54.7	78.7	111.6	303.9	61.0
169.8	169.5	70.9	77.5	46.9	144.7	244.4	86.7	170.9
16.4	−44.2	46.5	−247.6	−221.4	82.2	67.5	−112.4	−7.7
2691.7	**4321.4**	**6231.6**	**6774.3**	**7107.7**	**7667.2**	**8409.8**	**9895.2**	**10972.5**
881.5	1001.4	1241.8	1310.1	1375.6	1484.3	1484.4	1774.3	1837.6
728.1	1189.9	1506.8	1596.5	1636.8	1731.3	1830.5	2004.8	2091.3
133.0	118.2	178.1	195.9	223.1	252.0	276.2	333.1	386.6
709.4	1246.6	2221.7	2543.8	2671.0	2964.8	3485.2	4182.2	5019.4
22.5	103.6	260.9	255.9	268.1	280.8	355.5	419.0	486.0
217.0	645.7	759.7	803.7	853.9	870.0	890.0	1068.0	1015.1
	16.1	62.7	68.4	79.2	83.9	87.9	113.7	136.4
2564.8	4070.0	6016.2	6546.6	6867.3	7441.2	8138.5	9560.2	10605.7
601.2	938.5	1291.4	1368.8	1396.4	1505.3	1559.2	1669.9	1724.5
126.9	251.4	215.5	227.7	240.4	226.0	271.3	334.92	366.7
124.5	204.9	215.5	227.7	240.4	226.0	271.3	334.92	366.7
2.4	46.6							
−2.3	82.7	−27.4	32.2	164.4	55.2	57.8	53.28	0.1

4-12 液化石油气平衡表

单位: 万吨

项 目	Item	1980	1985
可供量	**Total Energy Available for Consumption**	**122.5**	**157.3**
生产量	Output	122.5	159.7
进口量	Imports		
出口量(-)	Exports (-)		1.9
年初年末库存差额	Stock Changes in the Year		-0.5
消费量	**Total Energy Consumption**	**119.6**	**155.7**
在消费量中:	Consumption by Sector		
1. 农、林、牧、渔业	Farming, Forestry, Animal Husbandry, Fishery Conservancy		
2. 工业	Industry	76.1	59.9
3. 建筑业	Construction		
4. 交通运输、仓储和邮政业	Transport, Storage and Post		
5. 批发、零售业和住宿、餐饮业	Wholesale, Retail Trade and Hotel, Restaurants		0.5
6. 其他	Other	0.4	4.5
7. 生活消费	Residential Consumption	43.1	90.8
平衡差额	**Balance**	**2.9**	**1.6**

LPG BALANCE SHEET

(10 000 ton)

1990	1995	1999	2000	2001	2002	2003	2004	2005
258.5	**774.3**	**1146.6**	**1396.2**	**1428.0**	**1663.6**	**1836.2**	**2051.1**	**2052.2**
261.6	540.8	816.6	916.6	952.3	1036.8	1211.7	1417.0	1432.7
	232.6	322.3	481.7	488.9	626.2	636.7	641.0	617.0
1.1	7.1	7.5	1.6	2.1	5.6	2.4	3.2	2.67
−2.0	8.0	−1.5	−0.6	−11.1	6.3	−9.9	−3.7	5.2
254.2	**750.6**	**1208.5**	**1366.7**	**1411.0**	**1625.4**	**1796.6**	**2016.1**	**2016.1**
	0.1		0.4	0.3			5.1	5.0
82.0	192.5	254.0	276.1	291.7	320.5	361.6	491.6	531.9
1.0	0.5	7.9	8.9	9.5	12.8	8.9	8.7	6.3
	0.5	2.0	16.5	17.0	28.6	36.1	35.9	48.7
6.6	17.4	47.9	55.5	60.4	62.6	64.4	91.3	99.0
6.1	5.7	17.9	21.0	26.2	31.9	32.9	32.9	25.8
158.5	534.0	878.5	988.3	1006.0	1169.1	1292.7	1350.5	1328.7
4.3	**23.7**	**−61.6**	**29.5**	**16.9**	**38.2**	**39.6**	**35.0**	**6.7**

4－13 天然气平衡表

单位：亿立方米

项 目	Item	1980	1985
可供量	**Total Energy Available for Consumption**	**142.7**	**129.3**
生产量	Output	142.7	129.3
进口量	Imports		
出口量（－）	Exports（－）		
年初年末库存差额	Stock Changes in the Year		
消费量	**Total Energy Consumption**	**140.6**	**129.3**
在消费量中：	Consumption by Sector		
1. 农、林、牧、渔业	Farming, Forestry, Animal Husbandry, Fishery Conservancy		
2. 工业	Industry	131.4	109.6
3. 建筑业	Construction	6.0	14.1
4. 交通运输、仓储和邮政业	Transport, Storage and Post	0.7	0.8
5. 批发、零售业和住宿、餐饮业 Wholesale, Retail Trade and Hotel, Restaurants			
6. 其他	Other	0.5	0.5
7. 生活消费	Residential Consumption	2.0	4.3
平衡差额	**Balance**	**2.1**	

NATURAL GAS BALANCE SHEET

(100 million cu. m)

1990	1995	1999	2000	2001	2002	2003	2004	2005
153.0	**179.5**	**218.2**	**240.6**	**272.9**	**294.6**	**331.42**	**390.2**	**463.51**
153.0	179.5	252.0	272.0	303.3	326.6	350.15	414.6	493.20
		33.8	31.4	30.4	32.0	18.73	24.4	29.69
152.5	**177.4**	**214.9**	**245.0**	**274.3**	**291.8**	**339.1**	**396.7**	**467.63**
120.2	154.4	180.2	202.0	217.8	227.5	267.8	293.6	353.79
10.6	0.3	0.7	0.8	0.7	0.7	0.7	1.4	1.49
1.9	1.6	4.8	5.8	6.0	6.4	6.8	11.2	13.01
	0.6	2.9	3.4	5.0	6.1	6.9	9.2	10.79
1.2	1.2	0.6	0.6	0.7	0.0	0.0	14.1	9.12
18.6	19.4	25.7	32.3	44.1	51.2	56.9	67.2	79.43
0.5	**2.1**	**3.3**	**−4.4**	**−1.4**	**2.7**	**−7.7**	**−6.5**	**−4.12**

4-14 电力平衡表

单位:亿千瓦小时

项 目	Item	1980	1985
可供量	**Total Energy Available for Consumption**	**3006.3**	**4117.6**
生产量	Output	3006.3	4106.9
水 电	Hydropower	582.1	923.7
火 电	Thermal Power	2424.2	3183.2
核 电	Nuclear Power		
进口量	Imports		11.1
出口量(-)	Exports (-)		0.4
消费量	**Total Energy Consumption**	**3006.3**	**4117.6**
在消费量中:	Consumption by Sector		
1. 农、林、牧、渔 业	Farming, Forestry, Animal Husbandry, Fishery Conservancy	270	317.4
2. 工 业	Industry	2471.9	3283.4
3. 建筑业	Construction	47.1	71.2
4. 交通运输、仓储和邮政业	Transport, Storage and Post	26.5	63.4
5. 批发、零售业和住宿、餐饮业	Wholesale, Retail Trade and Hotel, Restaurants	16.8	38.0
6. 其他	Others	68.8	121.7
7. 生活消费	Residential Consumption	105.2	222.5
在消费量中:	Consumption by Usage		
(一)终端消费	(I) Final Consumption	2763.4	3813.3
#工 业	Industry	2229.0	2979.1
(二)输配电损失量	(II) Losses in Transmission	242.9	304.3

ELECTRICITY BALANCE SHEET

(100 million kW · h)

1990	1995	1999	2000	2001	2002	2003	2004	2005
6230.4	**10023.4**	**12305.2**	**13472.7**	**14724.1**	**16466.0**	**19032.2**	**21972.3**	**24940.8**
6212.0	10077.3	12393.0	13556.0	14808.0	16540.0	19105.8	22033.1	25002.6
1267.2	1905.8	2038.1	2224.1	2774.3	2879.7	2836.8	3535.4	3970.2
4944.8	8043.2	10205.4	11141.9	11834.3	13381.4	15803.6	17955.9	20473.4
	128.3	149.5	167.4	174.7	251.3	433.4	504.7	530.9
19.3	6.4	3.7	15.5	18.0	23.0	29.8	34.0	50.1
0.9	60.3	91.5	98.8	101.9	97.0	103.4	94.8	111.9
6230.4	**10023.4**	**12305.2**	**13471.4**	**14723.5**	**16465.5**	**19031.6**	**21971.4**	**24940.4**
426.8	582.4	660.4	673.0	762.4	776.2	773.2	808.9	876.3
4873.3	7659.8	8832.7	9653.6	10534.7	11927.2	13899.7	16254.3	18481.7
65.0	159.6	142.3	154.8	144.9	164.1	189.8	222.1	233.9
105.9	182.3	254.8	281.2	309.3	338.0	396.9	449.6	430.3
76.2	199.5	342.8	393.7	444.9	500.0	623.0	735.4	752.3
202.4	234.2	591.4	643.2	688.1	758.5	911.0	1036.6	1340.9
480.8	1005.6	1480.8	1672.0	1839.2	2001.4	2238.0	2464.5	2824.8
5795.8	9278.9	11443.3	12534.7	13690.0	15296.8	17770.9	20550.8	23233.8
4438.7	6915.3	7970.8	8716.9	9501.2	10758.5	12639.0	14833.7	16775.2
434.6	**744.5**	**861.9**	**936.7**	**1033.5**	**1168.7**	**1260.7**	**1420.6**	**1706.5**

五、能源消费

Chapter 5　Energy Consumption

5−1 能源消费总量和构成
PRIMARY ENERGY COMPOSITION AND ITS COMPOSITION

项　目　Item	1995	2000	2001	2002	2003	2004	2005
能源消费总量（万吨标煤）（电热当量计算法） Total Energy Consumption（10⁴ tce） （calorific value calculation）	125763	132469	135765	144155	167273	193990	214466
能源消费总量（万吨标煤）（发电煤耗计算法） Total Energy Consumption（10⁴ tce） （coal equivalent calculation）	131176	138553	143199	151797	174990	203227	224682
煤炭（万吨）Coal（10⁴ tn）	137677	132000	135000	141601	169232	193596	216723
石油（万吨）Petroleum（10⁴ tn）	16065	22439	22838	24787	27126	31700	32535
天然气（亿立方米）Natural Gas（10⁸ cu. m）	177	245	274	292	339	397	479
水电（亿千瓦时）Hydro Power（10⁸ kW·h）	1906	2224	2774	2880	2837	3535	3970
核电（亿千瓦时）Nuclear Power（10⁸ kW·h）	128	167	175	251	433	505	531
构成（电热当量计算法）（%） As Percentage of Primary Energy Production（%） （calorific value calculation）							
煤炭 Coal	77.40	71.02	70.50	69.96	71.63	71.31	72.76
石油 Petroleum	18.30	24.28	24.12	24.66	23.24	23.39	21.74
天然气 Natural Gas	1.88	2.46	2.69	2.69	2.70	2.72	2.90
水电 Hydro Power	1.84	2.08	2.53	2.48	2.11	2.26	2.30
核电 Nuclear Power	0.13	0.16	0.16	0.21	0.32	0.32	0.30
构成（发电煤耗计算法）（%） As percentage of primary energy production（%） （coal equivalent calculation）							
煤炭 Coal	74.60	67.75	66.69	66.32	68.38	67.99	69.11
石油 Petroleum	17.50	23.21	22.87	23.41	22.21	22.33	21.00
天然气 Natural Gas	1.80	2.35	2.55	2.56	2.58	2.60	2.80
水电 Hydro Power	5.71	6.23	7.43	7.10	5.93	6.20	6.26
核电 Nuclear Power	0.39	0.46	0.46	0.61	0.90	0.88	0.83

5-2 工业分行业终端能源消费量(实物量)-2005

行 业	Sector	煤合计 (万吨) Coal Total (10^4 tn)	原煤 (万吨) Raw Coal (10^4 tn)
工业	Industry	48040.74	41018.77
(一)采掘业	**Mining and Quarrying**	5051.80	4561.35
煤炭开采和洗选业	Mining and Washing of Coal	4346.40	3886.90
石油和天然气开采业	Extraction of Petroleum and Natural Gas	134.52	134.47
黑色金属矿采选业	Mining and Processing of Ferrous Metal Ores	112.12	104.52
有色金属矿采选业	Mining and Processing of Noe-Ferrous Metal Ores	88.09	78.35
非金属矿采选业	Mining and Processing of Nonmetal Ores	369.02	355.46
其他采矿业	Mining of Other Ores	1.66	1.66
(二)制造业	**Manufacturing**	40225.62	33785.86
农副食品加工业	Processing of Food from Agricultural Products	973.93	902.03
食品制造业	Manufacture of Foods	612.56	600.65
饮料制造业	Manufacture of Beverages	610.89	594.76
烟草制品业	Manufacture of Tobacco	106.69	102.67
纺织业	Manufacture of Textile	1579.08	1559.71
纺织服装、鞋、帽制造业	Manufacture of Textile Wearing Apparel,Footware,and Caps	176.21	171.27
皮革、毛皮、羽毛(绒)及其制品业	Manufacture of Leather,Fur,Feather and Related Products	80.52	79.73
木材加工及木、竹、藤、棕、草制品业	Processing of Timber,Manufacture of Wood,Bamboo,Rattan,Palm,and Straw Products	338.41	333.24
家具制造业	Manufacture of Furniture	25.72	25.37
造纸及纸制品业	Manufacture of Paper and Paper Products	1634.52	1546.12
印刷业和记录媒介的复制	Printing,Reproduction of Recording Media	35.74	35.46
文教体育用品制造业	Manufacture of Articles For Culture,Education and Sport Activity	16.57	16.38
石油加工、炼焦及核燃料加工业	Processing of Petroleum,Coking,Processing of Nuclear Fuel	1129.28	839.35
化学原料及化学制品制造业	Manufacture of Raw Chemical Materials and Chemical Products	6949.45	6372.50
医药制造业	Manufacture of Medicines	441.75	422.23
化学纤维制造业	Manufacture of Chemical Fibers	201.64	199.43
橡胶制品业	Manufacture of Rubber	309.01	300.67
塑料制品业	Manufacture of Plastics	217.87	213.92
非金属矿物制品业	Manufacture of Noe-metallic Mineral Products	16411.48	12260.45
黑色金属冶炼及压延加工业	Smelting and Pressing of Ferrous Metals	5338.20	4416.56
有色金属冶炼及压延加工业	Smelting and Pressing of Noe-ferrous Metals	1068.74	932.57
金属制品业	Manufacture of Metal Products	254.32	240.89
通用设备制造业	Manufacture of General Purpose Machinery	284.10	266.44
专用设备制造业	Manufacture of Special Purpose Machinery	395.89	361.22
交通运输设备制造业	Manufacture of Transport Equipment	519.86	508.64
电气机械及器材制造业	Manufacture of Electrical Machinery and Equipment	136.01	131.01
通信设备、计算机及其他电子设备制造业	Manufacture of Communication Equipment,Computers and Other Electronic Equipment	88.19	86.22
仪器仪表及文化、办公用机械制造业	Manufacture of Measuring Instruments and Machinery for Cultural Activity and Office Work	19.76	18.55
工艺品及其他制造业	Manufacture of Artwork and Other Manufacturing	263.21	243.83
废弃资源和废旧材料回收加工业	Recycling and Disposal of Waste	6.02	4.00
(三)电力、煤气及水生产和供应业	**Electric Power,Gas and Water Production and Supply**	2763.32	2671.55
电力、热力的生产和供应业	Production and Distribution of Electric Power and Heat Power	2656.71	2565.36
燃气生产和供应业	Production and Distribution of Gas	77.04	76.64
水的生产和供应业	Production and Distribution of Water	29.58	29.55

FINAL ENERGY CONSUMPTION BY INDUSTRIAL SECTOR – 2005
(PHYSICAL QUANTITY)

洗精煤（万吨）Cleaned Coal (10⁴ tn)	其他洗煤（万吨）Other Washed Coal (10⁴ tn)	焦炭（万吨）Coke (10⁴ tn)	焦炉煤气（亿立方米）Coke Oven Gas (10⁸ cu. m)	其他煤气（亿立方米）Other Gas (10⁸ cu. m)	其他焦化产品（万吨）Other Coking Products (10⁴ tn)	油品合计（万吨）Petroleum Products Total (10⁴ tn)	原油（万吨）Crude Oil (10⁴ tn)
2064.00	4813.42	23133.01	373.75	590.36	389.76	11245.03	870.36
189.58	300.87	140.83	1.54	2.67	2.94	1041.09	503.65
167.11	292.39	34.55	1.04	2.60	2.94	90.76	
0.05		0.28		0.01		817.92	503.65
4.60	3.00	78.61	0.50	0.07		42.25	
7.64	2.10	15.32				18.87	0.00
10.17	3.38	12.07				70.21	
						1.08	
1870.22	4425.97	22984.77	364.57	583.05	383.65	9981.76	366.28
7.03	64.87	8.00	0.02			101.26	0.07
7.02	4.90	5.03	0.01	0.14		52.34	0.10
10.33	5.80	0.97	0.00			36.74	0.50
1.90	2.12	0.01	0.01	0.14		8.26	
10.86	8.51	2.81	0.31	0.05		109.63	0.20
3.53	1.41	1.25	0.02	0.05		48.12	0.24
0.21	0.58	0.29	0.01	0.01		32.13	0.04
3.17	2.00	1.70		0.01		20.84	0.12
0.09	0.26	0.97				13.32	0.03
30.47	57.93	4.09	0.17	0.01		71.73	0.51
0.10	0.18	0.14	0.00	0.06		17.77	
0.06	0.126	3.35				19.99	0.09
235.84	54.09	61.71	43.91	5.01	42.00	4738.19	154.67
328.40	172.74	1608.97	8.24	5.63	146.96	2336.92	182.38
16.77	2.75	1.06	0.07	0.06		23.61	
1.81	0.40	48.10				56.18	10.62
4.34	3.99	1.66	0.00	0.05		40.77	0.82
1.93	2.02	2.46	0.01			83.58	0.08
325.37	3793.66	195.59	3.55	16.17	39.73	951.65	14.17
749.39	157.55	20012.53	299.51	520.05	128.04	326.72	0.13
59.00	62.95	345.15	6.30	19.54	26.92	232.75	0.31
7.95	5.49	73.56	0.29	0.27		104.19	0.06
7.88	5.99	427.78	0.79	3.39		110.29	0.15
32.67	2.00	64.69	0.67	10.44		56.29	0.11
6.75	4.47	88.19	0.31	0.75		142.39	0.15
3.82	1.18	15.73	0.29	0.75		101.96	0.26
1.75	0.22	0.64	0.07	0.12		98.99	0.40
0.03	1.18	2.58	0.01	0.00		14.51	0.05
11.74	4.61	3.56	0.01	0.16		27.99	0.01
0.02	2.00	2.19		0.21		2.64	
4.19	86.59	7.41	7.63	4.63	3.17	222.18	0.43
4.00	86.35	5.75	0.61	0.67	1.38	115.70	0.17
0.18	0.22	1.60	7.02	3.96	1.78	100.81	0.26
0.01	0.02	0.06				5.67	0.00

行 业	Sector	汽油 (万吨) Gasoline (10^4 tn)	煤油 (万吨) Kerosene (10^4 tn)
工业	Industry	460.91	57.50
（一）采掘业	**Mining and Quarrying**	**54.20**	**6.40**
煤炭开采和洗选业	Mining and Washing of Coal	15.22	3.26
石油和天然气开采业	Extraction of Petroleum and Natural Gas	26.88	0.17
黑色金属矿采选业	Mining and Processing of Ferrous Metal Ores	4.81	1.42
有色金属矿采选业	Mining and Processing of Noe-Ferrous Metal Ores	3.45	0.74
非金属矿采选业	Mining and Processing of Nonmetal Ores	3.82	0.80
其他采矿业	Mining of Other Ores	0.02	0.01
（二）制造业	**Manufacturing**	**380.71**	**50.74**
农副食品加工业	Processing of Food from Agricultural Products	13.84	0.40
食品制造业	Manufacture of Foods	7.69	0.33
饮料制造业	Manufacture of Beverages	7.24	0.54
烟草制品业	Manufacture of Tobacco	0.78	0.03
纺织业	Manufacture of Textile	17.50	2.05
纺织服装、鞋、帽制造业	Manufacture of Textile Wearing Apparel,Footware,and Caps	9.70	0.70
皮革、毛皮、羽毛（绒）及其制品业	Manufacture of Leather,Fur,Feather and Related Products	4.50	0.37
木材加工及木、竹、藤、棕、草制品业	Processing of Timber,Manufacture of Wood, Bamboo,Rattan,Palm,and Straw Products	4.94	1.09
家具制造业	Manufacture of Furniture	2.86	0.24
造纸及纸制品业	Manufacture of Paper and Paper Products	8.42	0.91
印刷业和记录媒介的复制	Printing,Reproduction of Recording Media	6.94	0.74
文教体育用品制造业	Manufacture of Articles For Culture,Education and Sport Activity	3.87	0.35
石油加工、炼焦及核燃料加工业	Processing of Petroleum,Coking,Processing of Nuclear Fuel	21.80	2.06
化学原料及化学制品制造业	Manufacture of Raw Chemical Materials and Chemical Products	44.05	6.09
医药制造业	Manufacture of Medicines	7.67	0.52
化学纤维制造业	Manufacture of Chemical Fibers	1.15	0.50
橡胶制品业	Manufacture of Rubber	9.50	0.27
塑料制品业	Manufacture of Plastics	12.51	0.74
非金属矿物制品业	Manufacture of Noe-metallic Mineral Products	25.12	3.06
黑色金属冶炼及压延加工业	Smelting and Pressing of Ferrous Metals	22.13	1.92
有色金属冶炼及压延加工业	Smelting and Pressing of Noe-ferrous Metals	6.42	2.32
金属制品业	Manufacture of Metal Products	17.92	2.64
通用设备制造业	Manufacture of General Purpose Machinery	27.40	5.80
专用设备制造业	Manufacture of Special Purpose Machinery	16.56	1.69
交通运输设备制造业	Manufacture of Transport Equipment	36.50	11.08
电气机械及器材制造业	Manufacture of Electrical Machinery and Equipment	21.56	1.60
通信设备、计算机及其他电子设备制造业	Manufacture of Communication Equipment,Computers and Other Electronic Equipment	11.03	0.82
仪器仪表及文化、办公用机械制造业	Manufacture of Measuring Instruments and Machinery for Cultural Activity and Office Work	3.61	1.13
工艺品及其他制造业	Manufacture of Artwork and Other Manufacturing	7.18	0.70
废弃资源和废旧材料回收加工业	Recycling and Disposal of Waste	0.33	0.04
（三）电力、煤气及水生产和供应业	**Electric Power,Gas and Water Production and Supply**	**26.00**	**0.36**
电力、热力的生产和供应业	Production and Distribution of Electric Power and Heat Power	20.45	0.32
燃气生产和供应业	Production and Distribution of Gas	2.47	0.02
水的生产和供应业	Production and Distribution of Water	3.08	0.03

柴油 （万吨） Diesel Oil （10^4 tn）	燃料油 （万吨） Fuel Oil （10^4 tn）	液化石油气 （万吨） PLG （10^4 tn）	炼厂干气 （万吨） Refinery Gas （10^4 tn）	其他石油制品 （万吨） Other Petroleum Products （10^4 tn）	天然气 （万吨） Nature Gas （10^8 cu. m）	热力 （万百万千焦） Heat （10^{10} kJ）	电力 （亿千瓦小时） Electricity （10^8 kW·h）
1724.53	1732.59	528.60	791.35	5079.19	291.76	166267.92	16775.22
378.44	35.62	3.21	39.06	20.52	55.14	6745.56	1476.82
65.71	5.25	0.25	0.00013	1.07	1.71	294.49	588.12
197.30	28.84	2.81	39.06	19.22	53.36	5181.82	384.43
35.34	0.65			0.03	0.02	0.76	205.14
14.28	0.25	0.10		0.05	0.02	0.06	157.28
64.76	0.63	0.05		0.15	0.03	1268.43	113.87
1.05							27.97
1277.19	1663.98	439.57	750.71	5052.58	231.52	148786.45	13094.79
58.00	12.40	3.00	11.44	2.11	0.30	2478.14	252.75
22.15	18.11	3.47		0.49	1.40	4003.47	114.54
15.12	13.04	0.30		0.55		1527.90	76.37
5.96	1.46	0.03		0.28		269.33	35.78
42.41	42.41	2.75	0.17	2.14	0.61	14644.83	821.61
29.59	6.68	0.62		0.60	0.10	619.76	87.40
14.93	11.90	0.26		0.14	0.03	165.12	54.72
11.79	2.62	0.19		0.10	0.12	476.27	105.32
8.81	0.28	1.09			0.04	54.00	24.22
25.37	28.08	8.33		0.12	0.54	9839.24	406.76
7.25	1.79	0.93		0.12	0.21	97.17	60.57
12.06	2.56	0.97		0.09		31.47	42.44
53.60	255.48	169.62	677.02	3403.94	14.76	28436.06	312.74
145.62	303.49	99.25	58.15	1497.89	151.59	44980.16	2124.70
9.13	5.49	0.50		0.30	1.06	4023.45	152.85
7.87	32.77	0.97	1.27	1.03	0.32	5011.55	232.65
10.38	17.69	1.10		1.01	0.38	831.76	208.80
39.19	18.03	1.90		11.13	0.60	353.54	321.65
268.45	525.64	73.11	2.09	40.01	26.04	624.96	1416.13
97.32	186.50	11.23		7.49	10.68	15354.83	2544.40
55.97	89.63	5.71		72.39	4.23	7585.50	1469.60
55.37	15.63	12.03		0.53	0.75	203.41	506.04
60.09	9.29	5.00		2.56	1.98	758.48	343.95
27.90	6.59	2.42		1.00	2.96	1529.94	182.47
72.40	11.65	8.09		2.53	5.28	2616.22	300.00
48.86	13.46	13.64	0.58	2.01	1.35	754.37	245.21
49.30	27.38	9.98		0.08	5.22	850.52	327.11
8.84	0.20	0.23		0.45	0.09	112.06	42.42
12.23	2.81	2.82		2.23	0.04	549.24	274.96
1.22	0.92	0.04		0.10		3.69	6.64
68.91	32.99	85.82	1.58	6.09	5.10	10735.91	2203.62
56.10	32.42	0.06	0.19	5.99	0.45	10454.62	1987.07
10.27	0.56	85.76	1.39	0.10	4.59	217.48	29.79
2.54	0.01	0.01		0.06		63.81	186.76

5-3 工业分行业终端能源消费量(标准量)-2005

单位:万吨标准煤

行 业	Sector	终端消费合计 Final Consumption Total	
		(发电煤耗计算法)(coal equivalent calculation)	(电热当量计算法)(calorific value calculation)
工业	**Industry**	**149638.92**	**109162.42**
(一)采掘业	**Mining and Quarrying**	**11828.33**	**8365.17**
煤炭开采和洗选业	Mining and Washing of Coal	5662.57	4313.78
石油和天然气开采业	Extraction of Petroleum and Natural Gas	3589.04	2644.03
黑色金属矿采选业	Mining and Processing of Ferrous Metal Ores	947.54	478.37
有色金属矿采选业	Mining and Processing of Noe-Ferrous Metal Ores	664.55	304.85
非金属矿采选业	Mining and Processing of Nonmetal Ores	863.42	586.89
其他采矿业	Mining of Other Ores	101.21	37.25
(二)制造业	**Manufacturing**	**126882.83**	**95045.51**
农副食品加工业	Processing of Food from Agricultural Products	2038.72	1429.22
食品制造业	Manufacture of Foods	1170.51	857.72
饮料制造业	Manufacture of Beverages	880.44	686.37
烟草制品业	Manufacture of Tobacco	238.00	152.76
纺织业	Manufacture of Textile	4983.70	2918.71
纺织服装、鞋、帽制造业	Manufacture of Textile Wearing Apparel, Footware, and Caps	547.41	339.67
皮革、毛皮、羽毛(绒)及其制品业	Manufacture of Leather, Fur, Feather and Related Products	310.51	183.26
木材加工及木、竹、藤、棕、草制品业	Processing of Timber, Manufacture of Wood, Bamboo, Rattan, Palm, and Straw Products	691.48	444.57
家具制造业	Manufacture of Furniture	128.98	72.90
造纸及纸制品业	Manufacture of Paper and Paper Products	3279.23	2224.02
印刷业和记录媒介的复制	Printing, Reproduction of Recording Media	274.81	135.05
文教体育用品制造业	Manufacture of Articles For Culture, Education and Sport Activity	196.14	98.68
石油加工、炼焦及核燃料加工业	Processing of Petroleum, Coking, Processing of Nuclear Fuel	10471.52	9395.17
化学原料及化学制品制造业	Manufacture of Raw Chemical Materials and Chemical Products	22007.48	16577.07
医药制造业	Manufacture of Medicines	1123.48	722.82
化学纤维制造业	Manufacture of Chemical Fibers	1343.45	747.74
橡胶制品业	Manufacture of Rubber	1080.78	592.69
塑料制品业	Manufacture of Plastics	1448.70	708.60
非金属矿物制品业	Manufacture of Noe-metallic Mineral Products	18985.62	15738.98
黑色金属冶炼及压延加工业	Smelting and Pressing of Ferrous Metals	36870.19	30856.14
有色金属冶炼及压延加工业	Smelting and Pressing of Noe-ferrous Metals	7183.27	3725.95
金属制品业	Manufacture of Metal Products	2223.58	1063.68
通用设备制造业	Manufacture of General Purpose Machinery	2068.18	1271.93
专用设备制造业	Manufacture of Special Purpose Machinery	1243.29	806.56
交通运输设备制造业	Manufacture of Transport Equipment	1950.69	1231.36
电气机械及器材制造业	Manufacture of Electrical Machinery and Equipment	1192.65	622.27
通信设备、计算机及其他电子设备制造业	Manufacture of Communication Equipment, Computers and Other Electronic Equipment	1476.22	717.30
仪器仪表及文化、办公用机械制造业	Manufacture of Measuring Instruments and Machinery for Cultural Activity and Office Work	194.47	96.03
工艺品及其他制造业	Manufacture of Artwork and Other Manufacturing	1245.15	609.34
废弃资源和废旧材料回收加工业	Recycling and Disposal of Waste	34.18	18.95
(三)电力、煤气及水生产和供应业	**Electric Power, Gas and Water Production and Supply**	**10927.76**	**5751.74**
电力、热力的生产和供应业	Production and Distribution of Electric Power and Heat Power	9772.23	5095.02
燃气生产和供应业	Production and Distribution of Gas	463.53	392.64
水的生产和供应业	Production and Distribution of Water	692.00	264.08

FINAL ENERGY CONSUMPTION BY INDUSTRIAL SECTOR – 2005
(STANDARD QUANTITY)

(10 000 tce)

煤合计 Coal Total	原煤 Raw Coal	洗精煤 Cleaned Coal	其他洗煤 Other Washed Coal	焦炭 Coke	焦炉煤气 Coke Oven Gas	其他煤气 Other Gas	其他焦化产品 Other Coking Products	油品合计 Petroleum Products Total
36646.13	32172.75	1857.60	2528.01	21581.73	2295.93	1697.75	449.78	15801.69
3906.30	3577.66	170.63	158.01	131.39	9.47	7.69	3.39	1504.75
3352.62	3048.66	150.40	153.56	32.23	6.39	7.48	3.39	132.27
105.51	105.47	0.05		0.26		0.01		1179.38
87.70	81.98	4.14	1.58	73.34	3.08	0.20		61.62
69.43	61.45	6.88	1.10	14.30				27.57
289.74	278.80	9.16	1.77	11.26				102.34
1.30	1.30							1.57
30594.57	26499.68	1683.20	2324.53	21443.42	2239.58	1676.75	442.74	13952.40
747.90	707.50	6.33	34.06	7.46	0.09			149.17
480.03	471.11	6.31	2.56	4.72	0.03	0.42		76.67
478.84	466.49	9.30	3.05	0.90	0.02			53.34
83.35	80.53	1.71	1.11	0.01	0.08	0.41		12.01
1237.59	1223.35	9.78	4.47	2.61	1.91	0.13		159.22
138.25	134.33	3.18	0.74	1.17	0.12	0.14		70.15
63.03	62.53	0.19	0.31	0.27	0.06	0.03		46.59
265.27	261.37	2.85	1.05	1.59		0.03		30.41
20.12	19.90	0.08	0.14	0.91				19.72
1270.53	1212.69	27.42	30.43	3.81	1.03	0.02		105.97
28.00	27.82	0.09	0.09	0.13		0.17		26.17
12.97	12.85	0.06	0.07	3.13				29.35
899.00	658.34	212.25	28.41	57.58	269.74	14.41	48.47	6515.68
5430.54	4998.22	295.56	90.72	1501.08	50.64	16.19	169.59	3205.03
347.71	331.17	15.01	1.44	0.99	0.40	0.17		34.45
158.26	156.42	1.63	0.21	44.87				80.89
241.83	235.83	3.91	2.10	1.55		0.16		59.15
170.59	167.79	1.74	1.06	2.29	0.06			120.32
11921.08	9616.39	292.83	1992.43	182.47	21.81	46.50	45.85	1384.86
4230.21	3464.09	674.45	82.75	18670.50	1839.89	1495.56	147.76	472.88
826.25	731.45	53.10	33.06	322.00	38.73	56.18	31.07	327.58
198.97	188.94	7.15	2.88	68.63	1.77	0.78		154.68
221.52	208.98	7.09	3.15	399.09	4.85	9.75		161.81
313.77	283.32	29.40	1.05	60.36	4.11	30.02		82.57
407.37	398.95	6.08	2.35	82.28	1.88	2.14		209.54
106.81	102.76	3.43	0.62	14.67	1.79	2.16		151.79
69.32	67.63	1.58	0.12	0.60	0.45	0.34		146.17
15.19	14.55	0.03	0.62	2.41	0.08	0.01		21.19
206.07	191.24	10.56	2.42	3.32	0.04	0.45		41.21
4.20	3.14	0.02	1.05	2.04		0.59		3.83
2145.26	2095.41	3.77	45.47	6.92	46.89	13.31	3.66	344.53
2061.68	2012.12	3.60	45.34	5.37	3.76	1.93	1.60	167.11
60.39	60.11	0.16	0.12	1.49	43.13	11.39	2.06	169.11
23.19	23.18	0.01	0.01	0.06				8.31

续表

单位:万吨标准煤

行 业	Sector	原油 Crude Oil	汽油 Gasoline
工业合计	**Industry Total**	1243.40	678.18
（一）采掘业	**Mining and Quarrying**	719.52	79.74
煤炭开采和洗选业	Mining and Washing of Coal		22.39
石油和天然气开采业	Extraction of Petroleum and Natural Gas	719.51	39.55
黑色金属矿采选业	Mining and Processing of Ferrous Metal Ores		7.07
有色金属矿采选业	Mining and Processing of Noe-Ferrous Metal Ores	0.00	5.08
非金属矿采选业	Mining and Processing of Nonmetal Ores		5.62
其他采矿业	Mining of Other Ores		0.03
（二）制造业	**Manufacturing**	523.26	560.18
农副食品加工业	Processing of Food from Agricultural Products	0.10	20.36
食品制造业	Manufacture of Foods	0.14	11.32
饮料制造业	Manufacture of Beverages	0.71	10.66
烟草制品业	Manufacture of Tobacco		1.15
纺织业	Manufacture of Textile	0.29	25.75
纺织服装、鞋、帽制造业	Manufacture of Textile Wearing Apparel, Footware, and Caps	0.34	14.27
皮革、毛皮、羽毛（绒）及其制品业	Manufacture of Leather, Fur, Feather and Related Products	0.05	6.61
木材加工及木、竹、藤、棕、草制品业	Processing of Timber, Manufacture of Wood, Bamboo, Rattan, Palm, and Straw Products	0.17	7.27
家具制造业	Manufacture of Furniture	0.04	4.21
造纸及纸制品业	Manufacture of Paper and Paper Products	0.73	12.39
印刷业和记录媒介的复制	Printing, Reproduction of Recording Media		10.21
文教体育用品制造业	Manufacture of Articles For Culture, Education and Sport Activity	0.13	5.69
石油加工、炼焦及核燃料加工业	Processing of Petroleum, Coking, Processing of Nuclear Fuel	220.97	32.08
化学原料及化学制品制造业	Manufacture of Raw Chemical Materials and Chemical Products	260.55	64.82
医药制造业	Manufacture of Medicines		11.29
化学纤维制造业	Manufacture of Chemical Fibers	15.17	1.69
橡胶制品业	Manufacture of Rubber	1.17	13.98
塑料制品业	Manufacture of Plastics	0.11	18.41
非金属矿物制品业	Manufacture of Noe-metallic Mineral Products	20.24	36.96
黑色金属冶炼及压延加工业	Smelting and Pressing of Ferrous Metals	0.19	32.57
有色金属冶炼及压延加工业	Smelting and Pressing of Noe-ferrous Metals	0.44	9.45
金属制品业	Manufacture of Metal Products	0.09	26.37
通用设备制造业	Manufacture of General Purpose Machinery	0.21	40.32
专用设备制造业	Manufacture of Special Purpose Machinery	0.16	24.37
交通运输设备制造业	Manufacture of Transport Equipment	0.21	53.71
电气机械及器材制造业	Manufacture of Electrical Machinery and Equipment	0.37	31.72
通信设备、计算机及其他电子设备制造业	Manufacture of Communication Equipment, Computers and Other Electronic Equipment	0.57	16.23
仪器仪表及文化、办公用机械制造业	Manufacture of Measuring Instruments and Machinery for Cultural Activity and Office Work	0.07	5.31
工艺品及其他制造业	Manufacture of Artwork and Other Manufacturing	0.01	10.57
废弃资源和废旧材料回收加工业	Recycling and Disposal of Waste		0.48
（三）电力、煤气及水生产和供应业	**Electric Power, Gas and Water Production and Supply**	**0.62**	**38.26**
电力、热力的生产和供应业	Production and Distribution of Electric Power and Heat Power	0.25	30.09
燃气生产和供应业	Production and Distribution of Gas	0.37	3.63
水的生产和供应业	Production and Distribution of Water	0.01	4.53

90

(10 000 tce)

煤油 Kerosene	柴油 Diesel Oil	燃料油 Fuel Oil	液化石油气 PLG	炼厂干气 Refinery Gas	其他石油制品 Other Petroleum Products	天然气 Nature Gas	热力 Heat	电力 Electricity
84.61	**2512.81**	**2475.18**	**906.18**	**1243.53**	**6657.81**	**3880.42**	**5669.74**	**20616.75**
9.41	**551.42**	**50.89**	**5.50**	**61.38**	**26.90**	**733.39**	**230.02**	**1815.01**
4.80	95.75	7.50	0.43	0.00	1.41	22.80	10.04	722.80
0.25	287.48	41.20	4.81	61.38	25.19	709.69	176.70	472.47
2.09	51.49	0.93			0.04	0.29	0.03	252.12
1.09	20.81	0.36	0.17		0.07	0.25	0.00	193.30
1.18	94.36	0.90	0.09		0.20	0.36	43.25	139.95
0.01	1.53							34.38
74.66	**1860.99**	**2377.16**	**753.55**	**1179.67**	**6622.92**	**3079.18**	**5073.62**	**16093.49**
0.59	84.51	17.71	5.15	17.98	2.76	3.99	84.50	310.63
0.49	32.28	25.87	5.94		0.64	18.62	136.52	140.77
0.79	22.03	18.63	0.51			7.32	52.10	93.86
0.05	8.68	2.09	0.04			3.76	9.18	43.97
3.02	61.79	60.59	4.72	0.27	2.81	8.10	499.39	1009.76
1.03	43.11	9.54	1.06		0.79	1.30	21.13	107.41
0.54	21.75	17.00	0.45		0.18	0.40	5.63	67.26
1.60	17.18	3.74	0.32		0.13	1.59	16.24	129.44
0.35	12.84	0.40	1.88			0.54	1.84	29.77
1.34	36.97	40.12	14.27		0.15	7.23	335.52	499.91
1.09	10.56	2.56	1.59		0.16	2.82	3.31	74.44
0.51	17.57	3.66	1.66		0.12		1.07	52.16
3.03	78.11	364.98	290.77	1063.86	4461.88	196.35	969.67	384.36
8.96	212.18	433.57	170.15	91.38	1963.43	2016.14	1533.82	2611.26
0.77	13.30	7.84	0.86		0.39	14.04	137.20	187.85
0.74	11.47	46.82	1.67	2.00	1.35	4.27	170.89	285.93
0.40	15.12	25.27	1.88		1.33	5.02	28.36	256.61
1.09	57.10	25.76	3.26		14.59	7.98	12.06	395.31
4.50	391.16	750.93	125.34	3.28	52.45	346.33	21.31	1740.42
2.83	141.80	266.43	19.25		9.82	142.04	523.60	3127.07
3.41	81.55	128.04	9.79		94.89	56.31	258.67	1806.14
3.89	80.69	22.33	20.63		0.70	9.99	6.94	621.92
8.53	87.55	13.27	8.56		3.36	26.33	25.86	422.71
2.49	40.66	9.42	4.15		1.32	39.30	52.17	224.25
16.30	105.49	16.64	13.87		3.32	70.25	89.21	368.70
2.35	71.19	19.23	23.38	0.90	2.63	17.96	25.72	301.37
1.21	71.83	39.12	17.11		0.10	69.42	29.00	402.02
1.66	12.88	0.29	0.39		0.59	1.20	3.82	52.13
1.04	17.83	4.01	4.83		2.92	0.60	18.73	337.93
0.07	1.78	1.31	0.06		0.13		0.13	8.16
0.53	**100.40**	**47.13**	**147.13**	**2.48**	**7.98**	**67.85**	**366.09**	**2708.25**
0.46	81.74	46.32	0.10	0.30	7.85	5.99	356.50	2442.11
0.02	14.96	0.80	147.01	2.18	0.13	61.05	7.42	36.61
0.04	3.70	0.02	0.01			0.82	2.18	229.53

5-4 分行业能源消费总量

单位:万吨标准煤

行　　　业	Sector	1995
消 费 总 量	**Total Consumption**	**131175.40**
农、林、牧、渔、水利业	**Farming, Forestry, Animal Husbandry, Fishery and Water Conservancy**	**5505.10**
工业	**Industry**	**96191.30**
采掘业	**Mining and Quarrying**	**9941.00**
煤炭开采和洗选业	Mining and Washing of Coal	5499.80
石油和天然气开采业	Extraction of Petroleum and Natural Gas	2812.60
黑色金属矿采选业	Mining and Processing of Ferrous Metal Ores	268.20
有色金属矿采选业	Mining and Processing of Noe-Ferrous Metal Ores	557.20
非金属矿采选业	Mining and Processing of Nonmetal Ores	553.40
其他采矿业	Mining of Other Ores	249.80
制造业	**Manufacturing**	**78368.20**
农副食品加工业	Processing of Food from Agricultural Products	1972.50
食品制造业	Manufacture of Foods	1208.00
饮料制造业	Manufacture of Beverages	1000.30
烟草制品业	Manufacture of Tobacco	223.80
纺织业	Manufacture of Textile	3531.30
纺织服装、鞋、帽制造业	Manufacture of Textile Wearing Apparel, Footware, and Caps	329.20
皮革、毛皮、羽毛(绒)及其制品业	Manufacture of Leather, Fur, Feather and Related Products	289.90
木材加工及木、竹、藤、棕、草制品业	Processing of Timber, Manufacture of Wood, Bamboo, Rattan, Palm, and Straw Products	380.00
家具制造业	Manufacture of Furniture	105.80
造纸及纸制品业	Manufacture of Paper and Paper Products	2138.40
印刷业和记录媒介的复制	Printing, Reproduction of Recording Media	203.40
文教体育用品制造业	Manufacture of Articles For Culture, Education and Sport Activity	62.00
石油加工、炼焦及核燃料加工业	Processing of Petroleum, Coking, Processing of Nuclear Fuel	5567.30
化学原料及化学制品制造业	Manufacture of Raw Chemical Materials and Chemical Products	15821.60
医药制造业	Manufacture of Medicines	1201.30
化学纤维制造业	Manufacture of Chemical Fibers	1278.00
橡胶制品业	Manufacture of Rubber	644.10
塑料制品业	Manufacture of Plastics	541.90
非金属矿物制品业	Manufacture of Noe-metallic Mineral Products	13058.00
黑色金属冶炼及压延加工业	Smelting and Pressing of Ferrous Metals	18532.80
有色金属冶炼及压延加工业	Smelting and Pressing of Noe-ferrous Metals	2841.70
金属制品业	Manufacture of Metal Products	993.90
通用设备制造业	Manufacture of General Purpose Machinery	1650.50
专用设备制造业	Manufacture of Special Purpose Machinery	1089.30
交通运输设备制造业	Manufacture of Transport Equipment	1376.30
电气机械及器材制造业	Manufacture of Electrical Machinery and Equipment	629.20
通信设备、计算机及其他电子设备制造业	Manufacture of Communication Equipment, Computers and Other Electronic Equipment	321.40
仪器仪表及文化、办公用机械制造业	Manufacture of Measuring Instruments and Machinery for Cultural Activity and Office Work	142.60
工艺品及其他制造业	Manufacture of Artwork and Other Manufacturing	1233.70
废弃资源和废旧材料回收加工业	Recycling and Disposal of Waste	
电力、煤气及水生产和供应业	**Electric Power, Gas and Water Production and Supply**	**7882.70**
电力、热力的生产和供应业	Production and Distribution of Electric Power and Heat Power	7052.70
燃气生产和供应业	Production and Distribution of Gas	341.30
水的生产和供应业	Production and Distribution of Water	488.70
建筑业	**Construction**	**1334.50**
交通运输、仓储和邮政业	**Transport, Storage and Post**	**5862.90**
批发、零售业和住宿、餐饮业	**Wholesale, Retail Trade and Hotel, Restaurants**	**2017.80**
其他行业	**Others**	**4519.00**
生活消费	**Residential Consumption**	**15744.80**

注:工业能源消费量中包括村办工业。

CONSUMPTION OF TOTAL ENERGY AND ITS MAIN VARIETIES BY SECTOR

(10 000 tce)

2000	2001	2002	2003	2004	2005
138552.6	**143199.30**	**151796.59**	**174951.64**	**203227.02**	**224681.99**
6045.26	**6400.00**	**6612.49**	**6716.00**	**7680.00**	**7918.35**
95442.80	**98273.30**	**104088.10**	**121731.86**	**143244.02**	**159491.63**
10294.15	**10728.75**	**10834.96**	**12432.52**	**12214.98**	**13051.88**
4864.850	5006.35	4591.22	5669.73	6343.26	6711.71
3856.521	4094.84	4550.31	4612.98	3625.65	3763.44
350.925	362.59	417.13	559.90	692.08	947.54
395.980	420.80	431.89	575.43	623.04	664.55
623.000	656.80	675.43	802.38	856.83	863.42
202.870	187.36	168.99	212.10	74.12	101.22
73824.29	**75710.21**	**80365.02**	**94880.15**	**115261.44**	**129291.33**
1517.745	1560.66	1662.70	1606.78	1820.78	2038.72
934.842	938.02	985.34	899.55	1026.11	1170.53
682.564	681.19	697.74	742.76	848.54	880.44
269.399	277.66	267.49	274.53	238.16	238.00
2714.437	2846.25	3095.79	3587.98	4550.25	4983.70
316.490	345.73	362.60	408.79	472.82	547.41
184.503	196.68	214.06	247.91	279.28	310.51
315.625	344.53	340.89	439.75	552.48	691.48
90.430	100.62	91.31	111.99	110.94	128.98
2004.484	2068.92	2281.77	2472.60	3081.35	3279.23
188.841	208.83	201.13	369.88	338.32	274.81
114.598	134.14	158.97	148.65	184.09	196.14
6961.567	7476.21	7644.04	8794.44	12173.85	118877.73
13164.921	13404.72	14786.61	17622.29	20346.88	22705.45
842.665	909.30	889.89	1072.84	1040.60	1123.48
1790.160	1791.17	1988.82	1741.78	1303.03	1343.45
621.921	679.72	662.63	759.45	883.72	1080.78
645.103	678.36	710.24	828.04	1129.29	1448.70
11694.318	11435.43	10864.31	13467.41	18088.40	19014.59
17820.391	18056.39	19658.35	24357.94	29702.49	37078.47
3835.097	4049.34	4495.85	5583.18	6403.53	7200.28
1121.491	1270.55	1497.09	1712.22	1966.62	2223.58
1156.368	1214.68	1351.57	1543.23	1705.51	2078.38
793.737	791.81	805.48	948.56	1146.52	1243.87
1371.568	1511.71	1632.57	1690.77	2079.64	1952.63
592.388	616.98	737.86	901.22	1119.35	1192.70
655.010	700.30	804.40	1050.09	1272.02	1476.20
145.262	151.60	171.77	201.65	171.55	194.47
1278.361	1268.72	1303.75	1293.86	1194.96	1282.44
0.000	0.00	0.00	38.57	30.35	34.18
11324.37	**11834.34**	**12888.12**	**14419.19**	**15767.60**	**17148.43**
10184.195	10759.99	11807.01	13360.38	14578.43	15826.77
552.191	488.92	535.06	507.37	535.75	629.64
587.981	585.43	546.05	551.44	653.41	692.01
2142.529	**2234.00**	**2544.00**	**2859.57**	**3259.00**	**3411.08**
10067.076	**10363.00**	**11171.00**	**12818.80**	**15104.00**	**16629.15**
3038.774	**3265.00**	**3520.00**	**4179.55**	**4820.00**	**5031.12**
5851.535	**6096.00**	**6334.00**	**6818.69**	**7839.00**	**8691.15**
15964.612	**16568.00**	**17527.00**	**19827.16**	**21281.00**	**23449.51**

a) The energy consumption by the industrial sector includes the consumption by village-run industry.

5-5 分行业煤炭消费总量

单位:万吨

行 业	Sector	1995
消 费 总 量	**Total Consumption**	**137676.50**
农、林、牧、渔、水利业	**Farming, Forestry, Animal Husbandry, Fishery and Water Conservancy**	**1856.70**
工业	**Industry**	**117570.70**
采掘业	**Mining and Quarrying**	**9861.00**
煤炭开采和洗选业	Mining and Washing of Coal	8290.70
石油和天然气开采业	Extraction of Petroleum and Natural Gas	637.20
黑色金属矿采选业	Mining and Processing of Ferrous Metal Ores	94.90
有色金属矿采选业	Mining and Processing of Noe-Ferrous Metal Ores	174.70
非金属矿采选业	Mining and Processing of Nonmetal Ores	434.40
其他采矿业	Mining of Other Ores	229.10
制造业	**Manufacturing**	**63109.40**
农副食品加工业	Processing of Food from Agricultural Products	1753.90
食品制造业	Manufacture of Foods	1214.50
饮料制造业	Manufacture of Beverages	983.30
烟草制品业	Manufacture of Tobacco	190.70
纺织业	Manufacture of Textile	2536.90
纺织服装、鞋、帽制造业	Manufacture of Textile Wearing Apparel, Footware, and Caps	117.30
皮革、毛皮、羽毛(绒)及其制品业	Manufacture of Leather, Fur, Feather and Related Products	239.00
木材加工及木、竹、藤、棕、草制品业	Processing of Timber, Manufacture of Wood, Bamboo, Rattan, Palm, and Straw Products	363.00
家具制造业	Manufacture of Furniture	62.70
造纸及纸制品业	Manufacture of Paper and Paper Products	2132.20
印刷业和记录媒介的复制	Printing, Reproduction of Recording Media	86.80
文教体育用品制造业	Manufacture of Articles For Culture, Education and Sport Activity	33.20
石油加工、炼焦及核燃料加工业	Processing of Petroleum, Coking, Processing of Nuclear Fuel	8025.10
化学原料及化学制品制造业	Manufacture of Raw Chemical Materials and Chemical Products	10803.50
医药制造业	Manufacture of Medicines	915.10
化学纤维制造业	Manufacture of Chemical Fibers	823.10
橡胶制品业	Manufacture of Rubber	566.40
塑料制品业	Manufacture of Plastics	311.50
非金属矿物制品业	Manufacture of Noe-metallic Mineral Products	13424.20
黑色金属冶炼及压延加工业	Smelting and Pressing of Ferrous Metals	12920.70
有色金属冶炼及压延加工业	Smelting and Pressing of Noe-ferrous Metals	1348.60
金属制品业	Manufacture of Metal Products	462.10
通用设备制造业	Manufacture of General Purpose Machinery	821.10
专用设备制造业	Manufacture of Special Purpose Machinery	652.50
交通运输设备制造业	Manufacture of Transport Equipment	860.20
电气机械及器材制造业	Manufacture of Electrical Machinery and Equipment	343.60
通信设备、计算机及其他电子设备制造业	Manufacture of Communication Equipment, Computers and Other Electronic Equipment	141.50
仪器仪表及文化、办公用机械制造业	Manufacture of Measuring Instruments and Machinery for Cultural Activity and Office Work	70.90
工艺品及其他制造业	Manufacture of Artwork and Other Manufacturing	905.90
废弃资源和废旧材料回收加工业	Recycling and Disposal of Waste	
电力、煤气及水生产和供应业	**Electric Power, Gas and Water Production and Supply**	**44600.30**
电力、热力的生产和供应业	Production and Distribution of Electric Power and Heat Power	43799.60
燃气生产和供应业	Production and Distribution of Gas	763.10
水的生产和供应业	Production and Distribution of Water	37.60
建筑业	**Construction**	**439.80**
交通运输、仓储和邮政业	**Transport, Storage and Post**	**1315.10**
批发、零售业和住宿、餐饮业	**Wholesale, Retail Trade and Hotel, Restaurants**	**977.40**
其他行业	**Others**	**1986.70**
生活消费	**Residential Consumption**	**13530.10**

CONSUMPTION OF COAL AND ITS MAIN VARIETIES BY SECTOR

(10 000 ton)

2000	2001	2002	2003	2004	2005
132000.00	**135000.05**	**141600.53**	**169232.05**	**193596.00**	**216722.51**
1647.68	**1599.64**	**1622.89**	**1683.33**	**2251.19**	**2315.24**
119300.65	**122518.30**	**129290.37**	**156168.48**	**180135.20**	**202609.12**
10858.37	**10463.70**	**9461.14**	**12724.07**	**11371.92**	**14214.20**
9388.47	8855.94	7793.82	10460.40	10364.73	13096.89
804.59	847.62	898.34	1139.03	355.81	338.07
65.14	64.09	80.71	98.80	92.59	112.12
83.41	88.52	82.57	85.04	90.11	91.24
402.84	482.67	505.23	730.13	467.02	574.22
113.92	124.86	100.47	210.68	1.66	1.66
50577.94	**50876.20**	**49686.36**	**59840.97**	**73097.33**	**81462.09**
1349.83	1406.90	1337.05	1463.46	1064.15	1152.72
606.73	609.10	562.51	536.62	770.98	814.83
576.40	613.97	571.03	621.10	698.13	682.08
117.57	129.27	124.74	132.57	126.01	107.97
1314.29	1334.15	1266.89	1422.78	1991.36	2141.14
110.26	120.98	107.88	121.78	171.20	191.54
63.64	66.25	62.85	64.89	84.41	84.04
210.07	209.41	204.31	250.86	352.69	348.52
38.70	42.55	38.82	46.26	26.25	26.01
1765.94	1741.22	1747.30	1835.91	2713.93	3027.87
45.86	48.68	46.72	60.11	36.21	36.22
15.80	17.36	15.32	17.01	16.63	16.57
8919.57	9794.02	10062.29	12927.00	15792.68	18919.09
7596.70	7604.43	7873.93	8940.11	9960.73	11209.03
497.81	498.56	483.20	545.93	539.29	573.50
872.50	840.51	720.23	753.44	778.88	760.15
246.53	262.11	251.72	268.28	354.33	363.18
134.25	136.44	104.16	134.94	225.52	223.61
11172.56	10681.44	8926.88	11259.01	16304.84	16764.28
11487.11	11243.99	11805.42	14730.74	16209.57	19186.70
1337.86	1401.79	1372.05	1596.65	2093.04	2238.11
214.50	223.35	217.27	202.44	269.45	273.28
335.63	347.95	330.34	317.44	340.35	340.58
309.65	301.83	266.83	368.86	450.60	456.52
699.14	724.60	729.60	668.48	802.90	730.35
174.73	171.36	159.39	155.57	149.70	137.82
65.82	60.21	57.73	66.64	137.62	132.29
28.97	25.60	24.77	31.48	20.54	19.76
269.52	218.17	215.13	200.60	608.94	498.32
0.00	0.00	0.00	100.00	6.39	6.02
57864.34	**61178.40**	**70142.87**	**83603.44**	**95665.95**	**106932.83**
56756.59	60162.23	69088.60	82503.01	94452.96	105606.07
1064.81	975.69	1018.69	1063.10	1182.70	1296.18
42.94	40.48	35.58	37.33	30.29	30.58
536.82	**534.98**	**553.54**	**577.15**	**601.53**	**603.56**
1132.24	**1041.28**	**1054.95**	**1067.33**	**832.12**	**815.34**
814.64	810.87	809.08	860.42	871.79	874.39
661.01	664.73	667.06	700.62	730.97	765.88
7906.96	7830.25	7602.64	8174.71	8173.20	8738.97

5-6 分行业焦炭消费总量

单位:万吨

行 业	Sector	1995
消费总量	**Total Consumption**	10725.28
农、林、牧、渔、水利业	**Farming, Forestry, Animal Husbandry, Fishery and Water Conservancy**	128.62
工业	**Industry**	10412.04
采掘业	**Mining and Quarrying**	151.42
煤炭开采和洗选业	Mining and Washing of Coal	41.97
石油和天然气开采业	Extraction of Petroleum and Natural Gas	1.21
黑色金属矿采选业	Mining and Processing of Ferrous Metal Ores	56.76
有色金属矿采选业	Mining and Processing of Noe-Ferrous Metal Ores	24.53
非金属矿采选业	Mining and Processing of Nonmetal Ores	26.14
其他采矿业	Mining of Other Ores	0.81
制造业	**Manufacturing**	10243.83
农副食品加工业	Processing of Food from Agricultural Products	15.37
食品制造业	Manufacture of Foods	10.43
饮料制造业	Manufacture of Beverages	4.98
烟草制品业	Manufacture of Tobacco	1.59
纺织业	Manufacture of Textile	5.78
纺织服装、鞋、帽制造业	Manufacture of Textile Wearing Apparel, Footware, and Caps	1.12
皮革、毛皮、羽毛(绒)及其制品业	Manufacture of Leather, Fur, Feather and Related Products	0.80
木材加工及木、竹、藤、棕、草制品业	Processing of Timber, Manufacture of Wood, Bamboo, Rattan, Palm, and Straw Products	1.13
家具制造业	Manufacture of Furniture	1.29
造纸及纸制品业	Manufacture of Paper and Paper Products	3.84
印刷业和记录媒介的复制	Printing, Reproduction of Recording Media	0.53
文教体育用品制造业	Manufacture of Articles For Culture, Education and Sport Activity	1.52
石油加工、炼焦及核燃料加工业	Processing of Petroleum, Coking, Processing of Nuclear Fuel	31.56
化学原料及化学制品制造业	Manufacture of Raw Chemical Materials and Chemical Products	1298.71
医药制造业	Manufacture of Medicines	2.64
化学纤维制造业	Manufacture of Chemical Fibers	23.53
橡胶制品业	Manufacture of Rubber	1.56
塑料制品业	Manufacture of Plastics	1.52
非金属矿物制品业	Manufacture of Noe-metallic Mineral Products	276.66
黑色金属冶炼及压延加工业	Smelting and Pressing of Ferrous Metals	7810.76
有色金属冶炼及压延加工业	Smelting and Pressing of Noe-ferrous Metals	195.09
金属制品业	Manufacture of Metal Products	123.24
通用设备制造业	Manufacture of General Purpose Machinery	237.13
专用设备制造业	Manufacture of Special Purpose Machinery	101.25
交通运输设备制造业	Manufacture of Transport Equipment	41.42
电气机械及器材制造业	Manufacture of Electrical Machinery and Equipment	15.59
通信设备、计算机及其他电子设备制造业	Manufacture of Communication Equipment, Computers and Other Electronic Equipment	1.05
仪器仪表及文化、办公用机械制造业	Manufacture of Measuring Instruments and Machinery for Cultural Activity and Office Work	3.42
工艺品及其他制造业	Manufacture of Artwork and Other Manufacturing	30.32
废弃资源和废旧材料回收加工业	Recycling and Disposal of Waste	
电力、煤气及水生产和供应业	**Electric Power, Gas and Water Production and Supply**	16.79
电力、热力的生产和供应业	Production and Distribution of Electric Power and Heat Power	3.80
燃气生产和供应业	Production and Distribution of Gas	12.88
水的生产和供应业	Production and Distribution of Water	0.11
建筑业	**Construction**	10.76
交通运输、仓储和邮政业	**Transport, Storage and Post**	10.10
批发、零售业和住宿、餐饮业	**Wholesale, Retail Trade and Hotel, Restaurants**	25.71
其他行业	**Others**	6.44
生活消费	**Residential Consumption**	131.61

CONSUMPTION OF COKE AND ITS MAIN VARIETIES BY SECTOR

(10 000 ton)

2000	2001	2002	2003	2004	2005
10440.01	**10999.23**	**12343.69**	**14503.76**	**17267.01**	**23605.84**
144.18	**139.23**	**140.98**	**140.98**	**98.69**	**63.47**
10080.55	**10638.40**	**11977.83**	**14149.85**	**16981.13**	**23360.92**
153.27	**149.90**	**165.77**	**157.00**	**129.88**	**165.38**
50.64	47.70	47.73	43.02	46.67	59.10
5.50	5.33	5.00	7.03	0.21	0.28
50.00	51.00	52.15	56.75	61.62	78.61
21.11	19.57	28.12	28.37	12.10	15.32
25.72	26.00	32.62	21.66	9.29	12.07
0.30	0.30	0.15	0.17	0.00	0.00
9890.50	**10448.79**	**11780.00**	**13951.34**	**16795.11**	**23130.99**
15.41	16.00	14.23	14.55	5.79	8.00
14.00	15.50	14.00	12.00	3.88	5.03
3.00	2.90	3.30	3.67	1.38	0.97
1.20	1.21	1.26	0.80	0.00	0.01
4.00	4.20	4.54	3.05	2.16	2.81
1.60	1.63	2.17	1.37	0.96	1.25
1.68	1.65	1.53	2.56	0.29	0.29
1.40	1.38	1.55	2.35	1.42	1.70
1.00	1.09	1.14	0.86	1.16	0.97
1.50	1.56	1.73	2.00	6.81	4.09
0.28	0.29	0.26	0.00	0.11	0.14
1.60	1.66	1.70	1.40	3.20	3.35
62.96	63.33	67.69	84.42	66.05	72.76
1054.89	1058.87	1169.03	1125.54	1131.81	1619.94
0.65	0.65	0.72	1.00	0.82	1.06
26.24	24.53	25.56	30.00	34.96	48.09
2.50	2.62	2.37	2.00	2.77	1.66
6.00	6.61	5.13	1.43	1.89	2.46
298.13	315.15	371.71	284.94	203.74	195.59
7720.00	8210.54	9319.68	11606.95	14596.00	20131.77
208.61	222.54	233.22	238.27	260.69	350.13
120.31	131.09	152.57	127.00	73.03	73.56
198.75	205.73	227.49	246.06	255.93	427.78
70.56	70.34	69.34	53.33	57.57	64.69
30.81	38.89	43.37	52.48	59.03	88.19
10.42	12.05	10.46	15.82	14.87	15.73
0.30	0.35	0.49	0.00	0.78	0.64
4.00	5.10	5.68	7.48	2.09	2.58
28.70	31.33	28.08	30.00	3.78	3.56
0.00	0.00		0.00	2.15	2.19
36.78	**39.71**	**32.06**	**41.51**	**56.13**	**64.55**
0.00	0.00		0.00	5.75	5.75
36.78	39.71	32.06	41.51	50.32	58.73
0.00	0.00		0.00	0.06	0.06
18.98	**23.91**	**23.38**	**20.79**	**16.79**	**18.38**
11.24	**11.68**	**11.44**	**10.79**	**1.79**	**1.07**
35.71	39.73	**42.60**	47.46	53.36	64.08
12.15	12.08	12.34	11.39	10.09	7.59
137.20	134.20	135.12	122.50	105.16	90.33

5-7 分行业原油消费总量

单位:万吨

行　　　　业	Sector	1995
消费总量	**Total Consumption**	**14886.39**
农、林、牧、渔、水利业	**Farming, Forestry, Animal Husbandry, Fishery and Water Conservancy**	**10.11**
工业	**Industry**	**14716.30**
采掘业	**Mining and Quarrying**	**1686.21**
煤炭开采和洗选业	Mining and Washing of Coal	
石油和天然气开采业	Extraction of Petroleum and Natural Gas	1686.16
黑色金属矿采选业	Mining and Processing of Ferrous Metal Ores	
有色金属矿采选业	Mining and Processing of Noe-Ferrous Metal Ores	0.05
非金属矿采选业	Mining and Processing of Nonmetal Ores	
其他采矿业	Mining of Other Ores	
制造业	**Manufacturing**	**12963.62**
农副食品加工业	Processing of Food from Agricultural Products	0.53
食品制造业	Manufacture of Foods	0.72
饮料制造业	Manufacture of Beverages	0.72
烟草制品业	Manufacture of Tobacco	
纺织业	Manufacture of Textile	1.29
纺织服装、鞋、帽制造业	Manufacture of Textile Wearing Apparel, Footware, and Caps	0.04
皮革、毛皮、羽毛(绒)及其制品业	Manufacture of Leather, Fur, Feather and Related Products	0.04
木材加工及木、竹、藤、棕、草制品业	Processing of Timber, Manufacture of Wood, Bamboo, Rattan, Palm, and Straw Products	
家具制造业	Manufacture of Furniture	
造纸及纸制品业	Manufacture of Paper and Paper Products	0.26
印刷业和记录媒介的复制	Printing, Reproduction of Recording Media	0.10
文教体育用品制造业	Manufacture of Articles For Culture, Education and Sport Activity	
石油加工、炼焦及核燃料加工业	Processing of Petroleum, Coking, Processing of Nuclear Fuel	11338.36
化学原料及化学制品制造业	Manufacture of Raw Chemical Materials and Chemical Products	1078.84
医药制造业	Manufacture of Medicines	0.12
化学纤维制造业	Manufacture of Chemical Fibers	478.22
橡胶制品业	Manufacture of Rubber	1.22
塑料制品业	Manufacture of Plastics	0.02
非金属矿物制品业	Manufacture of Noe-metallic Mineral Products	56.32
黑色金属冶炼及压延加工业	Smelting and Pressing of Ferrous Metals	3.17
有色金属冶炼及压延加工业	Smelting and Pressing of Noe-ferrous Metals	0.35
金属制品业	Manufacture of Metal Products	0.17
通用设备制造业	Manufacture of General Purpose Machinery	0.28
专用设备制造业	Manufacture of Special Purpose Machinery	0.20
交通运输设备制造业	Manufacture of Transport Equipment	0.57
电气机械及器材制造业	Manufacture of Electrical Machinery and Equipment	0.85
通信设备、计算机及其他电子设备制造业	Manufacture of Communication Equipment, Computers and Other Electronic Equipment	
仪器仪表及文化、办公用机械制造业	Manufacture of Measuring Instruments and Machinery for Cultural Activity and Office Work	
工艺品及其他制造业	Manufacture of Artwork and Other Manufacturing	1.23
废弃资源和废旧材料回收加工业	Recycling and Disposal of Waste	
电力、煤气及水生产和供应业	**Electric Power, Gas and Water Production and Supply**	**66.47**
电力、热力的生产和供应业	Production and Distribution of Electric Power and Heat Power	66.47
燃气生产和供应业	Production and Distribution of Gas	
水的生产和供应业	Production and Distribution of Water	
建筑业	**Construction**	**2.71**
交通运输、仓储和邮政业	**Transport, Storage and Post**	**156.77**
批发、零售业和住宿、餐饮业	**Wholesale, Retail Trade and Hotel, Restaurants**	**0.50**
其他行业	**Others**	
生活消费	**Residential Consumption**	

CONSUMPTION OF CRUDE OIL AND ITS MAIN VARIETIES BY SECTOR

(10 000 ton)

2000	2001	2002	2003	2004	2005
21232.01	21342.74	22541.05	24922.00	28749.31	30086.24
21052.08	21168.21	22357.50	24768.40	28625.49	29959.37
3196.35	3205.98	3378.87	3909.70	1313.74	1386.75
2.32	2.33	1.18	1.34		
3194.03	3203.65	3377.69	3908.36	1313.74	1386.75
				0.00	0.00
17779.14	17885.96	18909.36	20793.79	27302.48	28563.58
0.42	0.40	0.30	0.34	0.14	0.07
0.48	0.45	0.43	0.40	0.20	0.10
0.52	0.50	0.59	0.61	0.43	0.50
0.05	0.06	0.05	0.03	0.20	0.20
0.16	0.17	0.12	0.40	0.47	0.24
				0.07	0.04
				0.10	0.12
				0.04	0.03
0.48	0.51	0.50	0.63	0.38	0.51
0.10	0.11	0.09	0.10	0.07	0.09
15305.82	15383.52	16317.92	18008.32	25480.02	26021.27
1809.79	1823.31	1876.95	2002.53	1797.67	2513.08
594.71	611.31	646.40	712.78	8.48	10.62
0.05	0.06	0.06	0.10	0.72	0.82
0.40	0.35	0.50	0.90	0.10	0.08
53.54	53.12	49.61	55.80	11.62	14.17
10.25	9.85	13.47	8.39	0.11	0.13
0.80	0.77	1.00	1.00	0.44	0.31
0.03	0.03	0.04		0.10	0.06
0.11	0.12	0.09		0.25	0.15
0.27	0.26	0.25	0.27	0.08	0.11
0.06	0.07	0.05	0.27	0.10	0.15
0.50	0.45	0.50	0.53	0.16	0.26
				0.45	0.40
				0.06	0.05
0.60	0.54	0.44	0.40	0.02	0.01
76.59	76.27	69.27	64.92	9.26	9.04
76.59	76.27	69.27	64.92	8.74	8.78
				0.52	0.26
				0.00	0.00
3.30	3.37	4.20	4.00		
175.05	169.81	177.94	148.31	123.82	126.87
0.18	0.15	0.12	0.09		
1.40	1.20	1.29	1.20		

5-8 分行业汽油消费总量

单位:万吨

行　　业	Sector	1995
消费总量	**Total Consumption**	2909.59
农、林、牧、渔、水利业	**Farming, Forestry, Animal Husbandry, Fishery and Water Conservancy**	179.66
工业	**Industry**	812.43
采掘业	**Mining and Quarrying**	135.90
煤炭开采和洗选业	Mining and Washing of Coal	37.87
石油和天然气开采业	Extraction of Petroleum and Natural Gas	58.99
黑色金属矿采选业	Mining and Processing of Ferrous Metal Ores	4.74
有色金属矿采选业	Mining and Processing of Noe-Ferrous Metal Ores	8.18
非金属矿采选业	Mining and Processing of Nonmetal Ores	8.74
其他采矿业	Mining of Other Ores	17.38
制造业	**Manufacturing**	637.21
农副食品加工业	Processing of Food from Agricultural Products	37.56
食品制造业	Manufacture of Foods	16.33
饮料制造业	Manufacture of Beverages	14.91
烟草制品业	Manufacture of Tobacco	3.17
纺织业	Manufacture of Textile	42.72
纺织服装、鞋、帽制造业	Manufacture of Textile Wearing Apparel, Footware, and Caps	11.39
皮革、毛皮、羽毛(绒)及其制品业	Manufacture of Leather, Fur, Feather and Related Products	5.38
木材加工及木、竹、藤、棕、草制品业	Processing of Timber, Manufacture of Wood, Bamboo, Rattan, Palm, and Straw Products	4.68
家具制造业	Manufacture of Furniture	3.71
造纸及纸制品业	Manufacture of Paper and Paper Products	14.59
印刷业和记录媒介的复制	Printing, Reproduction of Recording Media	6.17
文教体育用品制造业	Manufacture of Articles For Culture, Education and Sport Activity	2.66
石油加工、炼焦及核燃料加工业	Processing of Petroleum, Coking, Processing of Nuclear Fuel	29.23
化学原料及化学制品制造业	Manufacture of Raw Chemical Materials and Chemical Products	62.64
医药制造业	Manufacture of Medicines	8.98
化学纤维制造业	Manufacture of Chemical Fibers	4.56
橡胶制品业	Manufacture of Rubber	14.41
塑料制品业	Manufacture of Plastics	17.47
非金属矿物制品业	Manufacture of Noe-metallic Mineral Products	82.14
黑色金属冶炼及压延加工业	Smelting and Pressing of Ferrous Metals	42.55
有色金属冶炼及压延加工业	Smelting and Pressing of Noe-ferrous Metals	12.71
金属制品业	Manufacture of Metal Products	18.19
通用设备制造业	Manufacture of General Purpose Machinery	58.65
专用设备制造业	Manufacture of Special Purpose Machinery	26.69
交通运输设备制造业	Manufacture of Transport Equipment	37.48
电气机械及器材制造业	Manufacture of Electrical Machinery and Equipment	24.07
通信设备、计算机及其他电子设备制造业	Manufacture of Communication Equipment, Computers and Other Electronic Equipment	9.15
仪器仪表及文化、办公用机械制造业	Manufacture of Measuring Instruments and Machinery for Cultural Activity and Office Work	4.69
工艺品及其他制造业	Manufacture of Artwork and Other Manufacturing	20.33
废弃资源和废旧材料回收加工业	Recycling and Disposal of Waste	
电力、煤气及水生产和供应业	**Electric Power, Gas and Water Production and Supply**	39.32
电力、热力的生产和供应业	Production and Distribution of Electric Power and Heat Power	33.85
燃气生产和供应业	Production and Distribution of Gas	3.21
水的生产和供应业	Production and Distribution of Water	2.26
建筑业	**Construction**	103.62
交通运输、仓储和邮政业	**Transport, Storage and Post**	982.30
批发、零售业和住宿、餐饮业	**Wholesale, Retail Trade and Hotel, Restaurants**	197.23
其他行业	**Others**	570.65
生活消费	**Residential Consumption**	63.70

CONSUMPTION OF GASOLINE AND ITS MAIN VARIETIES BY SECTOR

(10 000 ton)

2000	2001	2002	2003	2004	2005
3504.91	**3597.75**	**3749.70**	**4072.02**	**4695.76**	**4853.30**
184.51	**190.60**	**187.93**	**195.00**	**220.13**	**227.99**
601.98	**618.14**	**631.64**	**617.88**	**507.40**	**461.71**
106.59	**102.25**	**104.10**	**103.61**	**70.81**	**54.25**
32.05	30.93	30.10	32.26	17.79	15.27
40.05	38.23	39.10	38.14	36.56	26.88
6.01	5.17	6.18	5.84	6.77	4.81
5.18	4.90	4.87	4.87	3.07	3.45
8.00	8.20	8.57	8.19	6.58	3.82
15.30	14.82	15.28	14.30	0.03	0.02
466.65	**487.48**	**499.29**	**484.60**	**403.89**	**380.77**
30.04	31.87	30.66	21.23	16.07	13.84
12.02	12.80	13.18	8.15	7.80	7.69
10.02	9.35	8.46	8.00	8.05	7.24
30.04	30.00	30.54	27.31	0.93	0.78
35.02	37.05	35.44	25.62	21.26	17.50
7.01	8.17	8.06	9.08	7.95	9.70
5.01	4.94	4.81	3.96	4.05	4.50
3.25	4.00	3.00	3.00	3.43	4.94
3.50	3.57	3.87	4.46	2.28	2.86
12.02	12.20	15.65	18.65	8.88	8.42
6.01	6.17	6.51	6.12	5.89	6.94
2.25	2.73	2.86	2.72	3.33	3.87
14.70	15.46	15.98	22.15	25.10	21.82
45.05	50.01	55.03	44.11	45.72	44.05
9.02	10.35	10.65	13.24	7.67	7.67
3.80	3.55	3.64	2.95	0.74	1.15
8.55	8.04	8.29	8.73	9.75	9.54
12.12	11.35	11.68	9.73	14.80	12.51
45.66	47.39	55.70	57.74	34.41	25.12
30.04	30.87	31.22	35.97	22.13	22.13
11.02	11.20	11.02	11.65	7.06	6.42
18.02	21.52	19.78	21.47	19.92	17.92
21.02	21.70	22.14	27.97	30.37	27.40
30.11	28.87	27.48	23.66	23.66	16.56
20.03	18.70	19.79	21.00	28.46	36.50
16.02	17.52	18.19	22.59	20.69	21.56
8.00	9.35	9.70	11.48	10.41	11.03
3.00	3.30	3.03	6.24	5.35	3.61
14.30	15.45	12.93	5.63	7.33	7.18
0.00	0.00	0.00	0.00	0.41	0.33
28.74	**28.41**	**28.25**	**29.67**	**32.70**	**26.69**
24.97	24.31	24.34	25.21	27.23	21.14
1.72	1.60	1.47	1.08	1.63	2.47
2.05	2.50	2.44	3.39	3.84	3.08
115.55	**116.70**	**122.32**	**123.66**	**156.49**	**172.14**
1387.78	**1419.37**	**1503.50**	**1861.64**	**2308.46**	**2470.05**
209.84	**214.04**	**224.22**	**238.09**	**279.80**	**299.39**
877.67	**904.30**	**916.29**	**837.00**	**936.94**	**918.20**
127.58	**134.60**	**163.80**	**198.75**	**286.54**	**303.83**

5-9 分行业煤油消费总量

单位:万吨

行　　业	Sector	1995
消费总量	**Total Consumption**	**512.11**
农、林、牧、渔、水利业	**Farming, Forestry, Animal Husbandry, Fishery and Water Conservancy**	**3.57**
工业	**Industry**	**44.94**
采掘业	**Mining and Quarrying**	**2.92**
煤炭开采和洗选业	Mining and Washing of Coal	1.59
石油和天然气开采业	Extraction of Petroleum and Natural Gas	0.59
黑色金属矿采选业	Mining and Processing of Ferrous Metal Ores	0.08
有色金属矿采选业	Mining and Processing of Noe-Ferrous Metal Ores	0.40
非金属矿采选业	Mining and Processing of Nonmetal Ores	0.20
其他采矿业	Mining of Other Ores	0.06
制造业	**Manufacturing**	**40.41**
农副食品加工业	Processing of Food from Agricultural Products	0.26
食品制造业	Manufacture of Foods	0.33
饮料制造业	Manufacture of Beverages	0.23
烟草制品业	Manufacture of Tobacco	2.07
纺织业	Manufacture of Textile	2.91
纺织服装、鞋、帽制造业	Manufacture of Textile Wearing Apparel, Footware, and Caps	0.11
皮革、毛皮、羽毛(绒)及其制品业	Manufacture of Leather, Fur, Feather and Related Products	0.42
木材加工及木、竹、藤、棕、草制品业	Processing of Timber, Manufacture of Wood, Bamboo, Rattan, Palm, and Straw Products	1.17
家具制造业	Manufacture of Furniture	0.01
造纸及纸制品业	Manufacture of Paper and Paper Products	1.78
印刷业和记录媒介的复制	Printing, Reproduction of Recording Media	3.41
文教体育用品制造业	Manufacture of Articles For Culture, Education and Sport Activity	0.10
石油加工、炼焦及核燃料加工业	Processing of Petroleum, Coking, Processing of Nuclear Fuel	1.02
化学原料及化学制品制造业	Manufacture of Raw Chemical Materials and Chemical Products	8.10
医药制造业	Manufacture of Medicines	0.15
化学纤维制造业	Manufacture of Chemical Fibers	0.18
橡胶制品业	Manufacture of Rubber	0.16
塑料制品业	Manufacture of Plastics	0.39
非金属矿物制品业	Manufacture of Noe-metallic Mineral Products	2.59
黑色金属冶炼及压延加工业	Smelting and Pressing of Ferrous Metals	0.41
有色金属冶炼及压延加工业	Smelting and Pressing of Noe-ferrous Metals	0.57
金属制品业	Manufacture of Metal Products	3.37
通用设备制造业	Manufacture of General Purpose Machinery	3.05
专用设备制造业	Manufacture of Special Purpose Machinery	0.91
交通运输设备制造业	Manufacture of Transport Equipment	4.87
电气机械及器材制造业	Manufacture of Electrical Machinery and Equipment	0.50
通信设备、计算机及其他电子设备制造业	Manufacture of Communication Equipment, Computers and Other Electronic Equipment	0.23
仪器仪表及文化、办公用机械制造业	Manufacture of Measuring Instruments and Machinery for Cultural Activity and Office Work	0.12
工艺品及其他制造业	Manufacture of Artwork and Other Manufacturing	0.99
废弃资源和废旧材料回收加工业	Recycling and Disposal of Waste	
电力、煤气及水生产和供应业	**Electric Power, Gas and Water Production and Supply**	**1.61**
电力、热力的生产和供应业	Production and Distribution of Electric Power and Heat Power	1.30
燃气生产和供应业	Production and Distribution of Gas	0.11
水的生产和供应业	Production and Distribution of Water	0.20
建筑业	**Construction**	**3.51**
交通运输、仓储和邮政业	**Transport, Storage and Post**	**250.01**
批发、零售业和住宿、餐饮业	**Wholesale, Retail Trade and Hotel, Restaurants**	**8.51**
其他行业	**Others**	**137.32**
生活消费	**Residential Consumption**	**64.25**

CONSUMPTION OF KEROSENE   AND ITS MAIN VARIETIES BY SECTOR

(10 000 ton)

2000	2001	2002	2003	2004	2005
869.61	**890.27**	**919.20**	**921.61**	**1060.86**	**1076.84**
1.50	**1.52**	**1.40**	**1.35**	**1.08**	**1.60**
83.95	**86.00**	**87.35**	**87.77**	**60.89**	**57.50**
7.44	**7.59**	**8.15**	**8.09**	**6.80**	**6.40**
5.37	5.50	5.99	6.37	4.37	3.26
0.42	0.43	0.40	0.28	0.17	0.17
0.04	0.03	0.03	0.00	0.71	1.42
1.26	1.29	1.31	1.32	0.84	0.74
0.34	0.34	0.42	0.13	0.70	0.80
0.01	0.00	0.00	0.00	0.01	0.01
76.05	**77.92**	**78.66**	**79.14**	**53.83**	**50.74**
0.25	0.26	0.29	0.40	0.33	0.40
0.08	0.09	0.07	0.10	0.33	0.33
0.08	0.09	0.08	0.14	0.54	0.54
0.08	0.09	0.10	0.00	0.03	0.03
3.78	3.87	4.34	3.71	2.05	2.05
0.42	0.43	0.51	0.50	0.70	0.70
0.17	0.17	0.15	0.18	0.37	0.37
0.08	0.09	0.10	0.21	1.36	1.09
0.04	0.05	0.05	0.00	0.24	0.24
3.61	3.70	2.93	1.90	0.91	0.91
5.71	5.85	5.96	6.00	0.74	0.74
1.26	1.29	1.20	1.63	0.35	0.35
18.06	18.47	17.00	16.79	2.06	2.06
8.73	8.94	10.25	9.68	8.70	6.09
0.15	0.14	0.10	0.08	0.52	0.52
0.42	0.43	0.37	0.42	0.50	0.50
0.07	0.08	0.05	0.08	0.27	0.27
0.42	0.43	0.49	0.67	0.74	0.74
2.43	2.49	1.72	1.52	3.06	3.06
5.37	5.50	6.46	3.00	1.92	1.92
0.59	0.60	0.63	1.14	2.32	2.32
1.68	1.72	2.17	2.40	2.61	2.64
3.27	3.35	3.53	5.72	7.03	5.80
1.34	1.38	1.18	1.64	1.69	1.69
6.30	6.45	6.64	7.18	10.16	11.08
0.25	0.26	0.32	0.49	1.60	1.60
0.18	0.17	0.25	0.30	0.82	0.82
0.15	0.17	0.33	0.42	1.13	1.13
11.08	11.36	11.39	12.85	0.70	0.70
0.00	0.00	0.00	0.00	0.04	0.04
0.46	**0.49**	**0.54**	**0.53**	**0.26**	**0.36**
0.42	0.44	0.50	0.53	0.21	0.32
0.01	0.01	0.00	0.00	0.01	0.02
0.03	0.04	0.04	0.00	0.04	0.03
4.00	**3.50**	**0.00**	**0.00**	**0.00**	**0.00**
535.90	560.69	616.75	621.68	819.71	882.42
12.00	12.47	13.00	11.24	3.63	3.67
160.09	151.09	140.00	143.19	148.19	106.19
72.17	75.00	60.70	56.38	27.36	25.46

5-10 分行业柴油消费总量

单位：万吨

行　　　业	Sector	1995
消 费 总 量	**Total Consumption**	**4321.44**
农、林、牧、渔、水利业	**Farming, Forestry, Animal Husbandry, Fishery and Water Conservancy**	**1001.39**
工业	**Industry**	**1189.87**
采掘业	**Mining and Quarrying**	**229.63**
煤炭开采和洗选业	Mining and Washing of Coal	31.68
石油和天然气开采业	Extraction of Petroleum and Natural Gas	147.95
黑色金属矿采选业	Mining and Processing of Ferrous Metal Ores	5.41
有色金属矿采选业	Mining and Processing of Noe-Ferrous Metal Ores	12.62
非金属矿采选业	Mining and Processing of Nonmetal Ores	20.96
其他采矿业	Mining of Other Ores	11.01
制造业	**Manufacturing**	**722.25**
农副食品加工业	Processing of Food from Agricultural Products	33.65
食品制造业	Manufacture of Foods	18.15
饮料制造业	Manufacture of Beverages	8.04
烟草制品业	Manufacture of Tobacco	1.16
纺织业	Manufacture of Textile	36.39
纺织服装、鞋、帽制造业	Manufacture of Textile Wearing Apparel, Footware, and Caps	8.64
皮革、毛皮、羽毛(绒)及其制品业	Manufacture of Leather, Fur, Feather and Related Products	5.76
木材加工及木、竹、藤、棕、草制品业	Processing of Timber, Manufacture of Wood, Bamboo, Rattan, Palm, and Straw Products	6.10
家具制造业	Manufacture of Furniture	1.42
造纸及纸制品业	Manufacture of Paper and Paper Products	27.59
印刷业和记录媒介的复制	Printing, Reproduction of Recording Media	2.66
文教体育用品制造业	Manufacture of Articles For Culture, Education and Sport Activity	2.73
石油加工、炼焦及核燃料加工业	Processing of Petroleum, Coking, Processing of Nuclear Fuel	48.89
化学原料及化学制品制造业	Manufacture of Raw Chemical Materials and Chemical Products	94.41
医药制造业	Manufacture of Medicines	3.86
化学纤维制造业	Manufacture of Chemical Fibers	5.45
橡胶制品业	Manufacture of Rubber	4.04
塑料制品业	Manufacture of Plastics	21.02
非金属矿物制品业	Manufacture of Noe-metallic Mineral Products	149.29
黑色金属冶炼及压延加工业	Smelting and Pressing of Ferrous Metals	73.20
有色金属冶炼及压延加工业	Smelting and Pressing of Noe-ferrous Metals	21.66
金属制品业	Manufacture of Metal Products	23.40
通用设备制造业	Manufacture of General Purpose Machinery	31.18
专用设备制造业	Manufacture of Special Purpose Machinery	14.53
交通运输设备制造业	Manufacture of Transport Equipment	31.60
电气机械及器材制造业	Manufacture of Electrical Machinery and Equipment	17.14
通信设备、计算机及其他电子设备制造业	Manufacture of Communication Equipment, Computers and Other Electronic Equipment	10.73
仪器仪表及文化、办公用机械制造业	Manufacture of Measuring Instruments and Machinery for Cultural Activity and Office Work	3.94
工艺品及其他制造业	Manufacture of Artwork and Other Manufacturing	15.62
废弃资源和废旧材料回收加工业	Recycling and Disposal of Waste	
电力、煤气及水生产和供应业	**Electric Power, Gas and Water Production and Supply**	**237.99**
电力、热力的生产和供应业	Production and Distribution of Electric Power and Heat Power	234.44
燃气生产和供应业	Production and Distribution of Gas	2.12
水的生产和供应业	Production and Distribution of Water	1.43
建筑业	**Construction**	**118.19**
交通运输、仓储和邮政业	**Transport, Storage and Post**	**1246.56**
批发、零售业和住宿、餐饮业	**Wholesale, Retail Trade and Hotel, Restaurants**	**103.59**
其他行业	**Others**	**645.70**
生活消费	**Residential Consumption**	**16.14**

104

CONSUMPTION OF DIESEL OIL   AND ITS MAIN VARIETIES BY SECTOR

（ 10 000 ton）

2000	2001	2002	2003	2004	2005
6774.27	7107.65	7667.15	8409.76	9895.16	10972.46
1310.14	1375.64	1484.31	1484.40	1774.30	1837.64
1596.46	1636.80	1731.33	1830.51	2004.82	2091.27
270.13	279.49	317.02	309.82	347.22	382.47
50.75	50.86	54.80	50.06	65.07	68.31
155.62	161.79	187.36	169.13	176.45	198.73
11.69	12.14	15.52	19.38	32.67	35.34
12.78	12.00	13.72	15.92	16.68	14.28
27.39	31.50	34.11	44.01	55.16	64.76
11.90	11.20	11.51	11.31	1.19	1.05
1064.01	1084.85	1149.71	1208.61	1268.32	1296.57
37.56	30.61	33.07	32.35	42.96	58.30
16.67	16.72	19.86	21.19	20.95	22.65
10.02	11.00	11.84	9.02	13.40	15.14
4.00	3.55	4.55	5.14	6.38	5.96
43.75	44.64	43.94	42.08	57.55	45.39
13.69	14.50	15.35	18.34	28.42	31.09
14.55	17.11	14.05	18.50	18.10	15.57
6.50	6.80	6.09	7.00	9.22	11.79
2.40	2.70	3.29	4.00	5.72	8.81
22.54	22.20	29.73	35.81	25.70	26.60
7.18	7.68	7.87	6.84	7.79	7.35
11.37	14.25	15.68	17.08	15.24	13.06
69.18	70.38	75.76	88.46	90.92	54.60
115.21	118.11	125.34	132.62	134.15	145.82
6.69	7.00	6.81	5.00	9.75	9.13
9.70	10.08	10.55	9.90	8.07	7.89
7.69	7.10	7.34	8.63	10.41	10.53
39.44	43.41	40.55	42.74	45.10	41.19
298.33	296.18	301.64	292.03	231.84	268.70
68.95	73.53	81.10	95.27	84.10	97.65
41.09	41.83	42.81	52.18	61.15	56.23
37.15	40.89	43.63	44.24	52.72	55.57
31.23	26.01	31.83	35.00	61.45	60.19
12.69	10.96	11.18	18.18	35.98	28.68
47.81	51.09	42.20	48.20	70.68	72.60
24.12	24.20	27.44	31.07	51.22	51.86
35.26	41.82	60.94	50.14	44.55	51.43
9.69	10.10	11.46	17.18	8.96	9.34
19.55	20.40	23.81	20.09	14.56	12.23
0.00	0.00	0.00	0.33	1.30	1.22
262.32	272.46	264.60	312.08	389.29	412.23
253.02	262.46	251.24	297.49	370.21	399.42
6.69	7.60	11.00	12.00	17.11	10.27
2.61	2.40	2.36	2.58	1.96	2.54
195.86	223.08	251.99	276.23	333.13	386.64
2543.81	2671.00	2964.81	3485.20	4182.24	5019.41
255.94	268.07	280.79	355.53	418.99	486.03
803.70	853.89	870.00	890.00	1068.00	1015.06
68.36	79.17	83.92	87.89	113.67	136.40

105

5-11 分行业燃料油消费总量

单位:万吨

行　　　　业	Sector	1995
消费总量	**Total Consumption**	**3693.67**
农、林、牧、渔、水利业	**Farming, Forestry, Animal Husbandry, Fishery and Water Conservancy**	**8.37**
工业	**Industry**	**3406.16**
采掘业	**Mining and Quarrying**	**246.45**
煤炭开采和洗选业	Mining and Washing of Coal	1.16
石油和天然气开采业	Extraction of Petroleum and Natural Gas	226.71
黑色金属矿采选业	Mining and Processing of Ferrous Metal Ores	2.33
有色金属矿采选业	Mining and Processing of Noe-Ferrous Metal Ores	9.46
非金属矿采选业	Mining and Processing of Nonmetal Ores	6.79
其他采矿业	Mining of Other Ores	
制造业	**Manufacturing**	**2186.73**
农副食品加工业	Processing of Food from Agricultural Products	20.68
食品制造业	Manufacture of Foods	5.40
饮料制造业	Manufacture of Beverages	7.13
烟草制品业	Manufacture of Tobacco	1.34
纺织业	Manufacture of Textile	34.95
纺织服装、鞋、帽制造业	Manufacture of Textile Wearing Apparel, Footware, and Caps	2.07
皮革、毛皮、羽毛(绒)及其制品业	Manufacture of Leather, Fur, Feather and Related Products	1.49
木材加工及木、竹、藤、棕、草制品业	Processing of Timber, Manufacture of Wood, Bamboo, Rattan, Palm, and Straw Products	1.59
家具制造业	Manufacture of Furniture	0.83
造纸及纸制品业	Manufacture of Paper and Paper Products	16.62
印刷业和记录媒介的复制	Printing, Reproduction of Recording Media	0.23
文教体育用品制造业	Manufacture of Articles For Culture, Education and Sport Activity	0.06
石油加工、炼焦及核燃料加工业	Processing of Petroleum, Coking, Processing of Nuclear Fuel	611.91
化学原料及化学制品制造业	Manufacture of Raw Chemical Materials and Chemical Products	388.63
医药制造业	Manufacture of Medicines	38.86
化学纤维制造业	Manufacture of Chemical Fibers	90.23
橡胶制品业	Manufacture of Rubber	11.23
塑料制品业	Manufacture of Plastics	3.19
非金属矿物制品业	Manufacture of Noe-metallic Mineral Products	324.83
黑色金属冶炼及压延加工业	Smelting and Pressing of Ferrous Metals	464.93
有色金属冶炼及压延加工业	Smelting and Pressing of Noe-ferrous Metals	62.13
金属制品业	Manufacture of Metal Products	13.24
通用设备制造业	Manufacture of General Purpose Machinery	9.99
专用设备制造业	Manufacture of Special Purpose Machinery	22.57
交通运输设备制造业	Manufacture of Transport Equipment	15.93
电气机械及器材制造业	Manufacture of Electrical Machinery and Equipment	10.20
通信设备、计算机及其他电子设备制造业	Manufacture of Communication Equipment, Computers and Other Electronic Equipment	7.96
仪器仪表及文化、办公用机械制造业	Manufacture of Measuring Instruments and Machinery for Cultural Activity and Office Work	1.24
工艺品及其他制造业	Manufacture of Artwork and Other Manufacturing	17.27
废弃资源和废旧材料回收加工业	Recycling and Disposal of Waste	
电力、煤气及水生产和供应业	**Electric Power, Gas and Water Production and Supply**	**972.98**
电力、热力的生产和供应业	Production and Distribution of Electric Power and Heat Power	927.73
燃气生产和供应业	Production and Distribution of Gas	45.25
水的生产和供应业	Production and Distribution of Water	
建筑业	**Construction**	**14.24**
交通运输、仓储和邮政业	**Transport, Storage and Post**	**227.45**
批发、零售业和住宿、餐饮业	**Wholesale, Retail Trade and Hotel, Restaurants**	**6.62**
其他行业	**Others**	**30.83**
生活消费	**Residential Consumption**	

CONSUMPTION OF FUEL OIL AND ITS MAIN VARIETIES BY SECTOR

（10 000 ton）

2000	2001	2002	2003	2004	2005
3872.75	**3850.22**	**3873.87**	**4220.53**	**4783.48**	**4242.06**
0.40	**0.42**	**0.41**	**0.60**	**0.66**	**0.66**
2975.05	**2949.32**	**2950.86**	**3236.76**	**3570.40**	**3024.77**
209.96	**212.02**	**197.44**	**201.41**	**44.65**	**39.12**
5.77				6.15	5.25
202.77	210.52	196.30	176.32	36.16	32.34
				0.95	0.65
0.22	0.20	0.11		0.33	0.25
1.20	1.30	1.03	14.88	1.05	0.63
			10.21	0.01	
1928.46	**1895.59**	**1851.46**	**1986.79**	**2049.85**	**1828.77**
13.32	8.49	8.38	7.88	11.82	12.40
9.04	8.45	9.11	9.56	14.56	18.11
8.08	9.08	8.08	9.09	10.03	13.04
3.00	2.70	1.47	2.87	1.07	1.46
66.61	64.64	65.16	52.97	72.72	44.41
12.44	13.88	14.67	11.77	5.49	6.91
3.50	3.65	3.35	3.65	10.83	11.90
2.82	3.12	3.04	3.20	2.30	2.62
0.67	0.60	0.74	0.54	0.21	0.28
19.72	21.67	21.85	22.56	26.85	28.60
2.30	2.39	1.65	1.61	1.45	1.79
1.04	1.07	1.14	1.00	2.42	2.56
510.63	508.74	479.59	535.81	561.53	391.78
372.50	358.35	370.39	385.22	406.14	320.79
5.53	5.38	4.63	4.87	5.69	5.97
89.86	88.29	87.72	84.12	26.19	33.54
12.44	13.10	12.40	13.72	17.27	17.69
10.77	11.14	9.17	11.17	16.51	18.31
314.36	323.82	339.18	383.63	481.04	527.61
332.01	307.78	263.11	282.89	201.27	187.42
55.43	61.77	69.30	74.16	84.11	89.68
12.93	11.80	12.76	9.64	13.75	17.64
7.05	8.00	8.41	12.00	13.27	9.29
11.56	9.12	9.79	10.10	7.67	7.10
14.22	13.54	11.93	12.86	10.52	11.65
12.67	13.06	12.19	14.36	12.57	13.91
12.57	14.79	15.49	19.90	26.85	28.37
0.15	0.12	0.14	0.10	0.18	0.20
11.24	7.05	6.62	5.56	4.01	2.81
				1.53	0.92
836.63	**841.71**	**901.96**	**1048.56**	**1475.90**	**1156.88**
812.31	820.09	883.38	1028.04	1464.95	1141.92
24.31	21.60	18.56	20.49	10.94	14.95
0.01	0.02	0.02	0.02	0.01	0.01
16.71	**16.18**	**19.10**	**17.80**	**21.36**	**14.18**
850.00	**855.00**	**872.10**	**940.29**	**1150.44**	**1161.02**
11.59	**12.28**	**12.30**	**13.00**	**24.98**	**27.52**
19.00	**17.02**	**19.10**	**12.08**	**15.63**	**13.91**

5-12 分行业天然气消费总量

单位:亿立方米

行　　业	Sector	1995
消费总量	**Total Consumption**	**177.41**
农、林、牧、渔、水利业	**Farming, Forestry, Animal Husbandry, Fishery and Water Conservancy**	**0.02**
工业	**Industry**	**154.39**
采掘业	**Mining and Quarrying**	**51.87**
煤炭开采和洗选业	Mining and Washing of Coal	
石油和天然气开采业	Extraction of Petroleum and Natural Gas	50.58
黑色金属矿采选业	Mining and Processing of Ferrous Metal Ores	
有色金属矿采选业	Mining and Processing of Noe-Ferrous Metal Ores	0.59
非金属矿采选业	Mining and Processing of Nonmetal Ores	0.70
其他采矿业	Mining of Other Ores	
制造业	**Manufacturing**	**100.80**
农副食品加工业	Processing of Food from Agricultural Products	1.00
食品制造业	Manufacture of Foods	0.03
饮料制造业	Manufacture of Beverages	0.02
烟草制品业	Manufacture of Tobacco	
纺织业	Manufacture of Textile	3.97
纺织服装、鞋、帽制造业	Manufacture of Textile Wearing Apparel, Footware, and Caps	
皮革、毛皮、羽毛(绒)及其制品业	Manufacture of Leather, Fur, Feather and Related Products	
木材加工及木、竹、藤、棕、草制品业	Processing of Timber, Manufacture of Wood, Bamboo, Rattan, Palm, and Straw Products	
家具制造业	Manufacture of Furniture	
造纸及纸制品业	Manufacture of Paper and Paper Products	0.06
印刷业和记录媒介的复制	Printing, Reproduction of Recording Media	
文教体育用品制造业	Manufacture of Articles For Culture, Education and Sport Activity	
石油加工、炼焦及核燃料加工业	Processing of Petroleum, Coking, Processing of Nuclear Fuel	15.14
化学原料及化学制品制造业	Manufacture of Raw Chemical Materials and Chemical Products	63.36
医药制造业	Manufacture of Medicines	0.30
化学纤维制造业	Manufacture of Chemical Fibers	4.32
橡胶制品业	Manufacture of Rubber	
塑料制品业	Manufacture of Plastics	
非金属矿物制品业	Manufacture of Noe-metallic Mineral Products	2.27
黑色金属冶炼及压延加工业	Smelting and Pressing of Ferrous Metals	3.69
有色金属冶炼及压延加工业	Smelting and Pressing of Noe-ferrous Metals	0.50
金属制品业	Manufacture of Metal Products	0.45
通用设备制造业	Manufacture of General Purpose Machinery	0.14
专用设备制造业	Manufacture of Special Purpose Machinery	2.25
交通运输设备制造业	Manufacture of Transport Equipment	0.66
电气机械及器材制造业	Manufacture of Electrical Machinery and Equipment	0.74
通信设备、计算机及其他电子设备制造业	Manufacture of Communication Equipment, Computers and Other Electronic Equipment	1.01
仪器仪表及文化、办公用机械制造业	Manufacture of Measuring Instruments and Machinery for Cultural Activity and Office Work	0.01
工艺品及其他制造业	Manufacture of Artwork and Other Manufacturing	0.88
废弃资源和废旧材料回收加工业	Recycling and Disposal of Waste	
电力、煤气及水生产和供应业	**Electric Power, Gas and Water Production and Supply**	**1.72**
电力、热力的生产和供应业	Production and Distribution of Electric Power and Heat Power	1.14
燃气生产和供应业	Production and Distribution of Gas	0.58
水的生产和供应业	Production and Distribution of Water	
建筑业	**Construction**	**0.28**
交通运输、仓储和邮政业	**Transport, Storage and Post**	**1.57**
批发、零售业和住宿、餐饮业	**Wholesale, Retail Trade and Hotel, Restaurants**	**0.55**
其他行业	**Others**	**1.19**
生活消费	**Residential Consumption**	**19.41**

CONSUMPTION OF NATURAL GAS   AND ITS MAIN VARIETIES BY SECTOR

(100 million cu. m)

2000	2001	2002	2003	2004	2005
245.03	**274.30**	**291.84**	**339.08**	**396.72**	**467.63**
202.00	**217.81**	**227.53**	**267.82**	**293.63**	**353.79**
73.02	79.48	79.98	81.30	77.07	87.99
0.10				1.14	4.46
72.88	79.45	79.97	81.30	75.84	83.46
				0.04	0.02
				0.02	0.02
0.04	0.03	0.01		0.03	0.03
120.81	129.09	138.67	175.00	198.75	239.21
0.15	0.16	0.15		0.20	0.30
0.07	0.08	0.10		1.49	1.40
0.03	0.02	0.02		0.56	0.55
0.08	0.09	0.12		0.28	0.28
1.11	1.07	0.81	0.93	0.50	0.61
				0.10	0.10
				0.02	0.03
				0.08	0.12
				0.03	0.04
0.30	0.26	0.27		0.37	0.54
0.08	0.09	0.10		0.20	0.21
13.42	15.29	15.30	19.93	19.16	19.52
90.32	95.50	102.02	132.00	130.63	154.43
0.60	0.67	0.98	0.98	0.70	1.06
0.07				0.21	0.32
				0.38	0.38
0.10	0.09	0.10		0.40	0.60
2.50	2.80	3.50	3.86	19.56	26.04
1.71	1.67	2.30	3.26	7.64	10.68
0.50	0.53	0.66	0.82	2.82	4.23
0.60	0.75	0.82	1.00	0.80	0.75
0.20	0.17	0.22		1.32	1.98
1.31	1.60	2.22	2.43	1.97	2.96
1.71	2.05	1.79	1.89	3.65	5.37
0.80	0.70	1.02	1.27	0.90	1.35
3.41	3.98	4.83	5.62	4.68	5.22
0.02	0.03	0.03		0.06	0.09
1.72	1.49	1.31	1.00	0.03	0.04
8.17	9.24	8.88	11.52	17.81	26.60
6.44	7.29	6.93	7.55	12.77	18.81
1.71	1.92	1.93	3.97	5.00	7.72
0.02	0.03	0.02		0.04	0.06
0.82	0.72	0.68	0.70	1.39	1.49
5.81	5.96	6.37	6.82	11.16	13.01
3.44	5.00	6.10	6.85	9.18	10.79
0.64	0.70			14.14	9.12
32.32	44.11	51.16	56.89	67.22	79.43

5-13 分行业电力消费总量

单位:亿千瓦小时

行　　　业	Sector	1995
消费总量	**Total Consumption**	**10023.40**
农、林、牧、渔、水利业	**Farming,Forestry,Animal Husbandry,Fishery and Water Conservancy**	**582.42**
工业	**Industry**	**7659.81**
采掘业	**Mining and Quarrying**	**837.66**
煤炭开采和洗选业	Mining and Washing of Coal	392.38
石油和天然气开采业	Extraction of Petroleum and Natural Gas	258.85
黑色金属矿采选业	Mining and Processing of Ferrous Metal Ores	34.28
有色金属矿采选业	Mining and Processing of Noe-Ferrous Metal Ores	83.00
非金属矿采选业	Mining and Processing of Nonmetal Ores	52.76
其他采矿业	Mining of Other Ores	16.39
制造业	**Manufacturing**	**5156.10**
农副食品加工业	Processing of Food from Agricultural Products	181.00
食品制造业	Manufacture of Foods	72.15
饮料制造业	Manufacture of Beverages	52.62
烟草制品业	Manufacture of Tobacco	17.16
纺织业	Manufacture of Textile	335.22
纺织服装、鞋、帽制造业	Manufacture of Textile Wearing Apparel,Footware, and Caps	41.22
皮革、毛皮、羽毛(绒)及其制品业	Manufacture of Leather, Fur, Feather and Related Products	42.88
木材加工及木、竹、藤、棕、草制品业	Processing of Timber, Manufacture of Wood,　Bamboo, Rattan, Palm, and Straw Products	25.88
家具制造业	Manufacture of Furniture	13.16
造纸及纸制品业	Manufacture of Paper and Paper Products	169.06
印刷业和记录媒介的复制	Printing,Reproduction of Recording Media	31.19
文教体育用品制造业	Manufacture of Articles For Culture, Education and Sport Activity	7.09
石油加工、炼焦及核燃料加工业	Processing of Petroleum, Coking, Processing of Nuclear Fuel	156.06
化学原料及化学制品制造业	Manufacture of Raw Chemical Materials and Chemical Products	1028.05
医药制造业	Manufacture of Medicines	107.46
化学纤维制造业	Manufacture of Chemical Fibers	92.78
橡胶制品业	Manufacture of Rubber	53.80
塑料制品业	Manufacture of Plastics	71.36
非金属矿物制品业	Manufacture of Noe-metallic Mineral Products	599.61
黑色金属冶炼及压延加工业	Smelting and Pressing of Ferrous Metals	905.36
有色金属冶炼及压延加工业	Smelting and Pressing of Noe-ferrous Metals	425.61
金属制品业	Manufacture of Metal Products	113.51
通用设备制造业	Manufacture of General Purpose Machinery	136.30
专用设备制造业	Manufacture of Special Purpose Machinery	97.67
交通运输设备制造业	Manufacture of Transport Equipment	154.63
电气机械及器材制造业	Manufacture of Electrical Machinery and Equipment	64.96
通信设备、计算机及其他电子设备制造业	Manufacture of Communication Equipment, Computers and Other Electronic Equipment	38.64
仪器仪表及文化、办公用机械制造业	Manufacture of Measuring Instruments and Machinery for Cultural Activity and Office Work	17.12
工艺品及其他制造业	Manufacture of Artwork and Other Manufacturing	104.55
废弃资源和废旧材料回收加工业	Recycling and Disposal of Waste	
电力、煤气及水生产和供应业	**Electric Power, Gas and Water Production and Supply**	**1666.05**
电力、热力的生产和供应业	Production and Distribution of Electric Power and Heat Power	1539.76
燃气生产和供应业	Production and Distribution of Gas	10.83
水的生产和供应业	Production and Distribution of Water	115.46
建筑业	**Construction**	**159.62**
交通运输、仓储和邮政业	**Transport, Storage and Post**	**182.30**
批发、零售业和住宿、餐饮业	**Wholesale, Retail Trade and Hotel ,Restaurants**	**199.47**
其他行业	**Others**	**234.20**
生活消费	**Residential Consumption**	**1005.58**

CONSUMPTION OF ELECTRICITY AND ITS MAIN VARIETIES BY SECTOR

(100 million kW · h)

2000	2001	2002	2003	2004	2005
13471.38	**14723.46**	**16465.45**	**19031.60**	**21971.37**	**24940.39**
672.96	**762.39**	**776.23**	**773.15**	**808.87**	**876.40**
9653.62	**10534.66**	**11927.16**	**13899.68**	**16254.29**	**18481.69**
955.25	**1051.58**	**1127.86**	**1249.87**	**1371.36**	**1476.82**
401.01	448.02	498.82	522.82	576.15	588.12
309.19	340.83	349.51	349.34	358.95	384.43
61.00	64.95	75.55	109.00	140.04	205.14
77.66	85.78	88.00	127.00	144.52	157.28
81.55	89.31	95.55	112.51	131.60	113.87
24.84	22.69	20.43	29.20	20.11	27.97
6470.88	**7031.06**	**8011.57**	**9517.04**	**11303.02**	**13094.79**
155.00	170.01	195.19	170.56	202.03	252.75
95.00	94.11	113.69	93.04	100.05	114.54
56.70	60.11	67.85	65.00	66.71	76.37
31.58	32.50	31.23	31.37	31.25	35.78
356.08	385.87	454.11	544.80	719.32	821.61
47.17	54.11	58.97	65.86	72.57	87.40
26.07	30.00	35.70	42.46	45.44	54.72
30.99	37.00	37.59	53.30	61.56	105.32
12.00	14.00	11.21	15.04	20.59	24.22
228.22	251.35	284.97	311.62	359.33	406.76
30.00	35.00	33.80	78.00	78.37	60.57
20.00	25.00	32.05	29.00	38.32	42.44
236.09	266.34	330.62	335.61	412.85	312.74
1109.08	1184.83	1355.56	1630.34	1849.20	2124.70
84.94	99.22	97.93	124.00	130.92	152.85
187.25	196.22	206.46	207.54	225.33	232.65
94.92	106.66	108.87	127.70	149.41	208.80
116.14	127.14	143.53	171.00	230.16	321.65
734.18	793.05	879.64	1030.93	1209.25	1416.13
1077.69	1164.07	1323.11	1648.00	2063.63	2544.40
670.58	716.93	823.81	1071.66	1257.93	1469.60
188.70	223.55	282.10	355.85	432.79	506.04
154.55	168.22	201.52	248.00	279.78	343.95
90.83	94.11	102.86	120.00	152.31	182.47
195.55	228.22	258.53	282.51	357.67	300.00
87.17	98.11	129.98	169.00	222.92	245.21
121.01	130.11	150.15	217.00	277.21	327.11
24.39	26.00	32.04	35.85	35.35	42.42
209.00	219.22	228.50	232.00	215.66	274.96
0.00	0.00	0.00	10.00	5.11	6.64
2227.49	**2452.02**	**2787.73**	**3132.77**	**3579.91**	**3910.09**
2049.31	2268.46	2610.90	2959.16	3370.46	3693.54
33.08	37.06	36.95	29.19	34.33	29.79
145.10	146.50	139.88	144.43	175.13	186.76
154.77	**144.91**	**164.14**	**189.78**	**222.14**	**233.93**
281.20	**309.32**	**338.00**	**396.94**	**449.65**	**430.34**
393.68	**444.89**	**500.00**	**622.97**	**735.35**	**752.31**
643.20	**688.06**	**758.50**	**911.04**	**1036.58**	**1340.91**
1671.95	**1839.23**	**2001.42**	**2238.04**	**2464.49**	**2824.81**

5-14 分地区能源消费总量
TOTAL ENERGY CONSUMPTION BY REGION

单位:万吨标准煤 (10 000 tce)

地 区 Region	1990	1995	2000	2002	2003	2004	2005
北 京 Beijing	2709	3518	4144	4436	4648	5140	5522
天 津 Tianjin	2071	2569	2794	3022	3215	3697	4115
河 北 Hebei	6124	8990	11196	13405	15298	17348	19745
山 西 Shanxi	4710	8413	6728	9340	10386	11251	12312
内 蒙 古 Inner Mongolia	2424	2632	3549	4560	5778	7623	9643
辽 宁 Liaoning	7856	9671	10656	10602	11253	13074	14685
吉 林 Jilin	3523	4109	3766	4531	5174	5603	5958
黑 龙 江 Heilongjiang	5285	5935	6166	6004	6714	7466	8026
上 海 Shanghai	3175	4466	5499	6249	6796	7406	8069
江 苏 Jiangsu	5509	8047	8612	9609	11060	13652	16895
浙 江 Zhejiang	2580	4580	6560	8280	9523	10825	12032
安 徽 Anhui	2761	4194	4879	5316	5457	6017	6518
福 建 Fujian	1451	2280	3463	4236	4808	5449	6157
江 西 Jiangxi	1732	2392	2505	2933	3426	3814	4286
山 东 Shandong	6830	8780	11362	14599	16625	19624	23610
河 南 Henan	5206	6473	7919	9055	10595	13074	14625
湖 北 Hubei	3997	5655	6269	6713	7708	9120	9851
湖 南 Hunan	3821	5426	4071	5382	6298	7599	9110
广 东 Guangdong	4065	7345	9448	11355	13099	15210	17769
广 西 Guangxi	1309	2384	2669	3120	3523	4203	4981
海 南 Hainan	121	303	480	602	684	742	819
重 庆 Chongqing			2428	2696	3069	3670	4360
四 川 Sichuan	6353	9525	6518	7510	9204	10700	11301
贵 州 Guizhou	2133	3183	4279	4470	5534	6021	6429
云 南 Yunnan	1954	2641	3468	4131	4450	5210	6024
陕 西 Shaanxi	2239	3134	2731	3713	4170	4776	5424
甘 肃 Gansu	2172	2738	3012	3174	3525	3908	4368
青 海 Qinghai	507	688	897	1019	1123	1364	1670
宁 夏 Ningxia	707	759	1179	1378	2015	2322	2510
新 疆 Xinjiang	2063	2830	3328	3723	4177	4910	5507

注:1. 1996 年以前重庆包括在四川省内。

2. 由于折算系数的不同,故各地区相加数与全国数不等,以下同。

a) Prior to 1996, the consumption for Chongqing was included in Sichuan.

b) As the conversion factors, the sum of the data by region is not equal to the total. The same as in the following tables.

5-15 分地区煤炭消费量
COAL CONSUMPTION BY REGION

单位:万吨 (10 000 ton)

地 区 Region	1990	1995	2000	2002	2003	2004	2005
北 京 Beijing	2413	2692	2720	2531	2674	2939	3069
天 津 Tianjin	1788	2428	2473	2929	3205	3509	3801
河 北 Hebei	7875	10983	12115	13739	14851	17074	20542
山 西 Shanxi	7659	15015	14262	18055	20502	22433	25681
内 蒙 古 Inner Mongolia	3953	4420	5908	6864	9025	11391	13922
辽 宁 Liaoning	8252	9363	9582	9355	10454	11945	13070
吉 林 Jilin	4015	4816	4213	4664	5202	5715	6802
黑 龙 江 Heilongjiang	6517	6188	5815	5543	6490	7347	8560
上 海 Shanghai	2742	3944	4496	4737	5018	5144	5325
江 苏 Jiangsu	6223	8936	8770	9663	10849	13272	16779
浙 江 Zhejiang	2486	4231	5385	6595	7267	8362	9681
安 徽 Anhui	3428	4965	5909	6679	7489	7823	8340
福 建 Fujian	1307	1677	2160	2711	3272	3806	4857
江 西 Jiangxi	2266	3039	2469	2557	3089	3944	4243
山 东 Shandong	7256	9759	8698	12938	15166	18270	25248
河 南 Henan	6099	7960	8725	10333	11420	14938	18468
湖 北 Hubei	3343	5404	6051	6483	7238	8054	8653
湖 南 Hunan	3956	5591	3335	4287	4984	6040	8739
广 东 Guangdong	2991	4941	5890	6649	7910	8790	9942
广 西 Guangxi	1562	2330	2228	2133	2621	3367	3734
海 南 Hainan	68	168	192	0	607	477	342
重 庆 Chongqing			2942	3053	2646	2904	3335
四 川 Sichuan	6646	8909	4862	5462	7254	8189	7792
贵 州 Guizhou	2709	3946	5146	5199	6794	7994	8651
云 南 Yunnan	2194	2765	3062	3556	4614	5689	6682
陕 西 Shaanxi	2728	3779	2766	3451	3961	4958	6049
甘 肃 Gansu	1858	2547	2480	2798	3219	3479	3751
青 海 Qinghai	471	462	522	620	675	680	699
宁 夏 Ningxia	885	1079	1042	0	2965	2761	3249
新 疆 Xinjiang	1835	2448	2702	2898	3184	3632	3860

5-16 分地区焦炭消费量
COKE CONSUMPTION BY REGION

单位:万吨   (10 000 ton)

地　区 Region	1990	1995	2000	2002	2003	2004	2005
北　京 Beijing	231.43	500.71	449.08	378.00	438.25	455.73	397.40
天　津 Tianjin	137.06	149.45	143.68	149.49	143.15	328.04	329.75
河　北 Hebei	559.47	1135.79	1227.85	1808.02	2591.01	3243.46	4498.24
山　西 Shanxi	835.68	1287.03	1283.72	2761.58	3085.29	2724.31	2139.90
内 蒙 古 Inner Mongolia	234.93	339.33	286.47	393.58	477.34	577.98	814.03
辽　宁 Liaoning	889.23	987.59	878.12	1046.88	1131.02	821.02	1703.41
吉　林 Jilin	144.01	176.22	170.55	191.62	231.15	249.99	336.92
黑 龙 江 Heilongjiang	102.34	107.24	72.83	79.77	105.99	97.34	142.06
上　海 Shanghai	452.82	716.47	719.99	681.24	627.81	590.65	630.51
江　苏 Jiangsu	228.42	362.02	383.69	398.92	448.06	801.07	1593.12
浙　江 Zhejiang	85.46	127.76	117.46	125.56	126.93	149.21	163.59
安　徽 Anhui	260.36	440.72	533.27	556.20	599.66	544.29	538.39
福　建 Fujian	53.84	78.54	100.16	95.12	132.33	205.91	280.93
江　西 Jiangxi	157.25	187.87	205.94	261.39	297.68	379.57	452.86
山　东 Shandong	317.53	356.92	424.83	415.42	660.08	1235.5	1992.57
河　南 Henan	231.86	393.19	426.75	505.47	520.66	818.01	994.37
湖　北 Hubei	381.79	491.15	556.83	536.16	552.49	560.36	685.47
湖　南 Hunan	248.75	293.03	299.74	351.13	395.83	553.37	756.58
广　东 Guangdong	104.80	131.88	146.57	179.11	227.99	278.03	300.16
广　西 Guangxi	111.38	184.16	158.61	177.15	194.20	344.16	441.95
海　南 Hainan	3.21	1.61	3.47		5.92	3.51	1.61
重　庆 Chongqing			180.74	189.72	187.73	191.42	388.00
四　川 Sichuan	506.54	754.07	447.25	541.20	625.58	813.32	894.54
贵　州 Guizhou	133.01	201.71	238.86	234.40	239.99	269.06	333.86
云　南 Yunnan	253.19	370.85	360.00	590.14	759.23	1046.32	1223.36
陕　西 Shaanxi	98.43	304.04	134.27	175.94	188.88	249.65	251.10
甘　肃 Gansu	88.75	133.65	179.28	177.40	181.78	346.73	424.41
青　海 Qinghai	2.57	22.73	15.59	17.88	30.27	41.23	41.84
宁　夏 Ningxia	20.88	20.92	28.91		52.00	114.83	69.72
新　疆 Xinjiang	58.90	73.81	74.06	83.06	86.61	126.88	183.27

5–17 分地区原油消费量

CRUDE OIL CONSUMPTION BY REGION

单位:万吨 (10 000 ton)

地 区 Region	1990	1995	2000	2002	2003	2004	2005
北 京 Beijing	680.98	654.66	754.71	748.00	726.68	809.35	799.60
天 津 Tianjin	404.92	488.38	709.76	675.58	750.95	786.57	863.14
河 北 Hebei	312.97	498.50	747.37	697.59	835.19	939.39	1003.29
山 西 Shanxi							
内 蒙 古 Inner Mongolia	0.61	87.30	126.26	126.05	128.83	132.19	131.83
辽 宁 Liaoning	2387.08	2516.42	3938.74	4218.81	4560.41	5216.67	5410.89
吉 林 Jilin	470.15	493.30	702.63	731.42	885.24	833.01	968.36
黑 龙 江 Heilongjiang	997.15	1204.34	1601.27	1586.16	1619.14	1616.07	1785.01
上 海 Shanghai	828.27	976.04	1309.70	1424.91	1737.52	1842.29	1967.00
江 苏 Jiangsu	823.47	1010.80	1376.65	1407.68	1714.54	1875.39	2264.76
浙 江 Zhejiang	243.68	575.02	1112.48	1241.04	1425.16	1853.44	2113.04
安 徽 Anhui	257.34	277.04	345.06	307.99	334.92	419.79	414.49
福 建 Fujian		225.02	358.43	334.15	362.41	390.55	348.40
江 西 Jiangxi	155.1	230.56	331.18	297.27	314.07	363.41	368.02
山 东 Shandong	1170.34	1347.92	1771.22	1628.23	2213.73	3196.39	3300.36
河 南 Henan	222.79	401.96	610.58	601.64	37.12	704.54	668.82
湖 北 Hubei	508.55	511.36	669.77	595.43	637.14	754.01	822.13
湖 南 Hunan	322.11	348.87	541.05	470.92	507.82	615.79	660.86
广 东 Guangdong	912.94	1226.95	1956.41	1961.91	2095.15	2391.35	2388.37
广 西 Guangxi	5.88	42.44	61.41	70.24	73.19	82.36	97.71
海 南 Hainan		0.01	14.69		31.60	13.87	11.46
重 庆 Chongqing				0.25	0.27	0.48	2.86
四 川 Sichuan	16.68	30.60	38.89	57.78	75.67	114.99	140.81
贵 州 Guizhou							
云 南 Yunnan		32.16				0.06	0.07
陕 西 Shaanxi	60.99	153.94	521.61	704.25	869.97	1072.98	1242.42
甘 肃 Gansu	473.83	673.37	880.88	935.32	1017.98	1154.76	1229.26
青 海 Qinghai	31.64	83.96	62.17	62.43	66.73	83.41	95.02
宁 夏 Ningxia	11.62	67.86	92.62		200.40	159.10	167.05
新 疆 Xinjiang	483.73	727.61	1071.29	1128.01	1189.14	1314.13	1628.77

5-18 分地区燃料油消费量
FUEL OIL CONSUMPTION BY REGION

单位:万吨 (10 000 ton)

地 区 Region	1990	1995	2000	2002	2003	2004	2005
北 京 Beijing	228.49	196.20	89.62	71.00	66.10	66.96	65.88
天 津 Tianjin	227.88	155.73	79.51	88.98	113.48	113.9	112.69
河 北 Hebei	46.18	54.66	49.39	61.08	62.68	55.56	60.78
山 西 Shanxi	12.61	13.15	12.42	9.07	10.66	10.25	8.95
内 蒙 古 Inner Mongolia	25.54	15.91	30.99	39.06	39.37	47.97	25.34
辽 宁 Liaoning	642.38	499.65	296.73	237.58	192.54	193.29	189.88
吉 林 Jilin	101.07	75.76	50.96	32.03	28.95	38.45	53.13
黑 龙 江 Heilongjiang	235.48	187.51	135.38	76.77	63.32	47.68	39.89
上 海 Shanghai	434.28	364.71	494.20	519.71	616.07	657.95	765.95
江 苏 Jiangsu	189.98	161.95	202.44	181.52	216.31	328.2	257.72
浙 江 Zhejiang	102.20	106.47	182.52	192.42	261.60	292.31	303.66
安 徽 Anhui	42.37	47.02	46.91	47.52	53.81	23.92	23.88
福 建 Fujian	15.53	31.80	53.23	74.77	94.59	81.64	161.62
江 西 Jiangxi	23.38	26.70	34.20	46.15	39.73	46.88	31.08
山 东 Shandong	248.43	309.90	344.25	270.54	241.19	279.16	294.43
河 南 Henan	38.95	52.89	57.55	70.24	78.36	77.25	78.46
湖 北 Hubei	132.31	125.26	106.69	57.00	90.77	87.2	110.87
湖 南 Hunan	53.08	56.39	46.38	43.55	42.79	36.81	43.09
广 东 Guangdong	365.54	647.19	941.95	1154.19	1241.65	1533.95	1600.05
广 西 Guangxi	8.08	13.57	7.67	13.13	20.85	29.63	32.96
海 南 Hainan	0.51	4.19	9.39		5.24	5.88	5.24
重 庆 Chongqing			2.68	3.24	2.99	4.32	3.61
四 川 Sichuan	6.92	11.41	13.32	12.42	11.13	8.11	8.08
贵 州 Guizhou	4.77	5.34	7.51	7.67	9.94	10.34	10.39
云 南 Yunnan	1.80	2.80	11.17	8.53	5.69	7.54	3.91
陕 西 Shaanxi	22.40	28.19	80.05	120.19	57.15	39.85	4.43
甘 肃 Gansu	62.59	76.48	58.00	30.39	19.95	15.48	16.03
青 海 Qinghai	10.72	14.96	6.93	4.20	3.90	2.2	0.02
宁 夏 Ningxia	23.70	27.67	33.13		12.00	3.98	1.8
新 疆 Xinjiang	89.95	117.03	56.59	34.21	46.52	20.11	17.32

5-19 分 地 区 汽 油 消 费 量
GASOLINE OIL CONSUMPTION BY REGION

单位:万吨 (10 000 ton)

地　　区 Region	1990	1995	2000	2002	2003	2004	2005
北　京 Beijing	56.56	75.41	106.60	152.00	165.22	198.39	235.23
天　津 Tianjin	37.12	74.85	112.43	94.76	106.42	118.71	118.96
河　北 Hebei	96.55	132.24	136.44	147.41	157.00	169.86	221.91
山　西 Shanxi	70.95	97.51	88.84	89.23	89.27	79.78	95.23
内　蒙古 Inner Mongolia	33.50	49.62	64.81	79.35	96.63	151.30	192.41
辽　宁 Liaoning	103.06	119.75	149.47	236.10	227.94	229.18	357.17
吉　林 Jilin	55.58	82.71	90.67	96.99	103.41	111.12	166.94
黑龙江 Heilongjiang	93.33	184.44	244.04	258.57	310.17	321.58	312.19
上　海 Shanghai	49.96	78.84	133.25	191.73	202.24	221.02	242.34
江　苏 Jiangsu	90.94	164.07	187.30	293.39	339.17	364.23	420.13
浙　江 Zhejiang	58.33	123.96	196.19	231.44	262.15	278.66	368.53
安　徽 Anhui	44.10	58.38	68.54	73.90	76.70	78.18	86.41
福　建 Fujian	39.50	69.47	105.11	132.76	138.66	192.15	199.81
江　西 Jiangxi	42.31	42.06	58.46	82.19	59.63	61.82	64.49
山　东 Shandong	123.82	192.85	188.52	176.83	209.51	233.66	495.53
河　南 Henan	86.93	142.55	120.86	119.50	121.99	221.95	234.54
湖　北 Hubei	110.45	152.36	169.17	232.78	292.86	304.55	367.43
湖　南 Hunan	55.24	104.37	115.40	134.63	135.93	160.47	271.88
广　东 Guangdong	141.59	281.73	301.16	344.58	375.04	447.44	706.22
广　西 Guangxi	33.19	41.32	65.87	84.37	116.70	129.00	146.48
海　南 Hainan	11.98	20.88	30.93		19.79	34.21	39.48
重　庆 Chongqing			65.66	65.41	65.87	76.37	77.53
四　川 Sichuan	78.24	124.38	143.65	171.47	181.66	204.02	224.44
贵　州 Guizhou	46.07	52.00	46.46	50.48	58.94	67.23	67.52
云　南 Yunnan	53.71	64.92	90.79	97.60	106.10	111.47	122.95
陕　西 Shaanxi	46.49	82.39	103.51	95.00	105.43	144.96	196.70
甘　肃 Gansu	36.98	55.57	98.41	97.37	97.82	77.47	86.90
青　海 Qinghai	12.49	17.98	16.31	16.10	17.16	16.81	17.50
宁　夏 Ningxia	9.88	10.71	10.50		22.60	35.49	24.89
新　疆 Xinjiang	69.32	101.89	101.93	86.70	91.35	110.91	106.73

5-20 分 地 区 煤 油 消 费 量
KEROSENE OIL CONSUMPTION BY REGION

单位:万吨 (10 000 ton)

地 区 Region	1990	1995	2000	2002	2003	2004	2005
北 京 Beijing	43.17	65.84	117.60	145.00	137.94	182.82	189.36
天 津 Tianjin	1.96	3.79	18.82	15.63	18.61	15.02	15.12
河 北 Hebei	3.69	3.50	3.23	2.83	2.71	3.11	3.21
山 西 Shanxi	2.33	2.65	6.36	6.66	5.20	8.11	8.45
内 蒙 古 Inner Mongolia	1.48	0.40	1.55	1.58	1.76	1.94	0.40
辽 宁 Liaoning	6.13	11.56	18.55	20.27	18.42	21.53	26.40
吉 林 Jilin	1.28	2.55	3.28	3.89	4.07	10.29	15.85
黑 龙 江 Heilongjiang	2.46	5.17	8.74	10.61	7.06	8.94	7.28
上 海 Shanghai	20.53	37.56	55.71	103.62	103.44	168.15	188.32
江 苏 Jiangsu	12.65	8.61	38.94	6.52	14.92	20.18	21.55
浙 江 Zhejiang	6.59	7.29	11.25	9.37	10.40	10.55	40.98
安 徽 Anhui	8.55	5.36	2.56	2.70	7.53	8.49	10.52
福 建 Fujian	3.23	4.63	7.60	5.30	25.54	26.22	32.77
江 西 Jiangxi	5.31	3.19	2.81	0.82	5.32	8.66	7.14
山 东 Shandong	11.38	23.51	48.25	41.97	14.23	21.74	21.99
河 南 Henan	7.77	16.42	14.34	13.28	12.74	12.63	13.91
湖 北 Hubei	12.15	14.93	18.29	17.47	12.93	14.55	26.08
湖 南 Hunan	7.54	9.77	8.08	8.74	8.91	11.58	12.48
广 东 Guangdong	31.62	56.04	89.51	103.15	119.64	130.97	153.72
广 西 Guangxi	6.14	5.60	3.79	11.17	10.43	5.05	7.00
海 南 Hainan	1.27	11.01	28.13		52.20	54.26	62.50
重 庆 Chongqing			8.34	8.53	8.58	12.53	12.30
四 川 Sichuan	20.55	24.17	36.04	56.13	72.14	78.99	93.56
贵 州 Guizhou	4.90	7.49	9.37	2.29	2.55	2.69	8.41
云 南 Yunnan	5.84	9.15	19.24	18.95	20.02	23.50	28.71
陕 西 Shaanxi	8.11	17.26	19.49	28.03	36.01	48.46	34.81
甘 肃 Gansu	3.10	3.17	3.73	5.30	5.34	6.80	4.61
青 海 Qinghai	1.00	0.07	0.06				
宁 夏 Ningxia	0.33	0.42	0.04			4.13	2.01
新 疆 Xinjiang	4.62	16.10	21.31	16.61	15.61	18.20	26.12

118

5-21 分地区柴油消费量
DIESEL OIL CONSUMPTION BY REGION

单位:万吨   (10 000 ton)

地 区 Region	1990	1995	2000	2002	2003	2004	2005
北 京 Beijing	47.99	51.29	81.17	109.00	110.41	131.93	140.86
天 津 Tianjin	73.78	65.59	197.60	183.81	193.79	226.03	243.14
河 北 Hebei	136.67	189.91	181.28	169.52	173.82	210.52	438.68
山 西 Shanxi	50.31	63.22	80.67	127.33	141.05	190.53	246.42
内 蒙 古 Inner Mongolia	34.55	44.05	68.73	96.87	152.60	252.21	379.96
辽 宁 Liaoning	138.48	143.49	197.22	273.24	267.70	321.68	534.40
吉 林 Jilin	51.39	67.14	73.74	85.49	92.53	103.04	242.61
黑 龙 江 Heilongjiang	147.00	225.79	409.71	403.39	419.58	460.40	473.05
上 海 Shanghai	99.59	122.67	176.44	262.33	288.32	346.56	329.60
江 苏 Jiangsu	179.46	223.50	345.02	379.28	413.94	508.11	515.12
浙 江 Zhejiang	130.78	283.72	434.22	502.15	569.98	641.82	803.11
安 徽 Anhui	78.27	108.06	142.12	155.89	173.71	189.48	210.07
福 建 Fujian	62.27	156.91	213.50	250.13	266.38	324.33	368.96
江 西 Jiangxi	45.43	57.83	104.78	163.87	251.60	199.49	302.07
山 东 Shandong	226.65	309.78	343.87	248.72	521.01	582.30	1132.31
河 南 Henan	137.34	134.81	155.02	156.27	168.68	274.83	329.47
湖 北 Hubei	165.66	209.11	261.30	308.28	370.96	380.55	451.49
湖 南 Hunan	88.57	104.92	140.18	182.36	184.89	242.91	282.05
广 东 Guangdong	276.71	597.66	766.23	848.12	935.87	1023.69	1306.66
广 西 Guangxi	55.45	72.43	147.44	214.48	217.73	286.66	327.99
海 南 Hainan	9.92	38.99	46.20		50.73	53.98	43.09
重 庆 Chongqing			61.44	68.91	73.15	169.57	180.18
四 川 Sichuan	72.52	101.97	161.61	196.43	226.98	269.71	287.43
贵 州 Guizhou	27.46	29.82	57.81	89.23	104.41	108.40	139.04
云 南 Yunnan	34.61	46.89	55.46	179.35	207.45	238.69	283.90
陕 西 Shaanxi	46.29	72.52	94.76	147.38	162.56	197.75	180.28
甘 肃 Gansu	38.56	73.04	91.82	71.17	82.33	105.90	114.98
青 海 Qinghai	9.40	12.83	19.29	18.64	22.63	23.93	24.85
宁 夏 Ningxia	9.03	9.75	11.22		53.04	68.94	63.04
新 疆 Xinjiang	88.75	119.35	155.28	169.55	181.55	196.14	302.74

5-22 分地区天然气消费量
NATURAL GAS CONSUMPTION BY REGION

单位:亿立方米 （100 million cu. m）

地　区　Region	1990	1995	2000	2002	2003	2004	2005
北　京　Beijing	0.83	1.16	10.90	21.00	21.19	27.02	32.04
天　津　Tianjin	2.45	3.93	5.40	6.48	7.26	8.55	9.04
河　北　Hebei	6.07	6.89	7.72	7.74	8.28	9.73	9.14
山　西　Shanxi	0.60	0.47	1.14	1.92	2.50	2.96	3.24
内　蒙　古　Inner Mongolia			0.01	0.22	2.04	4.42	6.35
辽　宁　Liaoning	20.42	21.12	20.15	18.81	18.82	15.81	14.81
吉　林　Jilin	0.98	1.83	2.98	3.02	3.08	4.00	6.18
黑　龙　江　Heilongjiang	22.47	25.91	23.04	20.22	20.96	20.34	24.43
上　海　Shanghai			2.54	4.33	4.97	10.69	18.72
江　苏　Jiangsu	0.38	0.19	0.24	1.01	0.62	3.14	13.62
浙　江　Zhejiang						0.32	2.25
安　徽　Anhui						0.15	0.85
福　建　Fujian						0.60	0.51
江　西　Jiangxi					0.00	0.00	0.11
山　东　Shandong	14.44	12.85	4.53	4.63	9.61	11.71	17.89
河　南　Henan	10.73	9.37	11.23	14.63	16.77	20.29	23.71
湖　北　Hubei	0.58	0.76	0.91	0.91	0.94	0.94	6.11
湖　南　Hunan						0.06	1.00
广　东　Guangdong		1.02	1.43		1.26	1.62	2.49
广　西　Guangxi						0.02	1.12
海　南　Hainan			5.28		24.08	23.89	20.97
重　庆　Chongqing			33.26	27.33	28.75	30.34	35.50
四　川　Sichuan	57.51	68.92	58.67	69.96	74.68	80.64	89.52
贵　州　Guizhou	4.74	5.08	5.72	5.48	5.45	4.99	5.44
云　南　Yunnan	4.53	4.71	5.17	5.14	5.60	5.76	6.12
陕　西　Shaanxi	0.07	0.38	6.67	14.01	18.26	32.77	18.76
甘　肃　Gansu	0.26	0.62	0.85	2.76	7.37	8.53	9.62
青　海　Qinghai	0.39	0.64	3.91	11.27	15.15	17.91	22.11
宁　夏　Ningxia	0.07	0.15	0.12		10.10	6.77	6.63
新　疆　Xinjiang	5.02	11.48	23.44	34.57	40.55	54.01	56.46

5-23 分地区电力消费量
ELECTRICITY CONSUMPTION BY REGION

单位:亿千瓦小时 （100 million kW·h）

地 区 Region	1990	1995	2000	2002	2003	2004	2005
北 京 Beijing	174.13	261.74	384.48	436.00	461.24	510.11	567.04
天 津 Tianjin	124.15	178.99	236.55	281.00	313.00	350.97	396.33
河 北 Hebei	354.16	602.68	809.33	965.08	1098.99	1291.41	1501.93
山 西 Shanxi	255.47	399.16	506.09	628.83	731.77	841.55	946.32
内 蒙 古 Inner Mongolia	121.82	186.83	256.07	320.44	406.62	535.58	667.93
辽 宁 Liaoning	462.19	622.81	796.53	859.20	886.88	1058.10	1110.54
吉 林 Jilin	190.77	267.60	300.57	344.54	359.40	383.06	378.23
黑 龙 江 Heilongjiang	296.38	409.38	397.24	463.02	503.63	541.65	555.23
上 海 Shanghai	264.74	403.27	559.42	645.71	745.97	821.44	921.97
江 苏 Jiangsu	411.81	684.80	971.82	1244.60	1505.13	1820.08	2193.45
浙 江 Zhejiang	230.29	439.59	742.89	1015.84	1240.35	1419.53	1642.32
安 徽 Anhui	185.67	288.97	338.92	389.94	445.44	515.94	581.65
福 建 Fujian	136.66	261.28	403.02	497.86	585.35	664.35	756.59
江 西 Jiangxi	127.65	181.21	209.39	246.56	299.53	389.20	413.98
山 东 Shandong	448.69	741.07	1000.49	1230.02	1395.72	1693.71	2004.50
河 南 Henan	338.17	571.48	717.62	927.56	1054.64	1299.63	1387.49
湖 北 Hubei	281.33	414.99	503.02	567.43	629.20	699.41	804.41
湖 南 Hunan	226.73	374.76	406.20	476.00	546.95	662.61	674.42
广 东 Guangdong	359.00	787.66	1334.58	1687.83	2031.29	2387.14	2673.55
广 西 Guangxi	125.58	220.77	322.02	356.95	414.93	456.86	509.84
海 南 Hainan	13.96	32.00	42.23	49.00	59.30	68.66	82.04
重 庆 Chongqing			307.61	283.51	294.19	309.06	348.95
四 川 Sichuan	350.23	582.85	462.26	670.76	758.79	857.02	942.59
贵 州 Guizhou	103.21	203.70	334.76	491.67	551.07	583.26	554.47
云 南 Yunnan	124.55	223.71	317.25	393.46	409.79	475.19	557.25
陕 西 Shaanxi	170.29	239.68	314.39	373.86	421.92	459.78	516.00
甘 肃 Gansu	177.84	241.06	295.34	342.33	398.33	452.00	489.48
青 海 Qinghai	42.21	69.02	115.96	132.67	158.51	199.64	207.80
宁 夏 Ningxia	55.02	92.38	115.32	178.76	212.00	272.83	307.01
新 疆 Xinjiang	69.99	119.67	182.98	212.24	234.62	265.90	310.14

5-24 分地区农村非商品能源生活消费情况（沼气）
NON COMMERCIAL ENERGY CONSUMPTION FOR RURAL
RESIDENTIAL BY REGION（BIOGAS）

地 区 Region	实物（万立方米）Physical Unit（10^4 cu. m）				标准煤（万吨）Coal Equivalent Unit（10^4 tce）			
	2000	2003	2004	2005	2000	2003	2004	2005
全国总计 **National**	**227417.22**	**460590.27**	**558555.27**	**690113.54**	**162.29**	**330.21**	**398.85**	**492.66**
北 京 Beijing	1187.84	903.58	953.47	903.58	0.83	0.65	0.68	0.65
天 津 Tianjin	74.14	72.48	413.82	97.57	0.05	0.05	0.30	0.07
河 北 Hebei	6160.77	17033.41	23500.60	42348.06	4.41	13.52	16.77	30.23
山 西 Shanxi	774.21	1080.00	2397.00	4500.00	0.55	0.77	1.70	3.21
内 蒙 Inner Mongolia	41.82	13.94	556.05	1010.00	0.03	0.01	0.39	0.70
辽 宁 Liaoning	6033.19	7547.33	8594.42	8895.48	4.30	5.39	6.12	6.36
吉 林 Jilin	303.20	642.05	813.90	2167.97	0.22	0.46	0.58	1.55
黑龙江 Heilongjiang		410.10	1091.62	1565.22		0.30	0.79	1.12
上 海 Shanghai								
江 苏 Jiangsu	8122.01	8290.66	8406.17	10319.88	5.81	5.91	6.00	7.37
浙 江 Zhejiang	2288.46	2354.36	3459.97	4295.87	1.63	1.68	2.47	3.05
安 徽 Anhui	2040.76	6163.61	6606.33	7777.28	1.45	4.41	4.73	5.55
福 建 Fujian	4345.63	11312.05	12045.00	12322.45	3.11	8.08	8.60	8.78
江 西 Jiangxi	19591.83	27871.23	37183.77	47090.96	13.99	19.91	26.56	33.62
山 东 Shandong	9687.04	11746.92	12584.04	14693.95	6.90	8.38	8.99	10.49
河 南 Henan	2425.87	11147.14	24349.90	42982.73	1.73	7.94	17.39	30.67
湖 北 Hubei	19592.40	26588.65	31729.71	36534.25	13.97	19.00	22.66	26.09
湖 南 Hunan	30351.83	58436.58	71213.69	79524.03	21.66	41.72	50.85	56.78
广 东 Guangdong	6970.98	12440.21	13138.00	7364.73	4.98	8.87	9.37	5.27
广 西 Guangxi	42337.75	83737.39	89358.81	109101.35	30.22	59.78	63.84	77.92
海 南 Hainan	1181.67	7205.68	9414.80	10166.40	0.84	5.15	6.72	7.26
重 庆 Chongqing	8979.43	14916.37	16293.93	20622.43	6.40	10.66	11.63	14.72
四 川 Sichuan	30648.60	72256.97	86755.39	102112.03	21.88	51.56	61.94	72.91
贵 州 Guizhou	2525.11	17215.23	23246.04	36376.53	1.80	12.30	16.59	25.96
云 南 Yunnan	17512.20	51163.54	60956.20	70635.90	12.50	36.54	43.54	50.43
西 藏 Tibet								
陕 西 Shaanxi	3253.66	6762.73	8631.48	9930.05	2.32	4.83	6.17	7.07
甘 肃 Gansu	925.67	1898.22	2928.12	4298.59	0.67	1.36	2.09	3.07
青 海 Qinghai								
宁 夏 Ningxia	61.15	1187.62	1905.60	2337.60	0.04	0.84	1.36	1.67
新 疆 Xinjiang		27.44	27.44	138.27		0.02	0.02	0.09

资料来源：农业部
Source：Ministry of Agriculture, P. R. China.

5-25 分地区农村非商品能源生活消费情况（秸秆）
NON COMMERCIAL ENERGY CONSUMPTION FOR
RURAL RESIDENTIAL BY REGION (STALKS)

地 区	Region	实物（万吨）Physical Unit（10^4 tn）				标准煤（万吨）Coal Equivalent Unit（10^4 tce）			
		2000	2003	2004	2005	2000	2003	2004	2005
全国总计	**National**	**28812.08**	**33296.07**	**33985.63**	**37201.95**	**12360.35**	**14284.10**	**14579.87**	**15959.59**
北 京	Beijing	182.79	137.86	137.86	137.86	78.41	59.14	59.14	59.14
天 津	Tianjin	223.50	197.38	183.18	120.97	95.88	84.68	78.59	51.87
河 北	Hebei	1731.59	1793.21	1742.15	1808.44	742.85	769.32	747.39	775.82
山 西	Shanxi	307.50	950.00	447.29	550.00	131.92	407.55	191.88	235.95
内 蒙	Inner Mongolia	794.05	1409.97	1518.49	1147.76	340.66	604.88	651.43	492.36
辽 宁	Liaoning	1303.76	1292.16	1314.04	1282.99	559.32	554.35	563.74	550.42
吉 林	Jilin	1379.69	1246.40	1278.90	1337.92	591.89	534.70	548.66	573.97
黑龙江	Heilongjiang	1725.11	2224.87	2367.20	2372.25	740.07	954.47	1015.53	1017.70
上 海	Shanghai								
江 苏	Jiangsu	3151.88	2550.37	3278.78	3443.04	1352.16	1094.12	1406.59	1477.06
浙 江	Zhejiang	455.20	301.97	301.94	248.08	195.28	129.55	129.52	106.43
安 徽	Anhui	2393.05	2561.31	2607.31	2593.66	1026.62	1098.82	1118.54	1112.69
福 建	Fujian	39.05	208.18	201.94	151.58	16.75	89.31	86.63	65.03
江 西	Jiangxi	456.20	492.23	561.71	553.05	195.70	211.17	240.97	237.26
山 东	Shandong	3353.21	2993.67	2881.73	2784.47	1438.52	1284.29	1236.24	1194.52
河 南	Henan	1830.25	1789.01	2365.91	2581.38	785.17	767.47	1014.96	1107.38
湖 北	Hubei	1754.41	1494.03	1473.87	1396.73	752.64	640.94	632.31	599.20
湖 南	Hunan	713.89	749.86	728.89	732.91	306.26	321.69	312.71	314.42
广 东	Guangdong	723.70	1504.56	1490.91	1487.49	310.46	645.48	639.59	638.14
广 西	Guangxi	922.03	877.53	835.06	2441.79	395.57	376.45	358.24	1047.52
海 南	Hainan	828.66	260.07	216.07	213.50	355.51	111.56	92.69	91.59
重 庆	Chongqing	632.73	864.08	824.12	882.70	271.43	370.68	353.55	378.68
四 川	Sichuan	1434.96	3770.29	3542.62	4971.86	615.60	1617.46	1519.78	2132.93
贵 州	Guizhou	334.48	743.52	843.61	1019.18	143.48	318.99	361.93	437.24
云 南	Yunnan	298.33	612.60	517.66	555.22	127.98	262.80	222.09	238.19
西 藏	Tibet								
陕 西	Shaanxi	614.23	944.93	737.20	715.05	263.50	405.37	316.27	306.77
甘 肃	Gansu	632.74	707.43	648.20	639.73	271.43	303.49	278.07	274.44
青 海	Qinghai	127.53	127.53	127.53	127.53	54.71	54.71	54.71	54.71
宁 夏	Ningxia	80.82	240.63	300.63	321.19	34.67	103.24	128.97	137.79
新 疆	Xinjiang	386.74	250.40	510.83	583.62	165.91	107.42	219.15	250.37

资料来源：农业部

Source：Ministry of Agriculture，P. R. China.

123

5-26 分地区农村非商品能源生活消费情况(薪柴)
NON COMMERCIAL ENERGY CONSUMPTION FOR RURAL RESIDENTIAL BY REGION (FIREWOOD)

地 区	Region	实物(万立方米)Physical Unit (10⁴cu. m)				标准煤(万吨)Coal Equivalent Unit (10⁴tce)			
		2000	2003	2004	2005	2000	2003	2004	2005
全国总计	National	14100.90	20375.60	21091.93	18055.28	8051.68	11634.50	12043.45	10309.52
北 京	Beijing	40.53	43.76	43.76	43.76	23.15	24.99	24.99	24.99
天 津	Tianjin	0.63	0.57	0.55	0.36	0.36	0.33	0.31	0.21
河 北	Hebei	709.52	1336.55	1037.17	986.77	405.14	763.22	592.23	563.45
山 西	Shanxi	75.24	220.00	306.78	320.00	42.96	125.62	175.17	182.72
内 蒙	Inner Mongolia	129.93	177.46	311.18	304.93	74.19	101.33	177.70	174.12
辽 宁	Liaoning	534.83	570.30	728.08	666.25	305.38	325.65	415.73	380.43
吉 林	Jilin	324.82	283.11	269.63	261.87	185.47	161.65	153.95	149.53
黑龙江	Heilongjiang	371.84	304.39	330.23	368.45	212.33	173.82	188.57	210.38
上 海	Shanghai								
江 苏	Jiangsu	219.21	200.30	210.80	208.67	125.17	114.36	120.36	119.15
浙 江	Zhejiang	585.11	415.48	367.97	323.45	334.10	237.23	210.11	184.68
安 徽	Anhui	796.82	702.93	731.82	572.91	455.01	401.38	417.89	327.12
福 建	Fujian	32.46	2403.14	2800.01	240.58	18.53	1372.19	1598.81	137.37
江 西	Jiangxi	825.24	753.31	848.02	806.83	471.21	430.15	484.22	460.71
山 东	Shandong	459.76	501.25	471.71	481.73	262.52	286.20	269.33	275.07
河 南	Henan	440.20	437.35	427.25	434.46	251.36	249.72	243.97	248.08
湖 北	Hubei	1122.77	1172.59	1098.11	994.75	641.10	669.54	627.02	568.00
湖 南	Hunan	1372.36	1092.72	1279.63	1290.43	783.62	623.93	730.66	736.84
广 东	Guangdong	813.10	772.84	778.71	785.39	464.28	441.30	444.65	448.45
广 西	Guangxi	1154.26	1050.86	1115.74	2104.95	659.08	600.03	637.07	1201.93
海 南	Hainan	243.80	254.12	169.12	138.62	139.21	145.11	96.57	79.14
重 庆	Chongqing	438.75	736.62	670.05	1175.85	250.57	420.61	382.58	671.41
四 川	Sichuan	847.61	3021.09	3049.35	1543.09	483.99	1725.03	1741.16	881.08
贵 州	Guizhou	795.54	1834.50	1957.26	1912.17	454.25	1047.51	1117.60	1091.85
云 南	Yunnan	923.22	1116.69	1011.37	1014.71	527.16	637.63	577.48	579.38
西 藏	Tibet								
陕 西	Shaanxi	506.33	544.97	482.69	461.80	289.10	311.18	275.61	263.69
甘 肃	Gansu	186.53	214.71	230.58	247.57	106.50	122.60	131.65	141.36
青 海	Qinghai	33.39	33.39	33.39	33.39	19.07	19.07	19.07	19.07
宁 夏	Ningxia								
新 疆	Xinjiang	117.10	180.60	330.97	331.54	66.87	103.12	188.99	189.31

资料来源:农业部

Source:Ministry of Agriculture, P. R. China.

六、地区能源平衡表

Chapter 6　Energy Balance Table by Region

6-1 北京能源平衡表(实物量)-2005

项 目 Item	煤合计 (万吨) Coal Total (10^4 tn)	原煤 (万吨) Raw Coal (10^4 tn)
一.可供本地区消费的能源量 Total Primary Energy Supply	**3026.81**	**2563.37**
1.一次能源生产量 Indigenous Production	945.18	945.18
2.回收能 Recovery of Energy		
3.外省(区、市)调入量 Moving In from Other Provinces	2801.84	2340.00
4.进口量 Import	3.90	
5.我轮、机在外国加油量 Chinese Airplanes & Ships in Refueling Abroad		
6.本省(区、市)调出量(-) Sending Out to Other Provinces(-)	-522.06	-522.06
7.出口量(-) Export(-)	-174.91	-174.91
8.外轮、机在我国加油量(-) Foreign Airplanes & Ships in Refueling in China		
9.库存增(-)、减(+)量 Stock Change	-27.14	-24.84
二.加工转换投入(-)产出(+)量 Input(-) & Output(+) of Transformation	**-1754.26**	**-1293.35**
1.火力发电 Thermal Power	-904.32	-897.75
2.供热 Heating Supply	-394.90	-393.22
3.洗选煤 Coal Washing		
4.炼焦 Coking	-455.06	
5.炼油 Petroleum Refineries		
6.制气 Gas Works		
#焦炭再投入量(-) Coke Input(-)		
7.煤制品加工 Briquettes	0.02	-2.38
三.损失量 Loss		
四.终端消费量 Total Final Consumption	**1314.71**	**1312.02**
1.农、林、牧、渔、水利业 Farming, Forestry, Animal Husbandry, Fishery & Water Conservancy	43.11	43.11
2.工业 Industry	638.47	636.71
#用作原料、材料 Non-Energy Use	2.04	2.04
3.建筑业 Construction	19.29	19.29
4.交通运输、仓储和邮政业 Transport, Storage and Post	22.89	22.89
5.批发、零售业和住宿、餐饮业 Wholesale, Retail Trade and Hotel, Restaurants	41.87	41.87
6.生活消费 Residential Consumption	233.50	232.57
城镇 Urban	63.78	62.85
乡村 Rural	169.72	169.72
7.其他 Other	315.58	315.58
五.平衡差额 Statistical Difference	**-42.16**	**-42.00**
六.消费量合计 Sum of Consumption	**3068.97**	**2605.37**

ENERGY BALANCE OF BEIJING - 2005 (PHYSICAL QUANTITY)

洗精煤 （万吨） Cleaned Coal (10⁴ tn)	其他洗煤 （万吨） Other Washed Coal (10⁴ tn)	型煤 （万吨） Briquettes (10⁴ tn)	焦炭 （万吨） Coke (10⁴ tn)	焦炉煤气 （亿立方米） Coke Oven Gas (10⁸ cu. m)	其他煤气 （亿立方米） Other Gas (10⁸ cu. m)	油品合计 （万吨） Petroleum Products Total (10⁴ tn)	原油 （万吨） Crude Oil (10⁴ tn)	汽油 （万吨） Gasoline (10⁴ tn)
455.02	**8.42**		**49.15**			**1123.17**	**799.62**	**93.45**
453.56	8.28		125.65			1242.78	640.00	163.18
3.90						284.26	160.58	
						56.97		
			-35.85			-426.36		-85.65
			-25.70			-1.83		
						-55.61		
-2.44	0.14		-14.95			22.96	-0.96	15.92
-455.06	**-8.25**	**2.40**	**205.21**	**13.01**	**85.59**	**-98.77**	**-796.87**	**156.52**
	-6.57			-0.64	-16.09	-12.73		
	-1.68			-1.44	-15.88	-63.38		
-455.06			343.08	15.09				
						-22.66	-796.87	156.52
				117.56				
			-137.87					
		2.40						
				0.66		3.00	2.73	0.14
0.24	**0.03**	**2.42**	**259.53**	**12.29**	**85.74**	**1009.89**		**235.09**
						13.21		4.49
0.24	0.03	1.49	259.53	10.75	85.74	449.44		17.21
				0.96		316.27		0.77
						24.91		8.67
						294.77		48.46
				0.70		29.92		15.25
		0.93		0.34		140.95		103.40
		0.93		0.34		138.34		103.40
						2.61		
				0.50		56.69		37.61
-0.28	0.14	-0.02	-5.17	0.06	-0.15	11.51	0.02	14.74
455.30	8.28	2.42	397.40	15.03	117.71	1111.66	799.60	235.23

续表

项 目 Item		煤油 （万吨） Kerosene （10^4 tn）	柴油 （万吨） Diesel Oil （10^4 tn）
一. 可供本地区消费的能源量	Total Primary Energy Supply	**179.33**	**−27.83**
1. 一次能源生产量	Indigenous Production		
2. 回收能	Recovery of Energy		
3. 外省（区、市）调入量	Moving In from Other Provinces	154.26	149.39
4. 进口量	Import	123.68	
5. 我轮、机在外国加油量	Chinese Airplanes & Ships in Refueling Abroad	56.97	
6. 本省（区、市）调出量（−）	Sending Out to Other Provinces（−）	−98.71	−188.79
7. 出口量（−）	Export（−）		
8. 外轮、机在我国加油量（−）	Foreign Airplanes & Ships in Refueling in China	−55.61	
9. 库存增（−）、减（+）量	Stock Change	−1.26	11.57
二. 加工转换投入（−）产出（+）量	Input（−） & Output（+） of Transformation	**12.36**	**176.15**
1. 火力发电	Thermal Power		−0.48
2. 供热	Heating Supply		−0.17
3. 洗选煤	Coal Washing		
4. 炼焦	Coking		
5. 炼油	Petroleum Refineries	12.36	176.80
6. 制气	Gas Works		
#焦炭再投入量（−）	Coke Input（−）		
7. 煤制品加工	Briquettes		
三. 损 失 量	**Loss**	**0.02**	**0.08**
四. 终端消费量	**Total Final Consumption**	**189.34**	**140.13**
1. 农、林、牧、渔、水利业	Farming, Forestry, Animal Husbandry, Fishery & Water Conservancy		8.72
2. 工业	Industry	0.30	26.90
#用作原料、材料	Non-Energy Use		0.26
3. 建筑业	Construction		15.75
4. 交通运输、仓储和邮政业	Transport, Storage and Post	189.04	56.55
5. 批发、零售业和住宿、餐饮业	Wholesale, Retail Trade and Hotel, Restaurants		8.92
6. 生活消费	Residential Consumption		6.00
城镇	Urban		6.00
乡村	Rural		
7. 其他	Other		17.29
五. 平衡差额	**Statistical Difference**	**2.33**	**8.11**
六. 消费量合计	**Sum of Consumption**	**189.36**	**140.86**

128

燃料油 （万吨） Fuel Oil （10⁴tn）	液化石油气 （万吨） PLG （10⁴tn）	炼厂干气 （万吨） Refinery Gas （10⁴tn）	天然气 （亿立方米） Natural Gas （10⁸ cu. m）	其他石油制品 （万吨） Other Petroleum Products （10⁴tn）	其他焦化产品 （万吨） Other Coking Products （10⁴tn）	热力 （百亿千焦） Heat （10¹⁰ kJ）	电力 （亿千瓦时） Electricity （10⁸ kW · h）	其他能源 （万吨标煤） Other Energy （10⁴tce）
−6.20	−9.76		31.74	94.56	−8.98		358.26	30.50
							1.37	
15.49	12.10		31.74	108.36	2.37		357.69	31.24
−26.93	−21.74			−4.54	−12.08		−0.80	
				−1.83				
5.24	−0.12			−7.43	0.73			−0.74
22.70	47.34	41.76	−1.72	241.27	17.45	11335.69	209.80	−26.37
−12.25			−0.28				209.80	−8.58
−33.99		−4.31	−1.44	−24.91		11335.69		−17.79
					17.45			
68.94	47.34	46.07		266.18				
0.01	0.02		2.32			410.00	41.23	
19.63	46.08	41.76	28.00	337.86	5.43	11521.54	525.81	4.63
							11.43	
19.63	5.78	41.76	2.51	337.86	5.43	5690.26	209.91	4.63
				315.24				
	0.49		0.22			99.09	14.66	
	0.72		1.19			140.68	13.96	
	5.75		4.92			675.28	59.38	
	31.55		5.66			1991.28	88.92	
	28.94		5.66			1991.28	70.64	
	2.61						18.28	
	1.79		13.50			2924.95	127.55	
−3.14	−8.52		−0.30	−2.03	3.04	−595.85	1.02	−0.50
65.88	46.10	46.07	32.04	362.77	5.43	11931.54	567.04	31.00

6-2 天津能源平衡表（实物量）-2005

项 目 Item		煤合计 （万吨） Coal Total (10^4 tn)	原煤 （万吨） Raw Coal (10^4 tn)
一.可供本地区消费的能源量	Total Primary Energy Supply	**3801.18**	**3289.00**
1.一次能源生产量	Indigenous Production		
2.回收能	Recovery of Energy		
3.外省(区、市)调入量	Moving In from Other Provinces	3856.55	3334.00
4.进口量	Import		
5.我轮、机在外国加油量	Chinese Airplanes & Ships in Refueling Abroad		
6.本省(区、市)调出量(-)	Sending Out to Other Provinces (-)		
7.出口量(-)	Export (-)		
8.外轮、机在我国加油量(-)	Foreign Airplanes & Ships in Refueling in China		
9.库存增(-)、减(+)量	Stock Change	-55.37	-45.00
二.加工转换投入(-)产出(+)量	**Input (-) & Output (+) of Transformation**	**-2721.74**	**-2301.20**
1.火力发电	Thermal Power	-1675.20	-1675.20
2.供热	Heating Supply	-626.00	-626.00
3.洗 选 煤	Coal Washing		
4.炼焦	Coking	-420.54	
5.炼油	Petroleum Refineries		
6.制气	Gas Works		
#焦炭再投入量(-)	Coke Input (-)		
7.煤制品加工	Briquettes		
三.损 失 量	**Loss**	**9.59**	**9.59**
四.终端消费量	**Total Final Consumption**	**1070.12**	**978.48**
1.农、林、牧、渔、水利业	Farming, Forestry, Animal Husbandry, Fishery & Water Conservancy	14.31	14.31
2.工业	Industry	841.23	749.59
#用作原料、材料	Non-Energy Use		
3.建 筑 业	Construction	16.43	16.43
4.交通运输、仓储和邮政业	Transport, Storage and Post	21.67	21.67
5.批发、零售业和住宿、餐饮业	Wholesale, Retail Trade and Hotel, Restaurants	35.46	35.46
6.生活消费	Residential Consumption	88.98	88.98
城镇	Urban	47.58	47.58
乡村	Rural	41.40	41.40
7.其他	Other	52.04	52.04
五.平衡差额	**Statistical Difference**	**-0.27**	**-0.27**
六.消费量合计	**Sum of Consumption**	**3801.45**	**3289.27**

ENERGY BALANCE OF TIANJIN – 2005 (PHYSICAL QUANTITY)

洗精煤 (万吨) Cleaned Coal (10⁴ tn)	其他洗煤 (万吨) Other Washed Coal (10⁴ tn)	型煤 (万吨) Briquettes (10⁴ tn)	焦炭 (万吨) Coke (10⁴ tn)	焦炉煤气 (亿立方米) Coke Oven Gas (10⁸ cu. m)	其他煤气 (亿立方米) Other Gas (10⁸ cu. m)	油品合计 (万吨) Petroleum Products Total (10⁴ tn)	原油 (万吨) Crude Oil (10⁴ tn)	汽油 (万吨) Gasoline (10⁴ tn)
512.18			11.77	−0.22	21.55	765.32	863.17	−26.46
						1782.88	1782.88	
					21.55			
522.55			147.48			2498.10	77.83	758.92
						442.61	437.39	
						65.61		
			−109.28	−0.22		−3782.98	−1235.70	−785.77
			−22.14			−196.76	−194.95	
						−37.41		
−10.37			−4.29			−6.73	−4.28	0.39
−420.54			317.44	6.93	−14.11	−92.52	−829.17	145.42
				−0.75	−7.86			
						−1.70		
−420.54			317.44	7.68	−6.25			
						−90.82	−829.17	145.42
			0.69	0.40		10.49	10.49	
91.64			329.06	6.18	7.44	662.25	23.48	118.96
						21.73		4.99
91.64			329.06	5.19	7.44	251.64	23.48	9.39
						17.76		1.81
						204.42		49.14
				0.21		111.13		20.00
				0.74		34.61		21.94
				0.74		27.61		20.44
						7.00		1.50
				0.04		20.96		11.69
			−0.54	0.13		0.06	0.03	
512.18			329.75	7.33	15.30	765.26	863.14	118.96

续表

项 目	Item	煤油（万吨）Kerosene (10^4 tn)	柴油（万吨）Diesel Oil (10^4 tn)
一.可供本地区消费的能源量	**Total Primary Energy Supply**	−10.66	−121.89
1.一次能源生产量	Indigenous Production		
2.回收能	Recovery of Energy		
3.外省(区、市)调入量	Moving In from Other Provinces	94.25	1439.00
4.进口量	Import	3.36	0.06
5.我轮、机在外国加油量	Chinese Airplanes & Ships in Refueling Abroad		4.51
6.本省(区、市)调出量(−)	Sending Out to Other Provinces(−)	−107.42	−1559.13
7.出口量(−)	Export(−)	−1.81	
8.外轮、机在我国加油量(−)	Foreign Airplanes & Ships in Refueling in China		−3.40
9.库存增(−)、减(+)量	Stock Change	0.96	−2.93
二.加工转换投入(−)产出(+)量	**Input(−) & Output(+) of Transformation**	25.83	364.54
1.火力发电	Thermal Power		
2.供热	Heating Supply		
3.洗选煤	Coal Washing		
4.炼焦	Coking		
5.炼油	Petroleum Refineries	25.83	364.54
6.制气	Gas Works		
#焦炭再投入量(−)	Coke Input(−)		
7.煤制品加工	Briquettes		
三.损失量	**Loss**		
四.终端消费量	**Total Final Consumption**	15.12	243.14
1.农、林、牧、渔、水利业	Farming, Forestry, Animal Husbandry, Fishery & Water Conservancy	0.12	15.88
2.工业	Industry	0.97	24.11
#用作原料、材料	Non-Energy Use		
3.建筑业	Construction		15.95
4.交通运输、仓储和邮政业	Transport, Storage and Post	12.11	95.78
5.批发、零售业和住宿、餐饮业	Wholesale, Retail Trade and Hotel, Restaurants	0.50	79.78
6.生活消费	Residential Consumption		5.54
城镇	Urban		5.16
乡村	Rural		0.38
7.其他	Other	1.42	6.10
五.平衡差额	**Statistical Difference**	0.05	−0.49
六.消费量合计	**Sum of Consumption**	15.12	243.14

Continued

燃料油 （万吨） Fuel Oil （10⁴ tn）	液化石油气 （万吨） PLG （10⁴ tn）	炼厂干气 （万吨） Refinery Gas （10⁴ tn）	天然气 （亿立方米） Natural Gas （10⁸ cu. m）	其他石油制品 （万吨） Other Petroleum Products （10⁴ tn）	其他焦化产品 （万吨） Other Coking Products （10⁴ tn）	热力 （百亿千焦） Heat （10¹⁰ kJ）	电力 （亿千瓦时） Electricity （10⁸ kW·h）	其他能源 （万吨标煤） Other Energy （10⁴ tce）
107.00	**−16.62**		**9.05**	**−29.22**	**−11.43**		**19.97**	**7.77**
			8.79					
127.80	0.30		5.66				20.38	8.05
1.65	0.15							
61.10								
−51.59	−16.91		−5.40	−26.46	−11.17		−0.41	
−34.01								
2.05	−0.16			−2.76	−0.26			−0.28
3.98	**34.19**	**10.97**	**−0.13**	**151.72**	**19.05**	**10640.00**	**376.36**	**25.57**
			−0.08				376.36	
−1.70			−0.05			10640.00		
					19.05			
5.68	34.19	10.97		151.72				25.57
			0.35			50.58	22.96	
110.99	**17.09**	**10.97**	**8.56**	**122.50**	**7.62**	**10591.56**	**373.37**	**33.34**
0.74							9.73	
53.86	6.36	10.97	3.99	122.50	7.62	5325.54	269.53	33.34
						15.14	3.77	
47.39						72.56	6.52	
8.10	2.75		1.46			606.23	16.55	
	7.13		3.11			4482.00	37.96	
	2.01		3.11			4482.00	28.70	
	5.12						9.26	
0.90	0.85					90.09	29.31	
−0.01	**0.48**		**0.01**			**−2.14**		
112.69	**17.09**	**10.97**	**9.04**	**122.50**	**7.62**	**10642.14**	**396.33**	**33.34**

6-3 河北能源平衡表(实物量) - 2005

项 目	Item	煤合计 (万吨) Coal Total (10^4 tn)	原煤 (万吨) Raw Coal (10^4 tn)
一.可供本地区消费的能源量	**Total Primary Energy Supply**	**20542.39**	**19383.29**
1.一次能源生产量	Indigenous Production	8639.49	8639.49
2.回收能	Recovery of Energy		
3.外省(区、市)调入量	Moving In from Other Provinces	14197.86	12674.63
4.进口量	Import	16.62	16.62
5.我轮、机在外国加油量	Chinese Airplanes & Ships in Refueling Abroad		
6.本省(区、市)调出量(-)	Sending Out to Other Provinces(-)	-2174.41	-1969.96
7.出口量(-)	Export(-)	-64.33	-3.12
8.外轮、机在我国加油量(-)	Foreign Airplanes & Ships in Refueling in China		
9.库存增(-)、减(+)量	Stock Change	-72.84	25.63
二.加工转换投入(-)产出(+)量	**Input(-) & Output(+) of Transformation**	**-12550.27**	**-12693.83**
1.火力发电	Thermal Power	-6893.95	-6726.50
2.供 热	Heating Supply	-948.54	-920.49
3.洗 选 煤	Coal Washing	-1128.17	-4485.26
4.炼焦	Coking	-3586.60	-482.12
5.炼油	Petroleum Refineries		
6.制气	Gas Works	-4.46	-4.46
#焦炭再投入量(-)	Coke Input(-)		
7.煤制品加工	Briquettes	11.45	-75.00
三.损 失 量	**Loss**		
四.终端消费量	**Total Final Consumption**	**7992.12**	**6689.46**
1.农、林、牧、渔、水利业	Farming, Forestry, Animal Husbandry, Fishery & Water Conservancy	33.23	32.91
2.工业	Industry	6114.81	5483.23
#用作原料、材料	Non-Energy Use		
3.建 筑 业	Construction	34.74	34.24
4.交通运输、仓储和邮政业	Transport, Storage and Post	59.04	58.76
5.批发、零售业和住宿、餐饮业	Wholesale, Retail Trade and Hotel, Restaurants	63.67	61.48
6.生活消费	Residential Consumption	1420.54	755.43
城镇	Urban	499.92	262.42
乡村	Rural	920.62	493.01
7.其他	Other	266.09	263.41
五.平衡差额	**Statistical Difference**		
六.消费量合计	**Sum of Consumption**	**20542.39**	**19383.29**

ENERGY BALANCE OF HEBEI －2005 (PHYSICAL QUANTITY)

洗精煤 (万吨) Cleaned Coal (10^4 tn)	其他洗煤 (万吨) Other Washed Coal (10^4 tn)	型煤 (万吨) Briquettes (10^4 tn)	焦炭 (万吨) Coke (10^4 tn)	焦炉煤气 (亿立方米) Coke Oven Gas (10^8 cu. m)	其他煤气 (亿立方米) Other Gas (10^8 cu. m)	油品合计 (万吨) Petroleum Products Total (10^4 tn)	原油 (万吨) Crude Oil (10^4 tn)	汽油 (万吨) Gasoline (10^4 tn)
1073.21	85.89		1884.81		197.89	1031.78	1003.29	－8.73
						562.45	562.45	
					197.89			
1396.07	127.16		1975.58			480.02	222.18	116.80
						313.21	313.21	
						0.75		
－189.17	－15.28		－77.27			－319.13	－95.12	－123.69
－61.21								
						－0.70		
－72.48	－25.99		－13.50			－4.82	0.57	－1.84
－810.75	867.86	86.45	2613.43	42.85	－38.23	－53.09	－958.48	230.63
	－167.45			－0.62	－38.83	－12.80		－0.01
	－28.05					－5.88		
2293.73	1063.36							
－3104.48			2613.43	43.47				
						－34.41	－958.48	230.64
				0.60				
		86.45						
						14.63	14.55	
262.46	953.75	86.45	4498.24	42.85	159.66	964.06	30.26	221.90
		0.32	0.04			51.44		1.99
262.46	366.37	2.75	4497.53	35.31	159.66	290.71	30.26	43.11
		0.50	0.06			113.49		4.76
		0.28	0.04	0.01		381.39		114.48
		2.19	0.15	0.09		16.31		7.25
	587.38	77.73		7.36		76.39		20.93
	201.25	36.25		7.36		50.62		16.76
	386.13	41.48				25.77		4.17
		2.68	0.42	0.08		34.33		29.38
3366.94	1149.25	86.45	4498.24	43.47	198.49	1031.78	1003.29	221.91

项 目	Item	煤油（万吨）Kerosene (10^4 tn)	柴油（万吨）Diesel Oil (10^4 tn)
一.可供本地区消费的能源量	**Total Primary Energy Supply**	**−9.44**	**35.26**
1.一次能源生产量	Indigenous Production		
2.回收能	Recovery of Energy		
3.外省(区、市)调入量	Moving In from Other Provinces	2.45	89.12
4.进口量	Import		
5.我轮、机在外国加油量	Chinese Airplanes & Ships in Refueling Abroad		0.75
6.本省(区、市)调出量(−)	Sending Out to Other Provinces(−)	−11.93	−50.06
7.出口量(−)	Export(−)		
8.外轮、机在我国加油量(−)	Foreign Airplanes & Ships in Refueling in China		−0.70
9.库存增(−)、减(+)量	Stock Change	0.04	−3.85
二.加工转换投入(−)产出(+)量	**Input(−) & Output(+) of Transformation**	**12.65**	**399.41**
1.火力发电	Thermal Power		−3.54
2.供 热	Heating Supply		−0.47
3.洗 选 煤	Coal Washing		
4.炼焦	Coking		
5.炼油	Petroleum Refineries	12.65	403.42
6.制气	Gas Works		
#焦炭再投入量(−)	Coke Input(−)		
7.煤制品加工	Briquettes		
三.损 失 量	**Loss**		
四.终端消费量	**Total Final Consumption**	**3.21**	**434.67**
1.农、林、牧、渔、水利业	Farming, Forestry, Animal Husbandry, Fishery & Water Conservancy	0.09	48.97
2.工业	Industry	1.35	82.39
#用作原料、材料	Non-Energy Use		
3.建 筑 业	Construction	0.02	13.25
4.交通运输、仓储和邮政业	Transport, Storage and Post	0.15	261.35
5.批发、零售业和住宿、餐饮业	Wholesale, Retail Trade and Hotel, Restaurants	0.07	4.58
6.生活消费	Residential Consumption	1.37	20.24
城镇	Urban	0.01	5.68
乡村	Rural	1.36	14.56
7.其他	Other	0.16	3.89
五.平衡差额	**Statistical Difference**		
六.消费量合计	**Sum of Consumption**	**3.21**	**438.68**

燃料油 （万吨） Fuel Oil （10^4tn）	液化石油气 （万吨） PLG （10^4tn）	炼厂干气 （万吨） Refinery Gas （10^4tn）	天然气 （亿立方米） Natural Gas （10^8 cu. m）	其他石油制品 （万吨） Other Petroleum Products （10^4tn）	其他焦化产品 （万吨） Other Coking Products （10^4tn）	热力 （百亿千焦） Heat （10^{10} kJ）	电力 （亿千瓦时） Electricity （10^8 kW · h）	其他能源 （万吨标煤） Other Energy （10^4tce）
29. 69	**−18. 37**		**9. 14**	**0. 08**			**169. 47**	**249. 46**
			6. 90				6. 12	
								249. 46
49. 47			4. 88				163. 35	
−20. 17	−18. 16		−2. 64					
0. 39	−0. 21			0. 08				
30. 43	**61. 10**	**16. 95**		**154. 22**	**43. 18**	**12527. 58**	**1332. 46**	**−39. 26**
−0. 23		−9. 02				−768. 25	1332. 46	−32. 35
−0. 43		−4. 98				13295. 83		−6. 91
					43. 18			
31. 09	61. 10	30. 95		154. 22				
	0. 08						99. 91	
60. 12	42. 65	16. 95	9. 14	154. 30	43. 18	12527. 58	1402. 02	210. 20
0. 37	0. 02						116. 21	
52. 28	5. 15	16. 95	8. 27	59. 22	43. 18	7568. 50	1017. 71	210. 20
0. 29	0. 09			95. 08		41. 94	8. 69	
5. 35	0. 06					46. 69	35. 73	
1. 18	3. 23		0. 08			241. 94	23. 14	
	33. 85		0. 79			4103. 21	153. 05	
	28. 17		0. 79			4103. 21	72. 53	
	5. 68						80. 52	
0. 65	0. 25					525. 30	47. 49	
60. 78	42. 73	30. 95	9. 14	154. 30	43. 18	13295. 83	1501. 93	249. 46

6-4 山西能源平衡表(实物量)-2005

项 目 Item		煤合计 (万吨) Coal Total (10^4 tn)	原煤 (万吨) Raw Coal (10^4 tn)
一.可供本地区消费的能源量	**Total Primary Energy Supply**	**13681.40**	**16850.00**
1.一次能源生产量	Indigenous Production	55426.00	55426.00
2.回收能	Recovery of Energy		
3.外省(区、市)调入量	Moving In from Other Provinces	489.58	489.58
4.进口量	Import		
5.我轮、机在外国加油量	Chinese Airplanes & Ships in Refueling Abroad		
6.本省(区、市)调出量(-)	Sending Out to Other Provinces(-)	-39983.00	-36907.56
7.出口量(-)	Export(-)	-3294.00	-3294.00
8.外轮、机在我国加油量(-)	Foreign Airplanes & Ships in Refueling in China		
9.库存增(-)、减(+)量	Stock Change	1042.82	1135.98
二.加工转换投入(-)产出(+)量	**Input(-) & Output(+) of Transformation**	**-21390.75**	**-24050.00**
1.火力发电	Thermal Power	-6550.10	-6176.45
2.供热	Heating Supply	-430.10	-420.75
3.洗选煤	Coal Washing	-3049.59	-14652.96
4.炼焦	Coking	-11207.68	-2633.60
5.炼油	Petroleum Refineries		
6.制气	Gas Works	-150.78	-136.14
#焦炭再投入量(-)	Coke Input(-)		
7.煤制品加工	Briquettes	-2.50	-30.10
三.损失量	**Loss**		
四.终端消费量	**Total Final Consumption**	**4290.65**	**3800.00**
1.农、林、牧、渔、水利业	Farming, Forestry, Animal Husbandry, Fishery & Water Conservancy	140.00	140.00
2.工业	Industry	3112.02	2926.20
#用作原料、材料	Non-Energy Use		1051.80
3.建筑业	Construction	55.80	55.80
4.交通运输、仓储和邮政业	Transport, Storage and Post	68.00	68.00
5.批发、零售业和住宿、餐饮业	Wholesale, Retail Trade and Hotel, Restaurants	52.00	52.00
6.生活消费	Residential Consumption	817.83	513.00
城镇	Urban	240.40	152.00
乡村	Rural	577.43	361.00
7.其他	Other	45.00	45.00
五.平衡差额	**Statistical Difference**	**-12000.00**	**-11000.00**
六.消费量合计	**Sum of Consumption**	**25681.40**	**27850.00**

ENERGY BALANCE OF SHANXI – 2005（PHYSICAL QUANTITY）

洗精煤 （万吨） Cleaned Coal (10^4 tn)	其他洗煤 （万吨） Other Washed Coal (10^4 tn)	型煤 （万吨） Briquettes (10^4 tn)	焦炭 （万吨） Coke (10^4 tn)	焦炉煤气 （亿立方米） Coke Oven Gas (10^8 cu. m)	其他煤气 （亿立方米） Other Gas (10^8 cu. m)	油品合计 （万吨） Petroleum Products Total (10^4 tn)	原油 （万吨） Crude Oil (10^4 tn)	汽油 （万吨） Gasoline (10^4 tn)
−2704.72	−464.34	0.46	−5841.14		120.00	368.17		95.23
					120.00			
						379.31		99.07
−2598.89	−476.55		−4877.60			−0.92		−0.41
			−596.40					
−105.83	12.21	0.46	−367.14			−10.22		−3.43
1704.72	926.93	27.60	7981.04	122.83	31.91			
	−373.65				−21.08	−9.88		
	−9.35							
10275.88	1327.49							
−8571.16	−2.92		7981.04	143.91				
	−14.64				41.79			
			27.60					
						0.54		0.34
	462.59	28.06	2139.90	122.83	151.91	367.63		94.89
			20.00			35.89		9.20
	164.92	20.90	2040.50	110.12	146.81	85.85		15.83
			141.14			0.35		
			8.90			11.15		4.85
						200.35		46.01
			45.50	3.00	1.10	6.89		3.58
	297.67	7.16	25.00	9.71	4.00	9.01		3.61
	84.50	3.90	10.00	9.71	3.10	6.37		2.35
	213.17	3.26	15.00		0.90	2.64		1.26
						18.49		11.81
−1000.00								
8571.16	863.15	28.06	2139.90	143.91	161.79	368.17		95.23

续表

项 目	Item	煤油 （万吨） Kerosene （10⁴ tn）	柴油 （万吨） Diesel Oil （10⁴ tn）
一. 可供本地区消费的能源量	**Total Primary Energy Supply**	**8.45**	**246.42**
1. 一次能源生产量	Indigenous Production		
2. 回收能	Recovery of Energy		
3. 外省（区、市）调入量	Moving In from Other Provinces	8.33	255.17
4. 进口量	Import		
5. 我轮、机在外国加油量	Chinese Airplanes & Ships in Refueling Abroad		
6. 本省（区、市）调出量（－）	Sending Out to Other Provinces（－）		－0.51
7. 出口量（－）	Export（－）		
8. 外轮、机在我国加油量（－）	Foreign Airplanes & Ships in Refueling in China		
9. 库存增（－）、减（＋）量	Stock Change	0.12	－8.24
二. 加工转换投入（－）产出（＋）量	**Input（－）& Output（＋）of Transformation**		
1. 火力发电	Thermal Power		
2. 供 热	Heating Supply		
3. 洗 选 煤	Coal Washing		
4. 炼焦	Coking		
5. 炼油	Petroleum Refineries		
6. 制气	Gas Works		
#焦炭再投入量（－）	Coke Input（－）		
7. 煤制品加工	Briquettes		
三. 损 失 量	**Loss**		**0.20**
四. 终端消费量	**Total Final Consumption**	**8.45**	**246.22**
1. 农、林、牧、渔、水利业	Farming, Forestry, Animal Husbandry, Fishery & Water Conservancy	0.03	26.66
2. 工业	Industry	1.63	55.67
#用作原料、材料	Non-Energy Use		
3. 建 筑 业	Construction	0.02	6.28
4. 交通运输、仓储和邮政业	Transport, Storage and Post	6.04	148.30
5. 批发、零售业和住宿、餐饮业	Wholesale, Retail Trade and Hotel, Restaurants	0.18	2.85
6. 生活消费	Residential Consumption	0.33	
城镇	Urban	0.22	
乡村	Rural	0.11	
7. 其他	Other	0.22	6.46
五. 平衡差额	**Statistical Difference**		
六. 消费量合计	**Sum of Consumption**	**8.45**	**246.42**

140

燃料油（万吨）Fuel Oil (10⁴ tn)	液化石油气（万吨）PLG (10⁴ tn)	炼厂干气（万吨）Refinery Gas (10⁴ tn)	天然气（亿立方米）Natural Gas (10⁸ cu. m)	其他石油制品（万吨）Other Petroleum Products (10⁴ tn)	其他焦化产品（万吨）Other Coking Products (10⁴ tn)	热力（百亿千焦）Heat (10¹⁰ kJ)	电力（亿千瓦时）Electricity (10⁸ kW·h)	其他能源（万吨标煤）Other Energy (10⁴ tce)
8.95	5.94		3.24	3.18	0.95		−345.33	106.10
			3.24				20.32	
								104.34
7.44	5.94		3.36				3.61	
							−369.26	
1.51				−0.18	0.95			1.76
			−2.76		133.22	6020.60	1291.65	−77.51
			−2.76				1291.65	−69.31
						6020.60		−8.20
					133.22			
							53.86	
8.95	5.94		0.48	3.18	134.17	6020.60	892.46	28.59
							35.64	
8.95	0.59			3.18	134.17	3441.24	733.49	28.59
				0.35				
							4.95	
							31.07	
	0.28					34.64	15.49	
	5.07		0.48			2544.72	45.97	
	3.80		0.48			2544.72	28.10	
	1.27						17.87	
							25.85	
8.95	5.94		3.24	3.18	134.17	6020.60	946.32	106.10

6-5 内蒙古能源平衡表(实物量)-2005

项 目	Item	煤合计 (万吨) Coal Total (10^4 tn)	原煤 (万吨) Raw Coal (10^4 tn)
一. 可供本地区消费的能源量	**Total Primary Energy Supply**	**13706.67**	**13757.05**
1. 一次能源生产量	Indigenous Production	25607.69	25607.69
2. 回收能	Recovery of Energy		
3. 外省(区、市)调入量	Moving In from Other Provinces	1250.12	902.00
4. 进口量	Import	248.80	101.00
5. 我轮、机在外国加油量	Chinese Airplanes & Ships in Refueling Abroad		
6. 本省(区、市)调出量(-)	Sending Out to Other Provinces(-)	-12815.88	-12341.00
7. 出口量(-)	Export(-)		
8. 外轮、机在我国加油量(-)	Foreign Airplanes & Ships in Refueling in China		
9. 库存增(-)、减(+)量	Stock Change	-584.06	-512.64
二. 加工转换投入(-)产出(+)量	**Input(-) & Output(+) of Transformation**	**-9471.74**	**-9995.44**
1. 火力发电	Thermal Power	-6277.23	-6277.23
2. 供 热	Heating Supply	-808.20	-682.08
3. 洗 选 煤	Coal Washing	-794.29	-2564.65
4. 炼焦	Coking	-1590.07	-469.53
5. 炼油	Petroleum Refineries		
6. 制气	Gas Works	-1.96	-1.95
#焦炭再投入量(-)	Coke Input(-)		
7. 煤制品加工	Briquettes		
三. 损 失 量	**Loss**	**10.00**	**10.00**
四. 终端消费量	**Total Final Consumption**	**4440.07**	**3904.77**
1. 农、林、牧、渔、水利业	Farming, Forestry, Animal Husbandry, Fishery & Water Conservancy	127.82	92.42
2. 工业	Industry	2887.73	2587.23
#用作原料、材料	Non-Energy Use	803.45	803.45
3. 建 筑 业	Construction	76.96	71.25
4. 交通运输、仓储和邮政业	Transport, Storage and Post	178.67	122.12
5. 批发、零售业和住宿、餐饮业	Wholesale, Retail Trade and Hotel, Restaurants	187.24	131.41
6. 生活消费	Residential Consumption	811.25	801.24
城镇	Urban	509.93	501.12
乡村	Rural	301.32	300.12
7. 其他	Other	170.40	99.10
五. 平衡差额	**Statistical Difference**	**-215.14**	**-153.16**
六. 消费量合计	**Sum of Consumption**	**13921.81**	**13910.21**

ENERGY BALANCE OF INNER MONGOLIA – 2005 (PHYSICAL QUANTITY)

洗精煤 (万吨) Cleaned Coal (10^4 tn)	其他洗煤 (万吨) Other Washed Coal (10^4 tn)	型煤 (万吨) Briquettes (10^4 tn)	焦炭 (万吨) Coke (10^4 tn)	焦炉煤气 (亿立方米) Coke Oven Gas (10^8 cu. m)	其他煤气 (亿立方米) Other Gas (10^8 cu. m)	油品合计 (万吨) Petroleum Products Total (10^4 tn)	原油 (万吨) Crude Oil (10^4 tn)	汽油 (万吨) Gasoline (10^4 tn)
203.12	**−254.88**	**1.38**	**−220.16**		**118.14**	**636.53**	**131.83**	**147.42**
						146.92	146.92	
					118.14			
192.12	156.00					525.70		152.42
147.80						16.00	16.00	
−130.00	−344.88		−227.96			−29.70	−29.70	
			−0.01			−8.79		
−6.80	−66.00	1.38	7.81			−13.60	−1.39	−5.00
−116.16	639.86		897.17	14.41	**−33.98**	−7.29	**−120.37**	**44.99**
			−0.21	−0.39	−18.37	−0.91	−0.73	
−3.53	−122.59			−0.50	−18.46	−0.01		
979.05	791.31							
−1091.68	−28.86		1034.19					
						−6.37	−119.64	44.99
				15.30	2.85			
			−136.81					
86.96	446.96	1.38	677.01	14.41	84.16	629.24	11.46	192.41
	35.40		3.92			66.42		21.30
77.87	221.27	1.36	660.58	11.18	82.70	79.10	11.46	5.93
			150.09			0.52		0.23
3.41	2.30					21.67		7.44
5.68	50.87		1.77			333.95		102.20
	55.81	0.02	8.57			60.29		27.01
	10.01		2.17	3.23	1.46	29.26		7.21
	8.81		1.50	3.23	1.46	20.21		5.20
	1.20		0.67			9.05		2.01
	71.30					38.55		21.32
	−61.98							
1182.17	**598.41**	**1.38**	**814.03**	**15.30**	**120.99**	**636.53**	**131.83**	**192.41**

续表

项 目	Item	煤油 （万吨） Kerosene （10^4 tn）	柴油 （万吨） Diesel Oil （10^4 tn）
一.可供本地区消费的能源量	**Total Primary Energy Supply**	**0.40**	**338.95**
1.一次能源生产量	Indigenous Production		
2.回收能	Recovery of Energy		
3.外省（区、市）调入量	Moving In from Other Provinces	0.36	346.65
4.进口量	Import		
5.我轮、机在外国加油量	Chinese Airplanes & Ships in Refueling Abroad		
6.本省（区、市）调出量（ － ）	Sending Out to Other Provinces（ － ）		
7.出口量（ － ）	Export（ － ）		
8.外轮、机在我国加油量（ － ）	Foreign Airplanes & Ships in Refueling in China		
9.库存增（ － ）、减（ ＋ ）量	Stock Change	0.04	− 7.70
二.加工转换投入（ － ）产出（ ＋ ）量	**Input（ － ） & Output（ ＋ ） of Transformation**		**40.89**
1.火力发电	Thermal Power		− 0.12
2.供 热	Heating Supply		
3.洗 选 煤	Coal Washing		
4.炼焦	Coking		
5.炼油	Petroleum Refineries		41.01
6.制气	Gas Works		
#焦炭再投入量（ － ）	Coke Input（ － ）		
7.煤制品加工	Briquettes		
三.损 失 量	**Loss**		
四.终端消费量	**Total Final Consumption**	**0.40**	**379.84**
1.农、林、牧、渔、水利业	Farming, Forestry, Animal Husbandry, Fishery & Water Conservancy		45.12
2.工业	Industry	0.21	33.43
#用作原料、材料	Non-Energy Use	0.01	0.28
3.建 筑 业	Construction		12.13
4.交通运输、仓储和邮政业	Transport, Storage and Post	0.19	231.56
5.批发、零售业和住宿、餐饮业	Wholesale, Retail Trade and Hotel, Restaurants		30.43
6.生活消费	Residential Consumption		9.94
城镇	Urban		2.90
乡村	Rural		7.04
7.其他	Other		17.23
五.平衡差额	**Statistical Difference**		
六.消费量合计	**Sum of Consumption**	**0.40**	**379.96**

144

燃料油 （万吨） Fuel Oil （10⁴tn）	液化石油气 （万吨） PLG （10⁴tn）	炼厂干气 （万吨） Refinery Gas （10⁴tn）	天然气 （亿立方米） Natural Gas （10⁸ cu. m）	其他石油制品 （万吨） Other Petroleum Products （10⁴tn）	其他焦化产品 （万吨） Other Coking Products （10⁴tn）	热力 （百亿千焦） Heat （10¹⁰ kJ）	电力 （亿千瓦时） Electricity （10⁸ kW·h）	其他能源 （万吨标煤） Other Energy （10⁴tce）
11.78	**8.23**		**6.35**	**−2.08**	**−26.15**		**−342.28**	**51.58**
			38.57				15.06	
								51.58
11.40	8.31			6.56			32.99	
			−32.22		−28.19		−390.33	
	−0.09			−8.70				
0.38	0.01			0.06	2.04			
13.49	**6.95**	**3.21**		**3.55**	**63.34**	**9573.99**	**1010.21**	**−7.27**
	−0.06					−113.80	1010.21	−7.27
	−0.01					9687.79		
					63.34			
13.56	6.95	3.21		3.55				
25.27	**15.18**	**3.21**	**6.35**	**1.47**	**37.19**	**9573.99**	**667.93**	**44.31**
						90.52	27.73	
23.17	0.22	3.21	5.72	1.47	37.19	4328.23	566.67	44.31
			2.12		6.84			
2.10						123.12	2.43	
			0.17			798.44	6.14	
	2.85		0.07			784.33	8.75	
	12.11		0.19			2837.89	41.80	
	12.11		0.19			2837.89	26.38	
							15.42	
			0.20			611.46	14.41	
25.34	**15.18**	**3.21**	**6.35**	**1.47**	**37.19**	**9687.79**	**667.93**	**51.58**

6-6 辽宁能源平衡表(实物量)-2005

项 目	Item	煤合计 (万吨) Coal Total (10^4 tn)	原煤 (万吨) Raw Coal (10^4 tn)
一.可供本地区消费的能源量	**Total Primary Energy Supply**	**13069.67**	**12116.61**
1.一次能源生产量	Indigenous Production	6640.56	6640.56
2.回收能	Recovery of Energy		
3.外省(区、市)调入量	Moving In from Other Provinces	7246.33	5632.96
4.进口量	Import	109.53	90.21
5.我轮、机在外国加油量	Chinese Airplanes & Ships in Refueling Abroad		
6.本省(区、市)调出量(-)	Sending Out to Other Provinces(-)	-759.69	-42.42
7.出口量(-)	Export(-)		
8.外轮、机在我国加油量(-)	Foreign Airplanes & Ships in Refueling in China		
9.库存增(-)、减(+)量	Stock Change	-167.05	-204.69
二.加工转换投入(-)产出(+)量	**Input(-) & Output(+) of Transformation**	**-9437.94**	**-8980.36**
1.火力发电	Thermal Power	-4830.15	-4305.41
2.供 热	Heating Supply	-1886.21	-1766.13
3.洗 选 煤	Coal Washing	-712.19	-2709.68
4.炼焦	Coking	-1907.16	
5.炼油	Petroleum Refineries		
6.制气	Gas Works	-204.06	-199.14
#焦炭再投入量(-)	Coke Input(-)		
7.煤制品加工	Briquettes	-1.18	
三.损 失 量	**Loss**		
四.终端消费量	**Total Final Consumption**	**3631.73**	**3136.25**
1.农、林、牧、渔、水利业	Farming, Forestry, Animal Husbandry, Fishery & Water Conservancy	119.42	119.42
2.工业	Industry	2713.68	2379.94
#用作原料、材料	Non-Energy Use	13.85	13.79
3.建 筑 业	Construction	73.34	70.67
4.交通运输、仓储和邮政业	Transport, Storage and Post	95.12	95.12
5.批发、零售业和住宿、餐饮业	Wholesale, Retail Trade and Hotel, Restaurants	29.01	29.01
6.生活消费	Residential Consumption	547.16	388.09
城镇	Urban	326.92	200.12
乡村	Rural	220.24	187.97
7.其他	Other	54.00	54.00
五.平衡差额	**Statistical Difference**		
六.消费量合计	**Sum of Consumption**	**13069.67**	**12116.61**

ENERGY BALANCE OF LIAONING － 2005 （PHYSICAL QUANTITY）

洗精煤（万吨）Cleaned Coal (10⁴ tn)	其他洗煤（万吨）Other Washed Coal (10⁴ tn)	型煤（万吨）Briquettes (10⁴ tn)	焦炭（万吨）Coke (10⁴ tn)	焦炉煤气（亿立方米）Coke Oven Gas (10⁸ cu. m)	其他煤气（亿立方米）Other Gas (10⁸ cu. m)	油品合计（万吨）Petroleum Products Total (10⁴ tn)	原油（万吨）Crude Oil (10⁴ tn)	汽油（万吨）Gasoline (10⁴ tn)
1490.17	−536.79	−0.32	465.52			2209.16	5410.89	−609.58
						1260.96	1260.96	
1613.37			467.99			3671.52	3565.72	0.29
19.32						775.30	773.10	
						17.24		
−76.56	−640.71		−6.14			−3109.59	−13.83	−479.66
			−2.74			−240.27	−52.28	−147.29
						−75.03		
−65.96	103.92	−0.32	6.41			−90.97	−122.78	17.08
−1342.88	878.48	6.82	375.02	61.17	296.09	−461.88	−5286.14	966.75
	−524.74			−1.03	−12.62	−17.26	−1.16	
	−17.07			−3.10	−30.39	−39.38	−2.18	
569.20	1428.29							
−1907.16			1237.89	65.30				
						−392.59	−5282.80	966.75
−4.92			−862.87		339.10	−12.65		
	−8.00	6.82						
						27.37	26.99	0.38
147.29	341.69	6.50	840.54	61.17	296.09	1719.91	97.76	356.79
						83.05		35.07
147.29	179.95	6.50	840.54	61.17	283.44	791.93	87.79	25.70
	0.06		3.76	1.38		154.93		
	2.67					19.69		7.68
						431.04		258.54
					0.81	18.94		0.15
	159.07					54.67		
	126.80				10.59	43.58		
	32.27					11.09		
					1.25	48.16	9.97	29.65
2059.37	891.50	6.50	1703.41	65.30	339.10	2209.16	5410.89	357.17

续表

项 目	Item	煤油 （万吨） Kerosene （10⁴ tn）	柴油 （万吨） Diesel Oil （10⁴ tn）
一.可供本地区消费的能源量	**Total Primary Energy Supply**	**−193.70**	**−1359.25**
1.一次能源生产量	Indigenous Production		
2.回收能	Recovery of Energy		
3.外省(区、市)调入量	Moving In from Other Provinces	0.37	3.46
4.进口量	Import		1.04
5.我轮、机在外国加油量	Chinese Airplanes & Ships in Refueling Abroad	2.54	1.61
6.本省(区、市)调出量(−)	Sending Out to Other Provinces(−)	−195.53	−1282.61
7.出口量(−)	Export(−)	− 5.13	− 29.66
8.外轮、机在我国加油量(−)	Foreign Airplanes & Ships in Refueling in China	−2.00	−52.67
9.库存增(−)、减(+)量	Stock Change	6.05	− 0.42
二.加工转换投入(−)产出(+)量	**Input(−) & Output(+) of Transformation**	**220.10**	**1892.37**
1.火力发电	Thermal Power		− 1.18
2.供 热	Heating Supply		− 0.10
3.洗 选 煤	Coal Washing		
4.炼 焦	Coking		
5.炼油	Petroleum Refineries	220.10	1893.65
6.制气	Gas Works		
#焦炭再投入量(−)	Coke Input(−)		
7.煤制品加工	Briquettes		
三.损 失 量	**Loss**		
四.终端消费量	**Total Final Consumption**	**26.40**	**533.12**
1.农、林、牧、渔、水利业	Farming, Forestry, Animal Husbandry, Fishery & Water Conservancy		47.98
2.工业	Industry	4.13	79.59
#用作原料、材料	Non-Energy Use	0.29	0.06
3.建 筑 业	Construction		8.45
4.交通运输、仓储和邮政业	Transport, Storage and Post	22.27	391.57
5.批发、零售业和住宿、餐饮业	Wholesale, Retail Trade and Hotel ,Restaurants		4.23
6.生活消费	Residential Consumption		
城镇	Urban		
乡村	Rural		
7.其他	Other		1.30
五.平衡差额	**Statistical Difference**		
六.消费量合计	**Sum of Consumption**	**26.40**	**534.40**

148

燃料油（万吨）Fuel Oil (10⁴ tn)	液化石油气（万吨）PLG (10⁴ tn)	炼厂干气（万吨）Refinery Gas (10⁴ tn)	天然气（亿立方米）Natural Gas (10⁸ cu. m)	其他石油制品（万吨）Other Petroleum Products (10⁴ tn)	其他焦化产品（万吨）Other Coking Products (10⁴ tn)	热力（百亿千焦）Heat (10¹⁰ kJ)	电力（亿千瓦时）Electricity (10⁸ kW·h)	其他能源（万吨标煤）Other Energy (10⁴ tce)
-43.66	**-79.86**		**14.81**	**-915.68**	**-14.49**		**260.35**	**80.78**
			11.72				57.14	
								80.92
	0.81		3.09	100.87	4.66		242.69	
0.79	0.37							
13.09								
-41.13	-81.19			-1015.64	-18.09		-39.48	
-2.46				-3.45	-0.79			
-20.36								
6.41	0.15			2.54	-0.27			-0.14
197.43	**182.04**	**128.32**		**1237.25**	**81.92**	**29588.26**	**850.19**	**-18.28**
-9.32	-0.12	-5.48					850.19	-16.18
-20.96		-16.14				29588.26		-2.10
					81.92			
233.54	184.00	154.92		1237.25				
-5.83	-1.84	-4.98						
						100.23	62.07	
153.77	**102.18**	**128.32**	**14.81**	**321.57**	**67.43**	**29488.03**	**1048.47**	**62.50**
							19.20	
118.22	26.61	128.32	14.81	321.57	67.43	17821.09	783.32	62.50
0.80				153.78				0.57
	3.56					20.23	6.02	
31.09						30.65	22.35	
	14.56					46.53	32.10	
	54.67					11211.08	131.36	
	43.58					11211.08	82.26	
	11.09						49.10	
4.46	2.78					358.19	54.12	
189.88	**104.14**	**154.92**	**14.81**	**321.57**	**67.43**	**29588.26**	**1110.54**	**80.78**

6-7 吉林能源平衡表(实物量)-2005

项 目	Item	煤合计 (万吨) Coal Total (10^4 tn)	原煤 (万吨) Raw Coal (10^4 tn)
一.可供本地区消费的能源量	**Total Primary Energy Supply**	**6802.39**	**6458.06**
1.一次能源生产量	Indigenous Production	2715.11	2715.11
2.回收能	Recovery of Energy		
3.外省(区、市)调入量	Moving In from Other Provinces	4424.49	4093.00
4.进口量	Import	77.62	77.62
5.我轮、机在外国加油量	Chinese Airplanes & Ships in Refueling Abroad		
6.本省(区、市)调出量(-)	Sending Out to Other Provinces(-)	-429.06	-429.06
7.出口量(-)	Export(-)	-21.23	-21.23
8.外轮、机在我国加油量(-)	Foreign Airplanes & Ships in Refueling in China		
9.库存增(-)、减(+)量	Stock Change	35.46	22.62
二.加工转换投入(-)产出(+)量	**Input(-) & Output(+) of Transformation**	**-4171.02**	**-3905.51**
1.火力发电	Thermal Power	-2465.39	-2446.13
2.供 热	Heating Supply	-1212.00	-1166.62
3.洗 选 煤	Coal Washing	-51.93	-240.28
4.炼焦	Coking	-318.61	-33.86
5.炼油	Petroleum Refineries		
6.制气	Gas Works	-123.71	-10.71
#焦炭再投入量(-)	Coke Input(-)		
7.煤制品加工	Briquettes	0.62	-7.91
三.损 失 量	**Loss**		
四.终端消费量	**Total Final Consumption**	**2631.46**	**2552.64**
1.农、林、牧、渔、水利业	Farming, Forestry, Animal Husbandry, Fishery & Water Conservancy	68.05	68.05
2.工业	Industry	1710.31	1638.60
#用作原料、材料	Non-Energy Use	89.43	86.40
3.建 筑 业	Construction	69.90	69.90
4.交通运输、仓储和邮政业	Transport, Storage and Post	116.28	116.28
5.批发、零售业和住宿、餐饮业	Wholesale, Retail Trade and Hotel, Restaurants	180.52	180.52
6.生活消费	Residential Consumption	261.48	254.37
城镇	Urban	183.37	179.11
乡村	Rural	78.11	75.26
7.其他	Other	224.92	224.92
五.平衡差额	**Statistical Difference**	**-0.09**	**-0.09**
六.消费量合计	**Sum of Consumption**	**6802.48**	**6458.15**

洗精煤 （万吨） Cleaned Coal (10^4 tn)	其他洗煤 （万吨） Other Washed Coal (10^4 tn)	型煤 （万吨） Briquettes (10^4 tn)	焦炭 （万吨） Coke (10^4 tn)	焦炉煤气 （亿立方米） Coke Oven Gas (10^8 cu. m)	其他煤气 （亿立方米） Other Gas (10^8 cu. m)	油品合计 （万吨） Petroleum Products Total (10^4 tn)	原油 （万吨） Crude Oil (10^4 tn)	汽油 （万吨） Gasoline (10^4 tn)
250.19	**89.65**	**4.49**	**67.67**		**58.19**	**872.59**	**968.33**	**2.22**
						550.57	550.57	
					58.19			
237.88	89.12	4.49	62.76			453.18	399.24	
						0.10		
						−145.65		
			−4.54			−7.30		
12.31	0.53		9.45			21.69	18.52	2.22
−228.27	**−45.43**	**8.19**	**269.25**	**10.76**	**−10.29**	**−29.54**	**−740.75**	**164.72**
	−19.26			−3.57	−8.37	−3.94		
	−45.04	−0.34			−4.61	−17.24		
169.48	18.87							
−284.75			198.30	10.97	1.39			
						−8.36	−740.75	164.72
−113.00			70.95	3.36	1.30			
		8.53						
				0.02		**0.40**	**0.40**	
21.92	**44.22**	**12.68**	**336.92**	**10.74**	**47.90**	**842.68**	**227.21**	**166.94**
						84.43		6.32
21.92	44.22	5.57	336.92	6.61	47.90	443.19	227.21	27.65
3.03			7.94			218.16	189.62	0.02
						18.97		9.23
						97.36		34.41
						36.86		14.54
		7.11		4.13		84.46		24.97
		4.26		4.13		60.46		20.54
		2.85				24.00		4.43
						77.41		49.82
						−0.03	−0.03	
419.67	**108.52**	**13.02**	**336.92**	**14.33**	**60.88**	**872.62**	**968.36**	**166.94**

项 目	Item	煤油 (万吨) Kerosene (10⁴ tn)	柴油 (万吨) Diesel Oil (10⁴ tn)
一. 可供本地区消费的能源量	**Total Primary Energy Supply**	**15.85**	**－124.82**
1. 一次能源生产量	Indigenous Production		
2. 回收能	Recovery of Energy		
3. 外省(区、市)调入量	Moving In from Other Provinces	15.76	
4. 进口量	Import	0.10	
5. 我轮、机在外国加油量	Chinese Airplanes & Ships in Refueling Abroad		
6. 本省(区、市)调出量(－)	Sending Out to Other Provinces(－)		－124.43
7. 出口量(－)	Export(－)		
8. 外轮、机在我国加油量(－)	Foreign Airplanes & Ships in Refueling in China		
9. 库存增(－)、减(＋)量	Stock Change	－0.01	－0.39
二. 加工转换投入(－)产出(＋)量	**Input(－) & Output(＋) of Transformation**		**365.84**
1. 火力发电	Thermal Power		－1.48
2. 供 热	Heating Supply		－0.11
3. 洗 选 煤	Coal Washing		
4. 炼焦	Coking		
5. 炼油	Petroleum Refineries		367.43
6. 制气	Gas Works		
#焦炭再投入量(－)	Coke Input(－)		
7. 煤制品加工	Briquettes		
三. 损 失 量	**Loss**		
四. 终端消费量	**Total Final Consumption**	**15.85**	**241.02**
1. 农、林、牧、渔、水利业	Farming, Forestry, Animal Husbandry, Fishery & Water Conservancy		78.11
2. 工业	Industry	1.51	39.93
#用作原料、材料	Non-Energy Use	0.01	0.03
3. 建 筑 业	Construction		9.74
4. 交通运输、仓储和邮政业	Transport, Storage and Post	14.34	48.61
5. 批发、零售业和住宿、餐饮业	Wholesale, Retail Trade and Hotel, Restaurants		22.32
6. 生活消费	Residential Consumption		14.72
城镇	Urban		2.01
乡村	Rural		12.71
7. 其他	Other		27.59
五. 平衡差额	**Statistical Difference**		
六. 消费量合计	**Sum of Consumption**	**15.85**	**242.61**

燃料油 （万吨） Fuel Oil (10^4 tn)	液化石油气 （万吨） PLG (10^4 tn)	炼厂干气 （万吨） Refinery Gas (10^4 tn)	天然气 （亿立方米） Natural Gas (10^8 cu. m)	其他石油制品 （万吨） Other Petroleum Products (10^4 tn)	其他焦化产品 （万吨） Other Coking Products (10^4 tn)	热力 （百亿千焦） Heat (10^{10} kJ)	电力 （亿千瓦时） Electricity (10^8 kW·h)	其他能源 （万吨标煤） Other Energy (10^4 tce)
18.18	15.43	5.45	6.18	−28.05	−2.41		23.70	27.41
			5.40				78.90	
17.45	15.28	5.45	0.78				132.10	27.19
				−21.22	−2.41		−187.30	
				−7.30				
0.73	0.15			0.47				0.22
27.15	40.17	3.50	−0.88	109.83	6.77	15070.64	354.53	
−2.46			−0.84				354.53	
−5.34		−0.22	−0.04	−11.57		15070.64		
					6.77			
34.95	40.17	3.72	121.40					
						256.30		
45.33	55.60	8.95	5.30	81.78	4.36	14814.34	378.23	27.41
							6.57	
45.33	10.83	8.95	4.69	81.78	4.36	10682.22	261.97	27.41
28.46				0.02	2.35			
						43.72	2.49	
						235.05	12.98	
						85.90	12.22	
	44.77		0.61			3297.05	58.23	
	37.91		0.61			3297.05	36.18	
	6.86						22.05	
						470.40	23.77	
53.13	55.60	9.17	6.18	93.35	4.36	15070.64	378.23	27.41

燃料油 （万吨） Fuel Oil (10^4 tn)	液化石油气 （万吨） PLG (10^4 tn)	炼厂干气 （万吨） Refinery Gas (10^4 tn)	天然气 （亿立方米） Natural Gas (10^8 cu. m)	其他石油制品 （万吨） Other Petroleum Products (10^4 tn)	其他焦化产品 （万吨） Other Coking Products (10^4 tn)	热力 （百亿千焦） Heat (10^{10} kJ)	电力 （亿千瓦时） Electricity (10^8 kW·h)	其他能源 （万吨标煤） Other Energy (10^4 tce)

6-8 黑龙江能源平衡表(实物量)-2005

项 目 Item	煤合计 (万吨) Coal Total (10^4 tn)	原煤 (万吨) Raw Coal (10^4 tn)
一. 可供本地区消费的能源量 Total Primary Energy Supply	7686.15	9177.37
1. 一次能源生产量 Indigenous Production	9736.70	9736.70
2. 回收能 Recovery of Energy		
3. 外省(区、市)调入量 Moving In from Other Provinces	1530.00	1530.00
4. 进口量 Import	4.21	4.21
5. 我轮、机在外国加油量 Chinese Airplanes & Ships in Refueling Abroad		
6. 本省(区、市)调出量(-) Sending Out to Other Provinces(-)	-3490.86	-2001.50
7. 出口量(-) Export(-)	-14.41	-14.41
8. 外轮、机在我国加油量(-) Foreign Airplanes & Ships in Refueling in China		
9. 库存增(-)、减(+)量 Stock Change	-79.49	-77.63
二. 加工转换投入(-)产出(+)量 Input(-) & Output(+) of Transformation	-6600.81	-8916.76
1. 火力发电 Thermal Power	-3407.37	-3383.21
2. 供热 Heating Supply	-1016.87	-999.69
3. 洗选煤 Coal Washing	-1220.59	-4176.80
4. 炼焦 Coking	-774.70	-238.92
5. 炼油 Petroleum Refineries		
6. 制气 Gas Works	-181.28	-118.14
#焦炭再投入量(-) Coke Input(-)		
7. 煤制品加工 Briquettes		
三. 损失量 Loss		
四. 终端消费量 Total Final Consumption	1958.92	1134.19
1. 农、林、牧、渔、水利业 Farming, Forestry, Animal Husbandry, Fishery & Water Conservancy	11.69	11.69
2. 工业 Industry	1712.49	887.76
#用作原料、材料 Non-Energy Use	30.06	27.81
3. 建筑业 Construction	3.76	3.76
4. 交通运输、仓储和邮政业 Transport, Storage and Post	113.62	113.62
5. 批发、零售业和住宿、餐饮业 Wholesale, Retail Trade and Hotel, Restaurants		
6. 生活消费 Residential Consumption	117.36	117.36
城镇 Urban	89.36	89.36
乡村 Rural	28.00	28.00
7. 其他 Other		
五. 平衡差额 Statistical Difference	-873.58	-873.58
六. 消费量合计 Sum of Consumption	8559.73	10050.95

洗精煤 （万吨） Cleaned Coal (10^4 tn)	其他洗煤 （万吨） Other Washed Coal (10^4 tn)	型煤 （万吨） Briquettes (10^4 tn)	焦炭 （万吨） Coke (10^4 tn)	焦炉煤气 （亿立方米） Coke Oven Gas (10^8 cu. m)	其他煤气 （亿立方米） Other Gas (10^8 cu. m)	油品合计 （万吨） Petroleum Products Total (10^4 tn)	原油 （万吨） Crude Oil (10^4 tn)	汽油 （万吨） Gasoline (10^4 tn)
-892.72	-598.50		-315.96			1495.07	1785.01	-70.64
						4495.01	4495.01	
						353.20	353.20	
						34.40	34.40	
-882.40	-606.96		-308.86			-3332.02	-3045.62	-72.80
			-7.10			-57.70	-52.40	
-10.32	8.46					2.18	0.42	2.16
1231.20	1084.75		417.12	5.03	39.28	-145.44	-1536.51	382.83
	-24.16			-0.68		-3.44		
-0.68	-16.50					-93.01		
1830.80	1125.41							
-535.78			458.02					
						-48.99	-1536.51	382.83
-63.14			-40.90	5.71	39.28			
						53.94	53.94	
338.48	486.25		101.16	5.03	39.28	1295.69	194.56	312.19
						168.95		12.69
338.48	486.25		101.16	5.03	39.28	532.50	194.56	13.86
2.25			8.32	1.28	3.47	58.00		
						1.93		1.12
						236.85		118.42
						156.72		87.36
						155.79		37.85
						148.83		37.85
						6.96		
						42.95		40.89
938.08	526.91		142.06	5.71	39.28	1495.07	1785.01	312.19

续表

项 目	Item	煤油 （万吨） Kerosene （10^4 tn）	柴油 （万吨） Diesel Oil （10^4 tn）
一.可供本地区消费的能源量	**Total Primary Energy Supply**	−12.00	−150.87
1.一次能源生产量	Indigenous Production		
2.回收能	Recovery of Energy		
3.外省（区、市）调入量	Moving In from Other Provinces		
4.进口量	Import		
5.我轮、机在外国加油量	Chinese Airplanes & Ships in Refueling Abroad		
6.本省（区、市）调出量（−）	Sending Out to Other Provinces（−）	−12.00	−150.50
7.出口量（−）	Export（−）		
8.外轮、机在我国加油量（−）	Foreign Airplanes & Ships in Refueling in China		
9.库存增（−）、减（+）量	Stock Change		−0.37
二.加工转换投入（−）产出（+）量	**Input（−）& Output（+）of Transformation**	19.28	623.32
1.火力发电	Thermal Power		−0.57
2.供 热	Heating Supply		−0.03
3.洗 选 煤	Coal Washing		
4.炼焦	Coking		
5.炼油	Petroleum Refineries	19.28	623.92
6.制气	Gas Works		
#焦炭再投入量（−）	Coke Input（−）		
7.煤制品加工	Briquettes		
三.损 失 量	**Loss**		
四.终端消费量	**Total Final Consumption**	7.28	472.45
1.农、林、牧、渔、水利业	Farming, Forestry, Animal Husbandry, Fishery & Water Conservancy		156.26
2.工业	Industry	0.36	71.23
#用作原料、材料	Non-Energy Use		0.05
3.建 筑 业	Construction		0.81
4.交通运输、仓储和邮政业	Transport, Storage and Post	6.92	111.51
5.批发、零售业和住宿、餐饮业	Wholesale, Retail Trade and Hotel, Restaurants		69.36
6.生活消费	Residential Consumption		63.28
城镇	Urban		56.32
乡村	Rural		6.96
7.其他	Other		
五.平衡差额	**Statistical Difference**		
六.消费量合计	**Sum of Consumption**	7.28	473.05

燃料油 （万吨） Fuel Oil （10^4 tn）	液化石油气 （万吨） PLG （10^4 tn）	炼厂干气 （万吨） Refinery Gas （10^4 tn）	天然气 （亿立方米） Natural Gas （10^8 cu. m）	其他石油制品 （万吨） Other Petroleum Products （10^4 tn）	其他焦化产品 （万吨） Other Coking Products （10^4 tn）	热力 （百亿千焦） Heat （10^{10} kJ）	电力 （亿千瓦时） Electricity （10^8 kW·h）	其他能源 （万吨标煤） Other Energy （10^4 tce）
-0.19	-26.36		24.43	-29.88	0.04		-35.52	0.17
			24.43				13.38	
							1.30	
							59.58	
	-26.40			-24.70			-109.78	
				-5.30				
-0.19	0.04			0.12				0.17
10.79	**131.00**	**20.22**	**-5.59**	**203.63**	**8.22**	**12942.45**	**602.75**	**-5.77**
-1.55		-1.32	-2.24				602.75	
-27.74	-0.89	-29.45	-3.35	-34.90		12942.45		-5.77
40.08	131.89	50.99		238.53				
			2.00				20.65	
10.60	**104.64**	**20.22**	**16.84**	**173.75**	**8.26**	**12942.45**	**534.58**	**10.10**
							13.39	
8.54	49.98	20.22	14.78	173.75	8.26	7833.83	374.47	10.10
2.51			4.35	55.44				
							2.70	
							8.43	
							12.11	
	54.66		2.06			5108.62	88.30	
	54.66		2.06			5108.62	60.98	
							27.32	
2.06							35.18	
							12.00	-15.70
39.89	**105.53**	**50.99**	**24.43**	**208.65**	**8.26**	**12942.45**	**555.23**	**15.87**

6-9 上海能源平衡表(实物量) -2005

项 目 Item		煤合计 (万吨) Coal Total (10^4 tn)	原煤 (万吨) Raw Coal (10^4 tn)
一.可供本地区消费的能源量	**Total Primary Energy Supply**	**5322.57**	**4128.78**
1.一次能源生产量	Indigenous Production		
2.回收能	Recovery of Energy		
3.外省(区、市)调入量	Moving In from Other Provinces	6665.97	5491.00
4.进口量	Import	18.78	
5.我轮、机在外国加油量	Chinese Airplanes & Ships in Refueling Abroad		
6.本省(区、市)调出量(-)	Sending Out to Other Provinces(-)	-1376.37	-1376.37
7.出口量(-)	Export(-)		
8.外轮、机在我国加油量(-)	Foreign Airplanes & Ships in Refueling in China		
9.库存增(-)、减(+)量	Stock Change	14.19	14.15
二.加工转换投入(-)产出(+)量	**Input(-) & Output(+) of Transformation**	**-4265.79**	**-3134.33**
1.火力发电	Thermal Power	-2847.31	-2847.31
2.供 热	Heating Supply	-274.55	-274.55
3.洗 选 煤	Coal Washing		
4.炼焦	Coking	-1131.46	
5.炼油	Petroleum Refineries		
6.制气	Gas Works	-12.47	-12.47
#焦炭再投入量(-)	Coke Input(-)		
7.煤制品加工	Briquettes		
三.损 失 量	**Loss**	**2.31**	**2.31**
四.终端消费量	**Total Final Consumption**	**1056.42**	**992.09**
1.农、林、牧、渔、水利业	Farming, Forestry, Animal Husbandry, Fishery & Water Conservancy	11.69	11.69
2.工业	Industry	878.55	843.48
#用作原料、材料	Non-Energy Use		13.16
3.建 筑 业	Construction	10.08	6.78
4.交通运输、仓储和邮政业	Transport, Storage and Post	12.16	9.16
5.批发、零售业和住宿、餐饮业	Wholesale, Retail Trade and Hotel, Restaurants	33.12	26.50
6.生活消费	Residential Consumption	72.82	72.82
城镇	Urban	41.20	41.20
乡村	Rural	31.62	31.62
7.其他	Other	38.00	21.66
五.平衡差额	**Statistical Difference**	**-1.95**	**0.05**
六.消费量合计	**Sum of Consumption**	**5324.52**	**4128.73**

158

ENERGY BALANCE OF SHANGHAI – 2005 (PHYSICAL QUANTITY)

洗精煤 （万吨） Cleaned Coal $(10^4$ tn)	其他洗煤 （万吨） Other Washed Coal $(10^4$ tn)	型煤 （万吨） Briquettes $(10^4$ tn)	焦炭 （万吨） Coke $(10^4$ tn)	焦炉煤气 （亿立方米） Coke Oven Gas $(10^8$ cu. m)	其他煤气 （亿立方米） Other Gas $(10^8$ cu. m)	油品合计 （万吨） Petroleum Products Total $(10^4$ tn)	原油 （万吨） Crude Oil $(10^4$ tn)	汽油 （万吨） Gasoline $(10^4$ tn)
1159.79		**34.00**	**−140.46**		**92.00**	**2200.31**	**1967.00**	**−21.10**
						32.56	25.27	
					92.00			
1140.97		34.00	15.96			3710.35	20.61	1271.33
18.78						2202.01	1935.96	3.48
						489.39		
			−167.40			−4079.95	−10.02	−1250.79
			−6.23			−95.71		−53.10
						−96.37		
0.04			17.21			38.03	−4.82	7.98
−1131.46			743.42	21.64	−59.68	−66.80	−1960.39	263.45
				−1.68	−83.72	−82.21		
						−33.14		
−1131.46			770.77	28.06			−1960.39	263.45
						57.53		
			−27.35	−4.74	24.04	−8.98		
				0.07	2.83	11.18	6.61	1.15
29.09	1.53	33.71	603.16	21.62	29.50	2122.39		241.19
						47.92		18.43
29.09	1.53	4.45	603.16	21.34	11.75	786.85		34.07
				0.28		372.94		0.75
		3.30				92.39		19.96
		3.00				913.40		61.35
		6.62			2.82	78.95		26.65
				0.28	11.23	113.52		45.40
					11.23	66.27		34.30
				0.28		47.25		11.10
		16.34			3.70	91.06		35.33
−0.76	**−1.53**	0.29	−0.20	−0.05	−0.01	−0.06		0.01
1160.55	1.53	33.71	630.51	28.11	117.42	2200.37	1967.00	242.34

续表

项目 Item	煤油 （万吨） Kerosene (10^4 tn)	柴油 （万吨） Diesel Oil (10^4 tn)
一.可供本地区消费的能源量 Total Primary Energy Supply	44.07	−388.44
1.一次能源生产量 Indigenous Production		
2.回收能 Recovery of Energy		
3.外省（区、市）调入量 Moving In from Other Provinces	84.74	2036.27
4.进口量 Import	165.60	
5.我轮、机在外国加油量 Chinese Airplanes & Ships in Refueling Abroad	56.88	5.81
6.本省（区、市）调出量（−） Sending Out to Other Provinces（−）	−152.11	−2444.24
7.出口量（−） Export（−）	−18.62	−6.30
8.外轮、机在我国加油量（−） Foreign Airplanes & Ships in Refueling in China	−96.37	
9.库存增（−）、减（+）量 Stock Change	3.95	20.02
二.加工转换投入（−）产出（+）量 Input（−）& Output（+）of Transformation	144.25	715.02
1.火力发电 Thermal Power		−1.25
2.供 热 Heating Supply		−1.51
3.洗 选 煤 Coal Washing		
4.炼焦 Coking		
5.炼油 Petroleum Refineries	144.25	717.86
6.制气 Gas Works		−0.08
#焦炭再投入量（−） Coke Input（−）		
7.煤制品加工 Briquettes		
三.损 失 量 Loss		0.84
四.终端消费量 Total Final Consumption	188.32	325.92
1.农、林、牧、渔、水利业 Farming, Forestry, Animal Husbandry, Fishery & Water Conservancy		27.79
2.工业 Industry	2.46	64.80
#用作原料、材料 Non-Energy Use		
3.建 筑 业 Construction	0.01	45.82
4.交通运输、仓储和邮政业 Transport, Storage and Post	185.21	94.35
5.批发、零售业和住宿、餐饮业 Wholesale, Retail Trade and Hotel, Restaurants	0.35	35.05
6.生活消费 Residential Consumption	0.19	26.90
城镇 Urban	0.13	15.12
乡村 Rural	0.06	11.78
7.其他 Other	0.10	31.21
五.平衡差额 Statistical Difference		−0.18
六.消费量合计 Sum of Consumption	188.32	329.60

160

燃料油 （万吨） Fuel Oil （10^4 tn）	液化石油气 （万吨） PLG （10^4 tn）	炼厂干气 （万吨） Refinery Gas （10^4 tn）	天然气 （亿立方米） Natural Gas （10^8 cu. m）	其他石油制品 （万吨） Other Petroleum Products （10^4 tn）	其他焦化产品 （万吨） Other Coking Products （10^4 tn）	热力 （百亿千焦） Heat （10^{10} kJ）	电力 （亿千瓦时） Electricity （10^8 kW·h）	其他能源 （万吨标煤） Other Energy （10^4 tce）
646.35	**15.06**	**−1.90**	**18.74**	**−60.73**	**−14.45**	**488.71**	**181.27**	**13.40**
	7.29		6.04				0.24	
						488.71		12.36
245.54	3.03		12.70	48.83	8.40		201.43	1.04
60.02	31.61			5.34				
423.76				2.94				
−92.35	−27.94	−2.00		−100.50	−27.00		−20.40	
				−17.69				
9.38	1.07	0.10		0.35	4.15			
46.09	**63.84**	**124.43**	**−5.49**	**536.51**	**54.43**	**5651.90**	**740.70**	**−12.36**
−59.39		−0.57	−1.09	−21.00		−5.09	740.70	−12.36
−12.94		−0.64	−0.65	−18.05		5753.42		
					54.43			
119.68	64.35	127.28		581.05				
−1.26	−0.51	−1.64	−3.75	−5.49		−96.43		
0.52	**0.12**	**0.22**	**1.25**	**1.72**		**302.63**	**49.30**	
691.84	**78.78**	**122.44**	**11.98**	**473.90**	**40.20**	**5837.98**	**872.67**	**1.04**
				1.70			5.76	
130.42	39.99	122.44	7.04	392.67	40.20	5495.31	568.29	1.04
1.47	12.48			358.24	37.17			
8.83				17.77		20.81	9.97	
545.96	8.08		0.20	18.45		17.00	14.35	
5.34	3.38		0.60	8.18		97.35	58.09	
	25.32		2.89	15.71		141.45	109.20	
	5.71		2.65	11.01		141.45	102.08	
	19.61		0.24	4.70			7.12	
1.29	2.01		1.25	21.12		66.06	107.01	
0.08		**−0.13**	**0.02**	**0.16**	**−0.22**			
765.95	**79.41**	**125.51**	**18.72**	**520.16**	**40.20**	**6242.13**	**921.97**	**13.40**

燃料油 （万吨） Fuel Oil （10^4 tn）	液化石油气 （万吨） PLG （10^4 tn）	炼厂干气 （万吨） Refinery Gas （10^4 tn）	天然气 （亿立方米） Natural Gas （10^8 cu. m）	其他石油制品 （万吨） Other Petroleum Products （10^4 tn）	其他焦化产品 （万吨） Other Coking Products （10^4 tn）	热力 （百亿千焦） Heat （10^{10} kJ）	电力 （亿千瓦时） Electricity （10^8 kW·h）	其他能源 （万吨标煤） Other Energy （10^4 tce）

6-10 江苏能源平衡表(实物量)-2005

项 目	Item	煤合计 (万吨) Coal Total (10^4 tn)	原煤 (万吨) Raw Coal (10^4 tn)
一.可供本地区消费的能源量	**Total Primary Energy Supply**	**16778.57**	**15814.25**
1.一次能源生产量	Indigenous Production	2817.56	2817.56
2.回收能	Recovery of Energy		
3.外省(区、市)调入量	Moving In from Other Provinces	14495.78	13438.87
4.进口量	Import	296.00	256.00
5.我轮、机在外国加油量	Chinese Airplanes & Ships in Refueling Abroad		
6.本省(区、市)调出量(-)	Sending Out to Other Provinces(-)	-590.56	-494.95
7.出口量(-)	Export(-)	-200.55	-190.00
8.外轮、机在我国加油量(-)	Foreign Airplanes & Ships in Refueling in China		
9.库存增(-)、减(+)量	Stock Change	-39.66	-13.23
二.加工转换投入(-)产出(+)量	**Input(-) & Output(+) of Transformation**	**-12099.39**	**-11534.19**
1.火力发电	Thermal Power	-9888.06	-9888.06
2.供 热	Heating Supply	-1043.52	-1043.52
3.洗 选 煤	Coal Washing	-91.03	-568.44
4.炼焦	Coking	-1074.13	-30.84
5.炼油	Petroleum Refineries		
6.制气	Gas Works	-2.33	-0.81
#焦炭再投入量(-)	Coke Input(-)		
7.煤制品加工	Briquettes	-0.32	-2.52
三.损 失 量	**Loss**		
四.终端消费量	**Total Final Consumption**	**4679.18**	**4280.06**
1.农、林、牧、渔、水利业	Farming, Forestry, Animal Husbandry, Fishery & Water Conservancy	74.44	74.44
2.工业	Industry	4373.71	3988.94
#用作原料、材料	Non-Energy Use	166.08	166.08
3.建 筑 业	Construction	4.00	4.00
4.交通运输、仓储和邮政业	Transport, Storage and Post	50.68	50.68
5.批发、零售业和住宿、餐饮业	Wholesale, Retail Trade and Hotel, Restaurants	56.00	56.00
6.生活消费	Residential Consumption	120.35	106.00
城镇	Urban	58.41	53.35
乡村	Rural	61.94	52.65
7.其他	Other		
五.平衡差额	**Statistical Difference**		
六.消费量合计	**Sum of Consumption**	**16778.57**	**15814.25**

ENERGY BALANCE OF JIANGSU –2005 (PHYSICAL QUANTITY)

洗精煤（万吨）Cleaned Coal (10⁴ tn)	其他洗煤（万吨）Other Washed Coal (10⁴ tn)	型煤（万吨）Briquettes (10⁴ tn)	焦炭（万吨）Coke (10⁴ tn)	焦炉煤气（亿立方米）Coke Oven Gas (10⁸ cu. m)	其他煤气（亿立方米）Other Gas (10⁸ cu. m)	油品合计（万吨）Petroleum Products Total (10⁴ tn)	原油（万吨）Crude Oil (10⁴ tn)	汽油（万吨）Gasoline (10⁴ tn)
951.50	**−0.47**	**13.29**	**768.90**		**130.40**	**2218.51**	**2264.76**	**186.88**
						164.70	164.70	
				130.40				
1043.61		13.30	777.50			1352.81	701.71	272.21
40.00						1453.22	1410.30	
						6.26		
−95.61						−744.87	−8.86	−84.32
−10.55			−15.00			−18.91		−4.93
−25.95	−0.47	−0.01	6.40			5.30	−3.09	3.92
−753.51	**183.11**	**5.20**	**799.06**	**17.60**	**−28.59**	**−116.85**	**−2226.08**	**233.25**
				−1.38	−24.97	−38.43		
				−0.07	−6.57	−5.91		
291.30	186.11							
−1043.29			824.22	16.04	1.25			
						−72.02	−2226.08	233.25
−1.52			−25.16	3.01	1.70	−0.49		
	−3.00	5.20						
						13.64	10.43	1.44
197.99	**182.64**	**18.49**	**1567.96**	**17.60**	**101.81**	**2088.02**	**28.25**	**418.69**
						115.52		18.55
197.99	182.64	4.14	1567.96	12.95	99.81	1126.63	24.79	40.64
			19.73			112.60		0.75
						94.75		2.00
						551.68	3.46	259.78
				0.50		11.12		
		14.35		3.55	2.00	166.90		88.00
		5.06		3.55	2.00	160.37		88.00
		9.29				6.53		
				0.60		21.42		9.72
1242.80	**185.64**	**18.49**	**1593.12**	**19.05**	**133.35**	**2218.51**	**2264.76**	**420.13**

续表

项　目	Item	煤油 （万吨） Kerosene （10^4 tn）	柴油 （万吨） Diesel Oil （10^4 tn）
一.可供本地区消费的能源量	**Total Primary Energy Supply**	**−77.86**	**−210.56**
1.一次能源生产量	Indigenous Production		
2.回收能	Recovery of Energy		
3.外省（区、市）调入量	Moving In from Other Provinces	0.20	224.21
4.进口量	Import		
5.我轮、机在外国加油量	Chinese Airplanes & Ships in Refueling Abroad	0.79	0.64
6.本省（区、市）调出量（−）	Sending Out to Other Provinces（−）	−77.02	−421.71
7.出口量（−）	Export（−）	−2.53	−5.12
8.外轮、机在我国加油量（−）	Foreign Airplanes & Ships in Refueling in China		
9.库存增（−）、减（+）量	Stock Change	0.70	−8.58
二.加工转换投入（−）产出（+）量	**Input（−）& Output（+）of Transformation**	**99.41**	**709.65**
1.火力发电	Thermal Power		−16.00
2.供热	Heating Supply		−0.03
3.洗选煤	Coal Washing		
4.炼焦	Coking		
5.炼油	Petroleum Refineries	99.41	725.68
6.制气	Gas Works		
#焦炭再投入量（−）	Coke Input（−）		
7.煤制品加工	Briquettes		
三.损失量	**Loss**		**0.43**
四.终端消费量	**Total Final Consumption**	**21.55**	**498.66**
1.农、林、牧、渔、水利业	Farming, Forestry, Animal Husbandry, Fishery & Water Conservancy	0.07	96.90
2.工业	Industry	9.45	119.84
#用作原料、材料	Non-Energy Use	0.14	0.75
3.建筑业	Construction		10.00
4.交通运输、仓储和邮政业	Transport, Storage and Post	11.63	250.59
5.批发、零售业和住宿、餐饮业	Wholesale, Retail Trade and Hotel , Restaurants	0.10	11.00
6.生活消费	Residential Consumption		
城镇	Urban		
乡村	Rural		
7.其他	Other	0.30	10.33
五.平衡差额	**Statistical Difference**		
六.消费量合计	**Sum of Consumption**	**21.55**	**515.12**

Continued

燃料油 （万吨） Fuel Oil （10⁴tn）	液化石油气 （万吨） PLG （10⁴tn）	炼厂干气 （万吨） Refinery Gas （10⁴tn）	天然气 （亿立方米） Natural Gas （10⁸ cu. m）	其他石油制品 （万吨） Other Petroleum Products （10⁴tn）	其他焦化产品 （万吨） Other Coking Products （10⁴tn）	热力 （百亿千焦） Heat （10¹⁰ kJ）	电力 （亿千瓦时） Electricity （10⁸ kW·h）	其他能源 （万吨标煤） Other Energy （10⁴tce）
106.91	**33.49**		**13.62**	**−85.11**	**−0.43**		**76.73**	**2.03**
			0.64				3.27	
								2.03
92.61			12.98	61.87			319.79	
	40.92			2.00				
4.83								
−4.61	−7.12			−141.23			−246.33	
				−6.33				
14.08	−0.31			−1.42	−0.43			
137.59	**100.03**	**68.05**	**−3.41**	**761.25**	**29.95**	**18039.90**	**2116.72**	
−13.22		−0.83	−1.85	−8.38		−991.58	2116.72	
	−2.24	−0.43	−1.22	−3.21		19031.48		
					29.95			
150.81	102.76	69.31		772.84				
	−0.49		−0.34					
	1.34		0.13			951.57	172.27	
244.50	**132.18**	**68.05**	**10.08**	**676.14**	**29.52**	**17088.33**	**2021.18**	**2.03**
							29.12	
218.29	52.18	68.05	8.72	593.39	29.52	16732.66	1599.01	2.03
				110.96	6.21			
				82.75			22.06	
26.21	0.01						16.45	
	0.02						55.52	
	78.90		1.36			355.67	200.72	
	72.37		1.36			355.67	102.18	
	6.53						98.54	
	1.07						98.30	
257.72	**136.25**	**69.31**	**13.62**	**687.73**	**29.52**	**19031.48**	**2193.45**	**2.03**

6-11 浙江能源平衡表(实物量)-2005

项 目	Item	煤合计 (万吨) Coal Total (10^4 tn)	原煤 (万吨) Raw Coal (10^4 tn)
一. 可供本地区消费的能源量	**Total Primary Energy Supply**	**9680.64**	**9583.69**
1. 一次能源生产量	Indigenous Production	43.67	43.67
2. 回收能	Recovery of Energy		
3. 外省(区、市)调入量	Moving In from Other Provinces	9568.40	9471.70
4. 进口量	Import	174.55	174.55
5. 我轮、机在外国加油量	Chinese Airplanes & Ships in Refueling Abroad		
6. 本省(区、市)调出量(-)	Sending Out to Other Provinces(-)		
7. 出口量(-)	Export(-)		
8. 外轮、机在我国加油量(-)	Foreign Airplanes & Ships in Refueling in China		
9. 库存增(-)、减(+)量	Stock Change	-105.98	-106.23
二. 加工转换投入(-)产出(+)量	**Input(-) & Output(+) of Transformation**	**-6135.04**	**-6193.60**
1. 火力发电	Thermal Power	-4801.52	-4801.52
2. 供 热	Heating Supply	-1281.60	-1281.60
3. 洗 选 煤	Coal Washing		
4. 炼焦	Coking	-81.44	
5. 炼油	Petroleum Refineries		
6. 制气	Gas Works	-3.73	-3.73
#焦炭再投入量(-)	Coke Input(-)		
7. 煤制品加工	Briquettes	33.25	-106.75
三. 损 失 量	**Loss**		
四. 终端消费量	**Total Final Consumption**	**3545.76**	**3390.25**
1. 农、林、牧、渔、水利业	Farming, Forestry, Animal Husbandry, Fishery & Water Conservancy	6.99	6.99
2. 工业	Industry	3356.18	3336.00
#用作原料、材料	Non-Energy Use		
3. 建 筑 业	Construction	6.15	6.15
4. 交通运输、仓储和邮政业	Transport, Storage and Post	7.26	7.26
5. 批发、零售业和住宿、餐饮业	Wholesale, Retail Trade and Hotel, Restaurants	39.18	33.85
6. 生活消费	Residential Consumption	130.00	
城镇	Urban	52.00	
乡村	Rural	78.00	
7. 其他	Other		
五. 平衡差额	**Statistical Difference**	**-0.16**	**-0.16**
六. 消费量合计	**Sum of Consumption**	**9680.80**	**9583.85**

ENERGY BALANCE OF ZHEJIANG – 2005 (PHYSICAL QUANTITY)

洗精煤 (万吨) Cleaned Coal (10^4 tn)	其他洗煤 (万吨) Other Washed Coal (10^4 tn)	型煤 (万吨) Briquettes (10^4 tn)	焦炭 (万吨) Coke (10^4 tn)	焦炉煤气 (亿立方米) Coke Oven Gas (10^8 cu. m)	其他煤气 (亿立方米) Other Gas (10^8 cu. m)	油品合计 (万吨) Petroleum Products Total (10^4 tn)	原油 (万吨) Crude Oil (10^4 tn)	汽油 (万吨) Gasoline (10^4 tn)
96.93		**0.02**	**104.03**		**9.97**	**1931.94**	**2113.04**	**79.84**
					9.97			
96.70						1309.83	457.00	231.13
			105.85			1775.24	1663.26	
						-1093.30		-111.35
						-79.77		-40.84
0.23	0.02	-1.82				19.94	-7.22	0.90
-81.44		**140.00**	**58.57**	**2.27**	**-0.41**	**-214.74**	**-2112.58**	**288.69**
		-0.03			-0.06	-219.55	-27.01	
		-0.21		-0.10	-0.59	-42.81		
-81.44			57.76	2.37				
						47.62	-2085.57	288.69
		1.80		0.24				
		-0.75						
		140.00						
15.49		**140.02**	**162.60**	**2.23**	**9.50**	**1717.18**	**0.46**	**368.53**
						194.07		6.80
15.49	4.69		162.60	2.23	9.50	632.75	0.46	60.56
						84.84		12.38
						485.89		186.16
		5.33				47.73		10.63
		130.00				218.30		61.00
		52.00				130.70		34.00
		78.00				87.60		27.00
						53.60		31.00
				0.04	0.06	0.02		
96.93		**140.02**	**163.59**	**2.33**	**10.15**	**1931.92**	**2113.04**	**368.53**

续表

项 目	Item	煤油 （万吨） Kerosene （10^4 tn）	柴油 （万吨） Diesel Oil （10^4 tn）
一. 可供本地区消费的能源量	**Total Primary Energy Supply**	−89.99	75.47
1. 一次能源生产量	Indigenous Production		
2. 回收能	Recovery of Energy		
3. 外省（区、市）调入量	Moving In from Other Provinces	9.63	414.00
4. 进口量	Import		0.60
5. 我轮、机在外国加油量	Chinese Airplanes & Ships in Refueling Abroad		
6. 本省（区、市）调出量（−）	Sending Out to Other Provinces（−）	−83.23	−332.48
7. 出口量（−）	Export（−）	−16.47	−20.04
8. 外轮、机在我国加油量（−）	Foreign Airplanes & Ships in Refueling in China		
9. 库存增（−）、减（+）量	Stock Change	0.08	13.39
二. 加工转换投入（−）产出（+）量	**Input（−）& Output（+）of Transformation**	130.97	722.91
1. 火力发电	Thermal Power		−4.52
2. 供 热	Heating Supply		−0.12
3. 洗 选 煤	Coal Washing		
4. 炼焦	Coking		
5. 炼油	Petroleum Refineries	130.97	727.55
6. 制气	Gas Works		
#焦炭再投入量（−）	Coke Input（−）		
7. 煤制品加工	Briquettes		
三. 损 失 量	**Loss**		
四. 终端消费量	**Total Final Consumption**	40.98	798.47
1. 农、林、牧、渔、水利业	Farming, Forestry, Animal Husbandry, Fishery & Water Conservancy		187.27
2. 工业	Industry	6.76	255.54
#用作原料、材料	Non-Energy Use		
3. 建 筑 业	Construction		72.46
4. 交通运输、仓储和邮政业	Transport, Storage and Post	34.22	240.06
5. 批发、零售业和住宿、餐饮业	Wholesale, Retail Trade and Hotel, Restaurants		18.14
6. 生活消费	Residential Consumption		10.00
城镇	Urban		4.00
乡村	Rural		6.00
7. 其他	Other		15.00
五. 平衡差额	**Statistical Difference**		−0.09
六. 消费量合计	**Sum of Consumption**	40.98	803.11

燃料油 （万吨） Fuel Oil （10^4 tn）	液化石油气 （万吨） PLG （10^4 tn）	炼厂干气 （万吨） Refinery Gas （10^4 tn）	天然气 （亿立方米） Natural Gas （10^8 cu. m）	其他石油制品 （万吨） Other Petroleum Products （10^4 tn）	其他焦化产品 （万吨） Other Coking Products （10^4 tn）	热力 （百亿千焦） Heat （10^{10} kJ）	电力 （亿千瓦时） Electricity （10^8 kW · h）	其他能源 （万吨标煤） Other Energy （10^4 tce）
197.65	**64.56**		**2.27**	**-508.63**	**0.04**		**548.09**	**42.10**
							362.19	
								42.10
198.07			2.27				203.90	
0.27	111.11							
	-47.24			-519.00			-18.00	
				-2.42				
-0.69	0.69			12.79	0.04			
-48.48	**137.06**	**61.67**	**-0.62**	**605.02**	**4.84**	**24928.89**	**1094.23**	**-15.29**
-153.22			-0.62	-34.80			1094.23	-15.29
-1.27				-41.42		24928.89		
					4.73			
106.01	137.06	61.67		681.24				
					0.11			
							1096.87	102.32
149.17	201.62	61.65	1.63	96.30	4.73	23832.00	1540.00	26.81
							13.90	
123.72	27.76	61.65	0.91	96.30	4.73	20157.00	1188.71	26.81
							20.84	
25.45							12.13	
	18.96					3000.00	50.30	
	147.30		0.72				173.21	
	92.70		0.72				90.79	
	54.60						82.42	
	7.60					675.00	80.91	
		0.02	0.02	0.09	0.15	0.02		
303.66	201.62	61.65	2.25	172.52	4.73	24998.04	1642.32	42.10

6-12 安徽能源平衡表(实物量)-2005

项 目	Item	煤合计 (万吨) Coal Total (10^4 tn)	原煤 (万吨) Raw Coal (10^4 tn)
一.可供本地区消费的能源量	**Total Primary Energy Supply**	**8332.71**	**8497.59**
1.一次能源生产量	Indigenous Production	8634.50	8634.50
2.回收能	Recovery of Energy		
3.外省(区、市)调入量	Moving In from Other Provinces	2374.00	2060.00
4.进口量	Import		
5.我轮、机在外国加油量	Chinese Airplanes & Ships in Refueling Abroad		
6.本省(区、市)调出量(-)	Sending Out to Other Provinces(-)	-2565.58	-2100.00
7.出口量(-)	Export(-)	-26.66	
8.外轮、机在我国加油量(-)	Foreign Airplanes & Ships in Refueling in China		
9.库存增(-)、减(+)量	Stock Change	-83.55	-96.91
二.加工转换投入(-)产出(+)量	**Input(-) & Output(+) of Transformation**	**-4286.43**	**-5814.41**
1.火力发电	Thermal Power	-3082.90	-3082.90
2.供热	Heating Supply	-239.96	-239.96
3.洗选煤	Coal Washing	-259.33	-1944.40
4.炼焦	Coking	-768.37	-42.75
5.炼油	Petroleum Refineries		
6.制气	Gas Works	-11.47	
#焦炭再投入量(-)	Coke Input(-)		
7.煤制品加工	Briquettes	75.60	-504.40
三.损失量	**Loss**		
四.终端消费量	**Total Final Consumption**	**4053.21**	**2686.00**
1.农、林、牧、渔、水利业	Farming, Forestry, Animal Husbandry, Fishery & Water Conservancy	34.96	34.96
2.工业	Industry	3312.35	2525.14
#用作原料、材料	Non-Energy Use		355.00
3.建筑业	Construction	31.50	31.50
4.交通运输、仓储和邮政业	Transport, Storage and Post	13.40	13.40
5.批发、零售业和住宿、餐饮业	Wholesale, Retail Trade and Hotel, Restaurants	58.00	58.00
6.生活消费	Residential Consumption	580.00	
城镇	Urban	385.00	
乡村	Rural	195.00	
7.其他	Other	23.00	23.00
五.平衡差额	**Statistical Difference**	**-6.93**	**-2.82**
六.消费量合计	**Sum of Consumption**	**8339.64**	**8500.41**

170

ENERGY BALANCE OF ANHUI - 2005 (PHYSICAL QUANTITY)

洗精煤 (万吨) Cleaned Coal (10⁴ tn)	其他洗煤 (万吨) Other Washed Coal (10⁴ tn)	型煤 (万吨) Briquettes (10⁴ tn)	焦炭 (万吨) Coke (10⁴ tn)	焦炉煤气 (亿立方米) Coke Oven Gas (10⁸ cu. m)	其他煤气 (亿立方米) Other Gas (10⁸ cu. m)	油品合计 (万吨) Petroleum Products Total (10⁴ tn)	原油 (万吨) Crude Oil (10⁴ tn)	汽油 (万吨) Gasoline (10⁴ tn)
−166.66	1.78		50.41		40.00	475.81	414.43	0.38
					40.00			
314.00			38.00			488.22	263.80	33.70
						156.30	156.30	
−465.58						−163.37		−31.79
−26.66								
11.58	1.78		12.41			−5.34	−5.67	−1.53
202.21	745.77	580.00	486.98	14.06	−30.17	−12.33	−414.46	85.98
				−1.71	−30.00			
				−1.90	−0.29			
917.82	767.25							
−704.14	−21.48		479.33	17.42	0.12			
						−12.33	−414.46	85.98
−11.47			8.42	0.25				
			−0.77					
		580.00						
37.21	750.00	580.00	537.62	14.06	1.47	464.02	0.03	86.41
						56.51		8.90
37.21	750.00		537.62	11.66	1.47	171.01	0.03	7.11
151.00	24.00		19.00			2.42		0.15
						12.80		7.02
						184.87		54.00
						10.72		9.38
		580.00		2.40		28.11		
		385.00		2.40		17.11		
		195.00				11.00		
−1.66	−2.45		−0.23		8.36	−0.54	−0.06	−0.05
752.82	771.48	580.00	538.39	17.67	31.76	476.35	414.49	86.41

续表

项 目	Item	煤油（万吨）Kerosene (10^4 tn)	柴油（万吨）Diesel Oil (10^4 tn)
一. 可供本地区消费的能源量	**Total Primary Energy Supply**	**10.52**	**32.56**
1. 一次能源生产量	Indigenous Production		
2. 回收能	Recovery of Energy		
3. 外省（区、市）调入量	Moving In from Other Provinces	10.52	165.10
4. 进口量	Import		
5. 我轮、机在外国加油量	Chinese Airplanes & Ships in Refueling Abroad		
6. 本省（区、市）调出量（－）	Sending Out to Other Provinces（－）		−131.58
7. 出口量（－）	Export（－）		
8. 外轮、机在我国加油量（－）	Foreign Airplanes & Ships in Refueling in China		
9. 库存增（－）、减（＋）量	Stock Change		−0.96
二. 加工转换投入（－）产出（＋）量	**Input（－）& Output（＋）of Transformation**		**177.50**
1. 火力发电	Thermal Power		
2. 供 热	Heating Supply		
3. 洗 选 煤	Coal Washing		
4. 炼焦	Coking		
5. 炼油	Petroleum Refineries		177.50
6. 制气	Gas Works		
#焦炭再投入量（－）	Coke Input（－）		
7. 煤制品加工	Briquettes		
三. 损 失 量	**Loss**		
四. 终端消费量	**Total Final Consumption**	**10.52**	**210.07**
1. 农、林、牧、渔、水利业	Farming, Forestry, Animal Husbandry, Fishery & Water Conservancy		47.61
2. 工业	Industry	0.45	34.54
#用作原料、材料	Non-Energy Use		1.34
3. 建 筑 业	Construction		5.78
4. 交通运输、仓储和邮政业	Transport, Storage and Post	10.07	120.80
5. 批发、零售业和住宿、餐饮业	Wholesale, Retail Trade and Hotel, Restaurants		1.34
6. 生活消费	Residential Consumption		
城镇	Urban		
乡村	Rural		
7. 其他	Other		
五. 平衡差额	**Statistical Difference**		**−0.01**
六. 消费量合计	**Sum of Consumption**	**10.52**	**210.07**

172

燃料油 （万吨） Fuel Oil （10⁴tn）	液化石油气 （万吨） PLG （10⁴tn）	炼厂干气 （万吨） Refinery Gas （10⁴tn）	天然气 （亿立方米） Natural Gas （10⁸ cu. m）	其他石油制品 （万吨） Other Petroleum Products （10⁴tn）	其他焦化产品 （万吨） Other Coking Products （10⁴tn）	热力 （百亿千焦） Heat （10¹⁰ kJ）	电力 （亿千瓦时） Electricity （10⁸ kW·h）	其他能源 （万吨标煤） Other Energy （10⁴tce）
15.52		0.85		2.40			−53.25	
							13.48	
15.10		0.85					6.64	
							−73.37	
0.42				2.40				
8.30	29.78	15.71		84.86	32.41	4615.72	634.90	
						31.40	634.90	
						4584.32		
					31.96			
8.30	29.78	15.71		84.86				
					0.45			
23.88	29.71	15.48	0.85	87.92	32.41	4615.00	581.65	
							11.75	
23.88	1.60	15.48	0.45	87.92	32.41	3962.00	430.98	
0.85	0.08				25.00			
							4.88	
							4.98	
							12.57	
	28.11		0.40			653.00	89.70	
	17.11		0.40			653.00	47.97	
	11.00						41.73	
							26.79	
−0.06	0.07	0.23		−0.66			0.72	
23.88	29.71	15.48	0.85	87.92	32.41	4615.00	581.65	

6 – 13　福建能源平衡表(实物量) – 2005

项　　目	Item	煤合计 (万吨) Coal Total (10^4 tn)	原煤 (万吨) Raw Coal (10^4 tn)
一.可供本地区消费的能源量	**Total Primary Energy Supply**	**4857.13**	**4733.76**
1.一次能源生产量	Indigenous Production	2000.00	2000.00
2.回收能	Recovery of Energy		
3.外省(区、市)调入量	Moving In from Other Provinces	3056.26	2926.00
4.进口量	Import	83.76	83.76
5.我轮、机在外国加油量	Chinese Airplanes & Ships in Refueling Abroad		
6.本省(区、市)调出量(–)	Sending Out to Other Provinces(–)	– 206.90	– 201.00
7.出口量(–)	Export(–)		
8.外轮、机在我国加油量(–)	Foreign Airplanes & Ships in Refueling in China		
9.库存增(–)、减(+)量	Stock Change	– 75.99	– 75.00
二.加工转换投入(–)产出(+)量	**Input(–) & Output(+) of Transformation**	**– 2380.54**	**– 2276.50**
1.火力发电	Thermal Power	– 2107.69	– 2107.69
2.供 热	Heating Supply	– 150.56	– 150.56
3.洗 选 煤	Coal Washing	– 1.88	– 13.67
4.炼焦	Coking	– 117.76	– 1.93
5.炼油	Petroleum Refineries		
6.制气	Gas Works	– 2.65	– 2.65
#焦炭再投入量(–)	Coke Input(–)		
7.煤制品加工	Briquettes		
三.损 失 量	**Loss**		
四.终端消费量	**Total Final Consumption**	**2476.59**	**2457.26**
1.农、林、牧、渔、水利业	Farming, Forestry, Animal Husbandry, Fishery & Water Conservancy	84.45	84.45
2.工业	Industry	2055.63	2036.30
#用作原料、材料	Non-Energy Use		340.00
3.建 筑 业	Construction	18.40	18.40
4.交通运输、仓储和邮政业	Transport, Storage and Post	10.50	10.50
5.批发、零售业和住宿、餐饮业	Wholesale, Retail Trade and Hotel, Restaurants	31.70	31.70
6.生活消费	Residential Consumption	255.91	255.91
城镇	Urban	52.08	52.08
乡村	Rural	203.83	203.83
7.其他	Other	20.00	20.00
五.平衡差额	**Statistical Difference**		
六.消费量合计	**Sum of Consumption**	**4857.13**	**4733.76**

ENERGY BALANCE OF FUJIAN – 2005 (PHYSICAL QUANTITY)

洗精煤 （万吨） Cleaned Coal (10^4 tn)	其他洗煤 （万吨） Other Washed Coal (10^4 tn)	型煤 （万吨） Briquettes (10^4 tn)	焦炭 （万吨） Coke (10^4 tn)	焦炉煤气 （亿立方米） Coke Oven Gas (10^8 cu. m)	其他煤气 （亿立方米） Other Gas (10^8 cu. m)	油品合计 （万吨） Petroleum Products Total (10^4 tn)	原油 （万吨） Crude Oil (10^4 tn)	汽油 （万吨） Gasoline (10^4 tn)
115.93	**7.44**		**190.00**		**55.43**	**935.65**	**349.26**	**104.62**
					55.43			
122.68	7.58		193.89			928.54	343.82	104.82
−5.90								
−0.85	−0.14		−3.89			7.11	5.44	−0.20
−104.04			**85.80**	**3.76**	**0.48**	**−18.44**	**−348.40**	**95.19**
						−9.12		
						−1.26		
11.79								
−115.83			85.80	3.76				
						−8.06	−348.40	95.19
					0.48			
11.89	**7.44**		**280.93**	**3.76**	**55.91**	**916.05**		**199.81**
						129.56		14.79
11.89	7.44		280.93	3.76	55.91	335.34		13.36
0.25								
						13.74		4.55
						252.86		84.51
						30.65		15.29
						76.44		13.65
						57.89		11.46
						18.55		2.19
						77.46		53.66
			−5.13			1.16	0.86	
127.72	7.44		280.93	3.76	55.91	934.49	348.40	199.81

项　目 Item		煤油 （万吨） Kerosene (10^4 tn)	柴油 （万吨） Diesel Oil (10^4 tn)
一.可供本地区消费的能源量	**Total Primary Energy Supply**	**26.96**	**221.26**
1.一次能源生产量	Indigenous Production		
2.回收能	Recovery of Energy		
3.外省（区、市）调入量	Moving In from Other Provinces	30.10	216.15
4.进口量	Import		
5.我轮、机在外国加油量	Chinese Airplanes & Ships in Refueling Abroad		
6.本省（区、市）调出量（ - ）	Sending Out to Other Provinces(-)		
7.出口量（ - ）	Export(-)		
8.外轮、机在我国加油量（ - ）	Foreign Airplanes & Ships in Refueling in China		
9.库存增（ - ）、减（ + ）量	Stock Change	- 3.14	5.11
二.加工转换投入（ - ）产出（ + ）量	**Input(-) & Output(+) of Transformation**	**5.81**	**146.03**
1.火力发电	Thermal Power		- 1.67
2.供　热	Heating Supply		
3.洗　选　煤	Coal Washing		
4.炼焦	Coking		
5.炼油	Petroleum Refineries	5.81	147.70
6.制气	Gas Works		
#焦炭再投入量（ - ）	Coke Input(-)		
7.煤制品加工	Briquettes		
三.损　失　量	**Loss**		
四.终端消费量	**Total Final Consumption**	**32.77**	**367.29**
1.农、林、牧、渔、水利业	Farming, Forestry, Animal Husbandry, Fishery & Water Conservancy		114.77
2.工业	Industry	2.98	92.21
#用作原料、材料	Non-Energy Use		
3.建　筑　业	Construction		
4.交通运输、仓储和邮政业	Transport, Storage and Post	27.73	125.07
5.批发、零售业和住宿、餐饮业	Wholesale, Retail Trade and Hotel , Restaurants		7.86
6.生活消费	Residential Consumption	2.06	3.58
城镇	Urban	0.98	1.30
乡村	Rural	1.08	2.28
7.其他	Other		23.80
五.平衡差额	**Statistical Difference**		
六.消费量合计	**Sum of Consumption**	**32.77**	**368.96**

燃料油 （万吨） Fuel Oil （10⁴tn）	液化石油气 （万吨） PLG （10⁴tn）	炼厂干气 （万吨） Refinery Gas （10⁴tn）	天然气 （亿立方米） Natural Gas （10⁸ cu. m）	其他石油制品 （万吨） Other Petroleum Products （10⁴tn）	其他焦化产品 （万吨） Other Coking Products （10⁴tn）	热力 （百亿千焦） Heat （10¹⁰ kJ）	电力 （亿千瓦时） Electricity （10⁸ kW·h）	其他能源 （万吨标煤） Other Energy （10⁴tce）
153.06	**80.49**		**0.51**			**345.70**	**269.34**	**27.65**
							291.00	
						345.70		27.65
153.14	80.51		0.51				4.98	
							-26.64	
-0.08	-0.02							
0.15	**19.69**	**13.16**		**49.93**	**4.65**	**2428.12**	**486.90**	
-7.45							486.90	
-1.26						2428.12		
					4.65			
8.86	19.69	13.16		49.93				
							57.16	
152.91	**100.18**	**13.16**	**0.51**	**49.93**	**4.65**	**2773.82**	**699.43**	**27.65**
							8.78	
145.36	39.00	13.16	0.51	29.27	4.65	2773.82	480.74	27.65
				9.19			6.59	
7.55				8.00			11.44	
	7.50						23.20	
	53.68			3.47			121.97	
	43.68			0.47			70.19	
	10.00			3.00			51.78	
							46.71	
0.30							**-0.35**	
161.62	**100.18**	**13.16**	**0.51**	**49.93**	**4.65**	**2773.82**	**756.59**	**27.65**

6-14 江西能源平衡表（实物量）-2005

项 目 Item		煤合计 （万吨） Coal Total (10^4 tn)	原煤 （万吨） Raw Coal (10^4 tn)
一.可供本地区消费的能源量	Total Primary Energy Supply	4224.84	3798.22
1.一次能源生产量	Indigenous Production	2565.05	2565.05
2.回收能	Recovery of Energy		
3.外省（区、市）调入量	Moving In from Other Provinces	1834.39	1409.30
4.进口量	Import		
5.我轮、机在外国加油量	Chinese Airplanes & Ships in Refueling Abroad		
6.本省（区、市）调出量（-）	Sending Out to Other Provinces（-）	-97.90	-97.80
7.出口量（-）	Export（-）		
8.外轮、机在我国加油量（-）	Foreign Airplanes & Ships in Refueling in China		
9.库存增（-）、减（+）量	Stock Change	-76.70	-78.33
二.加工转换投入（-）产出（+）量	Input（-）& Output（+）of Transformation	-2733.96	-2679.49
1.火力发电	Thermal Power	-1869.31	-1869.29
2.供 热	Heating Supply	-89.85	-89.83
3.洗 选 煤	Coal Washing	-205.46	-490.15
4.炼焦	Coking	-323.06	-4.77
5.炼油	Petroleum Refineries		
6.制气	Gas Works	-294.82	-25.45
#焦炭再投入量（-）	Coke Input（-）		
7.煤制品加工	Briquettes	48.54	-200.00
三.损 失 量	Loss		
四.终端消费量	Total Final Consumption	1508.94	1135.58
1.农、林、牧、渔、水利业	Farming, Forestry, Animal Husbandry, Fishery & Water Conservancy	4.00	4.00
2.工业	Industry	1229.10	1084.02
#用作原料、材料	Non-Energy Use	71.45	63.60
3.建 筑 业	Construction		
4.交通运输、仓储和邮政业	Transport, Storage and Post	2.56	2.56
5.批发、零售业和住宿、餐饮业	Wholesale, Retail Trade and Hotel, Restaurants	10.00	10.00
6.生活消费	Residential Consumption	262.28	34.00
城镇	Urban	74.00	4.00
乡村	Rural	188.28	30.00
7.其他	Other	1.00	1.00
五.平衡差额	Statistical Difference	-18.06	-16.85
六.消费量合计	Sum of Consumption	4242.90	3815.07

洗精煤 (万吨) Cleaned Coal (10^4 tn)	其他洗煤 (万吨) Other Washed Coal (10^4 tn)	型煤 (万吨) Briquettes (10^4 tn)	焦炭 (万吨) Coke (10^4 tn)	焦炉煤气 (亿立方米) Coke Oven Gas (10^8 cu. m)	其他煤气 (亿立方米) Other Gas (10^8 cu. m)	油品合计 (万吨) Petroleum Products Total (10^4 tn)	原油 (万吨) Crude Oil (10^4 tn)	汽油 (万吨) Gasoline (10^4 tn)
418.05	7.44	1.13	56.16		4.89	510.20	368.02	−22.61
422.72	2.28	0.09	139.26		4.89	481.82	234.57	5.70
						138.34	138.34	
−0.10			−83.44			−106.58		−29.16
−4.57	5.16	1.04	0.34			−3.38	−4.89	0.85
−393.20	90.19	248.54	269.21	11.89	66.37	−33.19	−364.88	86.10
−0.02						−2.65		
	−0.02					−6.26		
192.72	91.97							
−318.29			267.48	2.85				
						−24.28	−364.88	86.10
−267.61	−1.76		129.22	9.04	66.37			
				−127.49				
		248.54						
						3.14	3.14	
26.06	97.63	249.67	325.37	10.62	71.26	474.96		64.49
						100.00		1.00
26.06	97.63	21.39	325.37	10.62	68.09	89.74		2.42
7.85								
						5.48		1.50
						211.49		34.28
					2.08	9.98		2.00
		228.28			1.09	41.48		12.00
		70.00			1.09	27.64		9.00
		158.28				13.84		3.00
						16.79		11.29
−1.21					1.27	−1.09		−1.00
611.98	99.41	249.67	452.86	10.62	71.26	511.29	368.02	64.49

续表

项　目	Item	煤油 （万吨） Kerosene （10^4 tn）	柴油 （万吨） Diesel Oil （10^4 tn）
一.可供本地区消费的能源量	**Total Primary Energy Supply**	**2.46**	**169.46**
1.一次能源生产量	Indigenous Production		
2.回收能	Recovery of Energy		
3.外省（区、市）调入量	Moving In from Other Provinces	4.11	209.46
4.进口量	Import		
5.我轮、机在外国加油量	Chinese Airplanes & Ships in Refueling Abroad		
6.本省（区、市）调出量（－）	Sending Out to Other Provinces（－）	－2.01	－39.13
7.出口量（－）	Export（－）		
8.外轮、机在我国加油量（－）	Foreign Airplanes & Ships in Refueling in China		
9.库存增（－）、减（＋）量	Stock Change	0.36	－0.87
二.加工转换投入（－）产出（＋）量	**Input（－）& Output（＋）of Transformation**	**4.67**	**131.19**
1.火力发电	Thermal Power		－1.30
2.供　热	Heating Supply		－0.04
3.洗 选 煤	Coal Washing		
4.炼焦	Coking		
5.炼油	Petroleum Refineries	4.67	132.53
6.制气	Gas Works		
#焦炭再投入量（－）	Coke Input（－）		
7.煤制品加工	Briquettes		
三.损 失 量	**Loss**		
四.终端消费量	**Total Final Consumption**	**7.14**	**300.73**
1.农、林、牧、渔、水利业	Farming, Forestry, Animal Husbandry, Fishery & Water Conservancy	0.10	98.65
2.工业	Industry	0.39	17.30
#用作原料、材料	Non-Energy Use		
3.建 筑 业	Construction	0.01	3.00
4.交通运输、仓储和邮政业	Transport, Storage and Post	6.36	168.78
5.批发、零售业和住宿、餐饮业	Wholesale, Retail Trade and Hotel, Restaurants	0.18	4.00
6.生活消费	Residential Consumption	0.10	5.00
城镇	Urban		3.00
乡村	Rural	0.10	2.00
7.其他	Other		4.00
五.平衡差额	**Statistical Difference**	**－0.01**	**－0.08**
六.消费量合计	**Sum of Consumption**	**7.14**	**302.07**

180

Continued

燃料油（万吨）Fuel Oil (10⁴tn)	液化石油气（万吨）PLG (10⁴tn)	炼厂干气（万吨）Refinery Gas (10⁴tn)	天然气（亿立方米）Natural Gas (10⁸ cu. m)	其他石油制品（万吨）Other Petroleum Products (10⁴tn)	其他焦化产品（万吨）Other Coking Products (10⁴tn)	热力（百亿千焦）Heat (10¹⁰ kJ)	电力（亿千瓦时）Electricity (10⁸ kW·h)	其他能源（万吨标煤）Other Energy (10⁴tce)
−8.45	2.42		0.11	−1.10			108.37	27.26
							89.88	
								27.26
9.54	13.00		0.11	5.44			19.75	
−16.84	−10.82			−8.62			−1.26	
−1.15	0.24			2.08				
36.98	26.90	7.19		38.66	12.02	1452.60	305.61	
−0.64		−0.71					305.61	
−1.91		−4.31				1452.60		
					12.02			
39.53	26.90	12.21		38.66				
							35.84	
28.53	29.32	7.19	0.11	37.56	0.15	1452.60	378.14	27.26
0.25							23.59	
24.27	2.17	7.19	0.01	36.00	0.15	1452.60	254.76	27.26
0.80				0.17			2.74	
1.91	0.01			0.15			4.35	
0.30	2.90		0.05	0.60			9.56	
	24.24		0.05	0.14			65.53	
	15.50		0.05	0.14			40.81	
	8.74						24.72	
1.00				0.50			17.61	
					11.87			
31.08	29.32	12.21	0.11	37.56	0.15	1452.60	413.98	27.26

6－15　山东能源平衡表(实物量)－2005

项　目	Item	煤合计 (万吨) Coal Total (10^4 tn)	原煤 (万吨) Raw Coal (10^4 tn)
一.可供本地区消费的能源量	**Total Primary Energy Supply**	**25140.60**	**28128.50**
1.一次能源生产量	Indigenous Production	14030.00	14030.00
2.回收能	Recovery of Energy		
3.外省(区、市)调入量	Moving In from Other Provinces	15164.00	15164.00
4.进口量	Import		
5.我轮、机在外国加油量	Chinese Airplanes & Ships in Refueling Abroad		
6.本省(区、市)调出量(-)	Sending Out to Other Provinces(-)	-2904.50	-729.00
7.出口量(-)	Export(-)	-801.00	
8.外轮、机在我国加油量(-)	Foreign Airplanes & Ships in Refueling in China		
9.库存增(-)、减(+)量	Stock Change	-347.90	-336.50
二.加工转换投入(-)产出(+)量	**Input(-) & Output(+) of Transformation**	**-15878.47**	**-19220.14**
1.火力发电	Thermal Power	-10556.27	-10405.40
2.供热	Heating Supply	-2147.36	-2142.00
3.洗选煤	Coal Washing	-1011.08	-6414.57
4.炼焦	Coking	-2091.21	-246.16
5.炼油	Petroleum Refineries		
6.制气	Gas Works	-71.35	-5.61
#焦炭再投入量(-)	Coke Input(-)		
7.煤制品加工	Briquettes	-1.20	-6.40
三.损失量	**Loss**		
四.终端消费量	**Total Final Consumption**	**9369.44**	**8992.05**
1.农、林、牧、渔、水利业	Farming, Forestry, Animal Husbandry, Fishery & Water Conservancy	258.00	258.00
2.工业	Industry	8146.34	7780.75
#用作原料、材料	Non-Energy Use		
3.建筑业	Construction	62.40	62.40
4.交通运输、仓储和邮政业	Transport, Storage and Post	109.80	109.80
5.批发、零售业和住宿、餐饮业	Wholesale, Retail Trade and Hotel, Restaurants	99.10	99.10
6.生活消费	Residential Consumption	622.80	611.00
城镇	Urban	224.30	215.00
乡村	Rural	398.50	396.00
7.其他	Other	71.00	71.00
五.平衡差额	**Statistical Difference**	**-107.31**	**-83.69**
六.消费量合计	**Sum of Consumption**	**25247.91**	**28212.19**

ENERGY BALANCE OF SHANDONG – 2005 (PHYSICAL QUANTITY)

洗精煤（万吨）Cleaned Coal (10^4 tn)	其他洗煤（万吨）Other Washed Coal (10^4 tn)	型煤（万吨）Briquettes (10^4 tn)	焦炭（万吨）Coke (10^4 tn)	焦炉煤气（亿立方米）Coke Oven Gas (10^8 cu. m)	其他煤气（亿立方米）Other Gas (10^8 cu. m)	油品合计（万吨）Petroleum Products Total (10^4 tn)	原油（万吨）Crude Oil (10^4 tn)	汽油（万吨）Gasoline (10^4 tn)
−2108.00	−879.68	−0.22	509.27			3270.38	3299.98	−2.84
						2694.50	2694.50	
			549.00			1437.86	483.00	96.66
						1380.56	1373.06	
−1298.50	−877.00					−2216.95	−1227.55	−97.00
−801.00								
−8.50	−2.68	−0.22	−39.73			−25.59	−23.03	−2.50
2411.82	922.85	7.00	1481.58	36.30	6.53	−298.63	−3149.59	498.77
−42.18	−108.69		−0.11					
−1.63	−3.74			−1.80				
4368.22	1035.27							
−1845.05			1483.18	38.10				
						−298.63	−3149.59	498.77
−65.74					6.53			
			−1.49					
−1.80		7.00						
303.71	42.62	31.06	1990.97	36.47	7.60	2981.02	150.77	495.53
						263.95		20.50
303.71	42.62	19.26	1990.97	26.67	7.60	902.13	150.77	50.00
						348.76		19.80
				0.80		1043.73		292.48
				3.00		103.90		29.00
		11.80		4.00		203.65		45.75
		9.30		4.00		170.40		36.30
		2.50				33.25		9.45
				2.00		114.90		38.00
0.11	0.55	−24.28	−0.12	−0.17	−1.07	−9.27	−0.38	0.40
2260.11	155.04	31.06	1992.57	38.27	7.60	3279.65	3300.36	495.53

项　目	Item	煤油（万吨）Kerosene（10^4 tn）	柴油（万吨）Diesel Oil（10^4 tn）
一.可供本地区消费的能源量	**Total Primary Energy Supply**	**−26.40**	**152.80**
1.一次能源生产量	Indigenous Production		
2.回收能	Recovery of Energy		
3.外省（区、市）调入量	Moving In from Other Provinces		323.00
4.进口量	Import		
5.我轮、机在外国加油量	Chinese Airplanes & Ships in Refueling Abroad		
6.本省（区、市）调出量（−）	Sending Out to Other Provinces（−）	−26.40	−170.00
7.出口量（−）	Export（−）		
8.外轮、机在我国加油量（−）	Foreign Airplanes & Ships in Refueling in China		
9.库存增（−）、减（+）量	Stock Change		−0.20
二.加工转换投入（−）产出（+）量	**Input（−）& Output（+）of Transformation**	**47.96**	**976.47**
1.火力发电	Thermal Power		
2.供　热	Heating Supply		
3.洗选煤	Coal Washing		
4.炼焦	Coking		
5.炼油	Petroleum Refineries	47.96	976.47
6.制气	Gas Works		
#焦炭再投入量（−）	Coke Input（−）		
7.煤制品加工	Briquettes		
三.损　失　量	**Loss**		
四.终端消费量	**Total Final Consumption**	**21.99**	**1132.31**
1.农、林、牧、渔、水利业	Farming, Forestry, Animal Husbandry, Fishery & Water Conservancy		242.60
2.工业	Industry	3.59	138.66
#用作原料、材料	Non-Energy Use		
3.建　筑　业	Construction		41.00
4.交通运输、仓储和邮政业	Transport, Storage and Post	18.40	568.95
5.批发、零售业和住宿、餐饮业	Wholesale, Retail Trade and Hotel, Restaurants		58.70
6.生活消费	Residential Consumption		9.40
城镇	Urban		7.10
乡村	Rural		2.30
7.其他	Other		73.00
五.平衡差额	**Statistical Difference**	**−0.43**	**−3.04**
六.消费量合计	**Sum of Consumption**	**21.99**	**1132.31**

Continued

燃料油 （万吨） Fuel Oil （10^4 tn）	液化石油气 （万吨） PLG （10^4 tn）	炼厂干气 （万吨） Refinery Gas （10^4 tn）	天然气 （亿立方米） Natural Gas （10^8 cu. m）	其他石油制品 （万吨） Other Petroleum Products （10^4 tn）	其他焦化产品 （万吨） Other Coking Products （10^4 tn）	热力 （百亿千焦） Heat （10^{10} kJ）	电力 （亿千瓦时） Electricity （10^8 kW·h）	其他能源 （万吨标煤） Other Energy （10^4 tce）
147.60	**94.84**		**17.85**	**−395.60**	**−57.94**		**0.28**	**256.17**
			9.25					
								260.72
376.00	95.00		8.60	64.20			0.28	
			7.50					
−229.00				−467.00	−56.50			
0.60	−0.16			−0.30	−1.44			−4.55
146.86	**122.50**	**47.00**		**1011.40**	**74.74**	**28805.00**	**1989.68**	**−125.80**
							1989.68	−118.90
						28805.00		−6.90
					74.74			
146.86	122.50	47.00		1011.40				
294.43	**221.63**	**47.28**	**17.89**	**617.08**	**15.88**	**27914.86**	**2004.50**	**130.37**
	0.85					312.00	47.20	
139.33	51.82	47.28	10.69	320.68	15.88	19448.86	1587.61	130.37
	1.56			286.40		477.00	13.22	
152.00	4.90		0.65	7.00		210.00	19.57	
3.10	10.10		1.00	3.00		1658.00	38.50	
	148.50		4.60			4768.00	210.00	
	127.00		4.60			3965.00	98.30	
	21.50					803.00	111.70	
	3.90		0.95			1041.00	88.40	
0.03	**−4.29**	**−0.28**	**−0.04**	**−1.28**	**0.92**	**890.14**	**−14.54**	
294.43	**221.63**	**47.28**	**17.89**	**617.08**	**15.88**	**27914.86**	**2004.50**	**256.17**

6-16 河南能源平衡表(实物量)-2005

项　目 Item	煤合计 (万吨) Coal Total (10^4 tn)	原煤 (万吨) Raw Coal (10^4 tn)
一.可供本地区消费的能源量　Total Primary Energy Supply	**16907.08**	**18653.40**
1.一次能源生产量　Indigenous Production	18761.42	18761.42
2.回收能　Recovery of Energy		
3.外省(区、市)调入量　Moving In from Other Provinces	3251.03	3251.03
4.进口量　Import		
5.我轮、机在外国加油量　Chinese Airplanes & Ships in Refueling Abroad		
6.本省(区、市)调出量(-)　Sending Out to Other Provinces(-)	-5836.55	-4130.55
7.出口量(-)　Export(-)		
8.外轮、机在我国加油量(-)　Foreign Airplanes & Ships in Refueling in China		
9.库存增(-)、减(+)量　Stock Change	731.18	771.50
二.加工转换投入(-)产出(+)量　**Input(-) & Output(+) of Transformation**	**-10941.27**	**-13016.52**
1.火力发电　Thermal Power	-7776.99	-7638.87
2.供 热　Heating Supply	-528.06	-528.06
3.洗 选 煤　Coal Washing	-557.04	-3680.13
4.炼焦　Coking	-1945.21	-1018.91
5.炼油　Petroleum Refineries		
6.制气　Gas Works	-128.97	-125.55
#焦炭再投入量(-)　Coke Input(-)		
7.煤制品加工　Briquettes	-5.00	-25.00
三.损 失 量　**Loss**		
四.终端消费量　**Total Final Consumption**	**7526.62**	**7199.00**
1.农、林、牧、渔、水利业　Farming, Forestry, Animal Husbandry, Fishery & Water Conservancy	100.00	100.00
2.工业　Industry	6176.53	5969.00
#用作原料、材料　Non-Energy Use	2261.88	2261.88
3.建 筑 业　Construction		
4.交通运输、仓储和邮政业　Transport, Storage and Post	20.00	20.00
5.批发、零售业和住宿、餐饮业　Wholesale, Retail Trade and Hotel, Restaurants	10.11	10.00
6.生活消费　Residential Consumption	1219.98	1100.00
城镇　Urban	519.98	400.00
乡村　Rural	700.00	700.00
7.其他　Other		
五.平衡差额　**Statistical Difference**	**-1560.81**	**-1562.12**
六.消费量合计　**Sum of Consumption**	**18467.89**	**20215.52**

洗精煤 （万吨） Cleaned Coal （10^4 tn）	其他洗煤 （万吨） Other Washed Coal （10^4 tn）	型煤 （万吨） Briquettes （10^4 tn）	焦炭 （万吨） Coke （10^4 tn）	焦炉煤气 （亿立方米） Coke Oven Gas （10^8 cu. m）	其他煤气 （亿立方米） Other Gas （10^8 cu. m）	油品合计 （万吨） Petroleum Products Total （10^4 tn）	原油 （万吨） Crude Oil （10^4 tn）	汽油 （万吨） Gasoline （10^4 tn）
−891.32	−855.97	0.97	−316.38		30.00	899.43	667.99	109.38
						507.16	507.16	
					30.00			
			105.00			368.37	32.67	122.00
						266.67	266.67	
−875.00	−831.00		−389.41			−262.70	−140.00	−11.38
−16.32	−24.97	0.97	−31.97			19.93	1.49	−1.24
996.25	1059.00	20.00	1188.05	9.18	68.80	−52.39	−636.82	127.01
	−138.12		−25.95		−10.20	−7.57	−0.82	−0.02
						−26.68	−23.00	
1921.42	1201.67							
−921.75	−4.55		1320.88	9.18				
						−18.14	−613.00	127.03
−3.42					79.00			
			−106.88					
		20.00						
				0.06	9.89	8.67	7.00	1.21
106.38	198.71	22.53	861.54	8.85	90.90	841.06	25.00	233.31
						97.11		7.00
100.00	85.00	22.53	861.54	8.08	90.37	295.60	25.00	27.00
			69.92			64.05		0.61
						33.36		0.26
						340.59		165.00
0.11						24.18		13.00
6.27	113.71			0.77	0.53	26.59		1.05
6.27	113.71			0.77	0.53	26.59		1.05
						23.63		20.00
−1.45	4.32	−1.56	10.13	0.27	−1.99	−2.69	−0.83	1.87
1031.55	341.38	22.53	994.37	8.91	110.99	902.12	668.82	234.54

续表

项 目	Item	煤油（万吨）Kerosene（10^4 tn）	柴油（万吨）Diesel Oil（10^4 tn）
一.可供本地区消费的能源量	**Total Primary Energy Supply**	**−6.35**	**95.27**
1.一次能源生产量	Indigenous Production		
2.回收能	Recovery of Energy		
3.外省（区、市）调入量	Moving In from Other Provinces	8.70	165.00
4.进口量	Import		
5.我轮、机在外国加油量	Chinese Airplanes & Ships in Refueling Abroad		
6.本省（区、市）调出量（−）	Sending Out to Other Provinces（−）	−14.73	−72.88
7.出口量（−）	Export（−）		
8.外轮、机在我国加油量（−）	Foreign Airplanes & Ships in Refueling in China		
9.库存增（−）、减（+）量	Stock Change	−0.32	3.15
二.加工转换投入（−）产出（+）量	**Input（−）& Output（+）of Transformation**	**20.07**	**231.29**
1.火力发电	Thermal Power		−3.03
2.供 热	Heating Supply		−0.06
3.洗 选 煤	Coal Washing		
4.炼焦	Coking		
5.炼油	Petroleum Refineries	20.07	234.38
6.制气	Gas Works		
#焦炭再投入量（−）	Coke Input（−）		
7.煤制品加工	Briquettes		
三.损 失 量	**Loss**	**0.03**	**0.35**
四.终端消费量	**Total Final Consumption**	**13.88**	**326.03**
1.农、林、牧、渔、水利业	Farming, Forestry, Animal Husbandry, Fishery & Water Conservancy	0.11	90.00
2.工业	Industry	2.30	55.00
#用作原料、材料	Non-Energy Use		1.58
3.建 筑 业	Construction	0.07	3.03
4.交通运输、仓储和邮政业	Transport, Storage and Post	10.59	165.00
5.批发、零售业和住宿、餐饮业	Wholesale, Retail Trade and Hotel, Restaurants	0.18	10.00
6.生活消费	Residential Consumption		
城镇	Urban		
乡村	Rural		
7.其他	Other	0.63	3.00
五.平衡差额	**Statistical Difference**	**−0.19**	**0.18**
六.消费量合计	**Sum of Consumption**	**13.91**	**329.47**

Continued

燃料油 （万吨） Fuel Oil （10⁴ tn）	液化石油气 （万吨） PLG （10⁴ tn）	炼厂干气 （万吨） Refinery Gas （10⁴ tn）	天然气 （亿立方米） Natural Gas （10⁸ cu. m）	其他石油制品 （万吨） Other Petroleum Products （10⁴ tn）	其他焦化产品 （万吨） Other Coking Products （10⁴ tn）	热力 （百亿千焦） Heat （10¹⁰ kJ）	电力 （亿千瓦时） Electricity （10⁸ kW·h）	其他能源 （万吨标煤） Other Energy （10⁴ tce）
37.53	−11.50	−0.45	23.93	7.56	0.24		38.79	15.00
			20.14				67.91	
								15.00
40.00			6.70				31.50	
−4.23	−11.36	−0.45	−2.91	−7.67			−60.62	
1.76	−0.14			15.23	0.24			
38.34	43.08	17.25	−1.01	107.39	23.30	9160.88	1346.79	−20.17
−0.29		−3.41					1346.79	−2.88
−1.44		−2.18	−1.01			9160.88		−1.23
					23.30			
40.07	43.08	22.84		107.39				−16.06
	0.08		0.89		4.00	619.63	86.57	
76.73	31.45	20.66	21.81	114.00	10.37	8519.31	1300.92	32.24
						13.60	62.00	
76.73	4.91	20.66	16.24	84.00	10.37	6747.36	998.00	32.24
	0.14	3.36	3.36	58.36	2.48			
				30.00			5.67	
			0.02			0.15	31.87	
	1.00		0.20			69.20	29.07	
	25.54		5.35			1689.00	125.60	
	25.54		5.35			1689.00	62.70	
							62.90	
							48.71	
−0.86	0.05	−3.86	0.22	0.95	9.17	21.94	−1.91	−37.41
78.46	31.53	26.25	23.71	114.00	14.37	9138.94	1387.49	52.41

6－17 湖北能源平衡表(实物量)－2005

项 目	Item	煤合计 (万吨) Coal Total (10^4 tn)	原煤 (万吨) Raw Coal (10^4 tn)
一.可供本地区消费的能源量	**Total Primary Energy Supply**	**8652.64**	**7689.66**
1.一次能源生产量	Indigenous Production	778.07	778.07
2.回收能	Recovery of Energy		
3.外省(区、市)调入量	Moving In from Other Provinces	8057.74	7085.90
4.进口量	Import		
5.我轮、机在外国加油量	Chinese Airplanes & Ships in Refueling Abroad		
6.本省(区、市)调出量(－)	Sending Out to Other Provinces(－)		
7.出口量(－)	Export(－)		
8.外轮、机在我国加油量(－)	Foreign Airplanes & Ships in Refueling in China		
9.库存增(－)、减(＋)量	Stock Change	－183.17	－174.31
二.加工转换投入(－)产出(＋)量	**Input(－) & Output(＋) of Transformation**	**－3978.67**	**－3044.31**
1.火力发电	Thermal Power	－2732.15	－2732.15
2.供 热	Heating Supply	－296.74	－296.74
3.洗 选 煤	Coal Washing		
4.炼焦	Coking	－929.61	
5.炼油	Petroleum Refineries		
6.制气	Gas Works	－20.17	－15.42
#焦炭再投入量(－)	Coke Input(－)		
7.煤制品加工	Briquettes		
三.损 失 量	**Loss**		
四.终端消费量	**Total Final Consumption**	**4673.97**	**4645.35**
1.农、林、牧、渔、水利业	Farming, Forestry, Animal Husbandry, Fishery & Water Conservancy	95.90	95.90
2.工业	Industry	3828.82	3800.20
#用作原料、材料	Non-Energy Use	672.98	672.98
3.建 筑 业	Construction	70.07	70.07
4.交通运输、仓储和邮政业	Transport, Storage and Post	105.67	105.67
5.批发、零售业和住宿、餐饮业	Wholesale, Retail Trade and Hotel, Restaurants	91.07	91.07
6.生活消费	Residential Consumption	468.00	468.00
城镇	Urban	187.70	187.70
乡村	Rural	280.30	280.30
7.其他	Other	14.44	14.44
五.平衡差额	**Statistical Difference**		
六.消费量合计	**Sum of Consumption**	**8652.64**	**7689.66**

ENERGY BALANCE OF HUBEI – 2005 (PHYSICAL QUANTITY)

洗精煤 （万吨） Cleaned Coal (10^4 tn)	其他洗煤 （万吨） Other Washed Coal (10^4 tn)	型煤 （万吨） Briquettes (10^4 tn)	焦炭 （万吨） Coke (10^4 tn)	焦炉煤气 （亿立方米） Coke Oven Gas (10^8 cu. m)	其他煤气 （亿立方米） Other Gas (10^8 cu. m)	油品合计 （万吨） Petroleum Products Total (10^4 tn)	原油 （万吨） Crude Oil (10^4 tn)	汽油 （万吨） Gasoline (10^4 tn)
960.08	**2.90**		**38.00**			**1252.95**	**822.13**	**188.56**
						78.11	78.11	
968.97	2.87		35.24			1111.37	741.61	178.25
-8.89	0.03		2.76			63.47	2.41	10.31
-934.36			645.75	29.94	6.00	-56.42	-811.12	178.87
				-1.15		-7.66	-0.36	
			-1.72	-0.12		-1.66		
-929.61			647.47	31.21	6.00			
						-47.10	-810.76	178.87
-4.75								
						5.06	5.06	
25.72	2.90		683.75	29.94	6.00	1191.47	5.95	367.43
						116.19		
25.72	2.90		683.75	29.94	6.00	412.79	5.95	25.31
						39.07		
						560.70		342.12
						17.31		
						45.41		
						34.63		
						10.78		
960.08	2.90		685.47	31.21	6.00	1252.95	822.13	367.43

续表

项 目	Item	煤油 （万吨） Kerosene （10^4 tn）	柴油 （万吨） Diesel Oil （10^4 tn）
一. 可供本地区消费的能源量	**Total Primary Energy Supply**	**17.23**	**121.59**
1. 一次能源生产量	Indigenous Production		
2. 回收能	Recovery of Energy		
3. 外省（区、市）调入量	Moving In from Other Provinces	9.20	114.59
4. 进口量	Import		
5. 我轮、机在外国加油量	Chinese Airplanes & Ships in Refueling Abroad		
6. 本省（区、市）调出量（ - ）	Sending Out to Other Provinces（ - ）		
7. 出口量（ - ）	Export（ - ）		
8. 外轮、机在我国加油量（ - ）	Foreign Airplanes & Ships in Refueling in China		
9. 库存增（ - ）、减（ + ）量	Stock Change	8.03	7.00
二. 加工转换投入（ - ）产出（ + ）量	**Input（ - ）& Output（ + ）of Transformation**	**8.85**	**327.46**
1. 火力发电	Thermal Power		- 2.39
2. 供 热	Heating Supply		- 0.05
3. 洗 选 煤	Coal Washing		
4. 炼焦	Coking		
5. 炼油	Petroleum Refineries	8.85	329.90
6. 制气	Gas Works		
#焦炭再投入量（ - ）	Coke Input（ - ）		
7. 煤制品加工	Briquettes		
三. 损 失 量	**Loss**		
四. 终端消费量	**Total Final Consumption**	**26.08**	**449.05**
1. 农、林、牧、渔、水利业	Farming, Forestry, Animal Husbandry, Fishery & Water Conservancy		116.19
2. 工业	Industry	4.97	106.10
#用作原料、材料	Non-Energy Use		
3. 建 筑 业	Construction		39.07
4. 交通运输、仓储和邮政业	Transport, Storage and Post	16.61	178.39
5. 批发、零售业和住宿、餐饮业	Wholesale, Retail Trade and Hotel, Restaurants		9.30
6. 生活消费	Residential Consumption	4.50	
城镇	Urban		
乡村	Rural	4.50	
7. 其他	Other		
五. 平衡差额	**Statistical Difference**		
六. 消费量合计	**Sum of Consumption**	**26.08**	**451.49**

燃料油 （万吨） Fuel Oil （10^4 tn）	液化石油气 （万吨） PLG （10^4 tn）	炼厂干气 （万吨） Refinery Gas （10^4 tn）	天然气 （亿立方米） Natural Gas （10^8 cu. m）	其他石油制品 （万吨） Other Petroleum Products （10^4 tn）	其他焦化产品 （万吨） Other Coking Products （10^4 tn）	热力 （百亿千焦） Heat （10^{10} kJ）	电力 （亿千瓦时） Electricity （10^8 kW·h）	其他能源 （万吨标煤） Other Energy （10^4 tce）
84.09	**0.64**	**6.11**		**18.71**	**0.15**		**358.69**	**121.50**
	1.11						860.28	121.50
67.72		5.00					77.97	
							−579.56	
16.37	0.64			18.71	0.15			
23.37	**52.79**	**28.76**		**134.60**	**6.46**	**4374.35**	**445.72**	
−3.15		−1.76				−81.51	445.72	
−0.26		−1.35				4455.86		
					6.46			
26.78	52.79	31.87		134.60				
107.46	**53.43**	**28.76**	**6.11**	**153.31**	**6.61**	**4374.35**	**804.41**	**121.50**
							35.12	
83.88	4.51	28.76	4.11	153.31	6.61	4374.35	562.54	121.50
							8.37	
23.58							13.71	
	8.01						26.43	
	40.91		2.00				112.91	
	34.63		2.00				77.35	
	6.28						35.56	
							45.33	
110.87	**53.43**	**31.87**	**6.11**	**153.31**	**6.61**	**4455.86**	**804.41**	**121.50**

6-18 湖南能源平衡表(实物量)-2005

项 目	Item	煤合计 (万吨) Coal Total (10^4 tn)	原煤 (万吨) Raw Coal (10^4 tn)
一.可供本地区消费的能源量	**Total Primary Energy Supply**	**8746.50**	**8154.19**
1.一次能源生产量	Indigenous Production	6904.39	6904.39
2.回收能	Recovery of Energy		
3.外省(区、市)调入量	Moving In from Other Provinces	3176.64	2541.91
4.进口量	Import		
5.我轮、机在外国加油量	Chinese Airplanes & Ships in Refueling Abroad		
6.本省(区、市)调出量(-)	Sending Out to Other Provinces(-)	-1228.17	-1188.69
7.出口量(-)	Export(-)		
8.外轮、机在我国加油量(-)	Foreign Airplanes & Ships in Refueling in China		
9.库存增(-)、减(+)量	Stock Change	-106.36	-103.42
二.加工转换投入(-)产出(+)量	**Input(-) & Output(+) of Transformation**	**-2852.37**	**-2760.99**
1.火力发电	Thermal Power	-1712.27	-1712.27
2.供 热	Heating Supply	-290.27	-290.27
3.洗 选 煤	Coal Washing	-152.37	-396.75
4.炼焦	Coking	-664.39	-94.87
5.炼油	Petroleum Refineries		
6.制气	Gas Works	-33.07	-11.83
#焦炭再投入量(-)	Coke Input(-)		
7.煤制品加工	Briquettes		-255.00
三.损 失 量	**Loss**		
四.终端消费量	**Total Final Consumption**	**5886.92**	**5385.99**
1.农、林、牧、渔、水利业	Farming, Forestry, Animal Husbandry, Fishery & Water Conservancy	383.06	383.06
2.工业	Industry	4532.49	4286.56
#用作原料、材料	Non-Energy Use	774.85	700.99
3.建 筑 业	Construction	24.63	24.63
4.交通运输、仓储和邮政业	Transport, Storage and Post	28.10	28.10
5.批发、零售业和住宿、餐饮业	Wholesale, Retail Trade and Hotel, Restaurants	298.38	298.38
6.生活消费	Residential Consumption	601.26	346.26
城镇	Urban	98.80	98.80
乡村	Rural	502.46	247.46
7.其他	Other	19.00	19.00
五.平衡差额	**Statistical Difference**	**7.21**	**7.21**
六.消费量合计	**Sum of Consumption**	**8739.29**	**8146.98**

洗精煤 （万吨） Cleaned Coal (10⁴ tn)	其他洗煤 （万吨） Other Washed Coal (10⁴ tn)	型煤 （万吨） Briquettes (10⁴ tn)	焦炭 （万吨） Coke (10⁴ tn)	焦炉煤气 （亿立方米） Coke Oven Gas (10⁸ cu. m)	其他煤气 （亿立方米） Other Gas (10⁸ cu. m)	油品合计 （万吨） Petroleum Products Total (10⁴ tn)	原油 （万吨） Crude Oil (10⁴ tn)	汽油 （万吨） Gasoline (10⁴ tn)
612.49	−33.93	13.75	366.15			849.46	652.28	144.31
623.55		11.18	437.98			924.30	655.83	158.30
						0.13		
−5.60	−33.88		−75.56			−64.83		−2.24
−5.46	−0.05	2.57	3.73			−10.14	−3.55	−11.75
−417.15	70.77	255.00	259.39	14.84	26.37	−62.78	−618.01	127.57
			−105.00			−3.85		
						−6.44		
169.85	74.53							
−565.76	−3.76		390.43	14.84				
						−52.08	−618.01	127.57
−21.24					26.37	−0.41		
			−26.04					
		255.00						
						9.50	9.50	
195.34	36.84	268.75	625.54	11.31	26.37	785.76	33.35	271.88
						13.87		8.55
195.34	36.84	13.75	625.54	11.31	26.37	223.17	33.35	14.41
70.10	3.76		16.07		0.03	32.43		0.96
						57.29		19.58
						377.79		178.51
						79.51		32.46
		255.00				34.13		18.37
						22.71		10.15
		255.00				11.42		8.22
				3.53		−8.58	−8.58	
782.34	40.60	268.75	756.58	11.31	26.37	858.04	660.86	271.88

续表

项 目	Item	煤油 （万吨） Kerosene (10^4 tn)	柴油 （万吨） Diesel Oil (10^4 tn)
一.可供本地区消费的能源量	**Total Primary Energy Supply**	**3.82**	**54.38**
1.一次能源生产量	Indigenous Production		
2.回收能	Recovery of Energy		
3.外省（区、市）调入量	Moving In from Other Provinces	3.59	60.99
4.进口量	Import		
5.我轮、机在外国加油量	Chinese Airplanes & Ships in Refueling Abroad	0.13	
6.本省（区、市）调出量（－）	Sending Out to Other Provinces（－）		−12.20
7.出口量（－）	Export（－）		
8.外轮、机在我国加油量（－）	Foreign Airplanes & Ships in Refueling in China		
9.库存增（－）、减（＋）量	Stock Change	0.10	5.59
二.加工转换投入（－）产出（＋）量	**Input（－）& Output（＋）of Transformation**	**8.66**	**226.22**
1.火力发电	Thermal Power		−1.39
2.供热	Heating Supply		−0.06
3.洗选煤	Coal Washing		
4.炼焦	Coking		
5.炼油	Petroleum Refineries	8.66	227.67
6.制气	Gas Works		
#焦炭再投入量（－）	Coke Input（－）		
7.煤制品加工	Briquettes		
三.损失量	**Loss**		
四.终端消费量	**Total Final Consumption**	**12.48**	**280.60**
1.农、林、牧、渔、水利业	Farming, Forestry, Animal Husbandry, Fishery & Water Conservancy		5.16
2.工业	Industry	1.86	30.76
#用作原料、材料	Non-Energy Use	0.05	0.79
3.建筑业	Construction	0.08	37.57
4.交通运输、仓储和邮政业	Transport, Storage and Post	10.11	175.67
5.批发、零售业和住宿、餐饮业	Wholesale, Retail Trade and Hotel, Restaurants	0.07	31.44
6.生活消费	Residential Consumption	0.36	
城镇	Urban		
乡村	Rural	0.36	
7.其他	Other		
五.平衡差额	**Statistical Difference**		
六.消费量合计	**Sum of Consumption**	**12.48**	**282.05**

燃料油 （万吨） Fuel Oil （10⁴tn）	液化石油气 （万吨） PLG （10⁴tn）	炼厂干气 （万吨） Refinery Gas （10⁴tn）	天然气 （亿立方米） Natural Gas （10⁸ cu. m）	其他石油制品 （万吨） Other Petroleum Products （10⁴tn）	其他焦化产品 （万吨） Other Coking Products （10⁴ tn）	热力 （百亿千焦） Heat （10¹⁰ kJ）	电力 （亿千瓦时） Electricity （10⁸ kW·h）	其他能源 （万吨标煤） Other Energy （10⁴tce）
10.93	**26.31**	**8.46**	**1.00**	**-51.03**	**4.34**		**271.34**	**210.79**
							243.56	
								122.00
10.80	26.33	8.46	1.00		4.17		65.13	89.54
				-50.39			-37.35	
0.13	-0.02			-0.64	0.17			-0.75
26.62	**55.40**	**9.18**		**101.58**	**12.69**	**4719.63**	**403.08**	**-30.13**
-1.68		-0.78			-1.50		403.08	-1.74
-3.86		-2.52				4719.63		
					14.19			
32.16	55.81	12.48		101.58				-27.98
	-0.41							-0.41
							58.83	
37.55	**81.71**	**17.64**	**1.00**	**50.55**	**17.03**	**4912.46**	**615.59**	**180.66**
				0.16			53.18	4.55
24.05	50.71	17.64	0.27	50.39	17.03	4912.46	380.11	54.11
2.88	0.74	1.83		25.18	0.50			0.43
	0.06		0.01				6.54	
13.50							19.05	
	15.54		0.42				16.41	
	15.40		0.30				110.54	122.00
	12.56		0.30				65.23	
	2.84						45.31	122.00
							29.76	
							-192.83	
43.09	**82.12**	**20.94**	**1.00**	**50.55**	**18.53**	**4912.46**	**674.42**	**210.79**

6-19 广东能源平衡表（实物量）-2005

项 目 Item	煤合计 （万吨） Coal Total (10^4 tn)	原煤 （万吨） Raw Coal (10^4 tn)
一. 可供本地区消费的能源量　Total Primary Energy Supply	9942.37	9683.05
1. 一次能源生产量　Indigenous Production	477.00	477.00
2. 回收能　Recovery of Energy		
3. 外省(区、市)调入量　Moving In from Other Provinces	8982.50	8709.74
4. 进口量　Import	711.92	711.92
5. 我轮、机在外国加油量　Chinese Airplanes & Ships in Refueling Abroad		
6. 本省(区、市)调出量(－)　Sending Out to Other Provinces(－)		
7. 出口量(－)　Export(－)	－76.71	－76.71
8. 外轮、机在我国加油量(－)　Foreign Airplanes & Ships in Refueling in China		
9. 库存增(－)、减(＋)量　Stock Change	－152.34	－138.90
二. 加工转换投入(－)产出(＋)量　Input(－) & Output(＋) of Transformation	－7071.26	－6878.38
1. 火力发电　Thermal Power	－6696.47	－6696.47
2. 供 热　Heating Supply	－124.79	－124.79
3. 洗 选 煤　Coal Washing	－15.04	－40.04
4. 炼焦　Coking	－172.54	
5. 炼油　Petroleum Refineries		
6. 制气　Gas Works	－16.75	－16.75
#焦炭再投入量(－)　Coke Input(－)		
7. 煤制品加工　Briquettes	－45.67	－0.33
三. 损 失 量　Loss	15.82	15.82
四. 终端消费量　Total Final Consumption	2855.29	2788.85
1. 农、林、牧、渔、水利业　Farming, Forestry, Animal Husbandry, Fishery & Water Conservancy	67.65	67.65
2. 工业　Industry	2664.55	2630.02
#用作原料、材料　Non-Energy Use	144.30	144.16
3. 建 筑 业　Construction	2.11	2.11
4. 交通运输、仓储和邮政业　Transport, Storage and Post	1.40	1.40
5. 批发、零售业和住宿、餐饮业　Wholesale, Retail Trade and Hotel, Restaurants	23.12	23.12
6. 生活消费　Residential Consumption	96.46	64.55
城镇　Urban	29.55	16.32
乡村　Rural	66.91	48.23
7. 其他　Other		
五. 平衡差额　Statistical Difference		
六. 消费量合计　Sum of Consumption	9942.37	9683.05

198

ENERGY BALANCE OF GUANGDONG – 2005 (PHYSICAL QUANTITY)

洗精煤 （万吨） Cleaned Coal （10⁴ tn）	其他洗煤 （万吨） Other Washed Coal （10⁴ tn）	型煤 （万吨） Briquettes （10⁴ tn）	焦炭 （万吨） Coke （10⁴ tn）	焦炉煤气 （亿立方米） Coke Oven Gas （10⁸ cu. m）	其他煤气 （亿立方米） Other Gas （10⁸ cu. m）	油品合计 （万吨） Petroleum Products Total （10⁴ tn）	原油 （万吨） Crude Oil （10⁴ tn）	汽油 （万吨） Gasoline （10⁴ tn）
213.08	**12.35**	**33.89**	**175.58**		**67.53**	**4968.12**	**2388.37**	**338.99**
						1470.03	1470.03	
					67.53			
228.18	10.93	33.65	154.02			1314.34		361.84
			0.01			2655.28	1130.97	
						28.59		
						-332.75	-151.97	
			-4.09			-72.85		-6.16
						-3.54		
-15.10	1.42	0.24	25.64			-90.98	-60.66	-16.69
-193.27		**0.39**	**118.52**	**4.37**	**7.78**	**-1015.84**	**-2377.02**	**366.55**
			-4.79		-1.87	-937.38	-10.91	-0.68
					-1.96	-55.30		
25.00								
-172.54			100.00	4.37	9.08			
						-7.49	-2366.11	367.23
			24.58		2.53	-15.67		
			-1.27					
-45.73		0.39						
						4.89	**4.83**	
19.81	**12.35**	**34.28**	**294.10**	**4.37**	**75.31**	**3947.39**	**6.52**	**705.54**
						132.06		14.80
19.81	12.35	2.37	294.10	4.37	65.32	1789.00	6.52	75.40
0.14			0.11			238.74		0.84
						46.09		23.78
						1236.21		373.08
					3.06	150.02		43.59
		31.91			6.93	544.82		133.36
		13.23			6.93	401.38		83.13
		18.68				143.44		50.23
						49.19		41.53
238.08	**12.35**	**34.28**	**300.16**	**4.37**	**79.14**	**4968.12**	**2388.37**	**706.22**

续表

项 目 Item		煤油 （万吨） Kerosene （10^4 tn）	柴油 （万吨） Diesel Oil （10^4 tn）
一. 可供本地区消费的能源量	Total Primary Energy Supply	−2.57	431.38
1. 一次能源生产量	Indigenous Production		
2. 回收能	Recovery of Energy		
3. 外省（区、市）调入量	Moving In from Other Provinces	1.45	462.33
4. 进口量	Import	22.60	5.32
5. 我轮、机在外国加油量	Chinese Airplanes & Ships in Refueling Abroad	28.59	
6. 本省（区、市）调出量（−）	Sending Out to Other Provinces（−）	−25.05	
7. 出口量（−）	Export（−）	−20.81	−3.09
8. 外轮、机在我国加油量（−）	Foreign Airplanes & Ships in Refueling in China	−3.54	
9. 库存增（−）、减（+）量	Stock Change	−5.81	−33.18
二. 加工转换投入（−）产出（+）量	Input（−）& Output（+）of Transformation	156.29	843.23
1. 火力发电	Thermal Power		−31.96
2. 供 热	Heating Supply		−0.06
3. 洗 选 煤	Coal Washing		
4. 炼焦	Coking		
5. 炼油	Petroleum Refineries	156.29	875.28
6. 制气	Gas Works		−0.03
#焦炭再投入量（−）	Coke Input（−）		
7. 煤制品加工	Briquettes		
三. 损 失 量	Loss		0.02
四. 终端消费量	Total Final Consumption	153.72	1274.59
1. 农、林、牧、渔、水利业	Farming, Forestry, Animal Husbandry, Fishery & Water Conservancy		96.65
2. 工业	Industry	7.74	445.46
#用作原料、材料	Non-Energy Use	0.27	2.29
3. 建 筑 业	Construction		21.75
4. 交通运输、仓储和邮政业	Transport, Storage and Post	143.00	615.39
5. 批发、零售业和住宿、餐饮业	Wholesale, Retail Trade and Hotel, Restaurants		80.29
6. 生活消费	Residential Consumption	2.98	8.93
城镇	Urban	0.23	1.56
乡村	Rural	2.75	7.37
7. 其他	Other		6.12
五. 平衡差额	Statistical Difference		
六. 消费量合计	Sum of Consumption	153.72	1306.66

Continued

燃料油 （万吨） Fuel Oil （10⁴tn）	液化石油气 （万吨） PLG （10⁴tn）	炼厂干气 （万吨） Refinery Gas （10⁴tn）	天然气 （亿立方米） Natural Gas （10⁸ cu. m）	其他石油制品 （万吨） Other Petroleum Products （10⁴ tn）	其他焦化产品 （万吨） Other Coking Products （10⁴ tn）	热力 （百亿千焦） Heat （10¹⁰ kJ）	电力 （亿千瓦时） Electricity （10⁸ kW·h）	其他能源 （万吨标煤） Other Energy （10⁴tce）
1352.38	**518.46**	**10.24**	**2.49**	**−69.13**	**3.10**		**833.26**	**116.98**
			44.75				438.29	
								113.44
317.81	124.32	10.24		36.35			471.08	
1038.89	390.75			66.75	26.85		44.95	
			−42.26	−155.73	−22.59		−7.93	
−28.68	−1.67			−12.44	−1.19		−113.13	
24.36	5.06			−4.06	0.03			3.54
−684.82	90.23	49.96	−1.09	539.74		4905.57	1840.29	−67.76
−887.21		−4.92	−0.93	−1.70		−30.92	1840.29	−104.66
−38.01		−2.25		−14.98		4936.49		−3.73
247.67	93.35	62.35		556.45				
−7.27	−3.12	−5.22	−0.16	−0.03				
								40.63
0.04							**130.56**	
667.52	**608.69**	**60.20**	**1.40**	**470.61**	**3.10**	**4905.57**	**2542.99**	**49.22**
14.83				5.78			65.23	
570.40	158.45	60.20	1.40	464.83	3.10	4905.57	1717.88	49.22
6.62	0.81			227.91	1.22			
	0.56						34.61	
74.21	30.53						30.44	
8.08	18.06						149.96	
	399.55						328.62	
	316.46						209.74	
	83.09						118.88	
	1.54						216.25	
1600.05	**611.81**	**72.59**	**2.49**	**487.32**	**3.10**	**4936.49**	**2673.55**	**157.61**

6-20 广西能源平衡表(实物量)-2005

项 目 Item		煤合计 (万吨) Coal Total (10^4 tn)	原煤 (万吨) Raw Coal (10^4 tn)
一. 可供本地区消费的能源量	**Total Primary Energy Supply**	**3734.93**	**3382.04**
1. 一次能源生产量	Indigenous Production	700.34	700.34
2. 回收能	Recovery of Energy		
3. 外省(区、市)调入量	Moving In from Other Provinces	3638.82	3275.00
4. 进口量	Import	266.00	266.00
5. 我轮、机在外国加油量	Chinese Airplanes & Ships in Refueling Abroad		
6. 本省(区、市)调出量(-)	Sending Out to Other Provinces(-)	-716.56	-716.56
7. 出口量(-)	Export(-)	-100.00	-100.00
8. 外轮、机在我国加油量(-)	Foreign Airplanes & Ships in Refueling in China		
9. 库存增(-)、减(+)量	Stock Change	-53.67	-42.74
二. 加工转换投入(-)产出(+)量	**Input(-) & Output(+) of Transformation**	**-1872.19**	**-1567.03**
1. 火力发电	Thermal Power	-1435.00	-1435.00
2. 供热	Heating Supply	-115.00	-115.00
3. 洗选煤	Coal Washing		
4. 炼焦	Coking	-305.16	
5. 炼油	Petroleum Refineries		
6. 制气	Gas Works	-17.03	-17.03
#焦炭再投入量(-)	Coke Input(-)		
7. 煤制品加工	Briquettes		
三. 损失量	**Loss**		
四. 终端消费量	**Total Final Consumption**	**1861.80**	**1813.64**
1. 农、林、牧、渔、水利业	Farming, Forestry, Animal Husbandry, Fishery & Water Conservancy	15.23	15.23
2. 工业	Industry	1774.14	1725.98
#用作原料、材料	Non-Energy Use	233.55	233.55
3. 建筑业	Construction	4.99	4.99
4. 交通运输、仓储和邮政业	Transport, Storage and Post	16.32	16.32
5. 批发、零售业和住宿、餐饮业	Wholesale, Retail Trade and Hotel, Restaurants	32.56	32.56
6. 生活消费	Residential Consumption	18.56	18.56
城镇	Urban	13.36	13.36
乡村	Rural	5.20	5.20
7. 其他	Other		
五. 平衡差额	**Statistical Difference**	**0.94**	**1.37**
六. 消费量合计	**Sum of Consumption**	**3733.99**	**3380.67**

ENERGY BALANCE OF GUANGXI – 2005 (PHYSICAL QUANTITY)

洗精煤 （万吨） Cleaned Coal (10⁴ tn)	其他洗煤 （万吨） Other Washed Coal (10⁴ tn)	型煤 （万吨） Briquettes (10⁴ tn)	焦炭 （万吨） Coke (10⁴ tn)	焦炉煤气 （亿立方米） Coke Oven Gas (10⁸ cu. m)	其他煤气 （亿立方米） Other Gas (10⁸ cu. m)	油品合计 （万吨） Petroleum Products Total (10⁴ tn)	原油 （万吨） Crude Oil (10⁴ tn)	汽油 （万吨） Gasoline (10⁴ tn)
349.98	**2.73**	**0.18**	**217.77**		**68.32**	**622.76**	**97.71**	**127.20**
						3.43	3.43	
				68.32				
361.13	2.54	0.15	208.35			652.32	93.96	126.00
						6.23		
						−39.23		
−11.15	0.19	0.03	9.42			0.01	0.32	1.20
−305.16			13.16	6.00	65.94	−14.41	−97.61	19.38
						−2.02		
−305.16			223.46	6.00		−12.39	−97.61	19.38
					65.94			
			−210.30					
						1.07		
45.26	**2.73**	**0.17**	**231.65**	**6.00**	**132.26**	**606.12**	**0.10**	**146.48**
						22.30		6.89
45.26	2.73	0.17	231.65	6.00	132.26	117.72	0.10	11.11
			41.00					
						9.32		4.10
						292.44		57.33
						28.90		6.53
						99.89		45.63
						80.88		32.74
						19.01		12.89
						35.55		14.89
−0.44		0.01	−0.72		2.00	1.16		0.10
350.42	2.73	0.17	441.95	6.00	132.26	621.60	97.71	146.48

项 目	Item	煤油 （万吨） Kerosene (10^4 tn)	柴油 （万吨） Diesel Oil (10^4 tn)
一.可供本地区消费的能源量	**Total Primary Energy Supply**	**6.79**	**291.23**
1.一次能源生产量	Indigenous Production		
2.回收能	Recovery of Energy		
3.外省（区、市）调入量	Moving In from Other Provinces	45.87	290.30
4.进口量	Import		
5.我轮、机在外国加油量	Chinese Airplanes & Ships in Refueling Abroad		
6.本省（区、市）调出量（−）	Sending Out to Other Provinces（−）		
7.出口量（−）	Export（−）		
8.外轮、机在我国加油量（−）	Foreign Airplanes & Ships in Refueling in China	−39.23	
9.库存增（−）、减（+）量	Stock Change	0.15	0.93
二.加工转换投入（−）产出（+）量	**Input（−）& Output（+）of Transformation**	**0.01**	**34.38**
1.火力发电	Thermal Power		−2.02
2.供 热	Heating Supply		
3.洗 选 煤	Coal Washing		
4.炼焦	Coking		
5.炼油	Petroleum Refineries	0.01	36.40
6.制气	Gas Works		
#焦炭再投入量（−）	Coke Input（−）		
7.煤制品加工	Briquettes		
三.损 失 量	**Loss**		**1.07**
四.终端消费量	**Total Final Consumption**	**7.00**	**324.90**
1.农、林、牧、渔、水利业	Farming, Forestry, Animal Husbandry, Fishery & Water Conservancy		11.29
2.工业	Industry	0.58	48.13
#用作原料、材料	Non-Energy Use		
3.建 筑 业	Construction		5.22
4.交通运输、仓储和邮政业	Transport, Storage and Post	6.42	228.69
5.批发、零售业和住宿、餐饮业	Wholesale, Retail Trade and Hotel, Restaurants		12.01
6.生活消费	Residential Consumption		
城镇	Urban		
乡村	Rural		
7.其他	Other		19.56
五.平衡差额	**Statistical Difference**	**−0.20**	**−0.36**
六.消费量合计	**Sum of Consumption**	**7.00**	**327.99**

Continued

燃料油（万吨）Fuel Oil (10^4 tn)	液化石油气（万吨）PLG (10^4 tn)	炼厂干气（万吨）Refinery Gas (10^4 tn)	天然气（亿立方米）Natural Gas (10^8 cu. m)	其他石油制品（万吨）Other Petroleum Products (10^4 tn)	其他焦化产品（万吨）Other Coking Products (10^4 tn)	热力（百亿千焦）Heat (10^{10} kJ)	电力（亿千瓦时）Electricity (10^8 kW·h)	其他能源（万吨标煤）Other Energy (10^4 tce)
24.28	**72.22**		**1.12**	**3.33**	**5.88**		**259.82**	**133.79**
							195.82	
					5.98			133.15
20.79	75.40		1.12				77.00	
2.81	0.07			3.35				
							−13.00	
0.68	−3.25			−0.02	−0.10			0.64
8.92	**6.63**	**1.83**		**12.05**	**8.78**	**1764.52**	**250.02**	**−133.15**
							250.02	−133.15
						1764.52		
					8.78			
8.92	6.63	1.83		12.05				
							37.88	
32.96	**77.70**	**1.83**	**1.12**	**15.15**	**14.56**	**1788.23**	**471.96**	
	4.12						13.86	
32.96	7.86	1.83		15.15	14.56	1788.23	341.90	
							5.02	
							6.78	
	10.36						6.59	
	54.26		1.12				69.44	
	48.14		1.12				40.65	
	6.12						28.79	
	1.10						28.37	
0.24	1.15			0.23	0.10	−23.71		0.64
32.96	77.70	1.83	1.12	15.15	14.56	1788.23	509.84	133.15

6-21 海南能源平衡表(实物量)-2005

项 目	Item	煤合计 (万吨) Coal Total (10^4 tn)	原煤 (万吨) Raw Coal (10^4 tn)
一.可供本地区消费的能源量	**Total Primary Energy Supply**	**341.60**	**341.60**
1.一次能源生产量	Indigenous Production		
2.回收能	Recovery of Energy		
3.外省(区、市)调入量	Moving In from Other Provinces	261.29	261.29
4.进口量	Import	71.03	71.03
5.我轮、机在外国加油量	Chinese Airplanes & Ships in Refueling Abroad		
6.本省(区、市)调出量(-)	Sending Out to Other Provinces(-)		
7.出口量(-)	Export(-)		
8.外轮、机在我国加油量(-)	Foreign Airplanes & Ships in Refueling in China		
9.库存增(-)、减(+)量	Stock Change	9.28	9.28
二.加工转换投入(-)产出(+)量	**Input(-) & Output(+) of Transformation**	**-228.95**	**-228.95**
1.火力发电	Thermal Power	-228.95	-228.95
2.供热	Heating Supply		
3.洗选煤	Coal Washing		
4.炼焦	Coking		
5.炼油	Petroleum Refineries		
6.制气	Gas Works		
#焦炭再投入量(-)	Coke Input(-)		
7.煤制品加工	Briquettes		
三.损失量	**Loss**	**1.20**	**1.20**
四.终端消费量	**Total Final Consumption**	**111.45**	**111.45**
1.农、林、牧、渔、水利业	Farming, Forestry, Animal Husbandry, Fishery & Water Conservancy	4.56	4.56
2.工业	Industry	95.86	95.86
#用作原料、材料	Non-Energy Use	2.02	2.02
3.建筑业	Construction		
4.交通运输、仓储和邮政业	Transport, Storage and Post	5.60	5.60
5.批发、零售业和住宿、餐饮业	Wholesale, Retail Trade and Hotel, Restaurants	5.43	5.43
6.生活消费	Residential Consumption		
城镇	Urban		
乡村	Rural		
7.其他	Other		
五.平衡差额	**Statistical Difference**		
六.消费量合计	**Sum of Consumption**	**341.60**	**341.60**

ENERGY BALANCE OF HAINAN －2005 (PHYSICAL QUANTITY)

洗精煤 （万吨） Cleaned Coal (10^4 tn)	其他洗煤 （万吨） Other Washed Coal (10^4 tn)	型煤 （万吨） Briquettes (10^4 tn)	焦炭 （万吨） Coke (10^4 tn)	焦炉煤气 （亿立方米） Coke Oven Gas (10^8 cu. m)	其他煤气 （亿立方米） Other Gas (10^8 cu. m)	油品合计 （万吨） Petroleum Products Total (10^4 tn)	原油 （万吨） Crude Oil (10^4 tn)	汽油 （万吨） Gasoline (10^4 tn)
			1.61			**168.52**	**11.46**	**39.48**
						0.03	0.03	
						10.07	10.07	
			1.61			118.59	2.64	39.48
						40.77		
						−0.94	−1.28	
						−1.62	**−11.44**	
						−1.50		
						−0.12	−11.44	
						0.20		0.09
			1.61			163.44	0.02	39.39
						23.05		4.50
			1.61			22.54	0.02	5.40
						0.13		
						6.60		2.50
						87.44		9.45
						4.35		4.35
						8.58		3.31
						7.37		2.10
						1.21		1.21
						10.88		9.88
						3.26		
			1.61			165.26	11.46	39.48

续表

项 目	Item	煤油（万吨）Kerosene（10⁴ tn）	柴油（万吨）Diesel Oil（10⁴ tn）
一. 可供本地区消费的能源量	**Total Primary Energy Supply**	**62.50**	**43.09**
1. 一次能源生产量	Indigenous Production		
2. 回收能	Recovery of Energy		
3. 外省（区、市）调入量	Moving In from Other Provinces	62.02	8.23
4. 进口量	Import		34.32
5. 我轮、机在外国加油量	Chinese Airplanes & Ships in Refueling Abroad		
6. 本省（区、市）调出量（－）	Sending Out to Other Provinces（－）		
7. 出口量（－）	Export（－）		
8. 外轮、机在我国加油量（－）	Foreign Airplanes & Ships in Refueling in China		
9. 库存增（－）、减（＋）量	Stock Change	0.48	0.54
二. 加工转换投入（－）产出（＋）量	**Input（－）& Output（＋）of Transformation**		**－1.50**
1. 火力发电	Thermal Power		－1.50
2. 供 热	Heating Supply		
3. 洗 选 煤	Coal Washing		
4. 炼焦	Coking		
5. 炼油	Petroleum Refineries		
6. 制气	Gas Works		
#焦炭再投入量（－）	Coke Input（－）		
7. 煤制品加工	Briquettes		
三. 损 失 量	**Loss**	**0.06**	**0.05**
四. 终端消费量	**Total Final Consumption**	**62.44**	**41.54**
1. 农、林、牧、渔、水利业	Farming, Forestry, Animal Husbandry, Fishery & Water Conservancy		18.55
2. 工业	Industry		13.41
#用作原料、材料	Non-Energy Use		0.13
3. 建 筑 业	Construction		4.10
4. 交通运输、仓储和邮政业	Transport, Storage and Post	62.44	4.48
5. 批发、零售业和住宿、餐饮业	Wholesale, Retail Trade and Hotel, Restaurants		
6. 生活消费	Residential Consumption		
城镇	Urban		
乡村	Rural		
7. 其他	Other		1.00
五. 平衡差额	**Statistical Difference**		
六. 消费量合计	**Sum of Consumption**	**62.50**	**43.09**

燃料油 （万吨） Fuel Oil （10⁴tn）	液化石油气 （万吨） PLG （10⁴tn）	炼厂干气 （万吨） Refinery Gas （10⁴tn）	天然气 （亿立方米） Natural Gas （10⁸ cu. m）	其他石油制品 （万吨） Other Petroleum Products （10⁴tn）	其他焦化产品 （万吨） Other Coking Products （10⁴tn）	热力 （百亿千焦） Heat （10¹⁰ kJ）	电力 （亿千瓦时） Electricity （10⁸ kW·h）	其他能源 （万吨标煤） Other Energy （10⁴tce）
4.14	**5.27**		**−213.44**	**2.58**			**10.50**	**14.72**
			1.66				10.50	
								14.73
4.77	1.08			0.37				
	4.18			2.27				
			−215.10					
−0.63	0.01			−0.06				−0.01
4.36			**−6.53**	**6.96**			**71.54**	
			−6.53				71.54	
4.36				6.96				
							6.90	
5.24	**5.27**		**14.44**	**9.54**			**75.14**	**14.72**
							4.62	
0.23			14.26	3.48			47.62	14.72
							0.60	
5.01				6.06			1.35	
			0.13				4.25	
	5.27		0.05				11.60	
	5.27		0.05				6.86	
							4.74	
							5.10	
3.26			−234.41					
5.24	**5.27**		**20.97**	**9.54**			**82.04**	**14.72**

6 – 22　重庆能源平衡表(实物量) – 2005

项　目	Item	煤合计 (万吨) Coal Total (10^4 tn)	原煤 (万吨) Raw Coal (10^4 tn)
一.可供本地区消费的能源量	**Total Primary Energy Supply**	**3335.20**	**3226.74**
1.一次能源生产量	Indigenous Production	3400.00	3400.00
2.回收能	Recovery of Energy		
3.外省(区、市)调入量	Moving In from Other Provinces	423.33	269.47
4.进口量	Import		
5.我轮、机在外国加油量	Chinese Airplanes & Ships in Refueling Abroad		
6.本省(区、市)调出量(-)	Sending Out to Other Provinces(-)	-489.82	-450.00
7.出口量(-)	Export(-)		
8.外轮、机在我国加油量(-)	Foreign Airplanes & Ships in Refueling in China		
9.库存增(-)、减(+)量	Stock Change	1.69	7.27
二.加工转换投入(-)产出(+)量	**Input(-) & Output(+) of Transformation**	**-1552.32**	**-1593.56**
1.火力发电	Thermal Power	-965.39	-875.40
2.供 热	Heating Supply	-115.92	-55.93
3.洗 选 煤	Coal Washing	-128.48	-573.49
4.炼焦	Coking	-342.53	-88.74
5.炼油	Petroleum Refineries		
6.制气	Gas Works		
#焦炭再投入量(-)	Coke Input(-)		
7.煤制品加工	Briquettes		
三.损 失 量	**Loss**		
四.终端消费量	**Total Final Consumption**	**1782.88**	**1633.18**
1.农、林、牧、渔、水利业	Farming, Forestry, Animal Husbandry, Fishery & Water Conservancy	216.00	216.00
2.工业	Industry	1372.70	1223.00
#用作原料、材料	Non-Energy Use		
3.建 筑 业	Construction	16.07	16.07
4.交通运输、仓储和邮政业	Transport, Storage and Post	21.26	21.26
5.批发、零售业和住宿、餐饮业	Wholesale, Retail Trade and Hotel, Restaurants	0.82	0.82
6.生活消费	Residential Consumption	155.00	155.00
城镇	Urban	1.58	1.58
乡村	Rural	153.42	153.42
7.其他	Other	1.03	1.03
五.平衡差额	**Statistical Difference**		
六.消费量合计	**Sum of Consumption**	**3335.20**	**3226.74**

ENERGY BALANCE OF CHONGQING – 2005 (PHYSICAL QUANTITY)

洗精煤 （万吨） Cleaned Coal (10^4 tn)	其他洗煤 （万吨） Other Washed Coal (10^4 tn)	型煤 （万吨） Briquettes (10^4 tn)	焦炭 （万吨） Coke (10^4 tn)	焦炉煤气 （亿立方米） Coke Oven Gas (10^8 cu. m)	其他煤气 （亿立方米） Other Gas (10^8 cu. m)	油品合计 （万吨） Petroleum Products Total (10^4 tn)	原油 （万吨） Crude Oil (10^4 tn)	汽油 （万吨） Gasoline (10^4 tn)
−39.96	140.58	7.84	181.44		3.21	284.38	2.86	77.53
				3.21				
	146.00	7.86	179.22			278.31	2.86	80.00
−39.82								
−0.14	−5.42	−0.02	2.22			6.07		−2.47
94.99	−53.75		206.56	0.18	−3.12	−2.30	−0.24	−0.02
	−89.99			−0.36	−3.12	−2.29		−0.02
	−59.99							
348.78	96.23							
−253.79			206.56	0.54				
						−0.01	−0.24	
55.03	86.83	7.84	388.00	0.18	0.09	282.08	2.62	77.51
			25.00			9.25		4.00
55.03	86.83	7.84	349.01	0.18	0.09	38.26	2.62	7.48
			10.00			8.49		3.94
			2.00			201.15		45.61
			0.50			12.03		8.74
			0.49			5.97		1.24
			0.40			0.66		0.65
			0.09			5.31		0.59
			1.00			6.93		6.50
308.82	236.81	7.84	388.00	0.54	3.21	284.38	2.86	77.53

项 目	Item	煤油（万吨）Kerosene（10^4 tn）	柴油（万吨）Diesel Oil（10^4 tn）
一.可供本地区消费的能源量	**Total Primary Energy Supply**	**12.30**	**180.18**
1.一次能源生产量	Indigenous Production		
2.回收能	Recovery of Energy		
3.外省（区、市）调入量	Moving In from Other Provinces	12.30	171.44
4.进口量	Import		
5.我轮、机在外国加油量	Chinese Airplanes & Ships in Refueling Abroad		
6.本省（区、市）调出量（－）	Sending Out to Other Provinces（－）		
7.出口量（－）	Export（－）		
8.外轮、机在我国加油量（－）	Foreign Airplanes & Ships in Refueling in China		
9.库存增（－）、减（＋）量	Stock Change		8.74
二.加工转换投入（－）产出（＋）量	**Input（－）& Output（＋）of Transformation**		**－1.38**
1.火力发电	Thermal Power		－1.38
2.供 热	Heating Supply		
3.洗 选 煤	Coal Washing		
4.炼焦	Coking		
5.炼油	Petroleum Refineries		
6.制气	Gas Works		
#焦炭再投入量（－）	Coke Input（－）		
7.煤制品加工	Briquettes		
三.损 失 量	**Loss**		
四.终端消费量	**Total Final Consumption**	**12.30**	**178.80**
1.农、林、牧、渔、水利业	Farming, Forestry, Animal Husbandry, Fishery & Water Conservancy		5.25
2.工业	Industry	0.93	16.38
#用作原料、材料	Non-Energy Use		
3.建 筑 业	Construction	0.04	4.51
4.交通运输、仓储和邮政业	Transport, Storage and Post	9.30	146.24
5.批发、零售业和住宿、餐饮业	Wholesale, Retail Trade and Hotel, Restaurants	0.10	3.19
6.生活消费	Residential Consumption	1.93	2.80
城镇	Urban		0.01
乡村	Rural	1.93	2.79
7.其他	Other		0.43
五.平衡差额	**Statistical Difference**		
六.消费量合计	**Sum of Consumption**	**12.30**	**180.18**

燃料油 （万吨） Fuel Oil （10^4 tn）	液化石油气 （万吨） PLG （10^4 tn）	炼厂干气 （万吨） Refinery Gas （10^4 tn）	天然气 （亿立方米） Natural Gas （10^8 cu. m）	其他石油制品 （万吨） Other Petroleum Products （10^4 tn）	其他焦化产品 （万吨） Other Coking Products （10^4 tn）	热力 （百亿千焦） Heat （10^{10} kJ）	电力 （亿千瓦时） Electricity （10^8 kW · h）	其他能源 （万吨标煤） Other Energy （10^4 tce）
3.61	**0.13**		**35.50**	**7.77**	**1.91**		**168.95**	**321.14**
			57.13				59.00	
								321.01
3.85	0.13		6.26	7.73	1.97		143.40	
			−27.89				−33.45	
−0.24				0.04	−0.06			0.13
−0.89			**−0.60**	**0.23**	**1.60**	**1462.91**	**180.00**	**−32.80**
−0.89							180.00	−32.80
			−0.60			1462.91		
					1.60			
				0.23				
							26.28	
2.72	**0.13**		**34.90**	**8.00**	**3.51**	**1462.91**	**322.67**	**288.34**
			0.44				4.00	
2.72	0.13		26.00	8.00	3.51	1462.91	208.65	288.34
			0.04				7.67	
			0.10				8.01	
			0.27				16.67	
			8.00				60.90	
			8.00				41.50	
							19.40	
			0.05				16.77	
3.61	**0.13**		**35.50**	**8.00**	**3.51**	**1462.91**	**348.95**	**321.14**

6-23 四川能源平衡表（实物量）-2005

项　目	Item	煤合计 （万吨） Coal Total （10^4 tn）	原煤 （万吨） Raw Coal （10^4 tn）
一. 可供本地区消费的能源量	**Total Primary Energy Supply**	**7791.93**	**7552.43**
1. 一次能源生产量	Indigenous Production	7905.21	7905.21
2. 回收能	Recovery of Energy		
3. 外省（区、市）调入量	Moving In from Other Provinces	651.38	410.65
4. 进口量	Import		
5. 我轮、机在外国加油量	Chinese Airplanes & Ships in Refueling Abroad		
6. 本省（区、市）调出量（－）	Sending Out to Other Provinces（－）	-781.70	-781.70
7. 出口量（－）	Export（－）	-11.76	-11.76
8. 外轮、机在我国加油量（－）	Foreign Airplanes & Ships in Refueling in China		
9. 库存增（－）、减（＋）量	Stock Change	28.80	30.03
二. 加工转换投入（－）产出（＋）量	**Input（－）& Output（＋）of Transformation**	**-4670.88**	**-4701.06**
1. 火力发电	Thermal Power	-2999.77	-2999.77
2. 供热	Heating Supply	-136.24	-136.24
3. 洗选煤	Coal Washing	-525.19	-1565.05
4. 炼焦	Coking	-1009.68	
5. 炼油	Petroleum Refineries		
6. 制气	Gas Works		
#焦炭再投入量（－）	Coke Input（－）		
7. 煤制品加工	Briquettes		
三. 损失量	**Loss**	**68.01**	**67.32**
四. 终端消费量	**Total Final Consumption**	**3053.04**	**2784.05**
1. 农、林、牧、渔、水利业	Farming, Forestry, Animal Husbandry, Fishery & Water Conservancy	34.14	34.14
2. 工业	Industry	2359.90	2091.34
#用作原料、材料	Non-Energy Use		200.12
3. 建筑业	Construction	14.06	14.06
4. 交通运输、仓储和邮政业	Transport, Storage and Post	11.01	10.98
5. 批发、零售业和住宿、餐饮业	Wholesale, Retail Trade and Hotel, Restaurants	42.27	41.96
6. 生活消费	Residential Consumption	579.60	579.60
城镇	Urban	108.96	108.96
乡村	Rural	470.64	470.64
7. 其他	Other	12.06	11.97
五. 平衡差额	**Statistical Difference**		
六. 消费量合计	**Sum of Consumption**	**7791.93**	**7552.43**

ENERGY BALANCE OF SICHUAN −2005 (PHYSICAL QUANTITY)

洗精煤 (万吨) Cleaned Coal (10⁴ tn)	其他洗煤 (万吨) Other Washed Coal (10⁴ tn)	型煤 (万吨) Briquettes (10⁴ tn)	焦炭 (万吨) Coke (10⁴ tn)	焦炉煤气 (亿立方米) Coke Oven Gas (10⁸ cu. m)	其他煤气 (亿立方米) Other Gas (10⁸ cu. m)	油品合计 (万吨) Petroleum Products Total (10⁴ tn)	原油 (万吨) Crude Oil (10⁴ tn)	汽油 (万吨) Gasoline (10⁴ tn)
238.64	0.86		66.60			675.05	140.81	195.84
						13.92	13.92	
240.73			65.63			668.65	126.99	195.75
						1.27		
						−2.30		
						−0.60		
−2.09	0.86		0.97			−5.89	−0.10	0.09
−229.78	259.96		827.94			−4.30	−139.34	28.60
						−2.22		
779.90	259.96							
−1009.68			827.94					
						−2.08	−139.34	28.60
0.48	0.21		1.24			1.05	0.45	0.07
8.38	260.61		893.30			669.70	1.02	224.37
						81.44		3.81
7.95	260.61		879.32			104.22	1.02	19.72
			7.28			35.24		17.27
0.03			0.12			346.58		133.97
0.31			6.16			46.61		9.37
			0.27			7.51		4.95
			0.07			4.57		3.27
			0.20			2.94		1.68
0.09			0.15			48.10		35.28
1018.54	260.82		894.54			675.05	140.81	224.44

洗精煤 (万吨) Cleaned Coal (10⁴ tn)	其他洗煤 (万吨) Other Washed Coal (10⁴ tn)	型煤 (万吨) Briquettes (10⁴ tn)	焦炭 (万吨) Coke (10⁴ tn)	焦炉煤气 (亿立方米) Coke Oven Gas (10⁸ cu. m)	其他煤气 (亿立方米) Other Gas (10⁸ cu. m)	油品合计 (万吨) Petroleum Products Total (10⁴ tn)	原油 (万吨) Crude Oil (10⁴ tn)	汽油 (万吨) Gasoline (10⁴ tn)

续表

项 目	Item	煤油 （万吨） Kerosene （10^4 tn）	柴油 （万吨） Diesel Oil （10^4 tn）
一.可供本地区消费的能源量	**Total Primary Energy Supply**	**92.12**	**238.20**
1.一次能源生产量	Indigenous Production		
2.回收能	Recovery of Energy		
3.外省（区、市）调入量	Moving In from Other Provinces	93.83	244.05
4.进口量	Import		
5.我轮、机在外国加油量	Chinese Airplanes & Ships in Refueling Abroad	1.27	
6.本省（区、市）调出量（－）	Sending Out to Other Provinces（－）	－2.30	
7.出口量（－）	Export（－）		
8.外轮、机在我国加油量（－）	Foreign Airplanes & Ships in Refueling in China	－0.60	
9.库存增（－）、减（＋）量	Stock Change	－0.08	－5.85
二.加工转换投入（－）产出（＋）量	**Input（－）& Output（＋）of Transformation**	**1.44**	**49.23**
1.火力发电	Thermal Power		
2.供 热	Heating Supply		
3.洗 选 煤	Coal Washing		
4.炼焦	Coking		
5.炼油	Petroleum Refineries	1.44	49.23
6.制气	Gas Works		
#焦炭再投入量（－）	Coke Input（－）		
7.煤制品加工	Briquettes		
三.损 失 量	**Loss**	**0.04**	**0.49**
四.终端消费量	**Total Final Consumption**	**93.52**	**286.94**
1.农、林、牧、渔、水利业	Farming, Forestry, Animal Husbandry, Fishery & Water Conservancy	0.09	77.45
2.工业	Industry	3.53	19.77
#用作原料、材料	Non-Energy Use		
3.建 筑 业	Construction	0.09	15.72
4.交通运输、仓储和邮政业	Transport, Storage and Post	87.07	125.54
5.批发、零售业和住宿、餐饮业	Wholesale, Retail Trade and Hotel, Restaurants	2.04	33.78
6.生活消费	Residential Consumption	0.55	2.01
城镇	Urban	0.11	1.19
乡村	Rural	0.44	0.82
7.其他	Other	0.15	12.67
五.平衡差额	**Statistical Difference**		
六.消费量合计	**Sum of Consumption**	**93.56**	**287.43**

Continued

燃料油 (万吨) Fuel Oil (10^4 tn)	液化石油气 (万吨) PLG (10^4 tn)	炼厂干气 (万吨) Refinery Gas (10^4 tn)	天然气 (亿立方米) Natural Gas (10^8 cu. m)	其他石油制品 (万吨) Other Petroleum Products (10^4 tn)	其他焦化产品 (万吨) Other Coking Products (10^4 tn)	热力 (百亿千焦) Heat (10^10 kJ)	电力 (亿千瓦时) Electricity (10^8 kW·h)	其他能源 (万吨标煤) Other Energy (10^4 tce)
8.08			**89.52**				**577.17**	
			137.74				653.34	
8.03							22.08	
			−48.22				−98.25	
0.05								
−2.22	**7.17**		**−3.24**	**50.82**		**2717.00**	**365.42**	
−2.22			−3.00				365.42	
			−0.24			2717.00		
	7.17			50.82				
			2.06			**10.05**	**95.22**	
5.86	**7.17**		**84.22**	**50.82**		**2706.95**	**847.37**	
0.09							21.78	
2.19	7.17		56.05	50.82		2706.95	582.46	
			46.94					
2.16			1.21				11.71	
			1.67				21.16	
1.42			3.33				26.70	
			21.85				143.46	
			21.85				85.01	
							58.45	
			0.11				40.10	
8.08	**7.17**		**89.52**	**50.82**		**2717.00**	**942.59**	

217

燃料油 (万吨) Fuel Oil (10^4 tn)	液化石油气 (万吨) PLG (10^4 tn)	炼厂干气 (万吨) Refinery Gas (10^4 tn)	天然气 (亿立方米) Natural Gas (10^8 cu. m)	其他石油制品 (万吨) Other Petroleum Products (10^4 tn)	其他焦化产品 (万吨) Other Coking Products (10^4 tn)	热力 (百亿千焦) Heat (10^10 kJ)	电力 (亿千瓦时) Electricity (10^8 kW·h)	其他能源 (万吨标煤) Other Energy (10^4 tce)

6 – 24　贵州能源平衡表(实物量) – 2005

项　目 Item	煤合计 (万吨) Coal Total (10^4 tn)	原煤 (万吨) Raw Coal (10^4 tn)
一. 可供本地区消费的能源量　Total Primary Energy Supply	**7657.78**	**8196.05**
1. 一次能源生产量　Indigenous Production	10615.20	10615.20
2. 回收能　Recovery of Energy		
3. 外省(区、市)调入量　Moving In from Other Provinces		
4. 进口量　Import		
5. 我轮、机在外国加油量　Chinese Airplanes & Ships in Refueling Abroad		
6. 本省(区、市)调出量(–)　Sending Out to Other Provinces(–)	– 3152.04	– 2617.15
7. 出口量(–)　Export(–)		
8. 外轮、机在我国加油量(–)　Foreign Airplanes & Ships in Refueling in China		
9. 库存增(–)、减(+)量　Stock Change	194.62	198.00
二. 加工转换投入(–)产出(+)量　**Input(–) & Output(+) of Transformation**	**– 4317.82**	**– 4980.01**
1. 火力发电　Thermal Power	– 3222.70	– 3212.31
2. 供 热　Heating Supply	– 28.29	– 28.29
3. 洗 选 煤　Coal Washing	– 495.59	– 1375.86
4. 炼焦　Coking	– 577.10	– 328.55
5. 炼油　Petroleum Refineries		
6. 制气　Gas Works		
#焦炭再投入量(–)　Coke Input(–)		
7. 煤制品加工　Briquettes	5.86	– 35.00
三. 损 失 量　**Loss**	**58.00**	**58.00**
四. 终端消费量　**Total Final Consumption**	**4275.62**	**4151.70**
1. 农、林、牧、渔、水利业　Farming, Forestry, Animal Husbandry, Fishery & Water Conservancy	249.30	249.30
2. 工业　Industry	2601.56	2518.50
#用作原料、材料　Non-Energy Use		592.60
3. 建 筑 业　Construction	7.30	7.30
4. 交通运输、仓储和邮政业　Transport, Storage and Post	9.50	9.50
5. 批发、零售业和住宿、餐饮业　Wholesale, Retail Trade and Hotel, Restaurants	151.88	149.50
6. 生活消费　Residential Consumption	1035.80	998.00
城镇　Urban	92.30	74.20
乡村　Rural	943.50	923.80
7. 其他　Other	220.28	219.60
五. 平衡差额　**Statistical Difference**	**– 993.66**	**– 993.66**
六. 消费量合计　**Sum of Consumption**	**8651.44**	**9189.71**

ENERGY BALANCE OF GUIZHOU - 2005 (PHYSICAL QUANTITY)

洗精煤 （万吨） Cleaned Coal (10⁴ tn)	其他洗煤 （万吨） Other Washed Coal (10⁴ tn)	型煤 （万吨） Briquettes (10⁴ tn)	焦炭 （万吨） Coke (10⁴ tn)	焦炉煤气 （亿立方米） Coke Oven Gas (10⁸ cu. m)	其他煤气 （亿立方米） Other Gas (10⁸ cu. m)	油品合计 （万吨） Petroleum Products Total (10⁴ tn)	原油 （万吨） Crude Oil (10⁴ tn)	汽油 （万吨） Gasoline (10⁴ tn)
-333.44	-204.83		-91.77			237.42		67.52
						235.99		66.05
-330.14	-204.75		-99.72					
-3.30	-0.08		7.95			1.43		1.47
407.84	213.49	40.86	425.63	7.09				
	-10.39							
656.39	223.88							
-248.55			425.63	7.09				
		40.86						
74.40	8.66	40.86	333.86	7.09		237.42		67.52
			28.20			8.11		2.16
74.40	8.66		294.38	5.54		32.06		8.63
			26.42					
			0.57			6.28		0.62
			0.18	0.39		133.16		44.57
		2.38	3.36	0.25		12.50		2.55
		37.80	1.82	0.91		7.03		
		18.10	1.82	0.91		6.53		
		19.70				0.50		
		0.68	5.35			38.28		8.99
322.95	19.05	40.86	333.86	7.09		237.42		67.52

续表

项　目	Item	煤油（万吨）Kerosene (10⁴ tn)	柴油（万吨）Diesel Oil (10⁴ tn)
一. 可供本地区消费的能源量	**Total Primary Energy Supply**	**8.41**	**139.04**
1. 一次能源生产量	Indigenous Production		
2. 回收能	Recovery of Energy		
3. 外省(区、市)调入量	Moving In from Other Provinces	8.40	138.83
4. 进口量	Import		
5. 我轮、机在外国加油量	Chinese Airplanes & Ships in Refueling Abroad		
6. 本省(区、市)调出量(-)	Sending Out to Other Provinces (-)		
7. 出口量(-)	Export(-)		
8. 外轮、机在我国加油量(-)	Foreign Airplanes & Ships in Refueling in China		
9. 库存增(-)、减(+)量	Stock Change	0.01	0.21
二. 加工转换投入(-)产出(+)量	**Input(-) & Output(+) of Transformation**		
1. 火力发电	Thermal Power		
2. 供 热	Heating Supply		
3. 洗 选 煤	Coal Washing		
4. 炼焦	Coking		
5. 炼油	Petroleum Refineries		
6. 制气	Gas Works		
#焦炭再投入量(-)	Coke Input(-)		
7. 煤制品加工	Briquettes		
三. 损 失 量	**Loss**		
四. 终端消费量	**Total Final Consumption**	**8.41**	**139.04**
1. 农、林、牧、渔、水利业	Farming, Forestry, Animal Husbandry, Fishery & Water Conservancy	0.05	5.90
2. 工业	Industry	0.78	12.26
#用作原料、材料	Non-Energy Use		
3. 建 筑 业	Construction		5.66
4. 交通运输、仓储和邮政业	Transport, Storage and Post	6.22	82.37
5. 批发、零售业和住宿、餐饮业	Wholesale, Retail Trade and Hotel, Restaurants	0.38	4.85
6. 生活消费	Residential Consumption	0.50	
城镇	Urban		
乡村	Rural	0.50	
7. 其他	Other	0.48	28.00
五. 平衡差额	**Statistical Difference**		
六. 消费量合计	**Sum of Consumption**	**8.41**	**139.04**

220

燃料油 （万吨） Fuel Oil （10^4 tn）	液化石油气 （万吨） PLG （10^4 tn）	炼厂干气 （万吨） Refinery Gas （10^4 tn）	天然气 （亿立方米） Natural Gas （10^8 cu. m）	其他石油制品 （万吨） Other Petroleum Products （10^4 tn）	其他焦化产品 （万吨） Other Coking Products （10^4 tn）	热力 （百亿千焦） Heat （10^{10} kJ）	电力 （亿千瓦时） Electricity （10^8 kW·h）	其他能源 （万吨标煤） Other Energy （10^4 tce）
10.39	**12.06**		**5.44**				**−15.10**	
							141.75	
10.65	12.06		5.44					
							−156.85	
−0.26								
						523.54	569.57	
							569.57	
						523.54		
						2.80	32.05	
10.39	12.06		5.44			520.74	522.42	
							17.52	
10.39			5.03			515.83	391.72	
							10.26	
							17.18	
	4.72						14.56	
	6.53	0.41				4.91	59.66	
	6.53	0.41				4.91	38.87	
							20.79	
	0.81						11.52	
10.39	**12.06**		**5.44**			**523.54**	**554.47**	

6-25 云南能源平衡表(实物量)-2005

项 目 Item		煤合计 (万吨) Coal Total (10^4 tn)	原煤 (万吨) Raw Coal (10^4 tn)
一.可供本地区消费的能源量	**Total Primary Energy Supply**	**6681.53**	**6550.89**
1.一次能源生产量	Indigenous Production	6462.14	6462.14
2.回收能	Recovery of Energy		
3.外省(区、市)调入量	Moving In from Other Provinces	832.33	509.35
4.进口量	Import		
5.我轮、机在外国加油量	Chinese Airplanes & Ships in Refueling Abroad		
6.本省(区、市)调出量(-)	Sending Out to Other Provinces(-)	-585.09	-405.73
7.出口量(-)	Export(-)		
8.外轮、机在我国加油量(-)	Foreign Airplanes & Ships in Refueling in China		
9.库存增(-)、减(+)量	Stock Change	-27.85	-14.87
二.加工转换投入(-)产出(+)量	**Input(-) & Output(+) of Transformation**	**-4053.53**	**-4136.45**
1.火力发电	Thermal Power	-2009.58	-1975.55
2.供热	Heating Supply	-39.91	-39.91
3.洗选煤	Coal Washing	-293.18	-1020.80
4.炼焦	Coking	-1624.50	-1074.50
5.炼油	Petroleum Refineries		
6.制气	Gas Works	-86.42	-15.27
#焦炭再投入量(-)	Coke Input(-)		
7.煤制品加工	Briquettes	0.06	-10.42
三.损失量	**Loss**		
四.终端消费量	**Total Final Consumption**	**2628.00**	**2414.43**
1.农、林、牧、渔、水利业	Farming, Forestry, Animal Husbandry, Fishery & Water Conservancy	196.71	196.71
2.工业	Industry	1928.46	1782.89
#用作原料、材料	Non-Energy Use		197.26
3.建筑业	Construction	25.96	25.28
4.交通运输、仓储和邮政业	Transport, Storage and Post	28.20	27.73
5.批发、零售业和住宿、餐饮业	Wholesale, Retail Trade and Hotel, Restaurants	28.67	28.67
6.生活消费	Residential Consumption	387.53	320.68
城镇	Urban	70.82	45.31
乡村	Rural	316.71	275.37
7.其他	Other	32.47	32.47
五.平衡差额	**Statistical Difference**		**0.01**
六.消费量合计	**Sum of Consumption**	**6681.53**	**6550.88**

ENERGY BALANCE OF YUNNAN – 2005 (PHYSICAL QUANTITY)

洗精煤 （万吨） Cleaned Coal （10^4 tn）	其他洗煤 （万吨） Other Washed Coal （10^4 tn）	型煤 （万吨） Briquettes （10^4 tn）	焦炭 （万吨） Coke （10^4 tn）	焦炉煤气 （亿立方米） Coke Oven Gas （10^8 cu. m）	其他煤气 （亿立方米） Other Gas （10^8 cu. m）	油品合计 （万吨） Petroleum Products Total （10^4 tn）	原油 （万吨） Crude Oil （10^4 tn）	汽油 （万吨） Gasoline （10^4 tn）
138.79	**−7.96**	**−0.19**	**9.66**			**457.88**	**0.07**	**122.91**
						0.09	0.09	
						0.01		
303.16	19.82		131.88			472.83		126.89
						0.31		
−169.33	−10.03		−85.01			−12.73		−0.24
						−0.31		
4.96	−17.75	−0.19	−37.21			−2.32	−0.02	−3.74
−67.57	**140.01**	**10.48**	**1129.30**	**7.92**	**48.40**	**−1.81**		
−0.15	−33.88		−8.05	−0.79	−15.96	−1.81		
550.80	176.82							
−547.07	−2.93		1213.72					
−71.15				8.71	64.36			
			−76.37					
		10.48						
					5.88			
71.22	**132.06**	**10.29**	**1138.94**	**8.05**	**42.52**	**456.10**	**0.07**	**122.95**
			0.41			20.11		6.33
71.22	70.59	3.76	1133.84	6.03	42.14	34.42	0.07	5.28
0.59	1.95		69.87			1.19		
	0.68		1.57			17.86		4.05
	0.47		0.61			337.99		89.03
			0.34			7.48		2.95
	60.32	6.53	0.50	2.02	0.38	26.18		10.28
	22.67	2.84	0.25	2.02	0.38	15.12		8.41
	37.65	3.69	0.25			11.06		1.87
			1.67			12.06		5.03
	−0.01		0.02	−0.13		−0.03		−0.04
689.59	**168.87**	**10.29**	**1223.36**	**8.84**	**64.36**	**457.91**	**0.07**	**122.95**

项 目	Item	煤油（万吨）Kerosene（10^4 tn）	柴油（万吨）Diesel Oil（10^4 tn）
一. 可供本地区消费的能源量	**Total Primary Energy Supply**	**28.71**	**283.90**
1. 一次能源生产量	Indigenous Production		
2. 回收能	Recovery of Energy		
3. 外省（区、市）调入量	Moving In from Other Provinces	28.65	294.40
4. 进口量	Import		
5. 我轮、机在外国加油量	Chinese Airplanes & Ships in Refueling Abroad	0.31	
6. 本省（区、市）调出量（-）	Sending Out to Other Provinces（-）	-0.02	-12.47
7. 出口量（-）	Export（-）		
8. 外轮、机在我国加油量（-）	Foreign Airplanes & Ships in Refueling in China	-0.31	
9. 库存增（-）、减（+）量	Stock Change	0.08	1.97
二. 加工转换投入（-）产出（+）量	**Input（-）& Output（+）of Transformation**		**-1.81**
1. 火力发电	Thermal Power		-1.81
2. 供 热	Heating Supply		
3. 洗 选 煤	Coal Washing		
4. 炼焦	Coking		
5. 炼油	Petroleum Refineries		
6. 制气	Gas Works		
#焦炭再投入量（-）	Coke Input（-）		
7. 煤制品加工	Briquettes		
三. 损 失 量	**Loss**		
四. 终端消费量	**Total Final Consumption**	**28.71**	**282.09**
1. 农、林、牧、渔、水利业	Farming, Forestry, Animal Husbandry, Fishery & Water Conservancy	0.43	13.35
2. 工业	Industry	0.57	20.89
#用作原料、材料	Non-Energy Use		
3. 建 筑 业	Construction	0.28	13.53
4. 交通运输、仓储和邮政业	Transport, Storage and Post	26.82	219.58
5. 批发、零售业和住宿、餐饮业	Wholesale, Retail Trade and Hotel, Restaurants	0.01	1.35
6. 生活消费	Residential Consumption	0.03	7.05
城镇	Urban	0.03	2.17
乡村	Rural		4.88
7. 其他	Other	0.57	6.34
五. 平衡差额	**Statistical Difference**		
六. 消费量合计	**Sum of Consumption**	**28.71**	**283.90**

燃料油（万吨）Fuel Oil (10^4 tn)	液化石油气（万吨）PLG (10^4 tn)	炼厂干气（万吨）Refinery Gas (10^4 tn)	天然气（亿立方米）Natural Gas (10^8 cu. m)	其他石油制品（万吨）Other Petroleum Products (10^4 tn)	其他焦化产品（万吨）Other Coking Products (10^4 tn)	热力（百亿千焦）Heat (10^{10} kJ)	电力（亿千瓦时）Electricity (10^8 kW · h)	其他能源（万吨标煤）Other Energy (10^4 tce)
3.91	**12.28**	**0.01**	**6.12**	**6.09**	**−0.26**		**282.23**	**236.09**
			0.22				349.19	236.05
		0.01						
3.91	12.71		5.90	6.27			1.31	
							−65.00	
							−3.27	
	−0.43			−0.18	−0.26			0.04
					17.78	**496.68**	**275.01**	**−59.72**
							275.01	−59.72
						496.68		
					17.78			
							51.57	
3.91	**12.28**		**6.12**	**6.09**	**17.62**	**497.32**	**505.68**	**176.37**
							8.79	64.58
3.91	0.29		5.92	3.41	16.42	497.32	374.37	70.15
0.05			5.77	1.14	3.47			4.42
					0.60		8.99	
					2.56		15.20	
	3.05			0.12	0.60		3.50	
	8.82		0.20				73.48	41.64
	4.51		0.20				53.19	0.73
	4.31						20.29	40.91
	0.12						21.35	
		0.01			−0.10	−0.64	−0.01	
3.91	**12.28**		**6.12**	**6.09**	**17.62**	**497.32**	**557.25**	**236.09**

6-26 陕西能源平衡表(实物量)-2005

项 目	Item	煤合计 (万吨) Coal Total (10^4 tn)	原煤 (万吨) Raw Coal (10^4 tn)
一.可供本地区消费的能源量	**Total Primary Energy Supply**	**10727.93**	**10183.35**
1.一次能源生产量	Indigenous Production	15246.00	15246.00
2.回收能	Recovery of Energy		
3.外省(区、市)调入量	Moving In from Other Provinces	980.00	260.00
4.进口量	Import		
5.我轮、机在外国加油量	Chinese Airplanes & Ships in Refueling Abroad		
6.本省(区、市)调出量(-)	Sending Out to Other Provinces(-)	-5390.00	-5200.00
7.出口量(-)	Export(-)		
8.外轮、机在我国加油量(-)	Foreign Airplanes & Ships in Refueling in China		
9.库存增(-)、减(+)量	Stock Change	-108.07	-122.65
二.加工转换投入(-)产出(+)量	**Input(-) & Output(+) of Transformation**	**-3264.55**	**-3123.29**
1.火力发电	Thermal Power	-2513.06	-2461.28
2.供 热	Heating Supply	-148.05	-148.05
3.洗 选 煤	Coal Washing	-112.42	-387.66
4.炼焦	Coking	-486.87	-122.15
5.炼油	Petroleum Refineries		
6.制气	Gas Works	-4.15	-4.15
#焦炭再投入量(-)	Coke Input(-)		
7.煤制品加工	Briquettes		
三.损 失 量	**Loss**		
四.终端消费量	**Total Final Consumption**	**2784.57**	**2395.68**
1.农、林、牧、渔、水利业	Farming, Forestry, Animal Husbandry, Fishery & Water Conservancy	8.50	8.50
2.工业	Industry	2011.03	1622.14
#用作原料、材料	Non-Energy Use	1043.63	914.63
3.建 筑 业	Construction	54.30	54.30
4.交通运输、仓储和邮政业	Transport, Storage and Post	19.65	19.65
5.批发、零售业和住宿、餐饮业	Wholesale, Retail Trade and Hotel, Restaurants	278.30	278.30
6.生活消费	Residential Consumption	400.29	400.29
城镇	Urban	380.29	380.29
乡村	Rural	20.00	20.00
7.其他	Other	12.50	12.50
五.平衡差额	**Statistical Difference**	**4678.81**	**4664.38**
六.消费量合计	**Sum of Consumption**	**6049.12**	**5518.97**

ENERGY BALANCE OF SHAANXI – 2005 (PHYSICAL QUANTITY)

洗精煤 （万吨） Cleaned Coal (10^4 tn)	其他洗煤 （万吨） Other Washed Coal (10^4 tn)	型煤 （万吨） Briquettes (10^4 tn)	焦炭 （万吨） Coke (10^4 tn)	焦炉煤气 （亿立方米） Coke Oven Gas (10^8 cu. m)	其他煤气 （亿立方米） Other Gas (10^8 cu. m)	油品合计 （万吨） Petroleum Products Total (10^4 tn)	原油 （万吨） Crude Oil (10^4 tn)	汽油 （万吨） Gasoline (10^4 tn)
541.21		3.37	−91.17	1.85	3.10	581.51	1243.95	−212.41
						1778.16	1778.16	
720.00				1.85	3.10	37.25		14.69
						0.02		0.02
−190.00			−119.30			−1312.03	−570.30	−230.00
			−3.94					
11.21		3.37	32.07			78.11	36.09	2.88
−153.14	11.88		350.27	0.37	1.11	−88.14	−1234.60	407.07
−16.22	−35.56		−3.23			−2.27		−0.02
						−0.04		
227.77	47.47							
−364.69	−0.03		353.50	0.37				
						−85.83	−1234.60	407.09
				1.11				
380.00	5.52	3.37	247.87	2.22	4.21	493.48	7.82	196.68
						28.56		3.56
380.00	5.52	3.37	247.87	2.22	0.42	60.42	7.82	7.89
126.00		3.00	22.15			9.14	7.82	0.06
						8.60		
						251.07		98.00
						45.00		35.00
					3.79	86.40		40.00
					3.79	59.50		31.80
						26.90		8.20
						13.43		12.23
8.07	6.36		11.23			−0.11	1.53	−2.02
760.91	41.11	3.37	251.10	2.22	4.21	581.62	1242.42	196.70

项 目	Item	煤油 （万吨） Kerosene （10^4 tn）	柴油 （万吨） Diesel Oil （10^4 tn）
一．可供本地区消费的能源量	**Total Primary Energy Supply**	**28.67**	**−349.67**
1．一次能源生产量	Indigenous Production		
2．回收能	Recovery of Energy		
3．外省（区、市）调入量	Moving In from Other Provinces	0.09	22.47
4．进口量	Import		
5．我轮、机在外国加油量	Chinese Airplanes & Ships in Refueling Abroad		
6．本省（区、市）调出量（−）	Sending Out to Other Provinces（−）		−380.00
7．出口量（−）	Export（−）		
8．外轮、机在我国加油量（−）	Foreign Airplanes & Ships in Refueling in China		
9．库存增（−）、减（+）量	Stock Change	28.58	7.86
二．加工转换投入（−）产出（+）量	**Input（−）& Output（+）of Transformation**	**6.14**	**527.75**
1．火力发电	Thermal Power		−2.24
2．供 热	Heating Supply		−0.04
3．洗 选 煤	Coal Washing		
4．炼焦	Coking		
5．炼油	Petroleum Refineries	6.14	530.03
6．制气	Gas Works		
#焦炭再投入量（−）	Coke Input（−）		
7．煤制品加工	Briquettes		
三．损 失 量	**Loss**		
四．终端消费量	**Total Final Consumption**	**34.81**	**178.00**
1．农、林、牧、渔、水利业	Farming, Forestry, Animal Husbandry, Fishery & Water Conservancy		25.00
2．工业	Industry	1.75	27.89
#用作原料、材料	Non-Energy Use	0.01	1.24
3．建 筑 业	Construction		8.60
4．交通运输、仓储和邮政业	Transport, Storage and Post	33.06	102.61
5．批发、零售业和住宿、餐饮业	Wholesale, Retail Trade and Hotel, Restaurants		10.00
6．生活消费	Residential Consumption		2.70
城镇	Urban		1.80
乡村	Rural		0.90
7．其他	Other		1.20
五．平衡差额	**Statistical Difference**		**0.08**
六．消费量合计	**Sum of Consumption**	**34.81**	**180.28**

燃料油 （万吨） Fuel Oil （10^4 tn）	液化石油气 （万吨） PLG （10^4 tn）	炼厂干气 （万吨） Refinery Gas （10^4 tn）	天然气 （亿立方米） Natural Gas （10^8 cu. m）	其他石油制品 （万吨） Other Petroleum Products （10^4 tn）	其他焦化产品 （万吨） Other Coking Products （10^4 tn）	热力 （百亿千焦） Heat （10^{10} kJ）	电力 （亿千瓦时） Electricity （10^8 kW·h）	其他能源 （万吨标煤） Other Energy （10^4 tce）
−81.18	−28.00		18.76	−19.85			−15.07	8.44
			80.59				46.68	
							21.25	
−83.88	−28.00		−61.83	−19.85			−83.00	
2.70								8.44
85.60	72.20	11.03	−2.04	36.67	5.85	2462.98	508.72	−8.24
−0.01			−1.46				508.72	−8.24
			−0.58			2462.98		
					5.85			
85.61	72.20	11.03		36.67				
							21.59	
4.42	43.90	11.03	16.72	16.82	7.36	2160.87	494.41	0.20
							31.10	
2.62	0.20	11.03	9.59	1.22	7.36	879.05	331.84	0.20
0.01			2.73		2.84			0.20
							4.66	
1.80			1.30	15.60		32.82	26.16	
			4.04			74.00	14.33	
	43.70		1.79			1107.00	55.35	
	25.90		1.79			1107.00	36.80	
	17.80						18.54	
						68.00	30.97	
	0.30				−1.51	302.11	−22.35	
4.43	43.90	11.03	18.76	16.82	7.36	2160.87	516.00	8.44

6-27 甘肃能源平衡表(实物量)-2005

项 目	Item	煤合计 (万吨) Coal Total (10^4 tn)	原煤 (万吨) Raw Coal (10^4 tn)
一.可供本地区消费的能源量	**Total Primary Energy Supply**	**3750.67**	**3424.50**
1.一次能源生产量	Indigenous Production	3620.00	3620.00
2.回收能	Recovery of Energy		
3.外省(区、市)调入量	Moving In from Other Provinces	1107.45	783.81
4.进口量	Import		
5.我轮、机在外国加油量	Chinese Airplanes & Ships in Refueling Abroad		
6.本省(区、市)调出量(-)	Sending Out to Other Provinces(-)	-964.00	-964.00
7.出口量(-)	Export(-)	-16.32	-16.32
8.外轮、机在我国加油量(-)	Foreign Airplanes & Ships in Refueling in China		
9.库存增(-)、减(+)量	Stock Change	3.54	1.01
二.加工转换投入(-)产出(+)量	**Input(-) & Output(+) of Transformation**	**-2269.87**	**-2026.65**
1.火力发电	Thermal Power	-1597.00	-1597.00
2.供 热	Heating Supply	-293.70	-293.70
3.洗 选 煤	Coal Washing	-13.50	-59.22
4.炼焦	Coking	-372.30	-38.24
5.炼油	Petroleum Refineries		
6.制气	Gas Works	-8.46	-0.03
#焦炭再投入量(-)	Coke Input(-)		
7.煤制品加工	Briquettes	15.09	-38.46
三.损 失 量	**Loss**		
四.终端消费量	**Total Final Consumption**	**1480.80**	**1397.85**
1.农、林、牧、渔、水利业	Farming, Forestry, Animal Husbandry, Fishery & Water Conservancy	35.01	35.01
2.工业	Industry	945.14	914.69
#用作原料、材料	Non-Energy Use		59.55
3.建 筑 业	Construction	23.80	23.80
4.交通运输、仓储和邮政业	Transport, Storage and Post	48.07	48.07
5.批发、零售业和住宿、餐饮业	Wholesale, Retail Trade and Hotel, Restaurants	21.08	21.08
6.生活消费	Residential Consumption	395.70	343.20
城镇	Urban	74.10	53.10
乡村	Rural	321.60	290.10
7.其他	Other	12.00	12.00
五.平衡差额	**Statistical Difference**		
六.消费量合计	**Sum of Consumption**	**3750.67**	**3424.50**

ENERGY BALANCE OF GANSU – 2005 (PHYSICAL QUANTITY)

洗精煤 (万吨) Cleaned Coal (10⁴ tn)	其他洗煤 (万吨) Other Washed Coal (10⁴ tn)	型煤 (万吨) Briquettes (10⁴ tn)	焦炭 (万吨) Coke (10⁴ tn)	焦炉煤气 (亿立方米) Coke Oven Gas (10⁸ cu. m)	其他煤气 (亿立方米) Other Gas (10⁸ cu. m)	油品合计 (万吨) Petroleum Products Total (10⁴ tn)	原油 (万吨) Crude Oil (10⁴ tn)	汽油 (万吨) Gasoline (10⁴ tn)
326.00	0.17		156.02		2.55	472.79	1229.26	−142.40
						304.55	304.55	
					2.55	9.12		
323.47	0.17		162.36			1032.19	949.73	35.77
						−847.36		−177.34
2.53			−6.34			−25.71	−25.02	−0.83
−296.77		53.55	268.09	7.61	3.44	−98.37	−1225.17	229.30
						−1.03		
				−1.19		−9.97		
45.72								
−334.06			268.39	8.80				
						−87.37	−1225.17	229.30
−8.43					3.44			
			−0.30					
		53.55						
						0.42	0.05	0.04
29.23	0.17	53.55	424.11	7.61	5.99	374.00	4.04	86.86
						25.41		3.20
29.23	0.17	1.05	424.11	7.24	5.97	182.68	4.04	8.41
			20.73			92.83		
						18.73		9.60
						130.86		55.97
						4.50		3.80
		52.50		0.37	0.02	5.85		0.92
		21.00		0.37	0.02	4.94		0.92
		31.50				0.91		
						5.97		4.96
371.72	0.17	53.55	424.41	8.80	5.99	472.79	1229.26	86.90

项　目	Item	煤油 （万吨） Kerosene （10⁴ tn）	柴油 （万吨） Diesel Oil （10⁴ tn）
一. 可供本地区消费的能源量	**Total Primary Energy Supply**	**-45.00**	**-420.69**
1. 一次能源生产量	Indigenous Production		
2. 回收能	Recovery of Energy		
3. 外省（区、市）调入量	Moving In from Other Provinces	4.17	42.52
4. 进口量	Import		
5. 我轮、机在外国加油量	Chinese Airplanes & Ships in Refueling Abroad		
6. 本省（区、市）调出量（-）	Sending Out to Other Provinces（-）	-49.65	-461.51
7. 出口量（-）	Export（-）		
8. 外轮、机在我国加油量（-）	Foreign Airplanes & Ships in Refueling in China		
9. 库存增（-）、减（+）量	Stock Change	0.48	-1.70
二. 加工转换投入（-）产出（+）量	**Input（-）& Output（+）of Transformation**	**49.61**	**535.20**
1. 火力发电	Thermal Power		-0.46
2. 供热	Heating Supply		-0.01
3. 洗选煤	Coal Washing		
4. 炼焦	Coking		
5. 炼油	Petroleum Refineries	49.61	535.67
6. 制气	Gas Works		
#焦炭再投入量（-）	Coke Input（-）		
7. 煤制品加工	Briquettes		
三. 损失量	**Loss**		**0.30**
四. 终端消费量	**Total Final Consumption**	**4.61**	**114.21**
1. 农、林、牧、渔、水利业	Farming, Forestry, Animal Husbandry, Fishery & Water Conservancy	0.01	22.20
2. 工业	Industry	0.31	11.80
#用作原料、材料	Non-Energy Use	0.06	
3. 建筑业	Construction	0.03	8.65
4. 交通运输、仓储和邮政业	Transport, Storage and Post	4.22	69.90
5. 批发、零售业和住宿、餐饮业	Wholesale, Retail Trade and Hotel, Restaurants	0.01	0.68
6. 生活消费	Residential Consumption	0.01	
城镇	Urban		
乡村	Rural	0.01	
7. 其他	Other	0.02	0.98
五. 平衡差额	**Statistical Difference**		
六. 消费量合计	**Sum of Consumption**	**4.61**	**114.98**

Continued

燃料油 （万吨） Fuel Oil $(10^4\,\text{tn})$	液化石油气 （万吨） PLG $(10^4\,\text{tn})$	炼厂干气 （万吨） Refinery Gas $(10^4\,\text{tn})$	天然气 （亿立方米） Natural Gas $(10^8\,\text{cu. m})$	其他石油制品 （万吨） Other Petroleum Products $(10^4\,\text{tn})$	其他焦化产品 （万吨） Other Coking Products $(10^4\,\text{tn})$	热力 （百亿千焦） Heat $(10^{10}\,\text{kJ})$	电力 （亿千瓦时） Electricity $(10^8\,\text{kW}\cdot\text{h})$	其他能源 （万吨标煤） Other Energy $(10^4\,\text{tce})$
−23.54	−25.90	9.12	9.62	−108.06	23.60		149.78	118.94
			1.60				162.08	
		9.12						114.53
			8.02		23.55		51.14	4.41
−24.43	−25.91			−108.52			−63.44	
0.89	0.01			0.46	0.05			
36.12	32.34	33.77	−0.66	210.46	8.70	5634.94	339.70	−1.30
−0.57			−0.52				339.70	−1.30
−2.88		−7.08	−0.14			5634.94		
					8.70			
39.57	32.34	40.85		210.46				
0.01	0.02						21.52	
12.57	6.42	42.89	8.96	102.40	32.30	5634.94	467.96	117.64
							51.70	3.11
12.56	0.75	42.89	7.34	101.92	32.30	3953.93	342.94	114.53
			4.73	92.77	1.44			
			0.01	0.45			4.08	
0.01	0.75		0.35	0.01			15.34	
			0.68	0.01			6.72	
		4.92	0.40			1681.01	32.46	
		4.02	0.40			1681.01	21.31	
		0.90					11.15	
			0.18	0.01			14.72	
16.03	6.44	49.97	9.62	102.40	32.30	5634.94	489.48	118.94

6-28 青海能源平衡表(实物量) - 2005

项 目	Item	煤合计 (万吨) Coal Total (10^4 tn)	原煤 (万吨) Raw Coal (10^4 tn)
一.可供本地区消费的能源量	**Total Primary Energy Supply**	**687.40**	**680.99**
1.一次能源生产量	Indigenous Production	554.85	554.85
2.回收能	Recovery of Energy		
3.外省(区、市)调入量	Moving In from Other Provinces	126.30	120.50
4.进口量	Import		
5.我轮、机在外国加油量	Chinese Airplanes & Ships in Refueling Abroad		
6.本省(区、市)调出量(-)	Sending Out to Other Provinces(-)		
7.出口量(-)	Export(-)		
8.外轮、机在我国加油量(-)	Foreign Airplanes & Ships in Refueling in China		
9.库存增(-)、减(+)量	Stock Change	6.25	5.64
二.加工转换投入(-)产出(+)量	**Input(-) & Output(+) of Transformation**	**-378.93**	**-379.50**
1.火力发电	Thermal Power	-345.10	-345.10
2.供 热	Heating Supply	-15.53	-15.53
3.洗 选 煤	Coal Washing	-0.53	-1.53
4.炼焦	Coking	-2.11	-1.68
5.炼油	Petroleum Refineries		
6.制气	Gas Works	-15.66	-15.66
#焦炭再投入量(-)	Coke Input(-)		
7.煤制品加工	Briquettes		
三.损 失 量	**Loss**	**1.98**	**1.98**
四.终端消费量	**Total Final Consumption**	**318.06**	**311.07**
1.农、林、牧、渔、水利业	Farming, Forestry, Animal Husbandry, Fishery & Water Conservancy	3.85	3.85
2.工业	Industry	209.99	203.00
#用作原料、材料	Non-Energy Use		
3.建 筑 业	Construction	2.37	2.37
4.交通运输、仓储和邮政业	Transport, Storage and Post	12.42	12.42
5.批发、零售业和住宿、餐饮业	Wholesale, Retail Trade and Hotel, Restaurants	2.35	2.35
6.生活消费	Residential Consumption	78.50	78.50
城镇	Urban	18.50	18.50
乡村	Rural	60.00	60.00
7.其他	Other	8.58	8.58
五.平衡差额	**Statistical Difference**	**-11.57**	**-11.56**
六.消费量合计	**Sum of Consumption**	**698.97**	**692.55**

ENERGY BALANCE OF QINGHAI – 2005 (PHYSICAL QUANTITY)

洗精煤 (万吨) Cleaned Coal (10^4 tn)	其他洗煤 (万吨) Other Washed Coal (10^4 tn)	型煤 (万吨) Briquettes (10^4 tn)	焦炭 (万吨) Coke (10^4 tn)	焦炉煤气 (亿立方米) Coke Oven Gas (10^8 cu. m)	其他煤气 (亿立方米) Other Gas (10^8 cu. m)	油品合计 (万吨) Petroleum Products Total (10^4 tn)	原油 (万吨) Crude Oil (10^4 tn)	汽油 (万吨) Gasoline (10^4 tn)
6.09		**0.32**	41.08			**71.53**	**94.99**	**−11.76**
						221.49	221.49	
5.50		0.30	33.30			18.81		
						14.50		14.50
						−190.93	−126.50	−25.50
0.59		0.02	7.78			7.66		−0.76
0.57		0.77			4.44	−10.19	−95.02	29.40
						−0.06		
1.00								
−0.43			0.77					
						−10.13	−95.02	29.40
					4.44			
		0.01				1.70		0.34
6.66		0.33	41.83		4.44	59.36		17.16
						2.97		1.22
6.66		0.33	41.83			27.63		1.28
			5.20			0.23		
						5.51		3.05
						14.32		5.71
						2.79		2.00
					4.44			
					4.44			
						6.14		3.90
	−0.01	0.01				0.28	−0.03	0.14
7.09		0.33	41.84		4.44	71.25	95.02	17.50

项　目	Item	煤油 （万吨） Kerosene （10⁴ tn）	柴油 （万吨） Diesel Oil （10⁴ tn）
一.可供本地区消费的能源量	**Total Primary Energy Supply**		−19.23
1.一次能源生产量	Indigenous Production		
2.回收能	Recovery of Energy		
3.外省（区、市）调入量	Moving In from Other Provinces		3.16
4.进口量	Import		
5.我轮、机在外国加油量	Chinese Airplanes & Ships in Refueling Abroad		
6.本省（区、市）调出量（−）	Sending Out to Other Provinces（−）		−30.00
7.出口量（−）	Export（−）		
8.外轮、机在我国加油量（−）	Foreign Airplanes & Ships in Refueling in China		
9.库存增（−）、减（+）量	Stock Change		7.61
二.加工转换投入（−）产出（+）量	**Input（−）& Output（+）of Transformation**		44.25
1.火力发电	Thermal Power		−0.06
2.供 热	Heating Supply		
3.洗 选 煤	Coal Washing		
4.炼焦	Coking		
5.炼油	Petroleum Refineries		44.31
6.制气	Gas Works		
#焦炭再投入量（−）	Coke Input（−）		
7.煤制品加工	Briquettes		
三.损 失 量	**Loss**		1.36
四.终端消费量	**Total Final Consumption**		23.43
1.农、林、牧、渔、水利业	Farming, Forestry, Animal Husbandry, Fishery & Water Conservancy		1.75
2.工业	Industry		7.58
#用作原料、材料	Non-Energy Use		0.23
3.建 筑 业	Construction		2.46
4.交通运输、仓储和邮政业	Transport, Storage and Post		8.61
5.批发、零售业和住宿、餐饮业	Wholesale, Retail Trade and Hotel, Restaurants		0.79
6.生活消费	Residential Consumption		
城镇	Urban		
乡村	Rural		
7.其他	Other		2.24
五.平衡差额	**Statistical Difference**		0.23
六.消费量合计	**Sum of Consumption**		24.85

燃料油 （万吨） Fuel Oil （10^4 tn）	液化石油气 （万吨） PLG （10^4 tn）	炼厂干气 （万吨） Refinery Gas （10^4 tn）	天然气 （亿立方米） Natural Gas （10^8 cu. m）	其他石油制品 （万吨） Other Petroleum Products （10^4 tn）	其他焦化产品 （万吨） Other Coking Products （10^4 tn）	热力 （百亿千焦） Heat （10^{10} kJ）	电力 （亿千瓦时） Electricity （10^8 kW · h）	其他能源 （万吨标煤） Other Energy （10^4 tce）
−2.19	−5.93		22.26	15.65	0.45		152.52	2.73
			22.26				157.52	
				15.65	0.45		15.50	2.73
−3.00	−5.93						−20.50	
0.81								
2.11	5.93	3.14	−2.07			124.68	55.63	
			−1.33				55.63	
			−0.74			124.68		
2.11	5.93	3.14						
			0.20			0.05	1.25	
0.02		3.14	19.84	15.61	0.47	124.50	206.55	2.73
							0.71	
0.02		3.14	3.72	15.61	0.47		187.78	2.73
			0.33		0.47			
							1.53	
			0.47				0.92	
			2.10				2.25	
			8.35			124.50	9.05	
			8.35			124.50	7.39	
							1.66	
			5.20				4.31	
−0.10			0.15	0.04	−0.02	0.13	0.35	
0.02		3.14	22.11	15.61	0.47	124.55	207.80	2.73

6-29 宁夏能源平衡表（实物量）-2005

项　　目	Item	煤合计 （万吨） Coal Total (10^4 tn)	原煤 （万吨） Raw Coal (10^4 tn)
一.可供本地区消费的能源量	**Total Primary Energy Supply**	**3248.93**	**3850.48**
1.一次能源生产量	Indigenous Production	2659.77	2659.77
2.回收能	Recovery of Energy		
3.外省(区、市)调入量	Moving In from Other Provinces	1788.14	1788.14
4.进口量	Import		
5.我轮、机在外国加油量	Chinese Airplanes & Ships in Refueling Abroad		
6.本省(区、市)调出量(－)	Sending Out to Other Provinces(－)	－1231.63	－607.40
7.出口量(－)	Export(－)	－27.70	
8.外轮、机在我国加油量(－)	Foreign Airplanes & Ships in Refueling in China		
9.库存增(－)、减(＋)量	Stock Change	60.35	9.97
二.加工转换投入(－)产出(＋)量	**Input(－) & Output(＋) of Transformation**	**－2109.67**	**－2840.31**
1.火力发电	Thermal Power	－1569.65	－1467.70
2.供　热	Heating Supply	－48.76	－43.89
3.洗　选　煤	Coal Washing	－281.61	－1243.07
4.炼焦	Coking	－198.87	－72.19
5.炼油	Petroleum Refineries		
6.制气	Gas Works	－9.00	－9.00
#焦炭再投入量(－)	Coke Input(－)		
7.煤制品加工	Briquettes	－1.78	－4.46
三.损　失　量	**Loss**	**6.00**	**6.00**
四.终端消费量	**Total Final Consumption**	**1133.26**	**1004.17**
1.农、林、牧、渔、水利业	Farming, Forestry, Animal Husbandry, Fishery & Water Conservancy	4.50	4.50
2.工业	Industry	960.00	830.91
#用作原料、材料	Non-Energy Use	242.06	180.00
3.建　筑　业	Construction	4.92	4.92
4.交通运输、仓储和邮政业	Transport, Storage and Post	12.13	12.13
5.批发、零售业和住宿、餐饮业	Wholesale, Retail Trade and Hotel, Restaurants	20.50	20.50
6.生活消费	Residential Consumption	120.21	120.21
城镇	Urban	27.94	27.94
乡村	Rural	92.27	92.27
7.其他	Other	11.00	11.00
五.平衡差额	**Statistical Difference**		
六.消费量合计	**Sum of Consumption**	**3248.93**	**3850.48**

ENERGY BALANCE OF NINGXIA −2005 (PHYSICAL QUANTITY)

洗精煤 （万吨） Cleaned Coal （10⁴ tn）	其他洗煤 （万吨） Other Washed Coal （10⁴ tn）	型煤 （万吨） Briquettes （10⁴ tn）	焦炭 （万吨） Coke （10⁴ tn）	焦炉煤气 （亿立方米） Coke Oven Gas （10⁸ cu. m）	其他煤气 （亿立方米） Other Gas （10⁸ cu. m）	油品合计 （万吨） Petroleum Products Total （10⁴ tn）	原油 （万吨） Crude Oil （10⁴ tn）	汽油 （万吨） Gasoline （10⁴ tn）
−595.39	−6.16		−40.60			145.49	167.05	−26.78
						4.00	4.00	
						181.49	161.85	
−607.77	−16.46		−42.57			−56.38		−33.62
−27.70			−4.30					
40.08	10.30		6.27			16.38	1.20	6.84
692.97	34.99	2.68	110.32	0.81		−19.48	−162.35	51.67
	−101.95							
−4.87								
824.52	136.94							
−126.68			110.32					
						−19.48	−162.35	51.67
				0.81				
		2.68						
97.58	28.83	2.68	69.72	0.81		126.01	4.70	24.89
						4.56		1.55
97.58	28.83	2.68	69.72	0.81		38.62	4.70	0.91
60.87	1.19		46.93					
						4.52		2.50
						64.50		11.87
						3.73		2.88
						5.40		2.18
						3.96		0.88
						1.44		1.30
						4.68		3.00
229.13	130.78	2.68	69.72	0.81		145.49	167.05	24.89

项 目 Item	煤油 （万吨） Kerosene （10^4 tn）	柴油 （万吨） Diesel Oil （10^4 tn）
一.可供本地区消费的能源量　Total Primary Energy Supply	**2.01**	**−7.85**
1.一次能源生产量　Indigenous Production		
2.回收能　Recovery of Energy		
3.外省（区、市）调入量　Moving In from Other Provinces	1.98	
4.进口量　Import		
5.我轮、机在外国加油量　Chinese Airplanes & Ships in Refueling Abroad		
6.本省（区、市）调出量（−）　Sending Out to Other Provinces（−）		−16.59
7.出口量（−）　Export（−）		
8.外轮、机在我国加油量（−）　Foreign Airplanes & Ships in Refueling in China		
9.库存增（−）、减（+）量　Stock Change	0.03	8.74
二.加工转换投入（−）产出（+）量　**Input（−）& Output（+）of Transformation**		**70.89**
1.火力发电　Thermal Power		
2.供 热　Heating Supply		
3.洗 选 煤　Coal Washing		
4.炼焦　Coking		
5.炼油　Petroleum Refineries		70.89
6.制气　Gas Works		
#焦炭再投入量（−）　Coke Input（−）		
7.煤制品加工　Briquettes		
三.损 失 量　**Loss**		
四.终端消费量　**Total Final Consumption**	**2.01**	**63.04**
1.农、林、牧、渔、水利业　Farming, Forestry, Animal Husbandry, Fishery & Water Conservancy		3.01
2.工业　Industry	0.03	4.83
#用作原料、材料　Non-Energy Use		
3.建 筑 业　Construction		2.02
4.交通运输、仓储和邮政业　Transport, Storage and Post	1.98	50.65
5.批发、零售业和住宿、餐饮业　Wholesale, Retail Trade and Hotel, Restaurants		0.85
6.生活消费　Residential Consumption		
城镇　Urban		
乡村　Rural		
7.其他　Other		1.68
五.平衡差额　**Statistical Difference**		
六.消费量合计　**Sum of Consumption**	**2.01**	**63.04**

Continued

燃料油 （万吨） Fuel Oil （10⁴tn）	液化石油气 （万吨） PLG （10⁴tn）	炼厂干气 （万吨） Refinery Gas （10⁴tn）	天然气 （亿立方米） Natural Gas （10⁸ cu. m）	其他石油制品 （万吨） Other Petroleum Products （10⁴tn）	其他焦化产品 （万吨） Other Coking Products （10⁴tn）	热力 （百亿千焦） Heat （10¹⁰ kJ）	电力 （亿千瓦时） Electricity （10⁸ kW·h）	其他能源 （万吨标煤） Other Energy （10⁴tce）
−0.86	−5.74		6.63	17.66	0.54		11.82	
			0.04				17.67	
			6.59	17.66	0.54		22.64	
	−6.17						−28.49	
−0.86	0.43							
2.66	8.96	5.18		3.51		802.59	295.19	6.29
							295.19	
						802.59		
2.66	8.96	5.18		3.51				6.29
							17.17	
1.80	3.22	5.18	6.63	21.17	0.54	802.59	289.84	6.29
							9.15	
1.80		5.18	6.14	21.17	0.54	410.92	260.10	6.29
			5.70					0.64
							1.08	
			0.15			10.00	4.52	
						25.00	2.24	
	3.22		0.21			275.00	9.95	
	3.08		0.21			275.00	7.02	
	0.14						2.93	
			0.13			81.67	2.80	
1.80	3.22	5.18	6.63	21.17	0.54	802.59	307.01	6.29

6 – 30 新疆能源平衡表(实物量) – 2005

项　目	Item	煤合计 (万吨) Coal Total (10^4 tn)	原煤 (万吨) Raw Coal (10^4 tn)
一. 可供本地区消费的能源量	**Total Primary Energy Supply**	**3714.27**	**3702.72**
1. 一次能源生产量	Indigenous Production	3942.29	3942.29
2. 回收能	Recovery of Energy		
3. 外省(区、市)调入量	Moving In from Other Provinces	32.35	
4. 进口量	Import	0.03	0.03
5. 我轮、机在外国加油量	Chinese Airplanes & Ships in Refueling Abroad		
6. 本省(区、市)调出量(−)	Sending Out to Other Provinces(−)	−323.47	−323.47
7. 出口量(−)	Export(−)	−0.01	−0.01
8. 外轮、机在我国加油量(−)	Foreign Airplanes & Ships in Refueling in China		
9. 库存增(−)、减(+)量	Stock Change	63.08	83.88
二. 加工转换投入(−)产出(+)量	**Input(−) & Output(+) of Transformation**	**−2369.40**	**−2362.02**
1. 火力发电	Thermal Power	−1368.29	−1358.09
2. 供　热	Heating Supply	−590.96	−572.01
3. 洗 选 煤	Coal Washing	−25.70	−212.59
4. 炼焦	Coking	−384.44	−200.00
5. 炼油	Petroleum Refineries		
6. 制气	Gas Works		
#焦炭再投入量(−)	Coke Input(−)		
7. 煤制品加工	Briquettes	−0.01	−19.33
三. 损 失 量	**Loss**		
四. 终端消费量	**Total Final Consumption**	**1484.79**	**1480.62**
1. 农、林、牧、渔、水利业	Farming, Forestry, Animal Husbandry, Fishery & Water Conservancy	103.30	103.30
2. 工业	Industry	805.59	801.42
#用作原料、材料	Non-Energy Use		
3. 建 筑 业	Construction	17.00	17.00
4. 交通运输、仓储和邮政业	Transport, Storage and Post	56.60	56.60
5. 批发、零售业和住宿、餐饮业	Wholesale, Retail Trade and Hotel, Restaurants	31.78	31.78
6. 生活消费	Residential Consumption	430.79	430.79
城镇	Urban	96.00	96.00
乡村	Rural	334.79	334.79
7. 其他	Other	39.73	39.73
五. 平衡差额	**Statistical Difference**	**−139.92**	**−139.92**
六. 消费量合计	**Sum of Consumption**	**3854.19**	**3842.64**

ENERGY BALANCE OF XINJIANG -2005 (PHYSICAL QUANTITY)

洗精煤 （万吨） Cleaned Coal （10⁴ tn）	其他洗煤 （万吨） Other Washed Coal （10⁴ tn）	型煤 （万吨） Briquettes （10⁴ tn）	焦炭 （万吨） Coke （10⁴ tn）	焦炉煤气 （亿立方米） Coke Oven Gas （10⁸ cu. m）	其他煤气 （亿立方米） Other Gas （10⁸ cu. m）	油品合计 （万吨） Petroleum Products Total （10⁴ tn）	原油 （万吨） Crude Oil （10⁴ tn）	汽油 （万吨） Gasoline （10⁴ tn）
30.55	−19.00		−112.69		42.41	1021.31	1628.77	−133.78
						2408.32	2408.32	
					42.41			
32.35			10.07			1.50		
						91.54	75.72	
						13.35		
			−63.33			−1525.72	−862.67	−143.42
			−54.86			−3.20		−0.28
						−1.98		
−1.80	−19.00		−4.57			37.50	7.40	9.92
−28.54	20.79	0.37	236.39	5.82		−47.37	−1500.59	240.50
	−10.20					−8.65	−0.18	−0.01
		−18.95				−1.04		
155.90	30.99							
−184.44			236.39	5.82				
						−37.68	−1500.41	240.51
		19.32						
						30.59	30.59	
2.01	1.79	0.37	179.18	5.82	42.41	936.88	97.59	106.72
						70.68		7.10
2.01	1.79	0.37	178.87	5.66	42.41	534.24	97.59	7.88
						15.36		3.36
			0.31			210.00		53.00
						31.91		8.40
				0.16		28.49		8.98
				0.16		27.09		8.98
						1.40		
						46.20		18.00
			−55.48			6.47		
186.45	11.99	19.32	179.18	5.82	42.41	1014.84	1628.77	106.73

项　目	Item	煤油 （万吨） Kerosene （10^4 tn）	柴油 （万吨） Diesel Oil （10^4 tn）
一.可供本地区消费的能源量	**Total Primary Energy Supply**	−5.54	−389.11
1.一次能源生产量	Indigenous Production		
2.回收能	Recovery of Energy		
3.外省（区、市）调入量	Moving In from Other Provinces		
4.进口量	Import		
5.我轮、机在外国加油量	Chinese Airplanes & Ships in Refueling Abroad	13.35	
6.本省（区、市）调出量（−）	Sending Out to Other Provinces（−）	−16.58	−401.87
7.出口量（−）	Export（−）		−0.24
8.外轮、机在我国加油量（−）	Foreign Airplanes & Ships in Refueling in China	−1.98	
9.库存增（−）、减（+）量	Stock Change	−0.33	13.00
二.加工转换投入（−）产出（+）量	**Input（−）& Output（+）of Transformation**	32.14	696.72
1.火力发电	Thermal Power		−0.50
2.供　热	Heating Supply		−0.01
3.洗 选 煤	Coal Washing		
4.炼焦	Coking		
5.炼油	Petroleum Refineries	32.14	697.23
6.制气	Gas Works		
#焦炭再投入量（−）	Coke Input（−）		
7.煤制品加工	Briquettes		
三.损 失 量	**Loss**		
四.终端消费量	**Total Final Consumption**	26.12	302.23
1.农、林、牧、渔、水利业	Farming, Forestry, Animal Husbandry, Fishery & Water Conservancy	0.50	59.44
2.工业	Industry	0.03	48.13
#用作原料、材料	Non-Energy Use		
3.建 筑 业	Construction		12.00
4.交通运输、仓储和邮政业	Transport, Storage and Post	23.44	131.56
5.批发、零售业和住宿、餐饮业	Wholesale, Retail Trade and Hotel , Restaurants	0.50	20.00
6.生活消费	Residential Consumption	0.55	6.00
城镇	Urban	0.15	5.00
乡村	Rural	0.40	1.00
7.其他	Other	1.10	25.10
五.平衡差额	**Statistical Difference**	0.48	5.38
六.消费量合计	**Sum of Consumption**	26.12	302.74

Continued

燃料油 （万吨） Fuel Oil (10⁴tn)	液化石油气 （万吨） PLG (10⁴tn)	炼厂干气 （万吨） Refinery Gas (10⁴tn)	天然气 （亿立方米） Natural Gas (10⁸ cu. m)	其他石油制品 （万吨） Other Petroleum Products (10⁴ tn)	其他焦化产品 （万吨） Other Coking Products (10⁴ tn)	热力 （百亿千焦） Heat (10¹⁰ kJ)	电力 （亿千瓦时） Electricity (10⁸ kW · h)	其他能源 （万吨标煤） Other Energy (10⁴tce)
14.86	**−14.72**		**56.46**	**−79.17**			**48.81**	
			106.64				48.81	
1.50								
15.82								
−6.08	−15.10		−50.18	−80.00				
−2.68								
6.30	0.38			0.83				
2.72	**51.58**	**40.75**	**−21.03**	**388.81**	**4.91**	**14190.72**	**261.33**	
−0.25		−7.71	−7.81				261.33	
−0.21		−0.82	−13.22			14190.72		
					4.91			
3.18	51.58	49.28		388.81				
			1.13			142.00	27.72	
16.86	**36.97**	**40.75**	**33.88**	**309.64**	**3.68**	**14048.80**	**282.42**	
				3.64			28.72	
16.86	17.00	40.75	27.96	306.00	3.68	9306.30	193.95	
						20.00	1.44	
	2.00		2.92			23.00	4.74	
	3.01		1.00			50.50	11.09	
	12.96		1.50			4619.00	27.10	
	12.96		1.50			4619.00	20.19	
							6.91	
	2.00		0.50			30.00	15.38	
0.72	**−0.11**		**0.42**		**1.23**		**−0.08**	
17.32	**36.97**	**49.28**	**56.04**	**309.64**	**3.68**	**14190.80**	**310.14**	

七、香港、澳门特别行政区能源数据

Chapter 7　Energy Data for Hong Kong and Macao Special Administrative Region

7-1 香港主要能源及相关指标
MAJOR ENERGY AND RELATED INDICATORS OF HONG KONG

项 目 Item	1990	1995	2000	2001	2002	2003	2004
一次能源供应总量（百万吨标准油） Total Primary Energy Supply（Mtoe）	10.66	13.77	15.45	16.28	16.38	16.51	17.12
净进口量（百万吨标准油） Net Imports（Mtoe）	11.93	15.69	18.91	19.99	21.22	21.70	24.90
油净进口量（百万吨标准油） Net Oil Imports（Mtoe）	6.58	9.55	12.4	12.26	13.24	13.26	15.95
油可供量（百万吨标准油） Oil Supply（Mtoe）	5.27	7.57	8.89	8.51	8.35	8.02	8.12
电消费量（十亿千瓦小时） Electricity Consumption（Twh）	23.83	29.86	36.3	37.26	38.09	38.46	39.23
能源最终消费量（百万吨标准油） Total Final Consumption of Energy（Mtoe）	7.12	9.9	11.92	11.6	11.5	11.2	11.4
年中人口数（万 人） Mid－year Population（10^4 persons）	570.0	615.6	666.5	672.5	678.7	680.3	690.0
国内生产总值（10 亿美元,2000 年价） GDP（109 US $,2000 price）	106.24	139.35	165.36	166.13	169.26	174.71	174.71
人均国内生产总值（美元,2000 年价） Per Capita GDP（US $,2000 price）	18639	22636	24810	24703	24939	25681	25320
人均能源供应量（吨标准油/人） TPES/Population（toe per capita）	1.87	2.24	2.32	2.42	2.41	2.43	2.48
人均电力消费量（千瓦小时/人） Per Capita Electricity Consumption（kwh/capita）	4178	4850	5446	5541	5612	5653	5686

资料来源：IEA《非 OECD 国家能源平衡》

Source：*IEA,Energy Balances of NON－OECD Countries.*

7-2 香港电力和煤气消费量
CONSUMPTION OF ELECTRICITY AND GAS OF HONG KONG

年 份 Year	电力（太焦耳）Electricity（terajoule）				煤气（太焦耳）Gas（terajoule）			
	住 宅 Residential	商 业 Commercial	工 业 Industrial	总 计 Total	住 宅 Residential	商 业 Commercial	工 业 Industrial	总 计 Total
1990	19037	41830	24934	85801	7596	6877	583	15056
1995	27063	60191	20222	107477	11408	9586	978	21972
2000	32234	80672	17769	130675	13866	11209	982	26057
2001	32799	84580	16759	134139	14493	11060	1011	26564
2002	33394	87606	16112	137112	14794	10860	987	26641
2003	34365	89218	14851	138435	15446	10542	1015	27002
2004	34134	91638	15430	141201	15237	10945	955	27137
2005	35811	93341	14636	144171	15444	10919	898	27261

资料来源：《香港能源统计》

Source：*Hong Kong Energy Statistics.*

7-3　香港油产品进口留用量
HONG KONG RETAINED IMPORTS OF OIL PRODUCTS

年　份 Year	航空汽油与煤油 （千公升） Aviation Gasoline and Kerosene（kilolitre）	车用汽油 （千公升） Motor Gasoline （kilolitre）		轻质柴油、重质 柴油与石脑油（千公升） Gas Oil, Diesel Oil and Naphtha（kilolitre）	燃料油 （千公升） Fuel Oil （kilolitre）	液化石油气和天然气 （公吨） LPG、Natural Gas （tonne）
1990	2303262	390577		2690712	1347198	169224
		含铅 Leaded Petrol	不含铅 Unleaded Petrol			
1995	3318386	171456	323351	4691324	1561524	147544
2000	4011029		486087	7802247	2140655	2363434
2001	4198740		524588	6920460	2394450	2459050
2002	4315798		473441	6810838	2973785	2420756
2003	3986920		458985	7094270	3216278	1689413
2004	4937314		458802	6989635	4626483	2299778
2005	5424882		454254	4992498	4975866	2310535

7-4　香港煤产品进口留用量
HONG KONG RETAINED IMPORTS OF COAL PRODUCTS

单位:公吨　　（tonne）

年　份 Year	蒸馏煤与其他煤产品 Steam Coal and Other Coal	木炭 Wood Charcoal	无烟煤 Anthracite	焦煤与半焦煤 Coke and Semi-coke
1990	8928614	16252	2053	1404
1995	9108994	13920		1063
2000	6057802	6050	1310	
2001	8033097	-4764	540	
2002	8717699	8142	201	
2003	10675881	8313	677	
2004	10691194	8052	396	-59
2005				

7-5　香港电力生产、消费及进出口
HONG KONG ELECTRICITY PRODUCTION, CONSUMPTION, IMPORTS AND EXPORTS

单位：太焦耳　　　　　　　　　　　　　　　　　　　　　　　　　　　　　　　　　　　　（terajoule）

年　份 Year	本地发电厂产电 Electricity Generated at Local Plant	由大陆进口 Imports to Mainland of China	系统损耗 System Loss	出口往大路 Exports of Mainland of China	由电表量度的本地电力耗用 Local Electricity Consumption as Measured at Meter Point
1990	104256		11985	6470	85801
1995	100496	27164	14843	5340	107477
2000	112783	36732	14587	4253	130675
2001	116745	37278	14192	5692	134139
2002	123522	36655	15235	7830	137112
2003	127822	37428	15988	10827	138435
2004	133663	35413	16763	11112	141201
2005	138414			16192	

资料来源:《香港能源统计》

Source: *Hong Kong Energy Statistics.*

7-6 澳门主要能源及相关指标
MAJOR ENERGY RELATED INDICATORS OF MACAO

项 目 Item	1990	1995	2000	2002	2003	2004
净进口量（太焦耳） Net Imports（10^{12} joules）	13955	17487	22742	25322	26340	32087
可供电量（百万千瓦小时） Electricity Supply（Gwh）		1335.1	1657.4	1795.7	1879.5	2028.4
电力消费量（百万千瓦小时） Electricity Consumption（Gwh）		1265.4	1570.1	1688.0	1771.5	1903.1
能源消费量（太焦耳） Energy Consumption（10^{12} joules）	8953	12120	12823	13435	13544	14709
年中人口数（万 人） Mid－year Population（10^4 persons）	33.50	40.93	43.1	43.9	44.5	45.7
国内生产总值（万澳门元,现价） GDP（104 MOP, Current Market Prices）	2617500	5227400	4897200	5481900	6356600	8310300
人均国内生产总值（澳门元,现价） Per Capita GDP（MOP,Current Market Prices）	78134	127716	113624	124872	142845	181845
人均能源消费量（百万焦耳） Per Capita Energy Consumption（10^8 joules）	26725	29612	29752	30604	30436	32186
人均电力消费量（千瓦小时／人） Per Capita Electricity Consumption（kwh／capita）		3092	3643	3845	3981	4164

7-7 澳门能源平衡表
MACAO ENERGY BALANCE TABLE

单位：太焦耳 （terajoules）

项 目	Item	1990	1995	2000	2002	2003	2004	2005
进口	Import							
总计	Total Energy	13975	17499	22742	25322	26340	32087	33605
#轻柴油	#Gas Oil and Diesel	3564	3257	3467	4243	5518	8529	7114
#重油	#Fuel Oil	8274	10325	11949	12962	12277	12618	14108
#电力	#Electricity	327	650	701	697	647	545	1227
#汽油	#Gasoline	752	1128	1340	1402	1450	1564	1758
出口	Export							
总计	Total Energy	20	12					
#电力	#Electricity	9	11					
#液化石油气	#LPG		1					
库存变化	Change in Stocks	252	−43	−487	−348	−187	728	−68
内部总消费	Gross Internal Consumption	13704	17670	19795	21601	21966	24529	26050
能源转化	Energy Transformation	−4461	−5124	−6458	−7533	−7728	−9075	−8558
电厂自耗和输电损失	Distribution and Transmission Loss	149	240	304	388	389	451	462
总消费量	Final Consumption	8953	12120	12823	13435	13544	14709	16748

资料来源：《澳门统计年鉴》

Source：*Macao Statistical Yearbook.*

八、附录
Chapter 8　Appendix

附录 1　台湾省能源数据
Appendix I Energy Data for Taiwan Province

附录 1-1　台湾省主要能源及相关指标
MAJOR ENERGY RELATED INDICATORS OF TAIWAN

项　目　Item	1990	1995	2000	2001	2002	2003	2004
能源生产量（百万吨标准油） Energy Production（Mtoe）	10.81	10.94	11.49	10.77	11.62	12.53	12.76
净进口量（百万吨标准油） Net Imports（Mtoe）	41.78	59.27	80.83	82.25	84.20	87.83	96.05
一次能源需求总量（百万吨标准油） Total Primary Energy Supply（Mtoe）	48.26	65.29	83.01	88.95	93.58	98.55	104.24
油净进口量（百万吨标准油） Net Oil Imports（Mtoe）	28.92	37.49	45.85	44.71	43.79	45.35	48.31
油可供量（百万吨标准油） Oil Supply（Mtoe）	26.00	34.47	37.32	41.46	42.45	43.47	45.87
电消费量（十亿千瓦小时） Electricity Consumption（tW·h）	85.12	128.20	184.74	188.95	198.52	201.14	210.20
一次能源消费总量（百万吨标准油） Total Primary Energy Consumption（Mtoe）	48.35	65.18	90.64	94.83	100.31	103.42	104.24
年中人口数（百万人） Mid-year Population（106 persons）	20.40	21.30	22.10	22.30	22.40	22.60	22.70
国内生产总值（10 亿美元,2000 年价） GDP（109 US $,2000 price）	157.12	221.60	292.90	286.46	296.77	306.56	323.70
人均国内生产总值（美元,2000 年价） Per Capita GDP（US $,2000 price）	7702.0	10403.8	13253.4	12845.7	13248.7	13564.6	14259.9
人均能源消费量（吨标准油/人） Per Capita Energy Consumption（toe/capita）	2.37	3.06	4.10	4.25	4.48	4.58	4.59
人均电力消费量（千瓦小时/人） Per Capita Electricity Consumption（kW·h/capita）	4173	6019	8359	8473	8863	8900	9260

资料来源：IEA《非 OECD 国家能源统计和平衡》。

Source：*IEA*, *Energy Statistics and Balances of NON - OECD Countries.*

附录 1-2　台湾省分行业电力消费量
TAIWAN ELECTRICITY CONSUMPTION BY SECTOR

单位：百万千瓦小时　　　　　　　　　　　　　　　　　　　　　　　　　　（100 million kW·h）

项　目　Item		1990	1995	2000	2001	2002	2003	2004
总计	Total	51841	68931	94768	94807	100435	106043	113293
农、林、牧、渔业	Farming,Forestry,Animal Husbandry,Fishery	1611	2042	2262	2229	2326	2416	2511
采掘业	Mining and Quarrying	171	209	319	293	367	431	444
制造业	Manufacturing	40698	50792	67378	66127	69696	73691	79267
建筑业	Construction	265	564	490	543	530	544	556
水电煤气卫生服务业	Electricity , Gas and Water Services	804	1037	1832	2065	2253	2415	2461
商业	Commerce	1987	3650	5809	6045	6407	6701	7034
运输仓储及通信业	Transportation, Storage, Post. &Tele. Services	1081	1571	2893	3014	3240	3326	3440
服务业	Services	4252	6763	10578	11165	12013	12718	13494
其他不能归类行业	Others	973	2299	3208	3324	3601	3801	4086

资料来源：中国台湾省编辑的《统计年鉴》。

Source：*Statistical Yearbook*, Taiwan Province of China.

附录 1-3 台湾省能源供给总量及构成
TAIWAN ENERGY SUPPLY AND COMPOSITION

年 份 Year	供给量总计 （千公升油当量） Total Supply （10^3 kl oil equivalent）	占供给总量的比重（%）As Percentage of Total Supply（%）				
		煤炭 Coal	石油 Petroleum	天然气 Natural Gas	水力发电 Hydropower	核能发电 Nuclear Power
1990	58198	23.45	55.17	3.86	3.49	14.03
1995	79620	26.20	54.30	5.80	2.80	11.00
2000	105043	31.30	50.90	6.80	2.10	9.10
2001	108521	32.30	50.40	7.10	2.10	8.12
2002	113230	33.10	49.25	7.00	1.40	8.68
2003	121220	32.56	50.76	7.30	1.41	7.97
2004	134060	32.50	51.00	8.00	1.20	7.30

附录 1-4 台湾省能源消费总量及分部门消费构成
TAIWAN ENERGY CONSUMPTION AND COMPOSITION BY SECTOR

年 份 Year	消费总计 （千公升油当量） Total Energy Consumption （10^3 kl oil equivalent）	占消费总量比重（%）As Percentage of Total Energy Consumption（%）						
		工业 Industry	运输 Transportation	农业 Agriculture	住宅 Residence	商业 Commerce	其他 Other	非能源消费 Non-energy Use
1990	52007	58.6	15.5	2.8	11.4	3.8	6.4	1.5
1995	68964	55.2	17.8	2.2	12.0	5.0	6.0	1.9
2000	90636	55.2	16.3	1.6	12.4	5.8	6.1	2.6
2001	94828	57.1	15.4	1.6	12.1	5.8	6.2	1.8
2002	100282	57.7	15.3	1.5	11.8	5.7	6.0	2.0
2003	103420	57.3	14.8	1.6	11.8	5.8	6.7	2.1
2004	104375	56.5	15.4	1.7	11.8	6.0	6.8	1.8

附录 1-5 台湾省电力生产量和消费量
TAIWAN ElECTRICITY PRODUCTION AND CONSUMPTION

单位：百万千瓦小时   （100 million kW·h）

年 份 Year	发电量 Electricity Generation				耗电量 Electricity Consumption			损失 Loss
	总计 Total	水力发电 Hydropower	火力发电 Thermal Power	核能发电 Nuclear Power	总计 Total	电力用电 Own Consumption	住户及 商业用电 Residence and Commerce	
1990	82350	8166	42629	31554	74345	51841	22504	5355
1995	117859	8858	75071	33931	105368	68931	36437	6848
2000	156511	8843	110672	36996	142413	94768	47644	8735
2001	158058	9138	114822	34094	143624	94807	48816	8610
2002	165901	6358	121526	38009	151193	100435	50758	9417
2003	173810	6863	129566	37371	159380	106043	53337	8751
2004	181245	6524	136770	37939	167478	113293	54185	8937

资料来源：中国台湾省编辑的《统计年鉴》。

Source：*Statistical Yearbook*，Taiwan Province of China.

附录 2　有关国家和地区能源数据
Appendix Ⅱ　Energy Data for Related Countries or Areas

附录 2 – 1　年中人口数
MID-YEAR POPULATION

单位：百万人　　　　　　　　　　　　　　　　　　　　　　　　　　　　　　　　　　（million）

国家和地区 Country or Area	2001	2002	2003	2004	人口比重% Percent of World
世界总计　World	**6120.9**	**6202.2**	**6277.9**	**6352.4**	**100.00**
OECD 合计　OECD Total	**1139.0**	**1148.0**	**1155.9**	**1163.9**	**18.32**
美国　United States	285.4	288.2	291.1	294.0	4.63
日本　Japan	127.3	127.4	127.6	127.7	2.01
墨西哥　Mexico	100.1	101.4	102.7	104.0	1.64
德国　Germany	82.3	82.5	82.5	82.5	1.30
法国　France	60.9	61.4	61.8	62.2	0.98
英国　United Kingdom	59.0	59.3	59.6	59.8	0.94
意大利　Italy	57.9	58.1	58.1	58.1	0.92
韩国　Korea	47.3	47.6	47.9	48.1	0.76
西班牙　Spain	40.3	41.3	42.0	42.7	0.67
加拿大　Canada	31.0	31.4	31.7	32.0	0.50
澳大利亚　Australia	19.5	19.8	20.0	20.2	0.32
荷兰　Netherlands	16.0	16.2	16.2	16.3	0.26
比利时　Belgium	10.3	10.3	10.4	10.4	0.16
瑞典　Sweden	8.9	8.9	9.0	9.0	0.14
瑞士　Switzerland	7.3	7.3	7.4	7.5	0.12
非 OECD 合计　NON-OECD Total	**4981.8**	**5054.3**	**5121.9**	**5188.5**	**81.68**
中国（大陆）　People's Rep. Of China	1271.9	1280.4	1288.4	1296.2	20.40
印度　India	1032.5	1048.6	1064.4	1079.7	17.00
印度尼西亚　Indonesia	209.0	211.8	214.7	217.6	3.43
巴西　Brazil	172.4	178.9	181.4	183.9	2.89
俄罗斯　Russia	144.8	145.3	144.6	143.9	2.27
埃及　Egypt	65.2	69.9	71.3	72.6	1.14
伊朗　Islamic Republic of Iran	64.5	65.5	66.4	67.0	1.05
泰国　Thailand	61.2	62.6	63.1	63.7	1.00
南非　South Africa	44.8	45.3	45.8	45.5	0.72
阿根廷　Argentina	36.2	37.6	38.0	38.4	0.60
委内瑞拉　Venezuela	24.8	25.2	25.7	26.1	0.41
沙特阿拉伯　Saudi Arabia	21.3	22.7	23.3	24.0	0.38
中国,台北　Chinese Taipei	22.4	22.5	22.6	22.7	0.36
中国,香港　Hong Kong, China	6.7	6.8	6.8	6.9	0.11
以色列　Israel	6.4	6.6	6.7	6.8	0.11

资料来源：国际能源机构统计年鉴-OECD 成员国能源平衡表，非 OECD 成员国能源平衡表。

Source：IEA STATISTICS-ENERGY BALANCES OF OECD COUNTRIES(2003 – 2004)，ENERGY BALANCES OF NON – OECD COUNTRIES(2003 – 2004)

附录 2-2 国内生产总值汇率算法(2000 年价格)
GROSS DOMESTIC PRODUCTS USING EXCHANGE RATES(US $ 2000)

单位:10 亿美元 （ billion US $ ）

国家和地区	Country or Area	2001	2002	2003	2004	GDP 比重% Percent of World
世界总计	**World**	**31919.7**	**32768.6**	**33641.4**	**35024.8**	**100.00**
OECD 合计	**OECD Total**	**25846.5**	**26299.6**	**26806.5**	**27698.0**	**79.08**
美国	United States	9838.9	9997.6	10269.3	10703.9	30.56
日本	Japan	4766.7	4741.3	4803.2	4932.5	14.08
德国	Germany	1886.0	1924.9	1921.3	1952.7	5.58
英国	United Kingdom	1471.3	1504.4	1542.2	1591.1	4.54
法国	France	1335.8	1371.8	1382.8	1414.8	4.04
意大利	Italy	1093.7	1097.9	1100.7	1114.2	3.18
加拿大	Canada	727.2	749.4	764.3	786.7	2.25
西班牙	Spain	578.2	617.4	635.9	655.6	1.87
墨西哥	Mexico	580.7	585.1	593.5	619.4	1.77
韩国	Korea	531.3	568.3	585.9	613.1	1.75
澳大利亚	Australia	402.6	428.2	445.2	455.6	1.30
荷兰	Netherlands	375.9	392.3	391.8	398.5	1.14
瑞典	Sweden	242.1	249.5	253.7	263.2	0.75
瑞士	Switzerland	248.6	249.4	248.7	253.8	0.72
比利时	Belgium	230.1	237.9	240.1	246.3	0.70
非 OECD 合计	**NON-OECD Total**	**6073.2**	**6469.0**	**6834.9**	**7326.8**	**20.92**
中国(大陆)	People's Rep. Of China	1161.8	1416.1	1557.7	1715.0	4.90
巴西	Brazil	609.6	621.4	624.8	655.4	1.87
印度	India	480.9	500.6	543.7	581.2	1.66
俄罗斯	Russia	272.9	285.9	306.9	328.8	0.94
中国,台北	Chinese Taipei	286.5	296.8	306.6	323.7	0.92
阿根廷	Argentina	271.7	242.1	263.5	287.1	0.82
沙特阿拉伯	Saudi Arabia	189.8	189.7	204.2	214.9	0.61
印度尼西亚	Indonesia	155.4	178.8	187.6	197.2	0.56
中国,香港	Hong Kong, China	166.1	169.3	174.7	188.9	0.54
南非	South Africa	131.5	141.4	145.3	150.7	0.43
泰国	Thailand	125.4	132.1	141.3	150.1	0.43
伊朗	Islamic Republic of Iran	99.5	113.9	119.6	126.3	0.36
以色列	Israel	115.1	113.8	115.8	120.9	0.35
委内瑞拉	Venezuela	124.6	110.4	101.9	120.1	0.34
埃及	Egypt	102.9	109.2	112.6	117.3	0.33

资料来源:国际能源机构统计年鉴-OECD 成员国能源平衡表, 非 OECD 成员国能源平衡表。

Source:IEA STATISTICS-ENERGY BALANCES OF OECD COUNTRIES(2003－2004), ENERGY BALANCES OF NON－OECD COUNTRIES(2003－2004)

附录2-3 国内生产总值购买力平价算法(2000年价格)
GROSS DOMESTIC PRODUCTS USING PURCHASING
POWER PARITIES(US $ 2000)

单位:10亿美元 　　　　　　　　　　　　　　　　　　　　　　　　　　　　　　　　(billion US $)

国家和地区	Country or Area	2001	2002	2003	2004	GDP 比重% Percent of World
世界总计	**World**	**46191.0**	**47938.7**	**49790.1**	**52289.2**	**100.00**
OECD 合计	**OECD Total**	**27409.7**	**27962.2**	**28522.2**	**29492.8**	**56.40**
美国	United States	9838.9	9997.6	10269.3	10703.9	20.47
日本	Japan	3323.0	3298.7	3341.7	3431.6	6.56
德国	Germany	2088.2	2129.3	2125.4	2160.0	4.13
法国	France	1584.6	1627.3	1640.3	1678.3	3.21
英国	United Kingdom	1537.6	1570.8	1610.3	1661.3	3.18
意大利	Italy	1469.6	1473.9	1477.7	1495.8	2.86
西班牙	Spain	845.7	902.2	929.2	958.0	1.83
墨西哥	Mexico	897.3	905.8	916.8	956.8	1.83
加拿大	Canada	875.5	902.0	920.0	946.9	1.81
韩国	Korea	798.1	853.4	879.8	920.7	1.76
澳大利亚	Australia	828.6	562.3	584.7	598.3	1.14
荷兰	Netherlands	441.3	460.2	459.6	467.5	0.89
比利时	Belgium	271.0	280.3	282.8	290.1	0.55
瑞典	Sweden	241.3	248.5	252.7	262.2	0.50
瑞士	Switzerland	221.3	221.8	221.2	225.8	0.43
非 OECD 合计	**NON-OECD Total**	**18781.3**	**19976.5**	**21267.9**	**22796.40**	**43.60**
中国(大陆)	People's Rep. Of China	5201.0	5849.0	6398.3	7023.7	13.43
印度	India	2572.6	2677.6	2907.3	3115.3	5.96
巴西	Brazil	1279.7	1322.7	1325.3	1385.1	2.65
俄罗斯	Russia	1094.2	1134.7	1232.5	1309.1	2.50
印度尼西亚	Indonesia	629.5	651.1	689.7	721.6	1.38
中国,台北	Chinese Taipei	428.5	443.9	458.5	484.2	0.93
泰国	Thailand	394.4	415.4	445.7	473.6	0.91
阿根廷	Argentina	421.0	401.9	431.9	469.0	0.90
南非	South Africa	429.9	445.8	460.8	468.1	0.90
伊朗	Islamic Republic of Iran	370.3	417.5	438.7	463.4	0.89
沙特阿拉伯	Saudi Arabia	263.0	268.2	290.6	304.3	0.58
埃及	Egypt	233.7	260.7	269.4	281.1	0.54
中国,香港	Hong Kong, China	170.0	176.8	179.5	195.0	0.37
以色列	Israel	126.7	144.3	146.1	152.3	0.29
委内瑞拉	Venezuela	141.8	132.6	122.3	145.1	0.28

资料来源:国际能源机构统计年鉴-OECD 成员国能源平衡表, 非 OECD 成员国能源平衡表。

Source: IEA STATISTICS-ENERGY BALANCES OF OECD COUNTRIES(2003 – 2004), ENERGY BALANCES OF NON – OECD COUNTRIES(2003 – 2004)

附录2-4 能源生产总量
TOTAL ENERGY PRODUCTION

单位：百万吨标准油   (million toe)

国家和地区	Country or Area	2001	2002	2003	2004	产量比重% Percent of World
世界总计	**World**	**10212.17**	**10294.74**	**10680.88**	**11213.42**	**100.00**
OECD 合计	**OECD Total**	**3868.90**	**3847.23**	**3806.28**	**3859.54**	**34.42**
美国	United States	1698.45	1666.04	1632.67	1641.04	14.63
加拿大	Canada	376.84	383.87	385.83	397.49	3.54
澳大利亚	Australia	248.88	254.49	253.75	261.77	2.33
墨西哥	Mexico	230.09	230.02	242.51	253.86	2.26
英国	United Kingdom	262.03	257.95	246.40	225.21	2.01
法国	France	132.83	134.65	136.22	137.42	1.23
德国	Germany	134.70	134.51	134.57	136.01	1.21
日本	Japan	105.45	98.67	85.46	96.76	0.86
荷兰	Netherlands	60.95	60.52	58.48	67.90	0.61
韩国	Korea	34.20	34.92	37.89	38.03	0.34
瑞典	Sweden	34.29	32.36	31.64	35.09	0.31
西班牙	Spain	33.47	31.79	32.95	32.53	0.29
意大利	Italy	26.92	27.45	27.59	30.14	0.27
比利时	Belgium	13.08	13.25	13.45	13.53	0.12
瑞士	Switzerland	12.36	11.58	11.79	11.82	0.11
非 OECD 合计	**NON-OECD Total**	**6343.28**	**6447.51**	**6874.60**	**7353.88**	**65.58**
中国(大陆)	People's Rep. Of China	1138.65	1202.31	1352.69	1536.78	13.70
俄罗斯	Russia	996.15	1034.48	1106.89	1158.46	10.33
沙特阿拉伯	Saudi Arabia	485.13	474.78	532.54	556.21	4.96
印度	India	430.68	436.45	450.57	466.87	4.16
伊朗	Islamic Republic of Iran	243.19	236.39	265.40	277.99	2.48
印度尼西亚	Indonesia	235.18	244.64	252.28	258.01	2.30
委内瑞拉	Venezuela	216.93	203.55	178.84	196.06	1.75
巴西	Brazil	146.88	162.01	171.67	176.31	1.57
南非	South Africa	144.40	143.07	152.92	156.00	1.39
阿根廷	Argentina	84.53	81.38	84.32	85.45	0.76
埃及	Egypt	56.74	60.88	64.43	64.66	0.58
泰国	Thailand	42.80	45.30	48.26	50.10	0.45
中国,台北	Chinese Taipei	10.77	11.62	12.53	12.76	0.11
以色列	Israel	0.69	0.72	0.75	1.71	0.02
中国,香港	Hong Kong, China	0.05	0.05	0.05	0.05	

资料来源：国际能源机构统计年鉴-OECD 成员国能源平衡表，非 OECD 成员国能源平衡表。

Source：IEA STATISTICS-ENERGY BALANCES OF OECD COUNTRIES(2003 – 2004)，ENERGY BALANCES OF NON – OECD COUNTRIES(2003 – 2004)

附录2-5 能源生产量/一次能源供应量(能源自给率)
ENERGY PRODUCTION/TPES(SELF SUFFICIENCY)

国家和地区	Country or Area	2001	2002	2003	2004
世界	**World**	**1.02**	**1.01**	**1.01**	**1.01**
OECD 合计	**OECD Total**	**0.7293**	**0.7195**	**0.7050**	**0.7007**
澳大利亚	Australia	2.2986	2.2742	2.2474	2.2610
墨西哥	Mexico	1.5150	1.4782	1.5160	1.5341
加拿大	Canada	1.5175	1.5353	1.4693	1.4774
英国	United Kingdom	1.1168	1.1288	1.0608	0.9637
荷兰	Netherlands	0.7829	0.7694	0.7226	0.8266
美国	United States	0.7520	0.7280	0.7158	0.7056
瑞典	Sweden	0.6657	0.6137	0.6119	0.6505
法国	France	0.4988	0.5060	0.5024	0.4994
瑞士	Switzerland	0.4413	0.4324	0.4389	0.4357
德国	Germany	0.3811	0.3896	0.3877	0.3908
比利时	Belgium	0.2232	0.2343	0.2272	0.2346
西班牙	Spain	0.2619	0.2415	0.2422	0.2288
日本	Japan	0.2025	0.1891	0.1656	0.1815
韩国	Korea	0.1765	0.1730	0.1837	0.1785
意大利	Italy	0.1553	0.1582	0.1522	0.1634
非 OECD 合计	**NON-OECD Total**	**1.35**	**1.32**	**1.33**	**1.32**
沙特阿拉伯	Saudi Arabia	4.07	3.78	4.09	3.96
委内瑞拉	Venezuela	3.73	3.52	3.37	3.49
伊朗	Islamic Republic of Iran	1.96	1.81	1.91	1.91
俄罗斯	Russia	1.60	1.67	1.73	1.81
印度尼西亚	Indonesia	1.55	1.52	1.53	1.48
阿根廷	Argentina	1.44	1.45	1.41	1.34
南非	South Africa	1.30	1.26	1.26	1.19
埃及	Egypt	1.16	1.16	1.19	1.14
中国(大陆)	People's Rep. Of China	1.00	0.99	0.98	0.95
巴西	Brazil	0.79	0.85	0.89	0.86
印度	India	0.82	0.82	0.82	0.82
泰国	Thailand	0.55	0.54	0.54	0.52
中国,台北	Chinese Taipei	0.12	0.12	0.13	0.12
以色列	Israel	0.03	0.04	0.04	0.08
中国,香港	Hong Kong, China				

资料来源：国际能源机构统计年鉴-OECD 成员国能源平衡表，非 OECD 成员国能源平衡表。

Source：IEA STATISTICS-ENERGY BALANCES OF OECD COUNTRIES(2003 – 2004)，ENERGY BALANCES OF NON – OECD COUNTRIES(2003 – 2004)

附录2-6 能源供应量/GDP(吨标准油/千美元2000年价格)

TPES/GDP(toe per thousand US $ 2000)

国家和地区	Country or Area	2001	2002	2003	2004
世界	World	**0.31**	**0.31**	**0.31**	**0.32**
OECD合计	OECD Total	**0.2053**	**0.2033**	**0.2014**	**0.1989**
瑞士	Switzerland	0.1127	0.1074	0.1080	0.1069
日本	Japan	0.1093	0.1100	0.1075	0.1081
英国	United Kingdom	0.1595	0.1519	0.1506	0.1469
意大利	Italy	0.1585	0.1580	0.1647	0.1656
德国	Germany	0.1874	0.1794	0.1807	0.1782
法国	France	0.1993	0.1940	0.1961	0.1945
瑞典	Sweden	0.2128	0.2114	0.2038	0.2049
荷兰	Netherlands	0.2071	0.2005	0.2066	0.2061
西班牙	Spain	0.2211	0.2132	0.2140	0.2169
美国	United States	0.2296	0.2289	0.2221	0.2173
比利时	Belgium	0.2548	0.2378	0.2456	0.2342
澳大利亚	Australia	0.2690	0.2613	0.2536	0.2541
墨西哥	Mexico	0.2615	0.2659	0.2695	0.2672
加拿大	Canada	0.3415	0.3336	0.3436	0.3420
韩国	Korea	0.3647	0.3552	0.3521	0.3475
非OECD合计	NON-OECD Total	**0.78**	**0.75**	**0.76**	**0.76**
中国,香港	Hong Kong, China	0.10	0.10	0.09	0.09
以色列	Israel	0.17	0.18	0.18	0.17
阿根廷	Argentina	0.22	0.23	0.23	0.22
巴西	Brazil	0.31	0.31	0.31	0.31
中国,台北	Chinese Taipei	0.31	0.32	0.32	0.32
委内瑞拉	Venezuela	0.47	0.52	0.52	0.47
埃及	Egypt	0.47	0.48	0.48	0.49
泰国	Thailand	0.62	0.63	0.63	0.65
沙特阿拉伯	Saudi Arabia	0.63	0.66	0.64	0.65
南非	South Africa	0.84	0.81	0.84	0.87
印度尼西亚	Indonesia	0.98	0.90	0.88	0.88
中国(大陆)	People's Rep. Of China	0.98	0.86	0.89	0.94
印度	India	1.09	1.07	1.01	0.99
伊朗	Islamic Republic of Iran	1.25	1.14	1.16	1.15
俄罗斯	Russia	2.28	2.16	2.08	1.95

资料来源:国际能源机构统计年鉴-OECD 成员国能源平衡表,非 OECD 成员国能源平衡表。

Source:IEA STATISTICS-ENERGY BALANCES OF OECD COUNTRIES(2003－2004), ENERGY BALANCES OF NON－OECD COUNTRIES(2003－2004)

附录2-7 人均能源供应量(吨标准油/人)
TPES/POPULATION(toe per capita)

国家和地区	Country or Area	2001	2002	2003	2004
世界	World	1.64	1.65	1.68	1.74
OECD 合计	OECD Total	4.6575	4.6582	4.6706	4.7322
加拿大	Canada	8.0050	7.9697	8.2944	8.4220
美国	United States	7.9151	7.9395	7.8358	7.9125
瑞典	Sweden	5.7904	5.9084	5.7725	5.9969
比利时	Belgium	5.7019	5.4754	5.7061	5.5380
澳大利亚	Australia	5.5443	5.6640	5.6500	5.7278
荷兰	Netherlands	4.8524	4.8711	4.9888	5.0481
法国	France	4.3710	4.3321	4.3874	4.4256
韩国	Korea	4.0929	4.2397	4.3114	4.4309
德国	Germany	4.2926	4.1858	4.2063	4.2186
日本	Japan	4.0915	4.0935	4.0441	4.1758
英国	United Kingdom	3.9745	3.8521	3.9002	3.9056
瑞士	Switzerland	3.8458	3.6462	3.6287	3.6260
西班牙	Spain	3.1748	3.1856	3.2391	3.3309
意大利	Italy	2.9948	2.9887	3.1222	3.1732
墨西哥	Mexico	1.5180	1.5346	1.5575	1.5911
非 OECD 合计	NON-OECD Total	0.95	0.97	1.01	1.07
沙特阿拉伯	Saudi Arabia	5.60	5.54	5.58	5.86
中国,台北	Chinese Taipei	3.97	4.16	4.36	4.59
俄罗斯	Russia	4.29	4.25	4.42	4.46
以色列	Israel	3.11	3.05	3.09	3.05
南非	South Africa	2.47	2.51	2.66	2.88
中国,香港	Hong Kong, China	2.42	2.41	2.43	2.49
伊朗	Islamic Republic of Iran	1.93	1.99	2.09	2.18
委内瑞拉	Venezuela	2.35	2.29	2.07	2.15
阿根廷	Argentina	1.62	1.49	1.57	1.66
泰国	Thailand	1.28	1.33	1.41	1.52
中国(大陆)	People's Rep. Of China	0.89	0.95	1.07	1.24
巴西	Brazil	1.08	1.07	1.07	1.11
印度尼西亚	Indonesia	0.73	0.76	0.77	0.80
埃及	Egypt	0.75	0.75	0.76	0.78
印度	India	0.51	0.51	0.52	0.53

资料来源：国际能源机构统计年鉴-OECD 成员国能源平衡表，非 OECD 成员国能源平衡表。

Source：IEA STATISTICS-ENERGY BALANCES OF OECD COUNTRIES(2003-2004)，ENERGY BALANCES OF NON-OECD COUNTRIES(2003-2004)

附录2-8 煤生产量
COAL PRODUCTION

单位:百万吨标准油 (Mtoe)

国家和地区 Country or Area		2001	2002	2003	2004	产量比重% Percent of World
世界总计	**World**	**2341.9**	**2375.3**	**2530.5**	**2750.2**	**100.00**
中国	PR of China	698.8	752.6	892.0	1053.0	38.29
美国	United States	574.1	555.1	526.1	546.6	19.87
澳大利亚	Australia	178.2	184.4	185.2	192.6	7.00
印度	India	156.2	156.8	166.3	177.9	6.47
南非	South Atrica	126.3	124.3	134.8	137.1	4.98
俄罗斯	Russia	122.1	117.8	127.3	130.1	4.73
印度尼西亚	Indonesia	56.9	63.6	70.9	81.4	2.96
波兰	Poland	71.4	71.2	70.8	69.8	2.54
德国	Germany	58.2	58.4	57.7	58.3	2.12
哈萨克斯坦	Kazakhstan	37.2	35.6	39.2	39.6	1.44
哥伦比亚	Colombia	28.2	26.1	32.8	35.2	1.28
加拿大	Canada	34.9	32.6	30.3	32.3	1.17
乌克兰	Ukraine	31.8	32.0	33.2	30.8	1.12
英国	United Kingdom	19.0	17.8	16.8	14.9	0.54

资料来源:国际能源机构统计年鉴-OECD 成员国能源平衡表, 非 OECD 成员国能源平衡表。

Source:IEA STATISTICS-ENERGY BALANCES OF OECD COUNTRIES, ENERGY BALANCES OF NON – OECD COUNTRIES

附录2-9 原油生产量
CRUDE OIL PRODUCTION

单位:千吨 (1000 ton)

国家和地区 Country or Area		2001	2002	2003	2004	产量比重% Percent of World
世界总计	**World**	**3622896**	**3591457**	**3707786**	**3870754**	**100.00**
石油输出国家组织	OPEC	1481719	1391835	1466662	1579209	40.80
沙特阿拉伯	Saudi Arabia	432144	418885	473663	492006	12.71
俄罗斯	Russia	345841	377173	418582	456253	11.79
美国	United States	286150	283395	280196	268014	6.92
伊朗	Iran	186149	172411	193687	202965	5.24
墨西哥	Mexico	162559	165964	176612	178280	4.61
中国	PR of China	164162	167219	169835	176156	4.55
委内瑞拉	Venezuela	171776	160363	137835	154424	3.99
挪威	Norway	157551	151681	147011	144627	3.74
尼日利亚	Nigeria	120116	102189	117666	128308	3.31
阿联酋	United Arab Emirates	114036	106477	119291	124593	3.22
科威特	Kuwait	102659	97381	111125	122474	3.16
加拿大	Canada	88279	91110	99256	102564	2.65
伊拉克	Iraq	116771	100469	65949	98951	2.56
英国	United Kingdom	108387	107430	97835	87516	2.26
阿尔及利亚	Algeria	66745	71035	79180	82720	2.14
利比亚	Libya	66681	62629	70781	77420	2.00
哈萨克斯坦	Kazakhstan	40091	47269	51451	59485	1.54
印度尼西亚	Indonesia	68288	62766	59356	54890	1.42
安哥拉	Angola	36469	44045	43083	49443	1.28
阿根廷	Argentina	42844	41576	40369	39424	1.02

资料来源:国际能源机构统计年鉴 – 非 OECD 国家能源统计。

Source:IEA STATISTICS – ENERGY STATISTICS OF NON – OECD,IEA STATISTICS – OIL INFORMATION

附录2-10 天然气生产量
NATURAL GAS PRODUCTION

单位:百万吨标准油 （Mtoe）

国家和地区	Country or Area	2001	2002	2003	2004	产量比重% Percent of World
世界总计	**World**	**2127.11**	**2170.12**	**2256.83**	**2320.69**	**100.00**
俄罗斯	Russia	468.63	479.41	499.69	509.17	21.94
美国	United States	459.25	442.34	448.05	438.37	18.89
加拿大	Canada	152.25	153.3	151.12	150.67	6.49
英国	United Kingdom	95.23	93.38	92.61	86.38	3.72
阿尔及利亚	Algeria	73.01	75.13	79.37	78.25	3.37
伊朗	Iran	53.58	58.48	65.57	68.73	2.96
印度尼西亚	Indonesia	60.81	65.87	68.90	66.92	2.88
荷兰	Netherland	55.7	54.26	53.20	61.57	2.65
沙特阿拉伯	Saudi Arabia	43.84	46.80	49.05	53.64	2.31
土库曼斯坦	Turkmenistan	41.77	43.56	48.17	48.04	2.07
乌兹别克斯坦	Uzbekistan	46.75	47.09	47.23	48.04	2.07
马来西亚	Malaysia	37.24	38.41	40.2	46.47	2.00
中国	PR of China	31.36	33.78	36.21	43.62	1.88
阿根廷	Argentina	33.48	32.16	35.76	39.12	1.69
阿联酋	United Arab Emirates	31.52	34.74	35.86	37.15	1.60
墨西哥	Mexico	31.58	32.39	33.94	35.49	1.53
卡塔尔	Qatar	23.63	25.95	27.61	34.51	1.49
澳大利亚	Australia	29.11	30.33	31.30	31.99	1.38
埃及	Egypt	18.37	23.14	26.09	28.18	1.21
巴基斯坦	Pakistan	17.41	17.84	22.15	24.05	1.04
印度	India	21.00	22.57	23.10	23.43	1.01
委内瑞拉	Venezuela	25.28	24.34	22.64	22.32	0.96
特立尼达和多巴哥	Trinidad and Tobago	11.78	13.72	20.88	22.01	0.95
泰国	Thailand	15.35	16.08	16.94	17.52	0.75
德国	Germany	15.93	15.98	15.92	14.73	0.63

资料来源:国际能源机构统计年鉴-OECD 成员国能源平衡表, 非 OECD 成员国能源平衡表。

Source:IEA STATISTICS-ENERGY BALANCES OF OECD COUNTRIES, ENERGY BALANCES OF NON-OECD COUNTRIES

附录 2-11 总发电量(2004 年)
TOTAL ELECTRICITY GENERATION(2004)

单位:百万千瓦小时 （million kW·h）

国家和地区	Country or Area	总发电量 百万千 瓦小时 Total Production of Electricity (million kwh)	发电量占 世界比重 % Percent of World	煤电比重 % Electricity Generation from Coal (% of total)	油电比重 % Electricity Generation from Oil (% of total)	气电比重 % Electricity Generation from Gas (% of total)	水电比重 % Electricity Generation from Hydro (% of total)	核电比重 % Electricity Generation from Nuclear (% of total)
世界总计	**World**	**17449817**	**100.00**	**39.80**	**6.71**	**19.59**	**16.09**	**15.69**
美国	United States	4147705	23.77	50.40	3.35	17.64	6.54	19.61
中国(大陆)	PR of China	2199601	12.61	77.89	3.26	0.36	16.07	2.26
日本	Japan	1071040	6.14	27.45	12.43	22.79	8.78	26.37
俄罗斯	Russia	929905	5.33	17.29	2.7	45.3	18.91	15.56
印度	India	667782	3.83	69.05	5.39	9.48	12.69	2.55
德国	Germany	609988	3.50	50.51	1.66	10.08	3.46	27.39
加拿大	Canada	598403	3.43	17.23	3.64	5.36	56.98	15.10
法国	France	567050	3.25	5.04	1.03	3.24	10.53	79.05
英国	United Kingdom	393204	2.25	34.06	1.25	40.59	1.25	20.35
巴西	Brazil	387452	2.22	2.68	3.18	4.97	82.8	3.00
韩国	Korea	366614	2.10	38.8	8.04	16.2	1.18	35.65
西班牙	Spain	277122	1.59	28.98	8.60	20.01	11.39	22.95
南非	South Africa	242186	1.39	93.23			0.91	5.52
墨西哥	Mexico	224077	1.28	10.66	31.06	38.85	11.25	4.10
中国,台北	Chinese Taipei	218384	1.25	53.20	7.10	17.07	3.01	18.08
乌克兰	Ukraine	182020	1.04	24.74	0.32	20.66	6.46	47.81
瑞典	Sweden	151672	0.87	1.65	1.29	0.49	39.64	51.09
荷兰	Netherlands	100770	0.58	26.04	2.80	60.55	0.09	3.79
阿根廷	Argentina	100260	0.57	1.67	4.03	54.75	30.45	7.85
比利时	Belgium	84353	0.48	13.61	1.99	25.46	0.38	56.09
芬兰	Finland	85817	0.49	27.46	0.71	14.86	17.56	26.47
捷克	Czech Republic	83790	0.48	60.29	0.42	4.57	2.41	31.42
巴基斯坦	Pakistan	85699	0.49	0.20	15.85	50.73	29.95	3.26
瑞士	Switzerland	63579	0.36		0.33	1.48	53.08	42.40
罗马尼亚	Romania	56499	0.32	38.54	3.89	18.52	29.23	9.82
保加利亚	Bulgaria	41426	0.24	46.12	1.98	3.61	7.65	40.59

资料来源:国际能源机构统计年鉴-OECD 成员国能源平衡表, 非 OECD 成员国能源平衡表。

Source:IEA STATISTICS-ENERGY BALANCES OF OECD COUNTRIES(2003 - 2004), ENERGY BALANCES OF NON - OECD COUNTRIES(2003 - 2004)

附录 2-12 能源最终消费量
TOTAL FINAL CONSUMPTION OF ENERGY

单位：百万吨标准油 (Mtoe)

国家和地区 Country or Area		2001	2002	2003	2004	消费比重% Percent of World
世界	**World**	**5983.56**	**6110.96**	**6304.83**	**6597.02**	**100.00**
OECD 合计	**OECD Total**	**3663.18**	**3569.52**	**3629.93**	**3700.95**	**56.10**
美国	United States	1538.61	1549.47	1570.09	1600.79	24.27
日本	Japan	349.58	352.48	349.34	354.32	5.37
德国	Germany	246.35	239.48	244.02	251.72	3.82
加拿大	Canada	184.45	190.01	197.32	201.74	3.06
法国	France	173.98	168.99	172.44	172.27	2.61
英国	United Kingdom	161.73	158.66	161.11	163.65	2.48
韩国	Korea	128.80	138.99	141.72	143.69	2.18
意大利	Italy	134.62	133.83	139.36	144.81	2.20
西班牙	Spain	93.29	94.44	99.89	103.48	1.57
墨西哥	Mexico	94.25	99.81	100.68	105.59	1.60
澳大利亚	Australia	72.94	70.96	72.30	73.95	1.12
荷兰	Netherlands	60.29	60.15	62.32	63.29	0.96
比利时	Belgium	43.05	40.93	42.65	41.27	0.63
瑞典	Sweden	35.32	35.72	35.87	35.71	0.54
瑞士	Switzerland	21.60	21.07	21.63	21.98	0.33
非 OECD 合计	**NON-OECD Total**	**2438.17**	**2541.44**	**2674.90**	**2896.07**	**43.90**
中国(大陆)	People's Rep. Of China	560.14	619.13	698.92	819.22	12.42
俄罗斯	Russia	422.29	409.62	419.47	422.55	6.41
印度	India	170.11	177.06	182.51	189.97	2.88
巴西	Brazil	118.34	120.02	118.81	125.15	1.90
伊朗	Islamic Republic of Iran	96.06	102.07	108.38	113.40	1.72
沙特阿拉伯	Saudi Arabia	71.59	76.95	79.75	87.71	1.33
印度尼西亚	Indonesia	72.87	75.57	74.41	84.64	1.28
中国,台北	Chinese Taipei	54.80	58.67	60.89	63.67	0.97
南非	South Africa	46.65	49.47	52.85	55.77	0.85
泰国	Thailand	44.48	47.25	49.95	53.91	0.82
阿根廷	Argentina	40.24	38.90	42.10	44.60	0.68
埃及	Egypt	32.75	34.87	35.69	38.72	0.59
委内瑞拉	Venezuela	36.47	36.27	34.83	36.54	0.55
以色列	Israel	12.40	12.22	12.69	13.33	0.20
中国,香港	Hong Kong, China	11.60	11.49	11.20	11.36	0.17

资料来源：国际能源机构统计年鉴-OECD 成员国能源平衡表，非 OECD 成员国能源平衡表。

Source：IEA STATISTICS-ENERGY BALANCES OF OECD COUNTRIES(2003-2004)，ENERGY BALANCES OF NON-OECD COUNTRIES(2003-2004)

附录 2 - 13 煤的一次供应量
PRIMARY SUPPLY OF COAL

单位:百万吨标准油 （Mtoe）

国家和地区	Country or Area	2001	2002	2003	2004	占世界比重% Percent of Word
世界	**World**	**2314.90**	**2380.83**	**2549.28**	**2775.72**	**100.00**
OECD 合计	**OECD Total**	**1089.91**	**1099.49**	**1103.51**	**1128.56**	**40.66**
美国	United States	534.77	542.16	531.17	545.36	19.65
日本	Japan	100.79	103.16	106.00	116.09	4.18
德国	Germany	86.45	84.10	85.02	85.83	3.09
韩国	Korea	42.85	45.67	47.09	50.09	1.80
澳大利亚	Australia	48.15	49.04	48.29	49.47	1.78
英国	United Kingdom	39.51	35.67	38.09	37.48	1.35
加拿大	Canada	30.53	30.54	30.34	28.71	1.03
西班牙	Spain	19.15	21.58	20.11	21.02	0.76
意大利	Italy	13.36	13.73	14.88	16.60	0.60
法国	France	12.66	13.57	14.36	14.05	0.51
荷兰	Netherlands	8.33	8.47	8.84	8.70	0.31
墨西哥	Mexico	7.06	7.43	8.23	7.13	0.26
比利时	Belgium	7.33	6.34	5.95	5.79	0.21
瑞典	Sweden	2.76	2.84	2.67	2.94	0.11
瑞士	Switzerland	0.15	0.14	0.14	0.13	
非 OECD 合计	**NON-OECD Total**	**1224.99**	**1281.34**	**1445.77**	**1647.16**	**59.34**
中国(大陆)	People's Rep. Of China	637.36	688.70	822.31	992.65	35.76
印度	India	172.09	173.58	178.95	195.54	7.04
俄罗斯	Russia	106.59	106.74	107.42	104.19	3.75
南非	South Africa	82.71	78.55	86.64	94.40	3.40
中国,台北	Chinese Taipei	31.43	33.31	36.05	37.46	1.35
印度尼西亚	Indonesia	16.76	17.95	18.82	22.26	0.80
巴西	Brazil	13.43	12.96	13.10	14.19	0.51
泰国	Thailand	8.62	8.99	9.40	10.38	0.37
以色列	Israel	7.23	7.85	7.98	8.11	0.29
中国,香港	Hong Kong, China	4.94	5.36	6.57	6.58	0.24
伊朗	Islamic Republic of Iran	1.06	1.14	1.11	1.05	0.04
埃及	Egypt	0.70	0.83	0.86	0.90	0.03
阿根廷	Argentina	0.52	0.45	0.51	0.57	0.02
委内瑞拉	Venezuela	0.05	0.02	0.04		
沙特阿拉伯	Saudi Arabia					

资料来源:国际能源机构统计年鉴-OECD 成员国能源平衡表, 非 OECD 成员国能源平衡表。

Source：IEA STATISTICS-ENERGY BALANCES OF OECD COUNTRIES(2003 - 2004), ENERGY BALANCES OF NON - OECD COUNTRIES(2003 - 2004)

附录2-14 石油的一次供应量
PRIMARY SUPPLY OF OIL

单位:百万吨标准油 　　　　　　　　　　　　　　　　　　　　　　　　　　　　　　　　（Mtoe）

国家和地区	Country or Area	2001	2002	2003	2004	占世界比重% Percent of Word
世界	**World**	**3544.04**	**3587.33**	**3656.19**	**3790.78**	**100.00**
OECD 合计	**OECD Total**	**2173.67**	**2172.52**	**2204.75**	**2241.54**	**59.13**
美国	United States	903.77	900.20	921.41	947.47	24.99
日本	Japan	252.76	258.15	258.26	255.01	6.73
德国	Germany	134.49	128.83	126.51	125.20	3.30
韩国	Korea	100.21	102.00	101.20	101.43	2.68
加拿大	Canada	88.44	86.37	92.84	98.24	2.59
墨西哥	Mexico	92.61	92.34	91.71	96.12	2.54
法国	France	93.85	91.27	91.13	92.13	2.43
英国	United Kingdom	81.54	80.51	81.84	83.66	2.21
意大利	Italy	87.03	87.45	87.44	83.47	2.20
西班牙	Spain	67.10	67.27	69.04	70.77	1.87
澳大利亚	Australia	33.22	34.57	35.93	37.04	0.98
荷兰	Netherlands	29.57	29.85	31.53	31.96	0.84
比利时	Belgium	24.26	22.90	24.76	23.02	0.61
瑞典	Sweden	14.49	16.52	15.75	15.50	0.41
瑞士	Switzerland	13.87	12.96	12.58	12.53	0.33
非 OECD 合计	**NON-OECD Total**	**1370.73**	**1414.81**	**1451.44**	**1549.24**	**40.87**
中国（大陆）	People's Rep. Of China	227.06	244.16	269.99	311.34	8.21
俄罗斯	Russia	132.97	128.35	131.53	130.85	3.45
印度	India	114.59	118.58	123.85	127.34	3.36
沙特阿拉伯	Saudi Arabia	75.26	78.94	81.16	86.77	2.29
巴西	Brazil	89.89	88.02	84.33	86.58	2.28
伊朗	Islamic Republic of Iran	66.93	65.80	68.24	72.13	1.90
印度尼西亚	Indonesia	55.74	58.71	58.48	64.40	1.70
中国,台北	Chinese Taipei	41.43	42.46	43.47	45.87	1.21
泰国	Thailand	35.47	37.90	40.61	45.65	1.20
埃及	Egypt	27.14	26.23	25.51	28.33	0.75
委内瑞拉	Venezuela	27.08	27.75	24.67	27.28	0.72
阿根廷	Argentina	21.63	20.19	20.54	23.58	0.62
南非	South Africa	10.12	16.82	17.60	18.54	0.49
以色列	Israel	12.29	11.59	12.08	11.09	0.29
中国,香港	Hong Kong, China	8.51	8.35	8.02	8.12	0.21

资料来源：国际能源机构统计年鉴-OECD 成员国能源平衡表，非 OECD 成员国能源平衡表。

Source：IEA STATISTICS-ENERGY BALANCES OF OECD COUNTRIES(2003-2004)，ENERGY BALANCES OF NON-OECD COUNTRIES(2003-2004)

附录 2 -15　天然气的一次供应量
PRIMARY SUPPLY OF GAS

单位:百万吨标准油 　　(Mtoe)

国家和地区	Country or Area	2001	2002	2003	2004	占世界比重% Percent of Word
世界	World	2105.68	2170.85	2255.65	2306.95	100.00
OECD 合计	OECD Total	1136.29	1167.30	1189.42	1197.23	51.90
美国	United States	515.44	535.66	519.98	514.78	22.31
英国	United Kingdom	86.63	85.83	85.86	87.36	3.79
德国	Germany	75.57	75.55	79.11	78.71	3.41
加拿大	Canada	71.86	73.33	79.71	78.04	3.38
日本	Japan	66.27	66.47	71.22	70.34	3.05
意大利	Italy	58.08	57.69	63.60	66.00	2.86
墨西哥	Mexico	34.49	38.33	41.97	43.70	1.89
法国	France	37.54	37.47	39.37	40.17	1.74
荷兰	Netherlands	35.54	35.83	35.99	36.73	1.59
韩国	Korea	18.74	21.20	22.00	25.28	1.10
西班牙	Spain	16.40	18.75	21.35	25.16	1.09
澳大利亚	Australia	20.31	21.45	22.15	22.74	0.99
比利时	Belgium	13.18	13.37	14.40	14.57	0.63
瑞士	Switzerland	2.53	2.49	2.63	2.71	0.12
瑞典	Sweden	0.88	0.89	0.89	0.88	0.04
非 OECD 合计	NON-OECD Total	969.39	1003.55	1066.23	1109.73	48.10
俄罗斯	Russia	325.22	325.56	342.50	346.56	15.02
伊朗	Islamic Republic of Iran	55.10	61.86	67.53	70.93	3.07
沙特阿拉伯	Saudi Arabia	43.84	46.80	49.05	53.64	2.33
中国(大陆)	People's Rep. Of China	29.34	31.85	34.97	41.83	1.81
印度尼西亚	Indonesia	31.93	32.98	35.43	33.74	1.46
阿根廷	Argentina	28.31	27.36	30.28	32.45	1.41
埃及	Egypt	18.37	23.14	25.43	25.17	1.09
泰国	Thailand	20.43	21.90	23.26	24.37	1.06
印度	India	21.00	22.57	23.10	23.43	1.02
委内瑞拉	Venezuela	25.28	24.34	22.64	22.32	0.97
巴西	Brazil	10.01	12.38	12.76	15.77	0.68
中国,台北	Chinese Taipei	6.01	6.95	7.21	8.89	0.39
中国,香港	Hong Kong, China	2.02	1.92	1.24	1.79	0.08
南非	South Africa	1.82	1.80	1.08	1.66	0.07
以色列	Israel	0.01	0.01	0.01	0.94	0.04

资料来源:国际能源机构统计年鉴-OECD 成员国能源平衡表, 非 OECD 成员国能源平衡表。

Source: IEA STATISTICS-ENERGY BALANCES OF OECD COUNTRIES(2003 -2004), ENERGY BALANCES OF NON – OECD COUNTRIES(2003 –2004)

附录 2-16 国内生产总值电耗(千瓦小时/美元 2000 年价)
ELECTRICITY CONSUMPTION/GDP(kW · h per US $ 2000)

国家和地区	Country or Area	2001	2002	2003	2004
世界	**World**	**0.44**	**0.45**	**0.45**	**0.46**
OECD 合计	**OECD Total**	**0.35**	**0.35**	**0.35**	**0.34**
OECD 北美区	OECD North America	0.40	0.40	0.39	0.38
OECD 太平洋区	OECD Pacific	0.26	0.27	0.27	0.27
OECD 欧洲区	OECD Europe	0.34	0.34	0.34	0.34
非 OECD 合计	**NON-OECD Total**	**0.85**	**0.85**	**0.87**	**0.88**
中国,香港	Hong Kong, China	0.22	0.22	0.22	0.21
阿根廷	Argentina	0.29	0.31	0.32	0.31
以色列	Israel	0.36	0.37	0.38	0.38
巴西	Brazil	0.51	0.52	0.55	0.55
印度尼西亚	Indonesia	0.57	0.51	0.50	0.53
委内瑞拉	Venezuela	0.54	0.61	0.67	0.60
中国,台北	Chinese Taipei	0.63	0.64	0.66	0.65
沙特阿拉伯	Saudi Arabia	0.66	0.70	0.71	0.69
埃及	Egypt	0.68	0.71	0.74	0.75
泰国	Thailand	0.76	0.78	0.78	0.79
印度	India	0.87	0.87	0.85	0.85
伊朗	Islamic Republic of Iran	1.09	1.03	1.06	1.08
中国(大陆)	People's Rep. Of China	1.17	1.07	1.14	1.20
南非	South Africa	1.46	1.46	1.50	1.50
俄罗斯	Russia	2.82	2.70	2.58	2.47

附录 2-17 人均电力消费量(千瓦小时/人)
ELECTRICITY CONSUMPTION/POPULATION(kW · h per capita)

国家和地区	Country or Area	2001	2002	2003	2004
世界	**World**	**2316**	**2365**	**2436**	**2516**
OECD 合计	**OECD Total**	**7891**	**7991**	**8076**	**8204**
OECD 北美区	OECD North America	10612	10689	10772	10833
OECD 太平洋区	OECD Pacific	7551	7946	7951	8236
OECD 欧洲区	OECD Europe	5858	5858	5962	6074
非 OECD 合计	**NON-OECD Total**	**1042**	**1087**	**1164**	**1241**
中国,台北	Chinese Taipei	8072	8441	8897	9264
以色列	Israel	6383	6486	6599	6808
沙特阿拉伯	Saudi Arabia	5924	5810	6259	6181
中国,香港	Hong Kong, China	5541	5612	5653	5699
俄罗斯	Russia	5319	5305	5480	5642
南非	South Africa	4288	4546	4757	4976
委内瑞拉	Venezuela	2720	2653	2664	2760
阿根廷	Argentina	2186	2017	2186	2301
巴西	Brazil	1794	1813	1885	1955
伊朗	Islamic Republic of Iran	1683	1782	1916	2045
泰国	Thailand	1563	1656	1752	1865
中国(大陆)	People's Rep. Of China	1069	1184	1379	1585
埃及	Egypt	1070	1103	1173	1215
印度尼西亚	Indonesia	422	428	440	478
印度	India	403	417	435	457

资料来源:国际能源机构统计年鉴-OECD 成员国能源平衡表, 非 OECD 成员国能源平衡表。
Source:IEA STATISTICS-ENERGY BALANCES OF OECD COUNTRIES, ENERGY BALANCES OF NON-OECD COUNTRIES

附录 2-18 煤净进口量
NET IMPORT OF COAL

单位：百万吨标准油 （Mtoe）

国家和地区	Country or Area	2001	2002	2003	2004
日本	Japan	99.58	102.58	106.04	116.09
韩国	Korea	39.00	43.95	45.42	50.25
中国台北	Chinese Taipei	32.02	34.15	35.98	39.73
德国	Germany	25.78	24.45	25.14	27.70
英国	United Kingdom	22.14	17.45	19.96	22.58
印度	India	13.50	15.48	14.11	17.45
西班牙	Spain	11.20	14.36	12.72	14.14
法国	France	11.18	12.60	11.76	13.27
巴西	Brazil	10.82	11.01	11.36	11.78
意大利	Italy	13.51	13.12	14.53	16.78
土耳其	Turkey	5.89	8.34	10.9	11.2
荷兰	Netherlands	8.40	8.24	9.23	8.58
以色列	Israel	7.15	7.98	7.70	8.02
比利时	Belgium	7.83	5.46	5.80	5.88
加拿大	Canada	-2.76	-1.46	-1.68	-3.92
美国	United States	-15.02	-11.49	-8.96	-7.34
波兰	Poland	-16.30	-15.60	-14.72	-14.97
哥伦比亚	Colombia	-25.06	-23.20	-29.63	-33.21
南非	South Africa	-44.79	-45.17	-46.69	-44.25
中国(大陆)	PR of China	-65.95	-57.4	-64.47	-55.61
印度尼西亚	Indonesia	-40.15	-45.62	-52.08	-59.14
澳大利亚	Australia	-125.24	-132.58	-135.50	-141.70

注：负数表示净出口。

a）Negative number show net export.

资料来源：国际能源机构统计年鉴-OECD 成员国能源平衡表，非 OECD 成员国能源平衡表。

Source：IEA STATISTICS-ENERGY BALANCES OF OECD COUNTRIES(2003-2004), ENERGY BALANCES OF NON-OECD COUNTRIES(2003-2004)

附录 2 - 19　石油净进口量
NET IMPORT OF OIL

单位:百万吨标准油

（Mtoe）

国家和地区	Country or Area	2001	2002	2003	2004
美国	United States	575.25	557.94	594.72	641.07
日本	Japan	253.51	259.08	260.46	256.85
中国(大陆)	PR of China	69.53	79.80	106.16	148.29
德国	Germany	132.9	124.45	126.3	122.41
韩国	Korea	106.39	106.47	108.69	107.84
法国	France	94.46	93.39	93.78	93.87
印度	India	77.63	80.35	85.35	88.23
意大利	Italy	83.82	85.49	83.97	81.29
西班牙	Spain	73.30	74.98	75.71	77.47
中国,台北	Chinese Taipei	44.69	43.79	45.35	48.31
荷兰	Netherlands	41.83	40.49	41.29	44.53
新加坡	Singapore	42.67	41.03	34.81	41.81
泰国	Thailand	27.86	28.36	30.98	35.91
比利时	Belgium	29.79	29.43	31.93	30.72
土耳其	Turkey	26.77	28.39	28.32	28.94
希腊	Greece	19.34	20.37	19.68	21.53
英国	United Kingdom	- 36.65	- 39.85	- 27.74	- 13.25
厄瓜多尔	Ecuador	- 13.46	- 12.64	- 13.36	- 19.36
卡塔尔	Qatar	- 34.47	- 32.12	- 32.42	- 37.02
阿曼	Oman	- 48.82	- 45.17	- 41.27	- 38.79
安哥拉	Angola	- 34.95	- 42.82	- 41.24	- 47.07
哈萨克斯坦	Kazakstan	- 30.19	- 38.05	- 43.36	- 47.94
加拿大	Canada	- 39.34	- 49.08	- 49.32	- 51.87
利比亚	Libya	- 55.68	- 51.25	- 59.34	- 66.20
伊拉克	Iraq	- 93.48	- 73.73	- 42.85	- 73.31
阿尔及利亚	Algeria	- 61.69	- 64.54	- 72.65	- 75.94
墨西哥	Mexico	- 81.78	- 81.73	- 94.4	- 97.77
阿联酋	United Arab Emirates	- 100.53	- 89.27	- 99.54	- 103.55
科威特	Kuwait	- 92.03	- 86.17	- 97.27	- 107.10
尼日利亚	Nigeria	- 108.14	- 90.67	- 107.62	- 119.02
伊朗	Iran	- 121.89	- 109.43	- 128.68	- 134.07
委内瑞拉	Venezuela	- 147.87	- 139.82	- 120.12	- 134.61
挪威	Norway	- 157.99	- 152.59	- 145.54	- 144.89
俄罗斯	Russia	- 214.00	- 250.44	- 290.38	- 326.22
沙特阿拉伯	Saudi Arabia	- 363.94	- 346.91	- 400.19	- 413.64

注:负数表示净出口。

a）Negative number show net export.

资料来源:国际能源机构统计年鉴-OECD 成员国能源平衡表,非 OECD 成员国能源平衡表。

Source：IEA STATISTICS-ENERGY BALANCES OF OECD COUNTRIES(2003 -2004)，ENERGY BALANCES OF NON – OECD COUNTRIES(2003 -2004)

附录 2 - 20 　 天然气净进口量
NET IMPORT OF GAS

单位：百万吨标准油 (Mtoe)

国家和地区	Country or Area	2001	2002	2003	2004
美国	United States	83.74	81.23	76.08	79.52
日本	Japan	63.74	64.46	68.56	67.82
德国	Germany	58.18	60.05	62.42	65.88
意大利	Italy	44.80	48.50	51.10	55.28
乌克兰	Ukraine	46.89	45.82	49.00	48.68
法国	France	34.94	36.73	37.59	38.69
韩国	Korea	18.91	20.85	22.73	25.91
西班牙	Spain	15.82	18.92	21.16	24.61
土耳其	Turkey	13.21	14.34	17.28	18.12
白俄罗斯	Belarus	14.33	14.59	15.03	16.30
比利时	Belgium	13.13	13.65	14.24	14.55
匈牙利	Hungary	7.78	8.70	9.94	9.28
波兰	Poland	7.18	6.68	7.50	8.12
中国,台北	Chinese Taipei	5.53	6.24	6.50	8.01
捷克	Czech Republic	7.73	7.92	7.70	7.09
泰国	Thailand	5.08	5.82	6.31	6.85
英国	United Kingdom	-8.34	-6.98	-7.02	1.46
乌兹别克斯坦	Uzbekistan	-4.68	-3.77	-3.04	-2.45
阿联酋	United Arab Emirates	-5.67	-5.73	-5.73	-5.91
阿根廷	Argentina	-5.17	-4.81	-5.48	-6.67
文莱	Brunei Darssalam	-7.85	-7.99	-8.39	-8.31
阿曼	Oman	-6.18	-6.85	-7.62	-8.45
澳大利亚	Australia	-8.8	-8.88	-9.15	-9.25
尼日利亚	Nigeria	-7.36	-6.64	-9.99	-10.67
卡塔尔	Qatar	-12.88	-15.03	-15.91	-20.36
马来西亚	Malaysia	-16.02	-16.99	-18.31	-25.98
印度尼西亚	Indonesia	-28.88	-32.88	-33.47	-33.18
土库曼斯坦	Turkmenistan	-30.37	-32.00	-35.34	-36.56
阿尔及利亚	Algeria	-54.05	-55.31	-57.60	-57.08
挪威	Norway	-43.45	-55.04	-60.93	-65.95
加拿大	Canada	-85.35	-82.78	-75.35	-77.36
俄罗斯	Russia	-142.72	-144.00	-145.87	-156.26

注：负数表示净出口。

a) Negative number show net export.

资料来源：国际能源机构统计年鉴-OECD 成员国能源平衡表, 非 OECD 成员国能源平衡表。

Source：IEA STATISTICS-ENERGY BALANCES OF OECD COUNTRIES(2003 -2004), ENERGY BALANCES OF NON - OECD COUNTRIES(2003 -2004)

附录2-21 主要高耗能产品单位能耗中外比较
ENERGY CONSUMPTION FOR MAIN ENERGY INTENSIVE PRODUCTS BY COMPARING CHINA WITH SELECTED COUNTRIES

1. 原煤耗电 Electricity Consumption for Coal

单位: 千瓦小时/吨 (kwh/tn)

国　家	Country	1980	1991	1994
中国①	China	24.27	29.82	31.19
英国②	United Kingdom	61.43	61.13	30.07
美国②	United States	20.26	17.45	16.99

资料来源(Source):1. UN. Annual Bulletin of Electric Energy Statistics 1994.

2.〔USA〕Coal Data 1996, The National Mining Association, June, 1996

注:①国有重点煤矿(key state-owned coal mines).

②商品煤, 占原煤比例美国86%, 英国72%(commercial coal, as % of raw coal: USA 86%, UK 72%).

2. 发电厂自用电率 Rate of Electricity Used by Power Plant

单位: % (%)

国　家	Country	1990	1995	1997	1998
中国 (6MW 及以上机组)	China(over 6MW)	6.90	6.78	6.80	6.66
欧盟平均	Average European	5.29	5.26	5.11	5.07

资料来源(Source):1. European Commission, 1999 Annual Energy Review, Jan. 2000.

3. 乙烯综合能耗 Fully Energy Consumption for Ethylene

单位: 千克标准煤/吨 (kgce/tn)

国家	Country	1980	1990	1995	2000	2003
中国	China	2013	1580	1277	1212	889.8
日本	Japan	1100	857	870	714	629

资料来源(Source):〔日〕节能总览, 通产资料调查会(〔Japan〕Energy Conservation)

4. 火电厂供电标准煤耗 Coal Consumption for Power Supply (Thermalpower Plant)

单位: 克/千瓦小时 (gce/kwh)

国家	Country	1980	1985	1990	1995	1998	1999	2000	2001	2003
中国 (6MW 及以上机组)	China(over 6MW)	448	431	427	412	404	399	392	385	380
美国	United States	378	376	373	376					
日本③	Japan	339	338	332	331	322	316	314	312	

资料来源(Source):日本电气事业手册(Japan Electricity Handbook, 2002)。

注:③ 九大电力公司平均(average level of 9 large electricity company).

5. 吨钢可比能耗　Energy Consumption for Steel Production

单位：千克标煤/吨　　　　　　　　　　　　　　　　　　　　　　　　　　　　（kgce/tn）

国家	Country	1980	1985	1990	1995	2000	2003
中国（重点企业）	China(key enterprises)	1201	1062	997	976	781	726
日本	Japan	705	640	629	656	646	646
美国	United States	880	761	757			
英国	United Kingdom	794	721	677	721（1994）		
法国	France	826	764	707	735（1994）		

资料来源(Source)：1. 日本能源学会志，2001，No.7.

　　　　　　　　2.〔日〕铁钢界

　　　　　　　　3. World Energy Council ,Energy Efficiency Improvement Utilising High Technology.

6. 合成氨综合能耗（大型装置）　Fully Energy Consumption for Sythetic Ammonia

单位：千克标准煤/吨　　　　　　　　　　　　　　　　　　　　　　　　　　（kgce/tn）

国家	Country	1980	1990	1995	1998	2000
中国	China	1431	1343	1284	1352	1200
美国	United States	1320	1000	970	970	970

资料来源（Source）：1.〔USA〕Hydrocarbon Processing.

　　　　　　　　2.〔USA〕Chemical Engineering ,Progress.

7. 水泥综合能耗　Fully Energy Consumption for Cement

单位：千克标准煤/吨　　　　　　　　　　　　　　　　　　　　　　　　　　（kgce/tn）

国家	Country	1980	1985	1990	1995	2000	2003
中国（大中型企业）	China(large,medium)	218.8	208	201	199.2	181	181
日本	Japan	135.7	123.4	122.6	124.4	125.7	128.4

资料来源(Source)：日本能源学会志，2001，No.7.

8. 铁路货运综合能耗　Fully Energy Consumption for Railway Freight Traffic

单位：千克标准煤/万吨公里　　　　　　　　　　　　　　　　　　　　　　（kgce/104tn – km）

国家	Country	1980	1985	1990	1995	2000
中国	China	147.4	118.7	84.2	74.0	72.5
日本	Japan	122.9	125.7	85.7	87.1	90.0

资料来源(Source)：日本能源经济统计手册（*Handbook of energy and economic statistics in Japan.*）

9. 载货汽车运输耗油　Oil Consumption for Trucks

单位：升/百吨公里　　　　　　　　　　　　　　　　　　　　　　　　　　（1/10^2 tn – km）

国家	Country	1980	1985	1990	1995	2000
中国	China					
汽油车	Gasoline Trucks	8.70	7.70	7.10	7.06	
柴油车	Diesel Oil Trucks	6.20	5.80	4.80	4.82	
美国	United States	3.43	3.36	3.50	3.54	

资料来源(Source)：〔USA〕DOE/EIA, *Annual Energy Outlook* 1997, Nov.1996 .

附录 3　主要统计指标解释

Appendix Ⅲ Explanatory Notes of
Main Statistical Indicators

主要统计指标解释

国内生产总值　是按市场价格计算的国内生产总值的简称。国内生产总值及其产业构成的资料,是由国家统计局国民经济核算司根据不同产业部门的特点和资料来源情况而采用不同的方法计算的,有的部门以生产法计算增加值为准,有的部门以收入法计算的增加值为准,最后将各产业部门增加值求和得到国内生产总值的标准数据。按支出法计算的国内生产总值等于总消费、总投资、货物和服务净出口之和,它与按上述方法计算的国内生产总值不相等,两者的差率一般在±3%以内。

三次产业　根据社会生产活动历史发展的顺序对产业结构的划分,产品直接取自自然界的部门称为第一产业。对初级产品进行再加工的部门称为第二产业。为生产和消费提供各种服务的部门称为第三产业。它是世界上通用的产业结构分类,但各国的划分不尽一致。我国的三次产业划分是:

第一产业:农业(包括种植业、林业、牧业、副业和渔业)

第二产业:工业(包括采掘业、制造业、自来水、电力、蒸汽、热水、煤气)和建筑业。

第三产业:除第一、第二产业以外的其他行业。

能源生产总量　指一定时期内全国(地区)一次能源生产量的总和,是观察全国(地区)能源生产水平、规模、过程构成和发展速度的总量指标。一次能源生产量包括原煤、原油、天然气、水电及其他动力能(如风能、地热能等)发电量。不包括低热值燃料生产量、生物质能、太阳能等的利用和由一次能源加工转换而成的二次能源产量。

能源消费总量　指一定时期内全国(地区)各行业和居民生活消费的各种能源的总观察能源消费水平、构成和增长速度的总量指标。能源消费总量包括原煤、原油及其制品、天然气、电力。不包括低热值燃料、生物质能和太阳能等的利用。能源消费总量分为三部分,即终端能源消费量、能源加工转换损失量和损失量。

(1)终端能源消费量　指一定时期内全国(地区)各行业和居民生活消费的各种能源在扣除了用于加工转换二次能源消费量和损失量以后的数量。

(2)能源加工转换损失量　指一定时期内全国(地区)投入加工转换的各种能源数量之和与产出各种能源产品之和的差额。它是观察能源在加工转换过程中损失量变化的指标。

(3)能源损失量　指一定时期内能源在输送、分配、储存过程中发生的损失和由客观原因造成的各种损失量。不包括各种气体能源放空、放散量。

能源生产弹性系数　是研究能源生产量的增长与国民经济增长之间关系的指标。计算公式:

$$能源生产弹性系数 = \frac{能源生产总量年平均增长速度}{国民经济年平均增长速度}$$

本资料采用国内生产总值指标计算国民经济年平均增长速度。

电力生产弹性系数 是研究电力生产量的增长与国民经济增长之间关系的指标。计算公式：

$$电力生产弹性系数 = \frac{电力生产量年平均增长速度}{国民经济年平均增长速度}$$

能源消费弹性系数 是反映能源消费增长速度与国民经济增长速度之间比例关系的指标。计算公式：

$$能源消费弹性系数 = \frac{能源消费总量年平均增长速度}{国民经济年平均增长速度}$$

电力消费弹性系数 是反映电力消费增长速度与国民经济增长速度之间比例关系的指标。计算公式：

$$电力消费弹性系数 = \frac{电力消费量年平均增长速度}{国民经济年平均增长速度}$$

能源加工转换效率 指一定时期内能源经过加工转换后,产出的各种能源产品的数量与投入加工转换的各种能源数量的比率。它是观察能源加工转换装置和生产工艺先进与落后、管理水平高低等的重要指标。计算公式：

$$能源加工转换效率 = \frac{加工转换产出量}{加工转换投入量} \times 100\%$$

Explanatory Notes on Main Statistical Indicators

Gross Domestic Product(GDP) : refers to gross domestic products calculated at market price. The data on GDP and its industrial composition are calculated by the Department of National Economic Accounting, State Statistical Bureau (SSB) with various approaches in the light of the features of various sectors and the data sources. The value added in some sectors is calculated with the production approach. The value added in other sectors is calculated with the income approach. Finally, the GDP is the result of the sum of the value added of various sectors. This is the standard data of GDP. The GDP calculated with the expenditure approach equals to the sum of total consumption, total investment and the net export of goods and services. However, it is not equal to the GDP calculated with the method mentioned above. The difference between the two figures is generally within $\pm 3\%$.

Three Industries : Industry structure has been classified according to the sequence of historical development of social production activities. Primary industry refers to extraction of natural resources; secondary industry involves processing of primary products; and tertiary industry provides services of various kinds for production and consumption. The above classification is universal although it to some extent from country to country. Industry classification in China comprises:

Primary Industry : agriculture (including farming, forestry, animal husbandry, sideline production and fishery).

Secondary Industry : industry (including mining and quarrying, manufacturing, water supply, electricity generation and supply, steam, hot water, gas) and construction.

Tertiary Industry : all other industries not included in primary and secondary industry.

Total Energy Production : refers to the total production of primary energy by all energy producing enterprises in the country (region) in a given period of time. It is a comprehensive indicator to show the capacity, scale, composition and development of energy production of the country (region). The production of primary energy includes that of coal, crude oil, natural gas, hydro power and electricity generated by other means such as wind power and geothermal power. However, it excludes the production of fuels of low calorific value, bioenergy, solar energy and the secondary energy converted from the primary energy.

Total Energy Consumption : refer to the total consumption of energy of various kinds by industry and residential in the country (region) in a given period of time. The total energy consumption includes that of coal, crude oil and their products, natural gas and electricity. However, it excludes the consumption of fuel of low calorific value, bioenergy and other non – commercial energy. Total energy consumption can be divided into three parts:

(1) Final Energy Consumption: refers to the total energy consumption by industry and residential in the country (re-

gion) in a given period of time, but excludes the consumption in conversion of the primary energy into the secondary energy and the loss in the process of energy transformation.

(2) Loss During Energy Transformation: refers to the total input of various kinds of energy for transformation, minus the total output of various kinds of energy in the country in a given period of time. It is an indicator to show the loss that occurs during the process of energy transformation.

(3) Loss: refers to the total of the loss of energy during the course of energy transport, distribution and storage and the loss caused by any objective reason in a given period of time. The loss of various kinds of gas due to gas discharges and stocktaking is excluded. Elasticity of Energy Production: is an indicator to show the relationship between the growth rate of energy production and the growth rate of the national economy. The formula is:

$$\text{Elasticity of Energy Production} = \frac{\text{average annual growth rate of energy production}}{\text{average annual growth rate of national economy}}$$

The gross domestic products (GDP) is used to calculate the growth rate of national economy in this book.

Elasticity of Electricity Production: is an indicator to show the relationship between the growth rate of electricity production and the growth rate of the national economy. The formula is:

$$\text{Elasticity of Electricity Production} = \frac{\text{average annual growth rate of electricity production}}{\text{average annual growth rate of national economy}}$$

Elasticity of Energy Consumption: is an indicator to show the relationship between the growth rate of energy consumption and the growth rate of the national economy. The formula is:

$$\text{Elasticity of Energy Consumption} = \frac{\text{average annual growth rate of energy consumption}}{\text{average annual growth rate of national economy}}$$

Elasticity of Electricity Consumption: is an indicator to show the relationship between the growth rate of electricity consumption and the growth rate of the national economy. The formula is:

$$\text{Elasticity of Electricity Consumption} = \frac{\text{average annual growth rate of electricity consumption}}{\text{average annual growth rate of national economy}}$$

Efficiency of Energy Transformation: refers to the ratio of the total output of energy products after transformation and the total input of energy for transformation in the same reference period. It is an indicator to show the current conditions of energy processing and conversion equipment, production technique and management. The formula is:

$$\text{Efficiency of Energy Transformation} = \frac{\text{output of energy from transformation}}{\text{input of energy for transformation}} \times 100\%$$

附录4 各种能源折标准煤参考系数

Appendix IV Conversion Factors from Physical Units to Coal Equivalent

各种能源折标准煤参考系数

能 源 名 称	平均低位发热量	折标准煤系数
原煤	20 908 千焦／（5 000 千卡）／千克	0.7143 千克标准煤／千克
洗 精 煤	26 344 千焦／（6 300 千卡）／千克	0.9000 千克标准煤／千克
其它洗煤		
洗 中 煤	8 363 千焦／（2 000 千卡）／千克	0.2857 千克标准煤／千克
煤 泥	8 363～12 545 千焦／（2 000～3 000 千卡）／千克	0.2857～0.4286 千克标准煤／千克
焦 炭	28 435 千焦／（6 800 千卡）／千克	0.9714 千克标准煤／千克
原油	41 816 千焦／（10 000 千卡）／千克	1.4286 千克标准煤／千克
燃 料 油	41 816 千焦／（10 000 千卡）／千克	1.4286 千克标准煤／千克
汽油	43 070 千焦／（10 300 千卡）／千克	1.4714 千克标准煤／千克
煤油	43 070 千焦／（10 300 千卡）／千克	1.4714 千克标准煤／千克
柴油	42 652 千焦／（10 200 千卡）／千克	1.4571 千克标准煤／千克
液化石油气	50 179 千焦／（12 000 千卡）／千克	1.7143 千克标准煤／千克
炼厂干气	46055 千焦／（11 000 千卡）／千克	1.5714 千克标准煤／千克
天 然 气	38 931 千焦／（9 310 千卡）／立方米	1.3300 千克标准煤／立方米
焦炉煤气	16 726～17 981 千焦／（4 000～4 300 千卡）／立方米	0.5714～0.6143 千克标准煤／立方米
其它煤气		
发 生 炉 煤 气	5 227 千焦／（1 250 千卡）／立方米	0.1786 千克标准煤／立方米
重油催化裂解煤气	19 235 千焦／（4 600 千卡）／立方米	0.6571 千克标准煤／立方米
重油热裂解煤气	35 544 千焦／（8 500 千卡）／立方米	1.2143 千克标准煤／立方米
焦 炭 制 气	16 308 千焦／（3 900 千卡）／立方米	0.5571 千克标准煤／立方米
压 力 气 化 煤 气	15 054 千焦／（3 600 千卡）／立方米	0.5143 千克标准煤／立方米
水 煤 气	10 454 千焦／（2 500 千卡）／立方米	0.3571 千克标准煤／立方米
煤焦油	33 453 千焦／（8 000 千卡）／千克	1.1429 千克标准煤／千克
粗苯	41 816 千焦／（10 000 千卡）／千克	1.4286 千克标准煤／千克
热力（当量）		0.03412 千克标准煤／百万焦耳 （0.14286 千克标准煤／1000 千卡）
电力（当量） 　（等价）	3 596 千焦／（860 千卡）／千瓦小时 按 当 年 火 电 发 电 标 准 煤 耗 计 算	0.1229 千克标准煤／千瓦小时
生物质能		
人粪	18 817 千焦／（4 500 千卡）／千克	0.643 千克标准煤／千克
牛粪	13 799 千焦／（3 300 千卡）／千克	0.471 千克标准煤／千克
猪粪	12 545 千焦／（3 000 千卡）／千克	0.429 千克标准煤／千克
羊、驴、马、骡粪	15 472 千焦／（3 700 千卡）／千克	0.529 千克标准煤／千克
鸡粪	18 817 千焦／（4 500 千卡）／千克	0.643 千克标准煤／千克
大豆秆、棉花秆	15 890 千焦／（3 800 千卡）／千克	0.543 千克标准煤／千克
稻秆	12 545 千焦／（3 000 千卡）／千克	0.429 千克标准煤／千克
麦秆	14 635 千焦／（3 500 千卡）／千克	0.500 千克标准煤／千克
玉 米 秆	15 472 千焦／（3 700 千卡）／千克	0.529 千克标准煤／千克
杂草	13 799 千焦／（3 300 千卡）／千克	0.471 千克标准煤／千克
树叶	14 635 千焦／（3 500 千卡）／千克	0.500 千克标准煤／千克
薪柴	16 726 千焦／（4 000 千卡）／千克	0.571 千克标准煤／千克
沼气	20 908 千焦／（5 000 千卡）／立方米	0.714 千克标准煤／立方米

Conversion Factors from Physical Unit to Coal Equivalent

Energy	Average Low Calorific Value	Conversion Factor
Raw Coal	20 908 kjoule / (5 000 kcal) / kg	0.7143 kgce / kg
Cleaned Coal	26 344 kjoule / (6 300 kcal) / kg	0.9000 kgce / kg
Other Washed Coal		
Middlings	8 363 kjoule / (2 000 kcal) / kg	0.2857 kgce / kg
Slimes	8 363 ~ 12 545 kjoule / (2 000 ~ 3 000kcal)/ kg	0.2857 ~ 0.4286 kgce / kg
Coke	28 435 kjoule / (6 800 kcal) / kg	0.9714 kgce / kg
Crude Oil	41 816 kjoule / (10 000 kcal) / kg	1.4286 kgce / kg
Fuel Oil	41 816 kjoule / (10 000 kcal) / kg	1.4286 kgce / kg
Gasoline	43 070 kjoule / (10 300 kcal) / kg	1.4714 kgce / kg
Kerosene	43 070 kjoule / (10 300 kcal) / kg	1.4714 kgce / kg
Diesel	42 652 kjoule / (10 200 kcal) / kg	1.4571 kgce / kg
Liquefied Petroleum Gas	50 179 kjoule / (12 000 kcal) / kg	1.7143 kgce / kg
Refinery Gas	46055 kjoule / (11 000 kcal) / kg	1.5714 kgce / kg
Natural Gas	38 931kjoule / (9 310 kcal) / cu. m	1.3300 kgce / cu. m
Coke Oven Gas	16 726 ~ 17 981kKjoule/ (4 000 ~ 4 300kcal)/ cu. m	0.5714 ~ 0.6143 kgce / cu. m
Other Coal Gas		
By Gas Furnace	5 227 kjoule / (1 250 kcal) / cu. m	0.1786 kgce / cu. m
By Heavy Oil Catalytic Cracking	19 235 kjoule / (4 600 kcal) / cu. m	0.6571 kgce / cu. m
By Heavy Oil Thermal Cracking	35 544 kjoule / (8 500 kcal) / cu. m	1.2143 kgce / cu. m
Coke Gas	16 308 kjoule / (3 900 kcal) / cu. m	0.5571 kgce / cu. m
By Pressure Gasification	15 054 kjoule / (3 600 kcal) / cu. m	0.5143 kgce / cu. m
Water Coal Gas	10 454 kjoule / (2 500 kcal) / cu. m	0.3571 kgce / cu. m
Coal Tar	33 453 kjoule / (8 000 kcal) / kg	1.1429 kgce / kg
Benzene	41 816 kjoule / (10 000 kcal) / kg	1.4286 kgce / kg
Heat (in calorific value)		0.03412 kgce / Mjoule
		(0.14286 kgce / 1000 kcal)
Electricity (in calorific value)	3 596 kjoule / (860 kcal) / kW · h	0.1229 kgce / kW · h
(in coal equivalent)	calculated by average coal input for thermal power generation in the year	
Biomass Energy		
Night Soil	18 817 kjoule / (4 500 kcal) / kg	0.643 kgce / kg
Cow Dung	13 799 kjoule / (3 300 kcal) / kg	0.471 kgce / kg
Pig Dung	12 545 kjoule / (3 000 kcal) / kg	0.429 kgce / kg
Sheep/Donkey/Horse/Mule Dung	15 472 kjoule / (3 700 kcal) / kg	0.529 kgce / kg
Poultry Manure	18 817 kjoule / (4 500 kcal) / kg	0.643 kgce / kg
Soybean Stalk, Cotton Stalk	15 890 kjoule / (3 800 kcal) / kg	0.543 kgce / kg
Paddy Stalk	12 545 kjoule / (3 000 kcal) / kg	0.429 kgce / kg
Wheat stalk	14 635 kjoule / (3 500 kcal) / kg	0.500 kgce / kg
Maize Stalk	15 472 kjoule / (3 700 kcal) / kg	0.529 kgce / kg
Fireweed	13 799 kjoule / (3 300 kcal) / kg	0.471 kgce / kg
Leaves	14 635 kjoule / (3 500 kcal) / kg	0.500 kgce / kg
Firewood	16 726 kjoule / (4 000 kcal) / kg	0.571 kgce / kg
Biogas	20 908 kjoule / (5 000 kcal) / cu. m	0.714 kgce / cu. m

企业风采

哈尔滨空调股份有限公司

哈尔滨空调股份有限公司是以生产石化空冷器、电站空冷器、电站（核）空调和节能换热设备为主的国有控股上市公司，是中国空冷器和空调器的发源地，已填补了48项产品空白。公司占地面积19万平方米，建筑面积9.1万平方米，在哈尔滨、上海拥有三个制造基地，资产总额10亿元。现有职工757人，其中工程技术人员208人，拥有各类专用生产设备1800多台（套）。公司主要产品为石化空冷器、电站空冷器、电站（核）空调和节能换热设备4大类、30余个品种、410多种规格。

现在，哈空调是国内电站辅机和石化通用设备制造行业的龙头企业，哈尔滨市利税大户之一。1995年，在国内同行业中率先通过了ISO9001质量体系认证；2002年取得了ASME标准认证；2002年9月，被中国工业经济联合会和中国机械工业联合会评为"中国工业企业核心竞争力100强企业"；2002年11月，被机械工业信息中心评为绩效管理A级企业；2006年进入中国上市公司综合竞争力百强榜（列57位）。

从"六五"到"十五"期间，在国家和地方政府的支持下，公司紧紧围绕国家在电力和石油化工等行业的发展，积极进行技术创新和技术改造，累计完成投资额40883万元，实施了十三项电站空冷器、石化空冷器、核电站空调的技术改造和重大技术装备国产化创新研制项目。这些项目提高了产品的科技含量和技术水准，实现了产品的更新换代，适应了市场需求，满足了国家电力和石油化工等支柱产业的发展要求，使公司在激烈的市场竞争中保持长久不衰。

电站空冷器是公司的主导产品之一，上世纪六十年代哈空调就开始了这方面的研究开发工作。1984年引进匈牙利海勒系统空冷器的设计制造技术，1992年引进德国GEA公司直冷系统空冷器的工艺制造技术及热浸锌工艺技术，经过消化创新和技术改造，公司已成为国内规模较大、技术领先的电站空冷器制造企业。其中在"十五"期间，是公司电站空冷器产品的重要发展时期，通过实施大型火电机组配套辅机尖峰冷却预热器技术改造（第二批国债项目）、工业循环水节水工程电站空冷器技术改造（第六批国债项目）和发展600MW直接空冷系统及大型核电空调机组项目（第一批东北老工业基地国债项目），完善了电站空冷器的生产制造技术，增加了换热元件品种，提高了空冷系统的设计能力，满足了用户需求。公司电站空冷器产品的设计水平、工艺装备水平、实验检测水平和产品质量得到了大幅度提高，市场竞争力进一步增强，形成了管束、风机、钢结

出口伊朗的产品

构和控制系统协调配套,形成了海勒式间接空冷器 3600MW、双排管直接空冷器 4500MW、大口径单排管直接空冷器 3600MW 的年配套能力。

在国家发改委能源局、工业司的直接协调和省市政府的大力支持下,在华能北方联合电力有限责任公司和中国电力投资集团公司的信

焓差法热工性能实验室

任和理解下,哈空调在2004年获得了北方联合电力乌拉山发电厂2×30万千瓦直冷系统和通辽第二发电有限公司1×60万千瓦机组两个国产化项目,打破了国外公司在该领域的垄断局面,使哈空调在大型直冷系统市场取得了实质性突破。之后,哈空调又取得了华能铜川电厂2×600MW、中电投霍林河电厂2×600MW 直接空冷系统的设计供货合同。经过两年的设计、制造、安装,乌拉山发电厂三期工程并网发电成功,这标志着哈空调在大型电站直冷系统国产化方面取得了重大成功,全面掌握了大型电站直冷系统的核心技术。哈空调因此荣获国家发改委颁发的"国家重大装备国产化先进集体"荣誉称号。

"十一五"期间公司针对存在的不足,继续加大投资力度,拟投资1.1亿元,实施大容量发电机组直接空冷系统及设备技术改造,重点进行直接空冷系统软件设计、空冷系统优化选型、先进换热组件研制、直接空冷系统防冻措施及大规模风机群自动控制系统开发和直接空冷系统支撑钢结构软件开发,并补充关键设备和生产作业面积的不足,形成年新增1000MW直冷系统空冷器的系统设计和生产能力。

公司坚持以市场为导向,围绕产品结构调整,改进质量、增加品种、提高效益和扩大出口,加强技术创新和技术改造,增强创新意识。积极推进多种形式的产、学、研联合,使院所与企业建立长期稳定的合作关系,推进以企业为主体的技术创新体系建设,逐步形成具有自主知识产权的技术、产品的开发能力和相关国际先进技术的消化吸收能力。

哈空调将以党的各中全会精神为指标,以技术创新和机制创新为动力,以国内外市场为导向,围绕公司改革改制和结构调整,积极进行转换机制,开发创新和资本运作,实施生产经营与资本经营并举、快速发展的扩张战略,把公司建设成为技术先进、管理科学、结构合理、资本雄厚、国际知名的大型企业集团。

哈空调生产基地

河南省电力公司

河南省电力公司是国家电网公司的全资子公司，下属 18 个市级供电公司、2 个调峰电厂、6 个设计施工修造企业等，代管 108 个县供电企业，其中改制控股 20 个县供电公司。截至 2005 年底，公司系统拥有员工 37247 人，资产总额 411.37 亿元；全省年发电量 1376 亿千瓦时，全社会年用电量 1353 亿千瓦时，公司年售电量 881 亿千瓦时；全年完成交换电量 175 亿千瓦时，外送电量达到 107.1 亿千瓦时。

河南电网位于华中电网的最北端，是西电东送、南北互供、全国联网的重要枢纽。河南电网覆盖面积 16.8 万平方公里，供电服务人口 9700 万，到 2005 年底，河南境内 500 千伏变电站 9 座，变电容量 750 万千伏安，线路 2036 千米；220 千伏变电站突破 100 座，变电容量 3172 万千伏安，线路 8417 千米。220 千伏及以上电网已经基本覆盖全省各县，电网结构和输送能力明显提高，为全省经济的快速发展提供了安全优质的电力保障。

河南省电力公司外景

现代化的河南电力调度中心

和谐发展的潮阳电力

潮阳电力工业局局长、党总支书记：马武雄

局领导班子共谋潮阳电网"十一五"规划发展蓝图

潮阳电力工业局电力调度中心

潮阳电力工业局办公大楼

潮阳电力工业局的供电管理工作覆盖着汕头市潮阳、潮南两区24个镇（街道办事处），总面积1271.12平方公里，总人口270多万人，供电用户近70万户的生产、生活用电的供应、管理和电力基础设施的规划、建设任务。"十五"期间，潮阳电力局的新领导班子始终保持共产党员先进性，努力践行"三个代表"重要思想，主动承担起更多的社会责任，团结一致，励精图治，更新观念，遵循南方电网公司"六个更加注重"的工作方针，积极带动全系统干部职工立足于服务地方经济发展和提高人民水平，紧紧围绕"更新观念，内强素质，外树形象，拓展市场，加快发展"的工作思路，坚持以电力建设为基础，以电力管理为核心，以电力经营为支柱，以服务社会为责任，全面推进电力事业的健康快速发展，改变了原来基础设施薄弱，供需矛盾尖锐的被动局面，较好地解决了严重制约社会经济发展的瓶颈，为地方经济快速发展和城乡人民群众生活的不断提高做出了积极的贡献，电力管理工作步上了科学规范的良好轨道，队伍建设得到加强，电力事业各方面的工作取得了重大成果，迈出了构建和谐企业的坚实步伐。企业的三个文明建设得到全面协调发展，多次被上级评为先进单位和光荣纳税大户。

"十五"期间，投入电力建设资金近15亿元，电力基础设施日臻完善，电网整体供电能力大大提高，安全生产不断增强，实现电网连续安全运行超6000天记录。至目前，潮阳电网拥有220千伏变电站3座，110千伏变电站13座，35千伏变电站3座。五年间系统累计完成购电量111亿千瓦时，是"九五"期间的3.9倍，上缴各项税费近3.5亿元，是"九五"期间的9.8倍。尤其是2005年上缴税费首次突破亿元大关，成为潮阳、潮南两区历史迄今为止唯一一个超亿元的企业纳税大户。

"十一五"期间，潮阳电力工业局在上级电网公司的正确领导下，团结和谐，开拓进取的领导班子正以新的精神状态、新的工作作风、新的工作思路和新的管理模式，绘制出了新的发展蓝图，潮阳电力发展将会出现更令人欣喜的新飞跃，一个崭新的具有强大的生命力和发展潜力的新潮阳电力将出现在世人面前。团结和谐的潮阳电力工业局领导班子和全系统干部职工将继续发扬艰苦奋斗的工作作风和奋发向上的革命精神，坚定信心，坚持改革促发展，以科学发展观引领电力工作，为构建社会主义和谐社会、和谐企业、建设社会主义新农村创造更加辉煌的业绩。

220千伏潮阳变电站

阳泉煤业（集团）有限责任公司

阳煤集团董事长、总经理　王体轩

阳煤集团党委书记、副董事长　石盛奎

综放采煤工作面

阳泉煤业（集团）有限责任公司，由始建于1950年的阳泉矿务局改制而成，是国家首批确认的特大型国有煤炭企业，长期位居中国企业500强之列。阳煤集团以卓尔不群的斐然业绩，荣膺全国"五一"劳动奖状、中国煤炭工业优秀企业奖、煤炭工业管理金石奖，被评为重合同守信用企业、质量标准化企业、AAA级信用度企业、山西省精神文明建设先进企业、山西省经济结构调整先进企业。

阳煤集团麾下拥有4个全资子公司，18个控股子公司，9个分公司。阳煤集团控股的国阳新能股份，成功上市后，业绩良好。集团公司具有160亿元优质存量资产和得天独厚的巨量资源赋存，并可凭倚畅达便利的交通条件和朴实开放的人文环境。在55年的奉献历程中，阳煤集团培育了门类齐全的济济人才和忠诚智勇的高素质队伍，形成了现代化的装备设施和雄厚的科技实力，锻造了严实精细的管理基础和深湛厚实的企业文化，蕴育了诚信的品牌美誉和卓越的企业形象。这些都是持续强盛的优势动力，为阳煤集团超常发展打开了广阔的成长空间。

阳煤热电

兆丰铝冶

　　阳煤集团实施"煤与非煤并重、做大与做优并举"的战略方针，"135"产业结构基本形成。煤炭产业如日中天，品质上乘的"阳优"煤行销海内外，倍受用户青睐。通过现有煤矿挖潜、新煤矿建设和兼并联营，到 2010 年阳煤集团煤炭产能将达到亿吨级水平，产量达到 8000 万吨，煤炭营业收入 166 亿元以上。电力、铝业、化工三个非煤主导产业，到 2010 年营业收入达到 147 亿元。其中：电力产业装机容量达到 368 万千瓦，年营业收入 19 亿元。铝产业，电解铝最终形成 22 万吨产能，同时完成 240 万吨铝土矿资源开发、120 万吨氧化铝、5 万吨铝加工项目、27 万吨炭素制品项目建设，营业收入达到 95 亿元。煤化工产业，完成 20 万吨聚氯乙烯配套 20 万吨烧碱、40 万吨合成氨配套 60 万吨尿素、20 万吨乙炔化工项目，营业收入 33 亿元。建筑房地产、煤机制造、磁材、建材、煤层气开发利用五个支持产业，到 2010 年营业收入达到 75 亿元。实现"以大搏强，十年三百亿"的战略目标。

　　阳煤集团始终以企业做大做强，确保股东权益最大化为己任。同时把企业员工利益作为发展的出发点和落脚点，给每个员工提供岗位成才的机会和平台，让员工与企业共荣共兴，使全体员工富裕安康。

　　"中国鲁尔，幸福家园"是阳煤人的共同愿景。

　　腾飞的阳煤集团，以国有特大型企业的卓越丰姿、骄人业绩和优质的产品服务，与投资者、客户和供应商共享资源、共赢市场，为优秀人才和每个员工提供成长成才的坚实舞台。

　　阳煤集团竭诚欢迎国内外朋友携手合作，共创辉煌。

现代化大型矿井

地址：中国山西阳泉北大街　　　　邮编：045000
电话：0353—7073112　7071412　　传真：0353—7071144
网址：www.ymjt.com.cn　　　　　　电子信箱：ymjt@ymjt.com.cn

中国电力山西神头发电有限责任公司

中国电力山西神头发电有限责任公司位于山西省朔州市朔城区神头镇，装机容量120万千瓦，其前身为神头第一发电厂。2005年5月，在企业内部体制改革过程中，成立神头发电有限责任公司。公司安装两台200MW原苏联机组，四台200MW原捷克斯洛伐克机组。1977年2月17日首台机组投产，1987年12月最后一台机组并网发电。截止2006年底，公司累计发电量1600亿千瓦时，为国民经济建设和电力工业的发展做出了巨大的贡献。2006年，公司发电量、综合厂用电率、发电煤耗、供电煤耗、燃油量、利用小时、非计划停运次数、售电量、利润总额、净资产收益率、上交投资收益、应收电费余额等十二项指标创历史最好水平。

党委书记兼总经理　杨福友

多年来，企业始终坚持两个文明建设一起抓，以经济效益为中心，认真贯彻"诚实、认真、细心、奉献"的企业精神，深化改革，强化管理，不断推进管理创新、机制创新和科技创新，企业管理水平得以加强，经济效益显著提高，两个文明建设取得了丰硕成果。先后被国家电力公司命名为"安全文明生产达标企业"、"双文明单位"；被山西省电力公司命名为"一流发电企业"；被山西省委、省政府授予"文明单位"、"山西省模范单位"、"文明单位标兵"、山西省"十大安全明星企业"，荣获山西省"五一劳动奖状"；被中央文明委命名为"全国精神文明建设先进单位"；2004年4月被中华全国总工会授予"全国五一劳动奖状"。

发展循环经济　建设生态园区

实现煤炭资源综合利用和矿区和谐发展

南煤集团现拥有两个生产矿井，五个非煤产业公司及两个直属分公司，员工8500多人，资产总额13亿元，矿区煤炭总储量10亿吨，年核定生产能力320万吨，规划年产量1200万吨，2005年全年收入10亿元。

在"十五"末实现销售收入10亿元，实现利润20715.02万元，实现利税30794.76万元的基础上，到2010年，产量达到700万吨，销售收入达30亿元以上。2015年，产量达到1300万吨，发电能力达270万KW，发电量160万亿度，其它非煤产业同步发展，届时全集团实现"十年百亿"目标。

一 整合资源，提升主业，最大限度地提高资源利用率

一是，提升煤炭开采的技术含量，提高资源回收率。

二是，大力进行煤炭的洗选加工，提高煤炭品质。

三是，积极推广新工艺、新技术，促进资源节约利用。

二 延伸产业链条，变废为宝，实现废弃物资源化、减量化、无害化

一是，坚持对煤矸石进行资源再生转化利用。

二是，大力发展低热值电厂。

三是，不断推进煤层气开发利用。

四是，大力实施矿井水复用工程。

三 梯度开发，持续发展，实现"十年百亿"战略目标

安阳市诚信矿业服务有限责任公司

安阳市诚信矿业服务有限责任公司位于河南省安阳市，成立于2002年12月，具有国家相关管理部门批准的探矿权和采矿权评估的资格，可从事探矿权和采矿权评估业务和矿业咨询服务。具有承担大型、复杂矿产地探矿权评估及矿产勘察、开发有关技术方面咨询服务的能力。

公司成立以来，本着"独立、客观、公平、公正、诚实、守信"的原则；坚持"质量第一"的宗旨，完成了多项探矿权评估报告和采矿权评估报告，同时，开展煤矿、铁矿、铝土矿、铅锌矿、建材矿及矿业技术咨询服务，为地方经济的发展起到了积极的作用。

安阳市诚信矿业服务有限责任公司热忱欢迎矿业相关单位与我公司开展矿业方面的合作！